THE SELECTED WORKS OF GORDON TULLOCK

VOLUME 9

Law and Economics

THE SELECTED WORKS OF GORDON TULLOCK

VOLUME 1 *Virginia Political Economy*

VOLUME 2 *The Calculus of Consent: Logical Foundations of Constitutional Democracy* (with James M. Buchanan)

VOLUME 3 *The Organization of Inquiry*

VOLUME 4 *The Economics of Politics*

VOLUME 5 *The Rent-Seeking Society*

VOLUME 6 *Bureaucracy*

VOLUME 7 *The Economics and Politics of Wealth Redistribution*

VOLUME 8 *The Social Dilemma: Of Autocracy, Revolution, Coup d'Etat, and War*

VOLUME 9 *Law and Economics*

VOLUME 10 *Economics without Frontiers* (includes a cumulative index for the series)

Gordon Tullock

THE SELECTED WORKS OF GORDON TULLOCK

VOLUME 9

Law and Economics

GORDON TULLOCK

Edited and with an Introduction by

CHARLES K. ROWLEY

Liberty Fund
Indianapolis

This book is published by Liberty Fund, Inc., a foundation established to encourage study of the ideal of a society of free and responsible individuals.

The cuneiform inscription that serves as our logo and as the design motif for our endpapers is the earliest-known written appearance of the word "freedom" (*amagi*), or "liberty." It is taken from a clay document written about 2300 B.C. in the Sumerian city-state of Lagash.

Printed in the United States of America

Paperback cover photo courtesy of the *American Economic Review*

Frontispiece courtesy of Center for Study of Public Choice, George Mason University, Fairfax, Virginia

09 08 07 06 05 C 5 4 3 2 1
09 08 07 06 05 P 5 4 3 2 1

Library of Congress Cataloging-in-Publication Data

Tullock, Gordon.
Law and economics / Gordon Tullock ; edited and with an introduction by Charles K. Rowley.
p. cm. — (Selected works of Gordon Tullock; v. 9)
Includes two previously published books by the author: The logic of the law and The case against the common law.
Includes bibliographical references and index.
ISBN 0-86597-528-0 (alk. paper) — ISBN 0-86597-539-6 (pbk. : alk. paper)
1. Law and economics. 2. Law reform—United States. 3. Common law—United States. 4. Social choice. I. Rowley, Charles Kershaw. II. Tullock, Gordon. Logic of the law. III. Tullock, Gordon. Case against the common law. IV. Title.

K487.E3T85 2005
340′.11—dc22

2004061511

LIBERTY FUND, INC.
8335 Allison Pointe Trail, Suite 300
Indianapolis, Indiana 46250-1684

CONTENTS

THE ECONOMICS OF LEGAL PROCEEDINGS

THE CASE AGAINST THE COMMON LAW

INTRODUCTION

Law and Economics brings together Gordon Tullock's innovative contributions to the economic and public choice analysis of law and legal institutions. This volume reproduces in full the contents of two books, namely, *The Logic of the Law* and *The Case against the Common Law.* It also includes selected chapters from *Trials on Trial* and a number of articles published in scholarly journals.[1] As will become apparent, Tullock's insights from public choice set his work radically apart from the mainstream literature of law and economics, which consistently emphasizes the efficiency of the common law and of the common law process.[2]

The Intellectual and Historical Background

The law-and-economics movement originated in the United States and was transmitted subsequently to other countries.[3] Almost inevitably, therefore, the immediate antecedents to the movement emanated from within the United States, even though the founding article, by Ronald Coase, was written by a quintessential Englishman who, at the age of forty-one, had migrated across the Atlantic only nine years earlier, when already in mid career.[4]

Since 1870, American jurisprudence has been characterized by a complex and changing pattern of ideas, with swings between legal formalism and legal realism that never completely ousted legal formalism, or the "black letter" law.[5] Yet, these swings opened up an avenue for the law-and-economics movement and, ultimately, for Tullock's contributions to the field.

Formalism was prevalent in many areas of knowledge during the late nine-

1. Gordon Tullock, *The Logic of the Law* (New York: Basic Books, 1971); Gordon Tullock, *The Case against the Common Law* (Fairfax, Va.: The Locke Institute, 1997); Gordon Tullock, *Trials on Trial* (New York: Columbia University Press, 1980).

2. See, especially, Richard A. Posner, *Economic Analysis of Law* (Boston: Little, Brown, 1973).

3. See Charles K. Rowley, "Law-and-Economics from the Perspective of Economics," in *The New Palgrave Dictionary of Economics and the Law*, ed. Peter Newman, vol. 2 (London and New York: Macmillan Reference, 1998), 474–85.

4. Ronald H. Coase, "The Problem of Social Cost," *Journal of Law and Economics* 3 (1960): 1–45.

5. Neil Duxbury, *Patterns of American Jurisprudence* (Oxford: Clarendon Press, 1995).

teenth century, as scholars sought to treat particular fields as if they were governed by "interrelated, fundamental and logically demonstrable principles of science."[6] This trend was discernible during the immediate post–Civil War period of American legal history and was subsequently reflected in two separate concepts: in the universities, there emerged the Langdellian science of law; in the courts, there emerged the philosophy of laissez-faire.

In 1870, Harvard University appointed Christopher Columbus Langdell to the newly created position of dean of the Harvard School of Law. Langdell quickly determined to resolve the perceived chaos of American jurisprudence by promoting legal science through the case method of legal instruction.

Langdell's legal science consisted of four elements: first, the rule of *stare decisis et non movere* (let existing laws stand), which in Langdell's judgment is the key to the science of law; second, the recognition that most reported cases are repetitious of extant legal principles and precedents; third, the fact that the number of fundamental doctrines is limited because only a small number of cases are truly relevant to the science of law; and fourth, the need to classify these legal doctrines and to demonstrate their logical interconnection.

Langdell's revolution in the method of instruction swept across the American academies and provided the basis for a legal formalism that dominated American legal education for at least half a century. It proved to be a tremendous force for harmonizing the American common law system at both the federal and the state levels.

The second facet of legal formalism—the tradition of laissez-faire—was a product of the courts. Laissez-faire was conceived of by the courts as the freedom of individuals to strike or not to strike a bargain. This was viewed as a cornerstone of a genuine legal science.[7] In particular, the U.S. courts were influenced by the writings of Herbert Spencer, whose books *Social Statics* and *The Man versus the State* ushered in the notion of social Darwinism, or the survival of the fittest.[8]

This concept involved the courts in ensuring that the burden of regulation was focused on the private realm of the market and not on the public realm of government. The appropriate framework for settling economic disputes

6. Ibid., 10.

7. Ibid., 26.

8. Herbert Spencer, *Social Statics: Or, the Conditions Essential to Human Happiness Specified and the First of Them Developed* (London: Chapman, 1851); and Herbert Spencer, *The Man versus the State* (1884; Caldwell, Idaho: Caxton Printers, 1940).

was private rather than public law. "Private relations between economic actors were to be governed, not by statutes, but by the contractual rights and duties accepted by those actors."[9]

From the U.S. Supreme Court downward in the federal court system and throughout the large majority of state court systems, the courts opposed government regulation of private economic relations and put in place a social Darwinist legal system that was to survive more or less intact until the mid 1930s. Inevitably, the judgments recorded by those courts became part of the science of law as discovered through the casebook method in the formalist U.S. academies.

As early as the late nineteenth century, however, social Darwinism was being challenged both in the academies and within the court system. Best known among the early legal challengers were Oliver Wendell Holmes Jr., Benjamin Nathan Cardozo, and Roscoe Pound. Although their attacks were directed more against social Darwinism than against legal formalism, in matters of economic regulation they could not attack the one without the other.

Perhaps the most famous early legal challenge to social Darwinism occurred in the dissenting opinion of Justice Holmes in the Supreme Court decision in *Lochner v. New York* (1905). In this case, the Court declared that a New York statute setting a ten-hour maximum workday for bakers violated the stipulation in the Fourteenth Amendment: "No state shall . . . deprive any person of life, liberty, or property, without due process of law." In dissent, Justice Holmes observed: "The Fourteenth Amendment does not enact Mr. Herbert Spencer's *Social Statics*." This sentence became something of a rallying cry for the legal realists when they came on the scene some fifteen years later.

By the end of World War I, formalism had become stale, leaving a void in American legal scholarship. The jurisprudence of legal realism evolved to fill this void, presenting a direct challenge to Langdellian science. It is important, however, not to exaggerate the skepticism of the legal realists. For the most part, they did not view the law simply as what judges do when settling disputes on the basis of the whim and fancy of the moment.

Rather, the mood of the realists was one of dissatisfaction with the notion that twentieth-century legal thought should be dominated by a nineteenth-century legal worldview. The key contributors to legal realism, Karl Llewellyn, Jerome Frank, Underhill Moore, William O. Douglas, and Robert Hale, did not always agree with one another on the meaning of realism itself, though

9. Duxbury, *Patterns of American Jurisprudence*, 30.

they coalesced in a dislike of Langdellian formalism. The law schools of Yale and Columbia universities became centers for this dissident approach.

Late-nineteenth-century developments in economics in the United States had challenged the validity of classical economics, most especially with respect to its support for the idea of free market exchange. An influential group of institutional economists, including Thorstein Veblen, John Bates Clark, Henry Carter Adams, Richard T. Ely, and E. R. A. Seligman, attacked the principle of laissez-faire on the grounds that it had failed to resolve problems of unemployment and poverty. They argued in favor of social justice, without socialism—namely, for economic regulation rather than for the widespread nationalization of the means of production.

As progressive lawyers became drawn to the methods of the social sciences, it is not surprising that institutional economics proved to be an attractive proposition. Thus it was that legal realism, following the intellectual lead provided by institutional economics, came to challenge legal formalism in the courts. Most important, during the 1930s, the legal realists, in support of New Deal legislation, contributed significantly to the demise of the private black letter law by helping to reverse a consistent five-to-four majority of Supreme Court justices, most notably, in the 1937 judgment in *West Coast Hotel v. Parrish*, which overturned a long line of precedents stretching back to *Lochner v. New York* (1905).

The intellectual significance of legal realism lies not in any concrete linkage between law and social sciences, for this did not occur before the beginning of World War II, when legal realism effectively disappeared and legal formalism reasserted its dominance. Rather, the legal realists sowed seeds that would germinate in the post–World War II period, initially with respect to antitrust law and economics and, later, with respect to the law-and-economics movement.

The law-and-economics movement developed at the University of Chicago during the 1960s, within an economics tradition far more favorable to the free-exchange model of classical political economy than was mainstream economics at that time. It was, moreover, an economics tradition markedly hostile to the interventionist, institutional approach that had so attracted the legal realists during the 1930s.

In a sense, it also turned out to be a movement that incorporated some of the formalism of the Langdellian era, albeit based on the notion that the common law should be, and is, economically efficient or wealth maximizing for society. From this perspective, *stare decisis*, properly interpreted, enables the law to evolve efficiently in conformity with changing economic conditions.

In 1960 Ronald H. Coase launched the law-and-economics research program, from the University of Virginia, with a seminal paper titled "The Problem of Social Cost." The paper was written in response to criticisms that Chicago economists leveled at his 1959 essay, "The Federal Communications Commission." "The Problem of Social Cost" was concerned "with those actions of business firms which have harmful effects on others." In essence, it was an attack on Pigou's solution to this problem as outlined in *The Economics of Welfare*:[10]

> The traditional approach has tended to obscure the nature of the choice that has been made. The question is commonly thought of as one in which A inflicts harm on B and what has to be decided is: how should we restrain A? But this is wrong. We are dealing with a problem of a reciprocal nature. To avoid the harm to B would inflict harm on A. The real question that has to be decided is: should A be allowed to harm B or should B be allowed to harm A? The problem is to avoid the more serious harm.[11]

On the assumption that the pricing system works smoothly and without cost, Coase deploys an example in which straying cattle destroy crops on neighboring land. The example demonstrates that the value of production will be maximized whether liability falls on the cattle owner or on the farmer. Under such circumstances, as long as the court assigns liability, the nature and direction of that assignment will not affect the final outcome in terms of economic efficiency.

Coase recognizes that the price system rarely works without cost and that the zero-transaction-cost assumption typically is inappropriate when evaluating the consequences of a legal dispute. Where transaction costs are high, the decision of the court—either in its choice of the direction of liability or in its choice between granting an injunction (a property rule) or imposing liability to pay damages (a liability rule)—may result in outcomes that do not maximize the value of production for society as a whole. A significant question then arises as to whether a particular common law system is economically efficient.

As the law-and-economics research program took off, during the 1960s and the 1970s, its focus shifted somewhat from the Coasian preoccupation with the implications of legal rules for economic efficiency toward the use

10. Coase, "The Problem of Social Cost"; Ronald H. Coase, "The Federal Communications Commission," *Journal of Law and Economics* 2 (1959): 1–40; ibid., 2; Arthur C. Pigou, *The Economics of Welfare* (London: Macmillan, 1920).

11. Coase, "The Problem of Social Cost," 2.

of economic theory to explain and to justify the common law system. Ultimately, Richard A. Posner emerged as the dominant "fast-second" figure in this program, in both its normative and its positive dimensions.[12] Tullock beat him to the punch, however, with his seminal book on law and economics, *The Logic of the Law*, published in 1971, two years before Posner's magnum opus.

Gordon Tullock's Contributions to Law and Economics

This volume demonstrates Tullock's independence from the mainstream law-and-economics research program and highlights, in particular, the full range of his critique of Posner's 1973 hypothesis that the common law is economically efficient.

The only formal training in economics that Tullock received was a one-semester course by Henry Simons at University of Chicago Law School. Simons is best known for his monograph *A Positive Program for Laissez-Faire*, published in 1934, during the Great Depression. Simons was a utopian, a disciple of Jeremy Bentham, whose 1776 monograph, *A Fragment on Government*, had first introduced utilitarian thinking to legal jurisprudence.[13]

Central to Bentham's utilitarian ethic was the axiom "It is the greatest happiness of the greatest number that is the measure of right and wrong." From that perspective, Bentham argued that the theory and practice of law could be reconstructed from first principles. Creating correct law would lead to happiness; and the creation of correct law meant reasoning from first principles rather than adopting "the piled up rubbish of ancient authority."

It is not surprising, in these circumstances, that Tullock's first contribution to law and economics, and the first contribution to this volume, *The Logic of the Law*, conveys a distinctly Benthamite tone. In *The Logic of the Law*, the first book ever published on law and economics, Tullock refers explicitly to Bentham's failed reforms of the English legal system and claims that "since we now have a vast collection of tools that was not available to Bentham, it is

12. See Posner, *Economic Analysis of Law*.

13. Henry Simons, *A Positive Program for Laissez-Faire: Some Proposals for Liberal Economic Policy* (Chicago: University of Chicago Press, 1934); Jeremy Bentham, *A Fragment on Government*, ed. J. H. Burns and H. L. A. Hart (1776; Cambridge: Cambridge University Press, 1988).

possible for us to improve on his work" and "hopefully this discussion, together with empirical research, will lead to significant reforms."[14]

The tools on which Tullock draws come from the new welfare economics, essentially the Pareto principle buttressed by the Kaldor-Hicks potential compensation test. This approach requires that, in order for that change to be acceptable to society, the gainers from any change in a legal rule must be able, in principle, to compensate the losers while themselves remaining better off from that change.

Drawing also on his work with James M. Buchanan in *The Calculus of Consent*,[15] Tullock focuses on the long-run application of the Pareto principle under conditions of uncertainty. He seeks, on this basis, to show that some legal reforms that may be expected to meet with short-run resistance from losers nevertheless may be accepted unanimously, if viewed as applying to the long run, given individuals' uncertainty regarding their own and their descendants' likely long-term relative positions in society.

On this basis, Tullock launches a review of the foundational principles of the law. He shows what happens when, abandoning the traditional view of the law as an extension of broad moral philosophy, we apply instead some of the concepts and procedures of Paretian welfare economics.

In a wide-ranging discussion that embraces all the major areas of U.S. law and law enforcement—from contract and negligence law to robbery and murder, from the treatment of minors and incompetents to the punishment of habitual offenders—Tullock derives optimal rules and procedures that differ markedly from those that prevailed in 1971.

Because *The Logic of the Law* represented a foundational challenge to the legal system of the United States rather than a textbook on law and economics that rationalized the existing legal system, Tullock's book failed to make the impact on the new discipline (especially on lawyers) that Posner's 1973 book surely would. In a fundamental sense, however, *The Logic of the Law* was the precursor to *Economic Analysis of Law* in its application of economic analysis to the U.S. legal system.

"The 'Dead Hand' of Monopoly," coauthored with James M. Buchanan, applies economic analysis to antitrust policy. Buchanan and Tullock explain that although those who initially obtain a monopoly, either through

14. Tullock, *The Logic of the Law*, xiv.

15. James M. Buchanan and Gordon Tullock, *The Calculus of Consent: Logical Foundations of Constitutional Democracy* (Ann Arbor: University of Michigan, 1962).

innovation or through government privilege, frequently benefit from that acquisition the benefits are quickly capitalized. Thus, current holders of the monopoly typically earn only a normal return on their investments.

If the monopoly is eliminated by antitrust policy without full compensation, the current holders of the privilege suffer an "unjust" capital loss. Buchanan and Tullock also demonstrate why *current* taxpayers will rationally resist providing such just compensation for removing a monopoly, thereby lowering commodity prices for a *future* generation of consumers.

In "Does Punishment Deter Crime?" Tullock compares two arguments in favor of punishing criminals, namely, that punishment deters crime and that punishment rehabilitates criminals. For the most part, economists writing during the 1960s and early 1970s favored the notion that punishment deterred crime, whereas sociologists did not. Tullock presents evidence from both sources that strongly supports the deterrence hypothesis. Sophisticated statistical studies demonstrate that several innocent lives are saved for each murderer who is executed. Tullock can find no evidence that rehabilitation programs deter crime. Under such circumstances, society must opt either for the deterrence method or for a higher rate of crime.

"Two Kinds of Legal Efficiency" notes that in discussing the efficiency of the law it is important to distinguish between two quite different issues. The first is whether the law itself is well designed to achieve goals that society regards as desirable. The second is whether the process of enforcing the law is efficient. Tullock notes that if the law itself is inefficient, inefficient enforcement of that law may be desirable. In deciding whether a law or its enforcement is efficient, Tullock argues that careful empirical research is essential, not least with respect to the magnitude of transaction costs.

"Optimal Procedure" outlines the characteristics of a desirable court system and evaluates the trade-offs between the various desirable characteristics. Tullock acknowledges that accuracy and low cost rank high among these characteristics. He demonstrates that the social value of these two characteristics is somewhat indirect and that the characteristics are difficult to measure. From this perspective, Tullock critically evaluates the efficiency of the Anglo-Saxon common law, where criminal cases must be proved beyond all reasonable doubt and where civil cases must be proved on the balance of probabilities.

"Technology: The Anglo-Saxons versus the Rest of the World" directly compares the adversary system deployed by the former with the inquisitorial system deployed by the latter with respect to accuracy and cost. The most significant legal costs of the adversary system are attorneys' costs. Those costs are under the direct control of the litigants. Yet, Tullock notes, because each litigant desires to win, competitive bidding raises attorneys' costs above the efficient floor. Moreover, the party who believes himself to be in the wrong has a strong incentive to elevate his litigation costs in order to lower the probability of an accurate judgment.

The most significant legal costs of the inquisitorial system are judges' costs. Greater outlays on the judiciary should increase the accuracy of legal judgments; however, the party who believes himself to be in the wrong has no incentive to increase judicial costs. Tullock argues, on efficiency grounds, for the replacement of the Anglo-Saxon by the inquisitorial legal system in the United States.

"Various Ways of Dealing with the Cost of Litigation" evaluates, from an economic viewpoint, methods of paying lawyers' fees as alternatives to the straightforward fee-for-service method (under the Anglo-Saxon system). Tullock explores the implications of the contingent fee arrangement, whereby attorneys offer their services to plaintiffs (but not to defendants) in return for a substantial share of any awarded damages. He explores the implications of the English system, whereby the losing party bears all the litigation costs, and of legal aid systems, whereby the government subsidizes some low-income litigants. Throughout, he weighs the implications of each remuneration system against the twin objectives of an accurate but a low-cost legal system.

"The Motivation of Judges" subjects judicial behavior, in both Anglo-Saxon and inquisitorial systems, to rational choice analysis. Tullock concludes that while both systems try to avoid negative incentives for high-cost, inaccurate outcomes it is extremely difficult to establish positive incentives for low-cost, accurate outcomes. In the case of contracts, parties may prefer to provide for arbitration rather than litigation. Tullock suggests that fee-based arbitration may be superior to litigation in terms of the economic efficiency of expected outcomes.

"Defending the Napoleonic Code over the Common Law" summarizes Tullock's overall assessment of the respective advantages and disadvantages of the two legal systems. On balance, he prefers the Napoleonic Code while acknowledging that there is scope for further research on the two legal systems. In making this judgment, Tullock focuses attention on three alleged deficiencies of the Anglo-Saxon system, namely, trial by jury, reliance on the accusatory rather than the inquisitorial method, and reliance on particular exclusionary laws of evidence that prevent juries from hearing relevant information.

"Negligence Again" analyzes the unrealistic assumptions used by law-and-economics scholars to justify, in terms of economic efficiency, the use of the negligence rule to decide accident cases. Tullock demonstrates that several other legal rules, including strict liability, also satisfy the efficiency criterion under these assumptions. Tullock notes that the probability of error, both in the calculations of risk by the parties and in the ex post determination of the outcome in the courts, is so high as to justify other, more rough-and-ready solutions, including that of no-fault liability, coupled with private insurance against accidents.

"Welfare and the Law" takes the arguments advanced in "Negligence Again" one stage further in a detailed challenge to the scholarship of Richard Posner. Specifically, Tullock argues in favor of utility maximization rather than wealth maximization (as advanced by Posner) as a desirable goal of the common law, but not as a highest-level goal (as also advanced by Posner). He argues that transaction costs of the law are more complex and widespread than those admitted by Posner and that they justify a much simpler and more limited legal code than that currently in existence.

The Case against the Common Law is a beautifully written monograph that summarizes Tullock's case against the Anglo-Saxon common law system. The monograph presents a powerful rational choice case for replacing the common law with a civil code system.

Central to the social functions and the foundational principles of the common law system, argues Tullock, was the concept of doctrinal stability encapsulated in the institutional principle of stare decisis, or binding precedent. The standard of doctrinal stability cannot survive significant deviations from the principle of stare decisis.

Tullock demonstrates how the twentieth-century retreat from stare decisis in the U.S. common law system was a predictable consequence of adverse institutional characteristics. He concludes that this withdrawal is now sufficiently extensive as to challenge the validity of the common law system itself. For what is now left—the surviving kernel of a once-robust system of law—is a high-cost, subjective, unresponsive, nonreplicable, and essentially illegitimate legal system predicated more on the rule of men than on the rule of law.

In part because of his public choice analysis of the U.S. legal system, and in part because of his insistence on viewing the common law courts as high-cost purveyors of legal error, Tullock is considered a maverick by both the law-and-economics scholars in particular and the legal profession in general.

Yet, Tullock's talent for careful observation of real-world institutions and his capacity to explain what he sees in terms of the rational choice model provide valuable, and often overlooked, insights into the true nature of the legal system.

CHARLES K. ROWLEY

Duncan Black Professor of Economics, George Mason University

Senior Fellow, James M. Buchanan Center for Political Economy, George Mason University

General Director, The Locke Institute

The Logic of the Law

PREFACE

Not long ago a British barrister told me that we should have drastic overhauls of the law, and completely re-examine legal procedures, only about every 200 years. Normally, he felt that the law should proceed by gradual development without any effort to return to first principles. I pointed out to him that the two-hundredth anniversary of the year when Jeremy Bentham first began to press for law reform was rapidly approaching, and that if any of the changes now proposed took as long to implement as the Benthamite changes, we would have another two-hundred-year interval until the time they come to pass if we started thinking about radical revision now. Since he had intended his argument essentially as a protest against any basic reconsideration of the law, my remark rather took him unawares. However, being one of the most rational of men, he conceded that upon his own premises it was time to begin to consider legal reform.

This volume is an effort to start such a basic reconsideration. At most times and, for that matter, at the present time, there is a great deal of public dissatisfaction with the law, and a good many proposals are being canvassed for reform. In general, however, this dissatisfaction and these proposals for reform take most of the law for granted and merely propose to change minor details. Bentham, of course, attempted to go back to basic principles and examine the law in its entirety. Although the changes Bentham eventually succeeded in implementing were fairly drastic, the foundations of the law are much the same as they were before he was born. It seems likely that any rethinking of the law will conclude that the law is fundamentally rational, and changes, even those as drastic as the Benthamite reforms, will leave a great deal of the basic legal structure intact.

A great many changes have occurred since Bentham's day, such as the great development of social science. Since we now have a vast collection of tools that was not available to Bentham, it is possible for us to improve on his work. Another modern advantage is the existence of a large community of scholars. The most desirable effect of this book would be to start a scientific discussion of the foundations of the law. Hopefully this discussion, together with empirical research, will lead to significant reforms. In any event, it is

The Logic of the Law (New York and London: Basic Books, 1971). Reprinted, with permission.

reasonable to look at the law *de novo*—to go back to basic principles and attempt to develop a logical structure. The conventional legal scholar will no doubt regard my methods as a radical departure from those to which he is accustomed. He will be correct. In a sense, my book is an attack upon the traditional methods of legal scholarship, which takes the form, however, not of direct criticism but of a presentation of a different procedure that I believe to be superior.

My own formal education was in the law (D.J., University of Chicago, 1947), but the methods used in this book are those of modern welfare economics. A few legal scholars—Calabresi, Blum, and Kalven come immediately to mind—have begun applying similar methods to various aspects of the law, but most law professors have never even thought of using them. This book makes no moral assumptions, and it is strictly utilitarian in its approach to legal institutions. In this I follow Bentham, but I have an advantage over him: that of modern welfare economics. As the reader will discover in Chapter 1, I even have a modification of welfare economics to suggest. It seems to me that these tools give us an advantage. Hopefully, this book will merely be a first step in the application of modern welfare economics to an analysis of legal problems. Our present legal system cries out for reform, and improved knowledge is a necessary prerequisite for genuine reform. It is my hope that many other scholars will push forward along the lines that I have followed.

This book is intended to begin discussion in a new field; it applies the latest tools of the social sciences to the law and to legal institutions. Eventually, after a number of other scholars have added their work to mine, it should be possible to improve our present legal institutions and our law. The substantive improvements, however, will probably not be gigantic. Although there are areas in which, if I am correct, our present law is far from optimal, the changes I propose in general are not of a revolutionary nature. In many cases, in fact, all I propose is that what we say be made to conform to what we actually do. To repeat, if the actual changes that I suggest are relatively modest, the foundations of my reasoning are radically different from the tradition.

Still, I feel confident that, at the very least, it is worthwhile to experiment with new techniques. The law is an important area and deserves every bit of light that can be shed upon it. Even those who think my light faint and flickering should agree that it will do at least some good. Economists are likely to feel that the tools I am using are correct. Indeed it is partly my own economic experience and partly my desire to attract economists into the field that have led me to use these tools in an extremely strict way. Actually, it is possible to achieve most of the conclusions of this book without such a rigorous adherence to the welfare economics schemata. People who are antagonistic to formal welfare economics could, strictly speaking, skip the first two chapters of the book and still find that they were able to agree with much of the rest of it.

Before closing this preface, I should like to explain why the institution of property is not thoroughly examined in the book, and why there is very little discussion of externality. The reason for leaving out externality is quite simple: I have written another book in this general field.* The reason for not discussing property is somewhat more complicated but basically similar. This is an extremely complex area in which welfare economics has a major role. Unfortunately, the complexities are so great that they would take another book to discuss them properly.

I should like to thank Donald Dewey for his thorough and penetrating criticism of an earlier draft of this book. I feel I should also thank Irving Kristol and Martin Kessler of Basic Books, Inc., for their willingness to publish a book that is fairly certain to receive vigorous, not to say acerbic, criticism.

*Gordon Tullock, *Private Wants, Public Means* (New York: Basic Books, 1970).

PART I

FUNDAMENTAL ASSUMPTIONS

CHAPTER I

LAW WITHOUT ETHICS

In recent years, "ethical science" has fallen into disrepute, not because we are necessarily less moral now or because we worry about ethical problems less, but because of the obvious flaws in the "scientific" treatises on the subject. From Plato and Aristotle to St. Thomas Aquinas and William James, numerous books of all degrees of profundity have been produced that purport to deduce an ethical system from a few basic postulates. The dearth of current books on the subject reflects neither disrespect for the great minds who have labored in the field nor a belief that they have solved the problem, but is merely an indication of simple skepticism. Any critical examination of these works indicates that their authors have made mistakes in logic that escaped their notice because they were morally convinced of the truth of their results. A man who firmly believes murder to be undesirable is not likely to be critical of a line of reasoning that leads to this conclusion.

In a way the modern skepticism about these classics, or about a modern attempt to repeat them, stems from our interest in different cultures. The knowledge that other people have different moral systems, although not really fully integrated into the reasoning of many students, has resulted in a more critical approach to the moral philosophers, and hence has contributed to the present lack of courses in "ethical science." In partial compensation, anthropologists have undertaken genuinely scientific studies of the ethical systems of different peoples and modern philosophers also study ethics in a more cautious and less sweeping way.

The philosophy of law is normally based on ethics. Although exceptions have occurred, most justifications of law are built upon an ethical base. These, until recently, were in much the same category as "ethical science," since they normally tried to justify the ethics. The more modern examples of legal philosophy simply assume an ethical system, either explicitly or implicitly, and then go on from there. Beginning in the 1930's, a school of legal positivists argued that the law was simply what the state decreed, and morals were not involved. The history of this movement would appear to indicate, however, that the positivists were unconsciously applying notions of natural law; they thought that the state was only going to enact laws of which they approved. The realization that states might enact laws that they violently disliked resulted in a fairly complete, albeit not necessarily publicly admitted, return to the natural law. Whatever else may be said about the Nuremberg trials, they marked the burial of legal positivism.

Recently legal positivism has had a limited and partial revival in the form of the view that the "Constitution is what the Supreme Court says it is." An analysis of the writing of the proponents of this view, however, will always uncover examples of Supreme Court decisions that they regard as incorrect. According to their strict argument, of course, this is impossible, and some higher standard is necessary. Again, the higher standard is simply a rather cloudy version of the natural law. In fact, it is more or less true that the whole present upsurge of apparent respect for the Supreme Court as a law-making body is based upon the fact that the decisions of the Court have recently tended closely to approximate the views on ethics held by a number of very articulate students.

This desperately brief and overcondensed discussion of recent developments in the field of legal and moral philosophy is intended to put the present study in perspective. In this book I intend to return to the approach of the nineteenth century, albeit with so many changes that Mill and Bentham might not recognize it. If the efforts to develop a science of norms were all unsuccessful, they were at least attempts to do something worthwhile. A system of behavioral rules deduced from a few realistic assumptions would be of great value. The men who tried to find it can be criticized for erroneously believing they had found it when they had not, but they were right to look.

This book, then, continues the quest. I am using radically different methods, but my goal is the same. Unfortunately, I cannot promise that I will find the grail. A set of general rules is "justified" by reasoning from basic principles, but they do not cover all of law and ethics. In part the limitation is self-imposed and is motivated by a desire not to bore either myself or the reader. I carry certain chains of reasoning only far enough to indicate their general direction without working out all of the details. In a more important part, however, the limitations on my reasoning are not matters of choice. The method that I propose as "the logical foundation of law and ethics" may eventually lead to a solution of many important legal and ethical problems or, then again, it may not. Be that as it may, at present it is merely a start. For some whole fields the method only gives the most feeble results. Thus, I present my method, apply it in the areas in which I can make it work, and hope that others will extend the reasoning to cover the areas that I must forego.

My first radical departure from that used in earlier studies is that it starts with law and then proceeds to ethics. Instead of deducing the law from previously deduced ethics, I shall attempt to deduce legal principles that are not based upon ethics, and then use these principles to produce a justification of ethics. This may seem an attempt to be paradoxical, but the procedure is not merely an effort to be clever. It is a different basic approach which, I feel, may avoid many of the difficulties that have stultified previous work.

The history of discussion of the law indicates that it is extremely difficult to avoid the unconscious use of ethical premises. I cannot, therefore, promise that I will not make such a mistake. All I can do is to say that I honestly tried to avoid it. The basic tools used in this book will be those of welfare economics. Like most welfare economists, I have always used the basic Paretian tools and have always felt a little unhappy about them.[1] In this book, I not only use the Paretian apparatus, but I should like to suggest a rather modest improvement in it; a somewhat simpler set of basic assumptions from which both welfare economics and the specific conclusions of this book can be deduced.

If we consider all possible changes in the state of the world, there will be some subset of those changes that is to my advantage. Furthermore, within this subset of possible changes is a further subset of changes that will also be to the advantage of you, the reader of this book. Last, but not least, within this second subset there is or at least may be another subset of possible changes that would be to the advantage of any person to whom you are talking. If this last subset is not an empty set, clearly I can argue that you should adopt it because it would be to your advantage and you can then argue with other people that they should adopt it because it would be to their advantage. Since I have put the matter in a perfectly general way, this amounts to saying that there may be some changes in the state of the world that are to everyone's advantage and that I can reasonably argue for them in terms of the advantage to other people, although my motive for doing so is self-interest. If such changes are possible, then we have an extremely elementary criterion for suggesting change. A proposed change within this set cannot be objectionable to anyone because if it is objectionable to anyone, it is not in the set.

Note that the converse is also true. In traditional discussion of Pareto optimality, changes that are desirable have been the principal theme and there has been little mention of changes that are clearly undesirable. Nevertheless, the traditional Paretian diagram shown in Figure 1.1 can be used to indicate undesirable changes.

1. See James M. Buchanan and Gordon Tullock, *The Calculus of Consent* (Ann Arbor: University of Michigan Press, 1962), especially pp. 85–99.

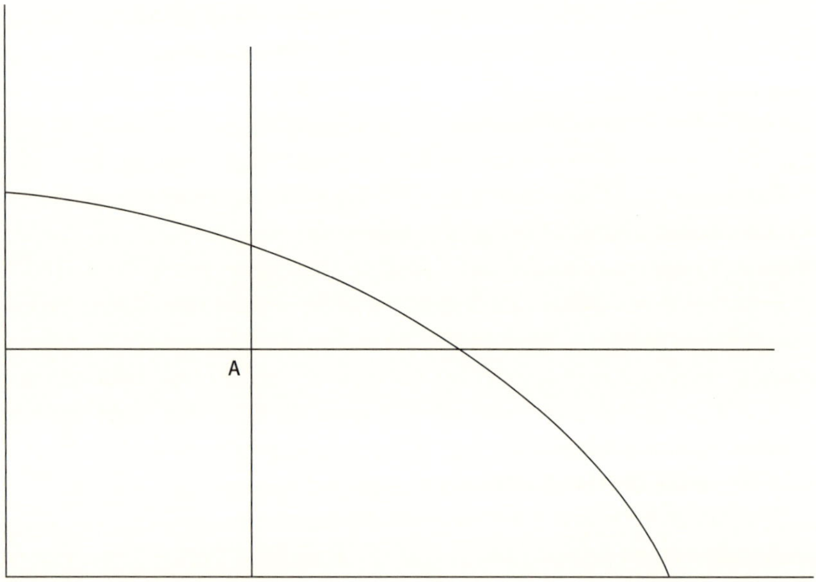

FIGURE 1.1
Conditional public welfare diagram

It is assumed that society is now at point A. The area of Pareto optimal changes shown by the triangle between the two lines through point A and the possibility frontier is, of course, the traditional area for desirable changes. The rectangle below and to the left of the point A, however, is an area of inefficient changes. Changes from point A to any point in that area injure at least one person and benefit no one. The two other areas, the second and fourth quadrants around point A, are areas of ambiguity. Strictly speaking, the economist cannot say anything about changes that will move into these two areas.

But if we have here a logically perfect method of selecting certain desirable policy changes, we still must ask if there are any possible policies that lie within the set. I think there are, and I am willing to argue that the policy of always undertaking Pareto optimal changes is an example. Suppose some change in the status quo is proposed and we discover by careful examination that it will injure no person and benefit at least one. Clearly my criteria do not indicate that everyone should favor it, although we could say that no one would be against it. Consider, however, a "constitutional" decision to adopt all changes that may be suggested that are Pareto optimal. Clearly each person would be guaranteed against harm by any such change and would have some finite probability of being benefited by one of these changes in the future; therefore, this policy would be in the self-interest of each of us. Thus the traditional Pareto optimal criteria can be "justified" by the new and more primitive criteria that I have suggested.

The converse of this situation is also easily dealt with. We can imagine a possible change in the status quo that injures me. It might be part of the set of those changes that also injures you and some of the joint members of these two sets that would injure substantially everyone. I can argue against such a change for the same reasons I can argue for generally beneficial changes. If we consider possible changes in the real world, clearly not all changes would fall either in that set of changes that benefits substantially everyone or in that set of changes that injures practically everyone. The possibility of compensation, however, convinces most economists that the set that falls in one or the other of these categories is sizable. In this book, we will devote ourselves mainly to discussing changes that are either in the subset of those that benefit everyone or in the subset of those that injure everyone.

However, I may have not yet convinced my readers that the set of all changes that meets my present criteria is not an empty one. There are people who believe that there is no such thing as a truly Pareto optimal change. It should be noted, then, that the criteria that I have proposed would also indicate that some changes that are not Pareto optimal should be made. Suppose we consider not an individual change but a policy for making changes in the future. Such a policy might well offer to every person a positive present discounted value *ex ante* while at the same time injure people in specific instances *ex post*. This type of Pareto optimality in the large was used as a foundation for *The Calculus of Consent* by James M. Buchanan and myself.[2] It can be used, however, for purposes other than developing a rationale for political institutions. One can imagine specific policies that would meet these criteria.

Martin Bailey once suggested that the federal government appoint an impartial board of cost-benefit analysts, which would then examine all proposals for public improvement in the United States. Those that the board found had a payoff higher than cost would be undertaken, and those in which the opposite relationship was found would not. Granting Bailey his implied assumptions about the ability of this committee to accurately analyze costs and benefits and to be free of bias, it is clear that an institution of this sort would

2. Ibid.

provide a positive discounted value for all of the citizens of the United States except possibly (and I emphasize possibly) some people who presently have a high prospect of obtaining a sizable gain from a project that is on the verge of implementation. Even this group, however, would be benefited if the proposal were to put Bailey's reform into operation ten years from today while permitting the present system to continue for ten years. I am sure that we could produce many further examples of general policies for making decisions in specific instances that would meet the criteria proposed.

It will, of course, be noted that these criteria carry within them a justification for welfare economics. If a proof has been developed that some particular change is Pareto optimal, then we can demonstrate, on the basis of our criteria, that this change should be adopted without any ethical presuppositions at all. In any event, this is the basic methodological tool that I shall use throughout the book. If, however, I am going to argue that any specific policy change or (as will be true in many cases in this book) a retention of our present policy is desirable for me, for you, and for any random person to whom you may speak, I must have some way of convincing you that this change is in accord with other people's preferences. This means, in a sense, that I must make some statement about everybody's ordering of preferences. These statements are contained in Chapter 2, and, in a sense, the theoretical work contained in the rest of the book is a development of these assumptions as to what people want. Explicit assumptions as to the shape of individual preference curves have not played much of a part in economic thought. I think, however, that a set of assumptions as simple and relatively obvious as the ones I propose to use has been implicit in much of the thinking that has gone on in this field.

CHAPTER 2

FUNDAMENTAL ASSUMPTIONS

A scientific theory consists of a logical structure proceeding from certain assumptions to certain conclusions. We hope that both the assumptions and the conclusions may be checked by comparing them with the real world; the more highly testable the theory, the better. Normally, however, certain parts of the theory are difficult to test. We are not unduly disturbed by this, since if parts of it survive tests, we assume that the untestable remainder is also true. The theory contained in this book raises exceptional problems in testing. Unfortunately, many of its implications are normative; that is, they simply indicate what people should do. This is an extraordinarily hard-to-test type of implication. I hope that it will turn out that these implications are difficult, but not impossible, to test; but I must confess that for many of them I can, at the moment, propose no tests. Of necessity, if I cannot propose many direct tests for the implications of my theory, I am rather more concerned with its assumptions than I would be were they more testable.

The three major assumptions upon which I base my discussion are fairly simple and should raise relatively few difficulties. Their content is so slight and so much in accord with ordinary experience that they are reasonably invulnerable. The reader should note that two of these assumptions are assumptions about *his* preferences. The fact that these assumptions are assumptions about the reader may seem surprising. Certainly if I am to make assumptions about any random reader of the book, these assumptions must be extremely general and primitive. Otherwise, they would not fit all possible readers. In fact, I shall occasionally point out special groups who might find that certain assumptions will not fit them in certain circumstances. In general, however, I think most of the readers will indeed find these assumptions are characteristic of their own situation.

In a sense, my argument for a given legal standard will be an appeal to the reader and will also be an argument that he could use in talking to other people. The other people, or, for that matter, the reader, could be drawn more or less at random from the entire population. The argument for the use of general standards instead of special laws for each individual person is simply that such laws can be urged in general debate. I cannot depend upon convincing anyone else that a special law giving me special powers is likely to be in his interest. If there is, however, some change in the law that would benefit substantially everyone, then it should be easier for me to argue for it. The person to whom I am speaking may have difficulty following a long train of reasoning, but at least no conflict of interest will result.

My first general assumption is that the reader is not in a position to assure himself of special legal treatment. That is, if I argue that you, the reader, should favor a law against theft, one of the basic assumptions is that you do not have a real opportunity to have a law enacted that prohibits theft by everyone else but leaves you free to steal. I am quite prepared to agree that such a law, with its special privilege for you, would be more to your advantage than general prohibition of theft. My argument applies only if you are in a position (as most of us are) wherein you have no real chance of securing such a special privilege. Dictators and kings would be differently placed, and the use of my logical system might lead them to enact such special laws. In point of fact, that "the law does not bind the sovereign" is a very old principle. In recent years, with the decline of the powers of kings and rulers in the English-speaking world, the rule has been modified to a very large extent. Still, even the most radical egalitarian of today would agree that the Supreme Court cannot bind itself. It can be argued, of course, that it should act as if it were bound. But these are special cases that do not include most readers.

For most readers, a rule that everyone except X should be prohibited from stealing would be worse than a rule prohibiting everyone from stealing, because most readers would have no possibility of being X.[1] The reader should favor *general* standards simply because a set of individually categorized standards is not likely to put him in a very favorable category. If he has a real chance of being put into a high category, such as a member of a legally privileged nobility, then I cannot argue that he should turn it down. In fact, my line of reasoning would suggest that the nobles have normally been sensible in trying to retain their privileges, just as the commonalty has been sensible in trying to reduce them.

While I can offer no argument for a set of general standards as against a set of special rules carefully designed to benefit the reader himself, I can warn him that historical evidence indicates that such systems have sometimes worked very badly. Furthermore, they sometimes turn out to be fraudulent. Often people have favored systems that they believed would give them a special position, only to later discover that they were deceived. The Bolsheviks, for example, promised the Russian proletariat a very special position in the state that

1. See "A and B," *The Mikado*, William Gilbert and Arthur Sullivan.

they proposed to construct. At least some of the proletariat presumably supported the Bolsheviks for this reason. It turned out that the special position that was valuable in the "new society" was that of Bolshevik, not proletarian. The system did, of course, discriminate against some nonproletarians, but that can hardly have been much consolation to the proletarians themselves.

But this is merely an historic example. Basically the argument for *general* standards must turn on the fact that the probability of being in a privileged minority is low. Parenthetically, it is also hard to propagandize for a system of special privilege. If you wish to publicly argue for a certain set of laws, you must either argue for laws that are, or appear to be, in the general interest, or that concentrate on a powerful group that can override the majority. The only other alternative is the Bolshevik one of a secret conspiracy, but this will seldom be effective. For most people this set of alternatives is unreal, and they must thus argue for general standards, not a set of categorized norms.

It should be noted that in one area special groups seem to be able to obtain special legislation *ad infinitum*. This is what we may call "economic legislation." The old common law was, in general, binding on all people and intended to control everyone's activity. Modern legal codes are filled with special economic privileges for special groups. I cannot, for example, become a barber without the permission of other barbers, who are permitted to manipulate this permission in such a way as to obtain cartel gains. As a professor, I cannot be fired because of pressures that university professors in general have succeeded in applying to the university structure. We could go on and on with such examples. The "protective" tariff system, the regulatory agencies—all are examples of special privileges for special groups that are part of the law.

As I stated previously, it is not possible for me to criticize special groups for favoring laws that give them special privileges. It is possible, however, to prove fairly readily that no one who is *not* a member of these special groups should favor these special privileges, and that probably most of the members of these special groups would be better off than they are now if *all* privileges—their own and the others that now exist—were abolished. The real question is how political systems permit certain small groups to obtain special economic legislation that discriminates in their favor. Since I have written a good deal on this subject, I will only briefly discuss it here.[2] I would

2. See James M. Buchanan and Gordon Tullock, *The Calculus of Consent* (Ann Arbor: University of Michigan Press, 1962), and Gordon Tullock, *Toward a Mathematics of Politics* (Ann Arbor: University of Michigan Press, 1967).

argue for a general rule prohibiting this type of special legislation. My argument clearly has not been accepted by any present-day government, but that does not mean it is incorrect.

If the first assumption indicates that most people should favor general legal standards, it does little to tell us what these standards should be. This situational assumption then plays only a minor explicit role in the discussion of specific laws that make up the remainder of the book. It will, however, underlie all of the proposals made herein, because without it there would be no argument for general laws at all. The two remaining major assumptions are about the preference schedule of the reader (any reader) of this book. In order to make use of the preference schedule of an unselected individual, I must obviously use only certain highly general aspects of the individual preference schedule, and must believe that these aspects are universal. The reader can check my basic assumptions very simply by considering introspectively whether they do or do not describe his own preferences. If they do not, then in my opinion either he has not understood what I have said or he needs help badly. In his opinion, I would be wrong.

Proceeding, then, I assume that the reader normally chooses what he prefers; that is, if he is presented the right to take either A or B and he prefers A, he will take A. This seems obvious, but it is sometimes alleged that an individual may want to take A, but, for reasons of ethics or duty, he actually takes B. I do not doubt the observation upon which this denial is based, but I contest its interpretation. The difference really concerns the word "prefer." My hypothetical critic believes that the word covers only part of the reasons why a man may do something. Thus a child seeing a candy bar may "prefer" to eat it but refrains from doing so because it is not his and he has been taught not to steal. This is, I think, a legitimate usage of the word "prefer," but I am employing another usage that is equally legitimate.[3] In this second use, "prefer" is much broader and takes in all influences upon a decision. The child "prefers" not to take the candy bar because the pleasure of eating it would not compensate him for breaking a rule of conduct. The distinction, of course, is familiar to economists. By a preferred action I mean one that lifts the individual to a higher indifference surface, regardless of the reasons for the "preference."

I should perhaps pause at this point in order to remove a possible suspicion that may be forming in the reader's mind. Since I am including moral drives in the individual's preference schedule, may I not, therefore, be sneaking

3. Paul A. Samuelson, *Economics*, 3rd ed. (New York: McGraw-Hill, 1955), pp. 432–35.

them into my reasoning? May I not urge that stealing should be made illegal because all people want it to be illegal? To set the reader's mind at rest, I do not use such preference for moral action in deducing my laws. Such a preference may turn up occasionally, but in a manner that is, I think, free from this criticism. If my system is to be realistic, I must recognize that real men have such drives, but I do not need to use them as the foundation of my theory.

My third basic postulate is that the individual normally prefers a choice to a lack of a choice. This principle, which is almost deducible from the prior one, is that an individual would prefer to be permitted to choose.[4] Given his choice between simply receiving A or being permitted to select either A or B, he will choose to select. It should be noted that, for the principle to apply, A and B must be different. If the individual knows that they are identical, he will not care. Furthermore, if A and B are not identical, the difference between them may still be less than the effort involved in making the choice. In this case, also, the individual will choose not to choose, not because he values the choice at zero, but because he values it less than the cost.

An example may clarify the matter. Suppose an Oriental monarch tells one of his subjects (in a kingdom from the Arabian Nights) that he may go to a room in the royal treasury and take the contents. Surely the subject would be gratified, but he would be even more gratified if told that he could inspect the contents of two rooms, and then take whichever one he wanted. Given the choice between simply taking the contents of the first room or choosing between it and a second room, he would surely prefer the second choice. Note, however, the necessity of efficient sets. For our assumption to apply, the larger collection of alternatives must include the smaller.

If, of course, the individual knew that he preferred the contents of the first room over that of the second, he would be completely indifferent; but in this case he has already chosen between the two rooms. For our purposes he must choose between having freedom of choice or not before making up his mind on the ultimate question. This is a simple logical requirement, since making up his mind on the ultimate question involves the choice under discussion. If he has already chosen between A and B, he must first have chosen to consider the matter and then made his choice.

4. Trout Rader argues quite strongly that, in fact, my third basic postulate is deducible from the second. "[The individual's] preference should be for final outcomes. If he is uncertain before making investigation, then he prefers a choice only because the expected outcome is thereby increased. Thusly interpreted, there is no logical problem and assumption three is implied by assumption two and the definition of choice." (From private communication.)

Our basic principle that individuals prefer choice, however, raises an apparent logical problem. Would an individual prefer to be given a choice between getting a choice and not getting a choice? The individual prefers being given a choice between A and B to simply receiving A. This means that he has chosen an alternative, let us call it X, which involves a choice between A and B over another alternative, let us call it Y, which involves only receiving A. Would the individual prefer a choice between X and Y to simply receiving X? At our present level of generality the answer is "yes." This appears to involve a contradiction, but it is merely an apparent one. If the individual has already in fact chosen between X and Y, then he may not wish to bother to repeat the operation. If, however, he actually has not chosen, he would prefer to do so. Once he has chosen X, then he becomes indifferent between simply receiving X or choosing it, but prior to his making the choice he should prefer freedom to coercion. The fact that we as outsiders can predict what choice he will make at every stage is irrelevant.

If we wish, we can easily construct an infinite series of choices for our individual. Thus M and N represent, respectively, a choice between X and Y or simply receiving X; would the individual prefer freedom of choice between them to simply receiving M? Clearly the series can be extended infinitely. This infinite regress, however, is something that we artificially construct, not something that impedes the individual's choice processes. At any stage we can give the long series of choices to the individual, and he will quickly work his way down to a definite final choice between A and B. The infinite series is infinite in an opposite direction from that in which the choosing individual would travel, and hence the possibility of infinite regression need not trouble him or us.

But would an individual continue to desire multiplication of his choices no matter how many there were? In our example, it is clear that the courtier would prefer to choose one out of two rooms full of treasure to being given one, but would he necessarily prefer to choose one out of 1,000 treasure rooms to one out of 999? The problem, obviously, is that a random sample of 999 is very similar to one of 1,000. Whether the choosing individual would regard the difference between these two alternatives as being great enough to justify the expenditure of energy used in making a choice would appear to be a matter upon which we cannot make any *a priori* judgment.

In order to analyze the situation, however, let us turn to the traditional probability apparatus of an urn filled with balls. Let us suppose that each ball has a number inside it and a wealthy man agrees to let a friend reach into the urn and remove a ball, the wealthy man being willing to pay the friend the amount of the number on the chosen ball in dollars. Clearly this would be a very advantageous proposition for the friend. Equally clearly, permission to select two, three, or more balls and collect the money for whichever had the largest number would be even more advantageous.

As the number of balls drawn increases, however, the likely gain from each one drawn goes down. The best of seven is likely to be greater than the best of six, but the probable gain is much smaller than between the better of two or the best of three. Thus, the net expected gain from the operation of drawing another ball out of the urn, opening it, and determining whether the number it contains is higher than any previously drawn ball declines steadily as the number of balls drawn increases. The actual work involved in drawing the balls, small though it is, does not decline. In fact, if the man who is drawing the balls is normal, the disutility of making the additional drawings will actually slowly increase. It is thus clear that eventually the friend will stop drawing the balls from the urn even if his wealthy benefactor tells him he may draw as many as he wants. This occurs not because he prefers a choice among 2,316 alternatives to a choice among 2,317 (which contain the original 2,316) but because he thinks the difference between a set of 2,316 and a set of 2,317 is trivial. He does not wish to draw one more ball from the urn, because the tiny disutility associated with the act of drawing is greater than the anticipated profit.

Even if the person who was to be permitted to draw the balls out of the urn thought that he was likely to stop after drawing 2,316 balls, this would not mean that he would be indifferent if the wealthy man proposed to restrict him to that amount. Firstly, he could not be certain when he would tire to the point of wishing to stop. Secondly, before he began drawing, he would not know anything about the distribution of the numbers on the balls. They might be distributed in such a way as to offer considerable inducements to continue much beyond 2,316 draws. If, for example, there were 1,000,000 balls in the urn and each of the numbers between 1 and 1,000,000 appeared on one of them, he might stop at 2,316. If, however, 99.9 percent of the balls had $1.00 on them and the remaining balls had one of the numbers 1,000, 2,000, 3,000, . . . , 1,000,000 on it, he might be motivated to continue on beyond 2,316 in spite of his ennui.[5]

5. In this case he might stop after eight or nine drawings unless he was somehow informed of the high value 0.1 percent.

Although the individual might not exhaust his opportunities, he would normally want no external restrictions on the area in which he can make choices. There is, however, one situation (and, practically, a most important one) in which he might choose a less extensive range of choices over a larger one. If the choices in the smaller range are preselected so that they are more favorable than those in the larger range, he might prefer the smaller area. Thus, if our wealthy man gave his friend the choice of drawing 1,000 balls out of his urn or of drawing 900 balls out of an urn that contained duplicates of the best half of the balls in the first urn, he would choose the second. The choice of 1,000 is not strictly comparable to the choice of 900, because the set of 900 is not contained in the set of 1,000.

The same line of reasoning indicates that the individual would not choose to extend his range of choice if the additional choices made it less likely that his final choice would be a high-value ball. Thus, a proposal to put another 100 balls into the urn, each of them with a sum between zero and $1.00 on it, would not be regarded as an improvement even though it does widen the apparent realm of choice. There might seem to be some contradiction between our basic assumption that an individual will always prefer to have his range of choice widened and our listing of areas where he will not choose to select from the widest possible assortment. In fact, he always prefers a wider choice, but this preference is limited; he can be paid to give it up. These payments can take the form of direct gifts, change in the structure of the alternatives, or simply the avoidance of the time-consuming task of making up one's mind between two substantially identical alternatives. In each case, the individual accepts a restriction on his choices in one area, but the "payment" he receives permits him to increase his area of choice somewhere else.

In order to explore this matter further, let us assume that the man in the Arabian Nights tale looking at rooms full of jewels is able to predict that, after looking at exactly 1,000 rooms, he will be unwilling to continue the search. He feels that the difference between the best of 1,001 and the best of 1,000 is small enough so that the time cost to him of examining the additional room would not be worth the benefit. Would he be perfectly happy if the Sultan specified 1,000 rooms? I do not think so. However, in this case the matter is somewhat dubious; it would depend upon the motives of the Sultan.

If the Sultan simply selected a collection of 1,000 rooms at random, my subject would presumably be indifferent between this and his own choice, although the possibility of perhaps simplifying his search by selecting rooms that were close together should also be considered. If, however, the subject suspected that the Sultan was beginning to regret his initial offer and that perhaps the 1,000 rooms pointed out were a negatively biased sample, he presumably would object strenuously to the change in conditions. On the other hand, if he felt confident that the Sultan was actually pointing out the 1,000 best rooms, he presumably would be very grateful.

We may consider it as a general rule that we would not wish to have our freedom of choice restricted by someone whose interests are contrary to ours. A restriction exactly the same as one we ourselves would impose (if this could somehow be worked out) would be something to which we would be indifferent, but anyone who claimed that he intended to do this would be suspect. A restriction that gave us a superior sample, however, might well be an improvement. Here our reasoning leads us to step back. If the Sultan pointed out 1,000 rooms to which his choice would be restricted, the individual would prefer to be given a choice between selecting his own 1,000 to accepting those pointed out by the Sultan. Thus, once again we move to a larger choice field from a narrower one. If he decided to accept the Sultan's 1,000 rooms, this would not contradict our general principle of wider choice being desired because this set is not contained within the alternative set.

This general principle has wide application to society in general. We frequently choose to patronize an establishment where a number of possible assortments of goods and services have been excluded by the management. Restaurants, for example, commonly are not purely à la carte, but have menus in which the entire meal is at least partially specified. In part this is the result of certain mechanical efficiencies that the restaurant can achieve with this type of organization, but in part it also proceeds from the desire of the restaurant keeper to provide superior food for his customers and his customers' knowledge that he is so motivated. Customers are willing to permit him to restrict their choice, because they assume that he will restrict them, on the whole, in a favorable manner.

Similarly, wealthy people frequently patronize stores that have a smaller variety of goods on display than the ones patronized by the less wealthy—not because they want their choice restricted in a pure sense, but because this smaller selection contains goods of a higher average quality than those available in the larger stores catering to the middle class. The wealthy man's advantage is that he has a choice between going to the large store dealing in a large range of goods or going to the smaller store with a superior selection. A movement toward greater wealth is thus a movement toward a wider range of choice.

The similarity between the statement that people want more freedom, more choices, and the common economic principle that people prefer more to less is of broad significance. In general, the structure of preferences that economists normally assume people to have can be deduced from our very general proposition. In particular, the view that an individual will always choose—assuming that he considers the matter carefully—that alternative that maximizes the present discounted value of his income stream is deducible from our premises.[6] Thus, frequently in the latter part of this book we prove something to be desirable simply by proving that it does increase the present discounted value of the lifetime income stream.

Our procedure, however, has an advantage over the standard economic approach; it can be applied in nonmarket areas. Increased political power may also bring a wider range of choice. What we normally refer to as personal freedom will usually, although not always, increase the total range of choice, and here again we can use the present discounted value technique. It must be admitted, however, that most of the applications of our greater freedom hypothesis are in areas customarily discussed in a study of economics and come down to choosing more rather than less.

The relationship of these propositions to the set of intersecting sets in the first chapter is, I presume, obvious. If my statements about individual preferences are correct, then the type of polity that meets our greater freedom hypothesis, or "the-more-rather-than-less-than" hypothesis of conventional economics, is within the set of propositions favored by everyone. Changes may also exist that are opposed by everyone and that would therefore be in a converse set. By starting with a general specification of the type of change in society that would be "sellable," we have pointed out that if there are changes in society from which substantially everyone would benefit, we may be able to convince people to make these changes. Then by specifying several very weak restrictions on individual preference functions, we find that there are indeed some cases within this set of desirable changes. The remainder of the book largely consists of exploring cases that fall within these categories.

Before closing our discussion of this particular subject it is necessary to point out a minor, more or less obvious but extremely important, corollary.

6. There are, of course, the problems of risk aversion here as in other economic reasoning. Fortunately, in most of the succeeding reasoning the choice that maximizes present discounted value also reduces risk. In those cases where it does not, special arrangements are proposed to take risk aversion into account.

Suppose an individual prefers a class of choices that we shall call A to another class of choices that we shall call B. As a normal rule, he would be willing to pay something, perhaps only a little, in order to receive class A instead of class B. In the marginal case this would not be so, but the marginal case is not a common phenomenon. Mainly, he will be willing to receive A minus some small payment in preference to B if he prefers A to B. This is of great importance to our later discussion because in general we demonstrate that the individual will be well advised to participate in the establishment of a social organization that guarantees him the receipt of some particular class of choices. Thus, he will have to pay for it. In general, we will not discuss the size of this payment, mainly because we lack empirical evidence in the field, but obviously this would also be a relevant matter.

In addition to these three major assumptions about individual preferences, three far less important assumptions should be dealt with before we turn to the law itself. These assumptions are much more dubious than the three we have discussed thus far, and it is fortunate that they are of less importance. A reader disagreeing with any one of them can disregard the portion of the book in which it is used and still accept most of our conclusions. The first is quite complicated and requires a fairly lengthy explanation. It is simplest to start with an example. When I taught at the University of South Carolina, the summer school was drastically reorganized. Among the new regulations was one that provided that any member of the teaching staff could have an appointment to teach in one of the two summer sessions, but that no one could teach in two sessions. I was rather critical of this provision, arguing that it simply reduced the freedom of choice of the professors. Instead of being given a free choice between no summer teaching, teaching in one session, or teaching in two sessions, professors were restricted to the first two alternatives.

Several of my colleagues disagreed with me quite vigorously, offering arguments that at the time I thought were stupid, but that now seem to me to have been quite sensible. They stated that they did not want to teach through the whole summer but that they feared that if the option of teaching two sessions were left open to them they would find the money for the second session too attractive, and hence would teach two sessions, which they did not want to do. Although I thought this just indicated intellectual confusion at the time, there is an assumption that makes their position defensible and explains many provisions of both law and contracts.

Consider an alcoholic. Some alcoholics are sober for considerable periods and only fall "off the wagon" occasionally. These people, when sober, normally are strongly opposed to their behavior when drunk, and will take precautions (usually unsuccessful) to prevent their next binge. Suppose we offered such people a commercial service, which, in return for an advance payment, provided a large, tough man to follow them around and physically stop them from drinking. I suspect that such a service would be quite popular if alcoholics could pay the price. In any event, surely some alcoholics would be interested.

This, however, appears to contradict our basic theorems. The individual is willing to undergo a reduction of his freedom of choice now, i.e., pay a fee, for the purpose of reducing his future freedom of choice. How do we explain this if individuals always prefer an increase in their freedom of choice? There does not appear to be an offsetting side payment. The alcoholic's freedom is reduced both now and in the future. It could, of course, be argued that the alcoholic is being "forced" to do something that he does not want to do by the alcohol, and the bodyguard merely counterbalances that force, thus leaving him free. This argument is not very appealing, however, and in any event it does not account for my colleagues who did not want to be permitted to teach two terms in the summer.

A better solution can be developed from a consideration of the discounting of future events. Economically, discounting appears simple. We simply apply market interest rates together with some allowance for the relative risk, which takes the form of a markup of the interest rate, and then compare the present value of the future events. For our present purposes, however, I would like to present normal economic discounting in a rather unusual way. Figure 2.1 is a graphic representation of the theory. The vertical axis drawn on a (logarithmic) scale represents the utility units to be obtained from any given action. The horizontal axis represents time with the origin at "now."

If the individual is contemplating immediate action X, he draws a line from the point representing the utility value of X on the vertical axis slanting upward at an angle determined by the appropriate rate of interest. Action X, if taken, will prevent the individual from performing some other action, say Z, in the future. He is, for example, buying a house, and if he puts his money into that, he will not have the money available to invest in a business opportunity in the fall. We plot action Z at its proper time and with the number of utility units it will produce at that time. If it is below the line originating at X units, then the individual should take action X. If, on the other hand, the second action were above the line, such as Y, the individual would logically refrain from action X and take action Y when the time was propitious. Suppose, however, that the individual is called upon now to make up his mind

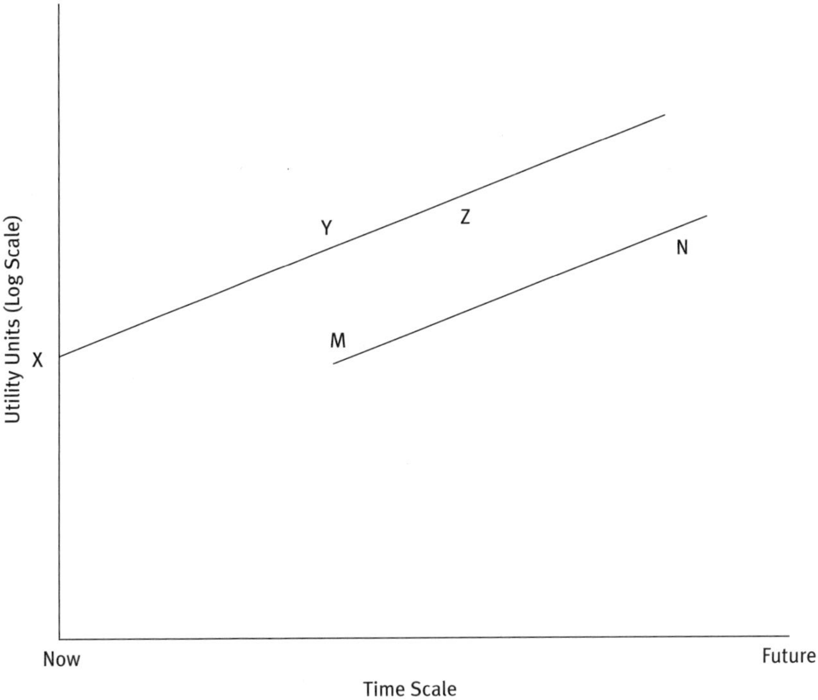

FIGURE 2.1
Classical time discounting

between two actions, M and N, both being in the future. We can deduce his decision quite simply. We simply plot the two points on our graph and draw a line from M at the slope of the rate of interest rate. If N is below this line, the individual will choose action M; if N is above the line, he will choose N.

All of this, however, assumes that we have an appropriate rate of interest. Since we are making our judgments in utility units, this would seldom be the case. The active businessman, interested in monetary matters, whose utility is highly correlated with his income, can easily use our model. He can simply take the market rate of interest for his discount rate, and he will come out ahead if he follows the rules we have shown. The market rate of interest, however, is the result of the interactions of a number of people and is not the subjective discounting factor of any individual. The businessman adjusts his actions so that his own margins match on this rate of interest, which is a given phenomenon to him. The fact that the choosing individual has a choice between X and Y on our diagram can be taken as evidence that, for at least some other person, the subjective values of these acts are sufficiently different so that this other person would prefer the present X to the distant Y.

In real life, very few people have access to short-term loans at the same rate of interest as longer-term loans. Thus, the part of our line that approaches the vertical axis is theoretical rather than real. In those cases where no actual market transaction is possible—and we shall turn to a number of such cases in Chapter 3—the individual must make his decisions in terms of his own subjective discounting formula. That is, he must weigh present against future gains by use of his own judgment. It seems likely that, for most people, the subjective time discounting schedule would not follow the straight line of Figure 2.1, but a curve of the type shown at X, in Figure 2.2. The axes of this graph are the same as those of 2.1, but it is assumed that the individual has no market rate of interest at which he can discount the particular transactions he is contemplating.

Being unable to use the money market, he is forced to make his own

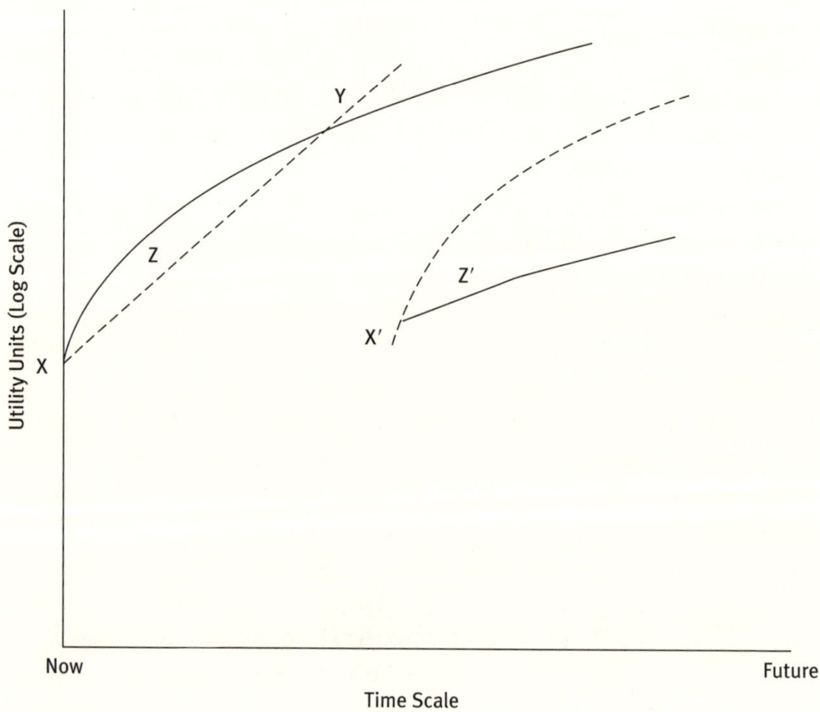

FIGURE 2.2
Logarithmic time discounting

judgments. The curve shown simply indicates that the individual's time discounting is not of the simple straight line sort that we find in the commercial market. Roughly, I have assumed that the individual discounts small differences in time more sharply when they are immediate than when they are far away. The individual would pay more to advance some pleasure from tomorrow to today than he would to advance it one day five years from now.

This assumption about the individual's preference schedule seems reasonable, and I shall shortly offer some arguments for its validity, but it plays a relatively minor role in the rest of the book. Its invalidity would result in destroying the proof of only a small minority of the propositions that are presented shortly. Thus, the reader who feels that his particular preference function does not have this shape can disagree with the propositions built upon it while accepting those in which it plays no part.[7] Most readers, however, will probably find that they do have a subjective time anticipation function of about this shape.

Given this sort of preference schedule, the individual will prefer the present satisfaction X to the near future satisfaction Z, but he will prefer the satisfaction Y in the more distant future to both of them in spite of the fact that a straight line connecting point X on the vertical axis and point Y (the dashed line) passes below point Z. I am not alleging any irrationality on the part of the individual, only that he regards the delay in the next few hours as being more significant than the delay of a few hours in the distant future. In a sense, the individual views future time on something like a logarithmic scale. For the individual, this may be very rational, but the market smooths individual preferences out to produce the straight line discounting function of Figure 2.1.[8] The market function is not more rational than the individual function hypothesized—it is merely the result of aggregating a large number of such functions.

This type of function, however, has a very real effect upon decisions about future choices. Suppose an individual at the "now" point of our diagram is contemplating the choice between X at the same time and Z a little later. Let

7. I have no strong feelings about the exact shape of the curve I have drawn. Presumably, it varies somewhat from individual to individual, and may be much more complicated than this one. My basic assumption is simply the greater steepness of the early section.

8. The difference between the discounting line in Figures 2.1 and 2.2 is mostly in the first segment. Since very short-term loans are more or less unobtainable in the real world, this segment in Figure 2.1 does not represent the real market situation.

us assume that X is the pleasure of taking one more drink and Z the pleasure of not having a hangover the next morning.[9] The individual will choose the extra drink. Suppose, however, that the individual is able to contemplate the desirability of taking a fourth cocktail at a party to be held next Saturday night (X′ on Figure 2.2) as compared with the pleasure of avoiding the hangover next Sunday morning (Z′). We construct another discounting function parallel to the one originating at X and running through X′ and observe that Z′ lies above it. The individual now prefers Z′ to X′.

If, however, we consider the individual at time X′, then his discounting curve would follow the dotted line, and he would prefer X′ to Z′. Thus, he now feels that he should not have the fourth cocktail next Saturday night; but he realizes that when the choice comes up, he will drink another. Clearly, he should be willing to make at least some sacrifice now to prevent himself from getting X–Z′. Thus, he should now be willing to reduce his freedom in order to put restraints on his freedom of choice at some time in the future. If he is successful in putting some restraint on his freedom of choice at time X′, then he will be unhappy about the restraint when the time comes. It does, however, increase the present discounted value of his future and probably will also seem like a good decision from time Z′.

This permits us to explain both the alcoholic who hires a man to stop him from drinking and my colleagues who did not want to be given a free choice as to how much of their summer they would spend teaching. In both cases, the individual now has a preference as to which choice he should make between two alternatives, both lying in the future. He can also predict that the change in perspective that will occur when the future becomes the present will change his preferences. He maximizes his present satisfaction by taking action that prevents him from obtaining his preference in the future.[10]

Our second minor assumption is that people are risk avoiders. This proposition has given economists a great deal of difficulty, because it would appear

9. It seems probable that one of the effects of drink, or any form of excitement, is to bend the discounting line even more sharply than its normal shape. Thus, it may be that the additional drink would not appear worth it in any event if the man were sober. It also seems possible that conduct referred to as "irrational" quite frequently is simply the result of a more sharply bent discounting curve than that possessed by the normal individual.

10. See Robert H. Strotz, "Myopia and Inconsistency in Dynamic Utility Maximization," *Review of Economics and Statistics* 23, No. 3 (1956): 165–80.

that people are also risk seekers.[11] The same person who buys insurance on his home also goes to Las Vegas and spends an evening gambling. Although attempting to reconcile these two behavioral patterns into one preference function has caused a great deal of trouble to many economists, for us, the problem is fortunately simpler. We can take the minimal assumption that some people are sometimes risk averters. Surely, no one will question that. The reason that we can use this modest assumption is that the institutional changes that we propose make it possible for people to reduce the risk if they choose. These changes will not make it impossible for them to increase the risk if that is their desire. Our objective is simply to separate the decision as to how much risk one will run from the decision on other matters.

As an example, at the present time when I drive I run a real danger that some other car will collide with me. If I am a risk avoider, I would like to have this risk reduced. If, on the other hand, I like risk, there is no reason why I cannot place near my bed a bomb with a random device that may or may not set it off. By suitable choice of the parameters of the random device, I can obtain any risk to life and limb that I desire without injuring or endangering anyone else.[12] Thus, reducing the likelihood of accidents would lower the risk for the risk averters but would still leave it open to the risk seekers to obtain whatever amount of risk they feel is best.

This assumption would seem to be fairly invulnerable to attack. Nevertheless, any individual who feels that it is not descriptive of the real world, who feels that all human beings always seek additional risk, will find it possible to modify the reasoning that follows by leaving this assumption out and still accepting many conclusions in the book.

Our third minor assumption is also one that the reader may disbelieve without rejecting the bulk of the conclusions in the book. It simply states that people do not get greater amounts of pleasure from inflicting injury or observing injury inflicted on others than the pain that they would suffer themselves if they were the victim. To clarify, let me give an imaginary example. Assume roughly that you would be unwilling to enter into a gambling agreement under which each of ten people drew a straw out of a hat and the short straw was subject to physical harm by the others. It seems to me that this is a

11. See Leonard J. Savage and Milton Friedman, "The Expected Utility Hypothesis and the Measurability of Utility," *Journal of Political Economy* 60 (December 1952): 463–74.

12. It might be wise to require individuals seeking this type of risk to either live in isolated areas or armor-plate their bedrooms.

fairly modest assumption and, indeed, a great many people receive pain rather than pleasure from observing injury inflicted on other people or from inflicting it themselves. Still, once again, this assumption is needed only for a small part of the reasoning of the latter part of the book.

As we proceed, various other special minor assumptions are used in the reasoning, which normally concern the situation covered by a particular law. In general, these should cause no great difficulty, but it is possible that one or more of them is incorrect, and in that event, of course, a particular theorem is false. Running through this part of the assumption set, however, is a complete set of assumptions mainly *im*plicit rather than *ex*plicit of very minor nature and having a considerable family resemblance. I doubt that they will upset any practical man, but conceivably some theorist may raise questions about them. Basically, these will be assumptions that people do not positively value certain types of activity to such a great extent that their practical inconveniences are overridden. More specifically, individuals do not get enough of a thrill from being robbed so that it more than compensates them for the loss of their money.

A person might favor making theft legal for several reasons, including the thought that he would gain from making theft legal because he would be able to commit more thefts on other people than would be committed on him. This one is discussed in the body of the book. I ignore the second possibility that he would get such a thrill out of being robbed that he would enjoy the process and would rather have it legally possible for people to steal from him. With respect to this particular possible preference ordering, however, there is no logical reason why the existence of some people who had this particular preference ordering could not be dealt with by a simple institutional change. Since I regard this as a highly unlikely preference set and the whole issue as unimportant, I have placed the demonstration of this point in an appendix. Thus, in the body of the book I assume that there is no one who has this particular preference ordering.

The third possibility, the existence of someone for whom a large number of thefts (not committed on him or by him) is a source of positive pleasure, is also ruled out. This pleasure would have to be sufficiently strong that he would be willing to accept a substantial reduction in his living standards in other respects in order to obtain this amount of theft. This type of preference ordering would cause very great difficulties for the reasoning in the book, and I shall assume there is no one of this sort around. In the real world, people like this would be disregarded, so their possible existence would have very little effect upon the application of my reasoning.

It would be possible to specify various other quasilunatic preference orderings that individuals might have that would conflict with the conclusions reached in this book. It is not possible for me to compile a list of all possible wildly deviant preference orderings and discuss them one at a time. Hence, I shall simply assume that they do not exist. This, as I said before, should cause no great difficulty for the practical man, but the purist may object. I am sorry in this respect that I am not able to demonstrate my point regardless of the preference orderings. It should be noted, however, that very few things can be demonstrated to be desirable if one assumes a complete and totally uncontrolled range of preferences. The oldest chestnut in economics is the demonstration that tariffs on the whole are undesirable. If we assume that there is one person in the world who positively likes tariffs *qua* tariffs, and whose liking for tariffs is so high that no possible payment would compensate him for eliminating them, this proof fails in pure welfare terms. Economists implicitly ignore the possible existence of such people. I see no reason why I should not behave similarly.

PART 2

CIVIL LAW

CHAPTER 3

CONTRACTS, SUBSTANTIVE LAW

A simple contract involves a promise by A to do something tomorrow in return for B's doing something today. A promise, however, can be broken. Would it be sensible to favor the establishment of a system for enforcing selected promises? Simply from our assumption that the individual will choose to extend his range of choice, it follows that it would. If confronted with the choice between situation A, in which promises are not "enforced," and situation B, in which promises may either be "enforced" or not, as the maker chooses, it would be rational to take the latter. It does not, after all, compel you to make enforceable promises, it only makes it possible. Situation A, on the other hand, limits you to unenforceable promises. Situation B is, of course, the existing law.

The fact that most legal codes permit the making of unenforceable promises is, for some reason, normally overlooked in discussions of the law. Since courts are largely engaged in dealing with enforceable contracts, the fact that not all promises are enforceable at law or in equity tends to be ignored. In fact, it is very easy to make an unenforceable promise. It seems likely that most promises that are made in day-to-day life are lacking in the technical characteristics that would give a court power to enforce them. If a promise might be enforceable, a simple statement that it is not to be legally binding will normally make it unenforceable.

Thus we have demonstrated that people should favor the establishment of a mechanism to make it possible for them to make enforceable promises. It is clear that situations in which making such an enforceable promise is desirable are fairly frequent. I wish to buy a house and do not have enough money to do so. Borrowing the money will improve my satisfaction, but in order to borrow I have to convince the lender that I will repay. Perhaps I can get away with an unenforceable promise, but for most people such loans are only possible if there is some mechanism to enforce the repayment.

At first glance, it would appear that we would favor a complete freedom to make any promise we wish under any conditions that we wish, and, indeed, the early utilitarians argued just that. A more careful examination of the problem indicates that there are possibly desirable limitations, and limitations and restrictions are contained in the present contract law. I do not wish to argue that the present body of contract law is ideal, but some limitations on unfettered freedom of contract are, as we shall see, sensible. The "optimum" restrictions, furthermore, would follow somewhat the same lines as those now in existence. On the other hand, it is clear that some of the existing contract rules are irrational, the results not of careful thought but of obscurantism and emotion.

As an example, once I have bought my house, I will obviously be better off if I can somehow avoid paying, or at least get better terms. If I have the normal human attitudes, I can easily convince myself that these desires are morally right, and that the mortgage holder is wicked. In recent times, the technical discussions of mortgages have normally been dominated by a sympathy for those mortgagees who have difficulty paying. Thus, a climate of opinion has emerged in which modifications of the mortgage contract by law should emerge in such a way as to benefit the mortgagee. Since the number of people who are currently paying off the mortgage on their houses is always much larger than the number who are in the business of lending money for such mortgages, or those who are currently contemplating borrowing, the possibility of modifying the contract for the benefit of the mortgagee is always present in a democracy.

This is, of course, not irrational. While it is sensible for me to want to be able to make an enforceable promise to repay the money loaned to me, once it is in my hands it is equally sensible for me to approve modifications in the contract in my favor. Once again our expansion of choice hypothesis is useful. Having the choice of repaying or not is obviously a superior position to not having this choice. Thus, the people who are now paying off their mortgages are likely to favor measures that reduce the security of the holders of the mortgages. The result has been the development of a set of laws that "protects" the debtor. These laws, however, do not compel people to issue mortgages. Naturally, they refrain from granting mortgages unless the interest rate compensates them for the additional risk. A full discussion of this problem requires tools that are introduced in Chapter 4, but the net result is that people who want to borrow money to buy houses have to pay higher interest rates to compensate the lenders for the additional risk imposed by rules supposed to help the borrowers. No doubt those who were paying off mortgages when the new regulations were enacted gained, but those who now try to borrow money would be better off if they had the choice of giving the lender better security at a lower rate.

In discussing limitations on freedom of contract, one of the first things to remember is that judges make mistakes. Since the problem of judicial procedure is the subject of several later chapters, serious discussion of this issue is deferred. An appreciation of the fact of such mistakes is, however, necessary. Most traditional institutions are surrounded with what anthropologists call "magic." They are thought of in unrealistic terms, the lack of realism having the effect of making us more satisfied with our environment by convincing us that it is better than it really is.[1] The courts are no exception. The view that the outcome of judicial process is "true" is widely held. Thus, I have been criticized for expressing the opinion that a person who has not been tried is guilty of a defalcation, the criticism taking the form of saying that he is not guilty until found so by a court. I may, of course, have been wrong, but the reason given for the criticism is irrational.

Most people do not really feel that the court's decision is always right. The decision in neither the Sacco-Vanzetti case nor the Hiss case was regarded as settling the matter by large and articulate groups in our intellectual community. On the other side, Judge Youngdahl's release of Owen Lattimore was not regarded as "clearing" the Johns Hopkins professor by a quite different group of persons. Regardless of what we may think of the specific facts in these cases, the refusal to accept the court's decision as necessarily determining the truth of the matter was clearly right. Courts do make mistakes, and the Supreme Court no less than others. We should hope for improvements in this regard, but we should not have any illusions about either the present (or likely future) efficiency and ability of our judges.

The judge and/or jury in a case have heard the case. They are in possession of more information, therefore, than most casual observers. The judge, furthermore, will normally be of above average intelligence. It must be assumed that the responsibilities connected with their decisions normally result in the judge's thinking seriously about the case. Their judgment, therefore, should be regarded with respect, and in easy cases (which make up the vast majority), we can accept their opinions as probably true. Furthermore, it is socially necessary to have some end to litigation. The fact that a given case has been settled in a given way legally ends it, regardless of the real rights and wrongs. But I have a perfect right to believe that a judicial decision is wrong. If I have made a careful study of the matter, my opinion may well be more authoritative than that of the court. Almost everyone can think of at least one decision that he regards as wrong, and his judgment in the matter may well be correct.

1. The psychological phenomenon of "reduction of cognitive dissonance" is closely connected to this social effect.

When I was in law school, our professor of Procedure related the following case. A wealthy woman saw an advertisement for an antique dining room set in the morning paper. She decided to buy it and mentioned that fact to her maid. When she arrived at the store and inspected the set, she changed her mind; but she spent the rest of the day shopping. During the afternoon, the set was delivered to her house and the maid signed a receipt. The store refused to take the set back and sued for the price. The law firm with which the wealthy lady normally dealt looked over the evidence and suggested settlement out of court on the basis of a partial payment. Righteously indignant, the lady turned to another lawyer and, by some coincidence, came into the hands of a shyster. When the case came to trial, the attorneys for the store put the salesman on the witness stand who testified that the woman had bought the set. The truck driver testified that it had been delivered and that the maid had expected it.

The woman thought she had been double-crossed by her attorney, who didn't even cross-examine these witnesses. When his turn came, however, he put three witnesses on the stand who testified that they had seen the defendant pay for the set. Having a great deal of experience in such matters, the three trained witnesses were able to defend themselves under vigorous, if rather confused, cross-examination. The jury found for the defendant; the lawyer took the dining room set for his fee, and (I suppose) substantial justice was done. But, clearly, this is not the type of court proceeding in which we can have high confidence. We must recognize, however, that it may be impossible to design courts so that this type of thing cannot and does not happen.

The possibility of erroneous court decisions must be taken into account in any discussion of the desirability of "enforcing" contracts. Someone must decide that the contract has been violated and take steps to enforce it. If that "someone" should be prone to frequent mistakes, then this fact must be taken into account when deciding whether or not contracts should be "enforced," and the extent to which that enforcement should be carried. Since judges are human, they will always make mistakes, although the number of these mistakes may possibly be reduced. What effect will this have on the desirability of making "enforcements" of contracts possible?

We can distinguish two main classes of error into which judges may fall in "enforcing" contracts. They may negatively fail to enforce a clause of a contract, or (positively) they may enforce a nonexistent clause. Thus, suppose A pays B a sum of money for some future act by B, and B refuses to carry out his promise. A goes to court and the court errs by agreeing with B that he has no legal liability. This is a negative error. For an example of a positive error, assume that A demands that B perform some additional act not provided for in the contract. The court errs by ordering B to carry out his nonexistent contractual obligation. Placed in this schematic form, these errors do not seem very likely. In fact, of course, contracts may be almost impossibly involved, and the occurrence of errors is certain. Simple cases are likely to be decided correctly, but not all cases are simple.

Positive errors are considerably less likely than negative ones, simply because it is more likely that an individual will try to get out of an existing obligation than that he will create a convincing obligation of someone else.[2] Note that the errors do not cancel out. A classic piece of legal wisdom holds that "you will lose some cases which you should have won, but, on the other hand, you will win some cases you should have lost." For the lawyer, it cancels out, but what about the clients? For the client who only goes to court a few times in his life, it is statistically unlikely that the errors will cancel. Even for those in continual litigation, however, the errors do not really cancel.

Imagine an importer who is engaged in commercial dealings, and for whom disagreements with other parties are frequent enough so that he can expect to become involved in 1,000 lawsuits during the course of his life. Suppose, furthermore, that courts dealing with cases of the degree of complexity represented by his litigation normally make errors 10 percent of the time. It might seem that with about 100 erroneous decisions, the likelihood that they will balance out would be fairly good. Assuming that the man is honest, this would not be so. If he never sues another man or forces someone else to sue him, except when his cause is just, then all of the errors will be against him.[3] It is only the man who sues when he has no case or who refuses to carry out a contract until he is sued who can hope to profit from miscarriages of justice. Between the just and the unjust, court errors always favor the "wrong" side.

This naturally raises the question of whether some institutional modification might not be helpful. Clearly, improving the efficiency of the courts is such an institutional modification, but a discussion of this must be deferred.

2. Third parties, i.e., legislators, may think of additional obligations and enact them into law.

3. Much the same general conclusions can be reached on less restrictive assumptions. If we assume that the man misjudges his own case as often as the judge does, or even twice as often, then the results are reached by more complicated chains of reasoning, but they are fundamentally the same.

Consideration of other possible modifications, such as making it harder to take a man's last dollar than his millionth, should also be deferred to some possible future occasion. This latter problem is really no different when the hardship is imposed as the result of an incorrect decision than in the case of a correct decision, and there are many reasons why decisions may fall in a gray area between the two extremes.

Suppose that I contract with a builder to add an extension to my house. After agreement on the plans and formal signature of the contract, a flood sweeps the town, and, in addition to doing other damage, it destroys my house. On re-examining the architectural drawings, I realize that by simply closing off the end of the "addition," which would normally face my house, with a few sheets of plywood, I will have housing that will serve to at least keep me warm until my house is rebuilt. I, therefore, appear in court and ask that the builder be forced to proceed with the contract. As a result of the flood, the builder, on the other hand, faces much higher costs because of the shortage of labor and materials, the changes to the topography of the site, the unavoidable delay in starting; hence, he can only finish by the contract date through the use of expensive overtime labor. He has also lost his own machinery in the flood and will have to buy or rent the necessary equipment.

He, therefore, argues that the contract called for the construction of an "addition," and that there is now nothing to be added to. I argue that I want him to produce the structure shown in the architect's drawings, and that the fact that there is now no longer a building located directly adjacent is irrelevant. Obviously, the judge is presented with a difficult problem.[4] The two parties certainly were not thinking about the flood when they entered into the original contract. There are no specific provisions in the contract that clearly cover the problem in dispute.

Any decision of the court will contain an element of arbitrariness, and it would be more or less impossible to say that any decision was, in the eyes of God, right or wrong. The court must somehow or other supplement the original contract. For this purpose it is likely, in the real world, to turn to some general rule for such cases. The rule chosen would depend mainly upon the nationality of the court. Let us, however, examine some of the possible rules.

4. All of this assumes that the addition can stand by itself. Many additions, of course, could not be built by themselves, because they depend upon the basic building for their support. Anyone who thinks that he sees an obvious solution should present the case to two or three other persons and see if they also reach the same conclusion.

The simplest rule would be to flip a coin, and there is an element of this in all other rules. No modern legal system, however, openly adopts this expedient. A second rule would be to say that if the contract did not directly refer to the circumstances that arose, it has no present effect. This would lead the court to give a decision in favor of the defendant. In this particular case, such an outcome does not seem to be bad, but in most cases of this sort, the difference between the situation that actually occurred and the one anticipated by the parties at the time the contract was signed is less extreme. Invalidating the contract because there is some minor difference does not seem very sensible.

A third possibility is to try to get some hint from the contract itself as to what the parties would have decided if the flood came (if they had any thought of it when they were making the original contract). Technically, this is "resolution by analogy." Thus, if the contract contained a provision canceling the entire arrangement if the house burned down, it would seem reasonable to assume that the parties would have put in a similar clause regarding floods if they had thought of it. Here again, we would get a decision for the defendant. Again, however, the relative ease of such a decision is a result of the simplicity of the case. Normally, no clause is as close to the contingency that actually occurs as fire is to flood. Courts trying to apply this general approach are frequently driven into the most extreme contortions in their attempts to find something in the contract that can be extended to cover the new situation.

A fourth possibility would be to try to find other evidence of the parties' intent. If, for example, in looking over the diagrams, I had said, "Gee, if the house burned down, I could actually live in the addition," and the contractor had replied, "You sure could," it would seem likely that the court would decide to force the contractor to build the addition. Once again, however, there is normally no such clear evidence of intent.[5] Lastly, the rule actually followed by most courts in the world is simply to apply general legal norms to the matter. Stated more simply, this approach assumes that the written contract between the two parties is only a part of their agreement. A body of legal decisions, statutes, and codes that provides a set of rules for what should be done in cases where there are no specific provisions in the contract will be in existence. Thus,

5. Modification of a contract by testimony about oral statements of the parties raises a series of difficult problems considered under the title of "Parole" in our legal system. The difficulty is that permitting such testimony is practically an invitation to perjury, particularly since courts, like other people, are not terribly good at detecting liars.

the court assumes that the contract was drawn up with the parties in actual, if not express, agreement that in any contingency not specifically covered by the contract, the rules provided by law will apply.

This approach also has the drawback that the contingency that arises may not be at all clearly covered by the existing laws. Thus, here again considerable contortions may be necessary to apply the procedure. The problem, however, is not as significant with this general approach. The contracting parties to the innumerable contracts that do exist tend to forget somewhat the same possible contingencies, with the result that rules originally developed for contracts of the past may very well fit. This procedure, of course, relieves the court from having to make up its mind on a difficult problem, which probably accounts for its popularity with judges.

Another advantage of this way of interpreting contracts when there is nothing in the text covering a contingency that has arisen is that it permits great economies in drawing up the contracts. The law of bills and notes, for example, is an extremely elaborate set of rules that fills many volumes. The contracts with which these rules deal may well take the form of one or two sentences printed on one side of a small piece of paper. If it were necessary to put into the actual contract all of the conditions that the law implies, no bill would be less than 100 pages long. Thus, the present situation provides a simple and quick contract, but it also provides definite rules that in effect elaborate that quick contract into a lengthy and complicated one.

The disadvantage of this method of interpreting contracts if some unprovided for contingency arises is that it results in the contract, in effect, being quite different from what the men have agreed to. If the contractor and I were not experts in the law and there was a large body of interpretive rules that would be applied by the courts, we might end up with a contract that surprised both of us. It might be, for example, that the rule in that jurisdiction was that, unless otherwise provided in the contract, a builder was responsible only for the structure itself, but not for the foundation. The court might thus rule that the contractor was not required to build the addition because I had not provided him with a foundation in proper time. This would please the contractor, but also would surprise him if he were not aware of the rule. Such ignorance on the part of the contractor would, of course, be unlikely, but the law of contracts has innumerable interpretive rules, and no one can possibly know all of them. Thus, the application of such rules must, at least occasionally, result in surprises.

What is perhaps more important, they may result in surprises for one party to the contract. Given the complexity of the rules surrounding contracts and the fact that they vary greatly from field to field, it is not unlikely that one party to a contract will know them fairly well and the other not at all. The second party, of course, may get legal advice, but this is expensive. The contractor, for example, would no doubt know about the rule on foundations hypothesized in the last example, but the purchaser might well not know this. Thus, this procedure encourages sharp practice. A and B enter into a contract that seems reasonable to A, who knows little of the specialized legal rules surrounding such a contract, but which is actually heavily weighted in favor of B. B has drawn the contract so that, when the standard legal interpretative rules are used, it is highly in his favor. In practice, the courts normally lean over backward to interpret rules in favor of whichever party seems to know the least about them. Still, the formal rule is that the "ignorance of the law is no excuse," and a good deal of sharp practice must be perpetuated under that rule.

But this has been a discussion of the situation as it now exists. Let us try to consider the problem in a more rigorous form. The judge, when he comes to a part of the contract that is not plain on its face, must make a decision according to some rule. As suggested previously, this rule might be flipping a coin, or it could be the application of some general rule dealing with all contracts of this sort. The difference between these two different techniques may not be significant from the standpoint of the litigants. Suppose Smith and I enter into a contract and we agree that Jones will decide any contractual disputes that may occur. Unknown to us, Jones has already decided with respect to one particular type of dispute how he will shape his verdict. From the standpoint of Smith and myself in making up the original contract, this decision is essentially unpredictable, since we did not know what Jones planned to do. Therefore, at the time we drew up the contract we were essentially facing the same situation we would have faced had the rule for this contingency been decided by flipping a coin.

It might, of course, have been possible for us to have predicted in some way the decision Jones would make. Even more likely, it might have been possible for us to feel that it was probable that he would decide in one particular way. We might feel, for example, that his decision on this matter would tend to be very similar to one we ourselves would make. We could hardly be certain of this, however, and in a sense, we would be making a guess that has a stochastic element. We might feel, for example, that the odds were three to one for the plaintiff. Although this would still be a stochastic model, it would require more than a single flip of a coin. Let us, however, ignore these intermediate stages between certainty and uncertainty, because they are simply a mixture of the two conditions, and confine our discussion entirely to those cases in which we can predict what the judge will do or in which we are totally uncertain. Real-world situations in which these two conditions are mixed can then be dealt with by mixing our two models.

With this model, we can now address ourselves to the question of how detailed the legal provisions for "interpreting" contracts should be. Note that we need say nothing, at this stage, about the substantive content of these provisions, because the parties to the contract can always avoid any particular substantive provision by simply putting an appropriate clause into their contract. Later in this chapter, we discuss limitations on freedom of contract that might well be part of our law, but at the moment we can confine ourselves to those areas where the contracting parties may reach any bargain that they wish. In this case, the substantive rules may perhaps be more efficient in one form than in another; that is, one particular set of legal rules as to what is done in the case of a contract that does not specifically cover a matter may lead more contracting parties to shorten their contracts than another set of rules. This is obvious, but I have nothing to add to the point and, hence, will turn to another matter—the optimal degree of detail for the law.

In order to approach this problem rationally let us begin by considering the amount of detail that the contracting parties should put into their contract in a situation in which everything that they clearly express in the contract will be carried out; those things that the contract clearly does not cover but in fact occur are dealt with in a stochastic manner that we may represent by the image of the flipped coin, and those issues that are related to the language but are not clearly covered by it will be dealt with by a mixture of certain and stochastic elements.

Suppose that I am buying a house and the seller and I have agreed on the price and a few other general matters, but have not completely and totally exhausted the possible items we could put into the contract of sale. Under these circumstances, I can weigh, on the one hand, the possibility that if some contingency not now covered by the contract occurs, I will lose in the essentially stochastical decision against the advantages and disadvantages of continuing the negotiations to get an additional clause covering the given contingency. The first thing to note, of course, is that the time spent in negotiations is a cost, and clearly if the contingency is unlikely enough, I would be well advised to leave the matter in the lap of the gods. Furthermore, it is by no means obvious that if I negotiate with my bargaining partner the certain clause that we end up with will be more to my advantage than flipping the coin. This might or might not be true, depending on whether there is some mutually advantageous way of dealing with this particular problem. If there is some provision that could be reached with respect to this particular problem that will be to both of us *ex ante* better than flipping a coin, we would, of course, do it; but there is no intrinsic reason to believe that this would be so for all the details of a contract. Furthermore, even if such a possibility for profit did exist, it might also exist after the contingency itself had occurred, and, therefore, we could make an agreement at that time rather than using the coin-flipping process.

This line of reasoning could, of course, be put in a highly rigorous form. It seems to me, however, that we have no great need to go further than the analysis thus far presented. The two parties under these circumstances would thus determine the length of the contract in full knowledge that some things were not covered. They would expect that those things would be determined by some process over which they had no control, because the cost of extending their joint control is greater than the present discounted value of the injury they might or, then again, might not suffer from the lack of control.

The same line of reasoning may be used to decide, in general, the proper degree of detail in the interpretive part of the law of contracts. The only real point of this part of the law is to save the parties the inconvenience of making their own contracts very long. Thus, it permits them to leave certain provisions out of their contract because they are covered by the law. Furthermore, since this technique in and of itself is more efficient than actually negotiating each contract clause step by step, one would assume that the parties would count it as a lower-cost way of obtaining certainty and, therefore, would prefer more details in this legally specified portion of the contract than in the part they actually negotiate between themselves. Still, it does seem likely that the amount of details they would require is not terribly high.

In particular, there is no reason why the parties should be concerned about the certainty or uncertainty of that part of the law that they do not know about. If there is a definite legal principle providing for the interpretation of a certain clause in a certain contingency, but this interpretation is not known to the parties, they are no better off than they would have been in my earlier example in which Jones had a secret rule. Only if the parties know and take into account the provision of the law is it of any advantage to them in reducing the hazard to which they are exposed. It is, in fact, true that many men engaged in practical activity know a great deal about the legal effects of contracts in their particular line of business. Thus, in these lines of business a rather long and detailed code would be reasonable.

Although we now have a set of principles for determining the desirable amount of detail in the interpretative portion of the law of contracts, there is no reason to believe that this set of principles has been applied in real life. Certainly, it has not been characteristic of the common law. Under the common law, each case that reaches an appellate court adds an additional bit of detail into the law. There is no effort on the part of anyone to decide how detailed the law should be. The result is a situation in which the person more learned in the law has the distinct advantage over the person less learned. In particular, it gives a major advantage to the lawyers. It is also helpful to the ego of the judges who are permitted to make the law for future contracts. Nevertheless, it cannot be said that it works any vast amount of harm. Substituting flipping coins for the details of our present interpretative law would be somewhat more efficient, but the difference would be minimal.

There is, however, something that can be said about the degree of detail in the law that should be of interest to the reader of this book (who, I presume, is an intellectual). Looking at the matter from our purely pragmatic, nonethical approach, obviously each reader should simply try to decide the degree of detail that would be best for him. The question really is which degree, over a period of time, will give him the widest range of choice. This means that he must consider the likelihood of his becoming involved in suits to enforce contracts in the future and then decide what rule will best suit him. Most readers will be people of above average intelligence, with literary and scholarly interests, and, probably, having research skills. For such people a maze of legal rules has decided advantages. If the system of interpreting contracts that do not clearly cover the given situation is to turn to a large body of legal rules containing a provision for a mass of such cases, then the average individual of normal intelligence, little patience for reading, and a complete lack of experience in library research is apt to be at a loss. He most assuredly will not find out what the rules are until it is too late. The intellectual, on the other hand, is much more likely to know what the rules are.[6]

6. This last statement is not necessarily true in the United States. It is one of the more remarkable characteristics of our law that a good deal of it is almost undiscoverable. Trained legal advice is frequently necessary, and even experienced lawyers are frequently wrong. In countries with civilized legal institutions, however, the problem is not so difficult. It is, doubtlessly, impossible to draw up the law in such a way that an untrained man can discover it easily, but we don't even make the attempt. In those countries in which a serious effort to state the law simply and concisely is made, the situation is far different from that in the United States.

This means, of course, that the intellectual has a real material interest in a detailed and complex set of rules. Since most of his contracts will be with nonintellectuals, this gives him a significant advantage. From this we could deduce that the intellectual should favor more detail than the common man. Furthermore, a system of written laws is something the intellectual can argue for openly. It does not appear on the surface to give a specific class an advantage, although it is in fact in the interest of the more intelligent and scholarly members of the community. In practice the common man sometimes realizes this, and has a considerable distrust both of the law and of lawyers.[7] Individuals who are trapped by provisions of the law of which they were ignorant are common in our fiction, and they are always treated sympathetically. The court may say "ignorance of the law is no excuse," but the novelists do not agree. The frequent pleas for settling cases on the "facts," "on the merits," or "by common sense" may also be efforts on the part of common men to avoid entering an arena in which the intellectuals have an obvious advantage. It is not at all apparent what decision would be made in our flood case on the "facts," on the "merits," or "by common sense," but it is clear that such a rule would give the intellectuals less advantage over the nonintellectuals.

Since, on the other hand, the intellectual normally dominates public debate, the long-run odds would appear to favor him in this clear-cut class difference. The judges, too, are intellectuals, who have the further advantage of being trained in the law. In his private contracts, the judge or any other lawyer who really knows the law of contracts has an advantage over almost anyone with whom he deals if contracts are interpreted by a complex set of legal rules. Further, this knowledge is a valuable piece of "capital." The judge can, therefore, be said to have a real interest in a detailed and complex system of interpretation.

Since we have not yet reached the portion of this book in which ethics are discussed, and since it seems fairly certain that we have here an area in which the individual reader might favor certain rules because they would benefit him, we might pause here to reconsider our first basic assumption. This assumption, it will be recalled, is that the individual reader is not in a situation whereby he can gain from rules designed to benefit a single class in society. It is only when this assumption is fulfilled that everyone can be expected to agree to a general rule. Rules that classify society and then give special privileges to

7. William Shakespeare, *King Henry IV*, part II, IV 2.86, "The first thing we do, let's kill all the lawyers."

some classes are obviously beneficial only to the favored class. These rules should thus be favored by members of the favored class, and opposed by members of other classes. In such an open and obvious situation, it is unlikely that such rules can be imposed unless the benefited class is, for some reason, stronger than the injured class or classes. The whites in South Africa, for example, are constitutionally in complete control of the government and are well armed and organized. They can, therefore, impose their rule on the blacks.

In addition to such overt class legislation, however, rules that appear to be general may, in fact, benefit special groups. Thus, a set of rules that has general application but that gives an advantage to the better educated as opposed to the less educated may be class legislation. The recent expansion of government-financed fellowships has been largely discussed in terms of general benefit, although it is obvious that only a tiny minority of the population can directly gain from them. Furthermore, this tiny minority is composed of people who, because of their intelligence, family background, and primary education, are likely to do very well in life anyway. More indirectly, the working man who has no plans to send his son to college is much less likely to benefit from a lavish provision of scholarship help than is the middle-class parent who is willing, if necessary, to make great sacrifices to see that his son receives a good education.[8]

But all of this merely illustrates the general problem. We have assumed that the individual does not have much of a chance of obtaining special "class" legislation that benefits him. For the average man, this is no doubt true. Furthermore, even the most influential people have little or no possibility of arranging for legislation that openly aims at their benefit. Deception, however, is possible. It is possible for people who have exceptional access to channels of influence and communication to benefit themselves to some extent. The father of an intelligent boy who would rather not pay his son's tuition in college can hardly hope to have a special bill passed. It is possible, however, that he, together with others similarly placed, can have a general bill passed that will reach the same end. Note, however, that the margin for this type of maneuver is narrow. Only if the special bill comports with generally held (if vague) ideas

8. In this discussion, I do not wish to deny the possible indirect benefits for the poorer classes of having the brighter members of society educated well. The public advocates of subsidization of higher education for a small, gifted minority, however, are almost all professional educators who will benefit from an expansion of the educational system, or middle- and upper-class intellectuals.

of proper governmental activity, and only if it does not appear to be specially geared to the interests of some group, can the trick be pulled off.[9]

Thus, the gains to be made from this sort of deception are quite limited. The intellectuals are best situated to get special legislation, but it is difficult even for them. They must, furthermore, work without overt coordination. All public references to the aid to education bill must be in terms of its general benefit. The fact that it is of special interest to the intellectuals and the upper class must not be mentioned. Still, for this particular type of problem, the first of our basic assumptions is probably not true for most potential readers of this book. They can, to some extent, give themselves an advantage by arguing for legal rules that appear to be general, but that in fact favor intellectuals. Nevertheless, the advantage to be gained would normally be small.

Is full freedom of contract desirable? Should it be possible to enter into any contract? It might appear that any reduction in the area of free contract would contravene our basic assumptions, but there are some situations where this is not true. We can begin by inquiring if there are any types of contracts that should simply be denied all enforcement. In our law no contract of enslavement is legal—is this provision desirable? At first glance it would appear to be a perfectly clear and unambiguous contravention of our basic principle. The individual who wishes to sell himself into slavery is prevented from doing so, and his freedom is thus restricted. This would seem to lead us into a direct conflict between two forms of freedom, but, fortunately, the conflict can be avoided.

Firstly, an individual desiring to sell himself into slavery would obviously be very rare. Once he is a slave, his new master could take back the price. In practical fact, most systems of slavery depend upon people's being sold into slavery by other persons. A will not regard a legal provision preventing B from selling him (A) into slavery as a restriction on his freedom of choice. This is equally true when B is an ancestor of A as when he is not. The right of an individual to sell himself into slavery may be argued for in terms of increasing his freedom of choice. His right to sell his children, including his unborn children, into slavery clearly reduces the freedom of choice of the children.[10]

9. Strictly selfish legislation is also possible. This, however, requires that the beneficiaries pay for their advantage by logrolling, and the total outcome, whatever else may be said about it, will not necessarily benefit a minority.

10. The issue of minors, morons, the insane, and other people who are not thought fully capable of handling their own affairs is a most difficult one, and I have substantially no

It is sometimes said that the Chinese may sell themselves into slavery during famines in order to obtain food for their families.[11] Clearly, this should be permitted. If a man has a choice between seeing his family starve or selling himself into slavery to feed them and chooses the latter, we should not impede his freedom of choice. A society in which a man confronts such a dilemma, however, is obviously one that is seriously ill. No one should ever be confronted with this dilemma. It seems dubious, in any event, that this ever really was a factor in the development of slavery. Real slaves were always born slaves, captured, or the victims of another process.

Readers of romantic literature about the Roman Empire are familiar with the character who had been "sold into slavery." In fact, this could happen under Roman law as the result of a voluntary contract, although it was probably less frequent than the novels imply. A man could borrow money and then post himself as part of the security; that is, he could agree that if a certain loan was not repaid, the creditor could not only proceed against the debtor's material assets, he could foreclose on the debtor himself. Why should we ban such contracts in which the individual pledges himself as part of the security for a loan? If we do not wish to take the risk ourselves, we need not do so, and the individual is likely to be the best judge of his own circumstances. Legally banning this form of contract clearly reduces the freedom of individuals to make choices and, hence, would appear to be decreasing freedom of choice. The freedom to decide now, in return for adequate compensation, to restrict my freedom in the future is a freedom, and we have deduced that its limitation would be a genuine reduction in the freedom of choice. Thus, it would appear that we should opt to retain the freedom to pledge ourselves as security for a loan.

The reason why we might decide to restrict our freedom to enter into such a loan contract in the future comes from our first minor assumption—that we discount future events in a manner that is not a linear function of time. Consider a businessman who is getting started in a retailing operation. He has begun well but is in what he feels confident is a temporary bind. A little more

---

suggestions for handling it. The guardian system, used in one form or another, has obvious defects, but nothing better has been suggested.

11. As far as I am aware, this factual allegation is incorrect. It arises out of the difficulties encountered in trying to understand an alien civilization. What actually happens is quite complicated and not really relevant for our present discussion. The case, however, is theoretically interesting even if it never happens in the real world.

time, he believes, which means a little more money, will carry him over until the business really begins to prosper. This stage is familiar to anyone who has studied the history of successful or unsuccessful businesses. In this situation, the businessman is likely to go to great extremes to obtain money. He will mortgage his house, his car, and anything else since he feels fairly certain that prosperity is "just around the corner." If he were given the opportunity to mortgage himself, he would probably do it.

Here, however, we have an example of the different rates of discounting that the same man may apply to the same situation at different times. The individual who would be willing to pledge himself in order to obtain additional capital the following year may this year think that it would be unwise. He knows that next year he would be likely to take a course of action which considered from this distant perspective of the present seems undesirable. Under the circumstances, he would like to bind himself today not to make such a mortgage agreement in the future. Hence, he would, if he had the assumed preference schedule, favor laws prohibiting such mortgages. The situation is the same as that of a compulsive drunkard who hires private detectives to forcibly prevent him from taking a drink. When considered calmly, most of us would agree that we should not take the risk of enslavement and also that we might make a fatal mistake some time in the future. Thus, a prohibition on contracts containing clauses involving enslavement is similar to voting for prohibition because we feel that we are too subject to temptation.

The same line of reasoning can be used to support bankruptcy laws and laws against imprisonment for debt. Surely, if I were in financial difficulties, I could get loans on better terms if I could agree not to avail myself of the benefits of bankruptcy. The bankruptcy laws, however, prohibit this and, hence, prevent me from committing possibly unwise acts in the future. Similarly, giving my creditor the option of having me sent to prison will surely make it easier to borrow money.[12] A determination now that I would rather pay a somewhat higher rate of interest in future transactions than take these risks is not necessarily irrational.

12. It should be stressed that imprisonment for debt was always at the option of the creditor. The argument against such imprisonment so often seen in textbooks—i.e., that a man in prison can hardly earn any money to pay back his debts, and, hence, the creditor does not gain by the right of imprisonment—is incorrect. The threat of imprisonment was a most potent debt-collecting device. An individual in prison because he could not pay his debts would not be able to earn money, but he would serve *pour l'encouragement des autres*.

Limitations can be placed on the application of this line of reasoning. In many areas I might suspect that my judgment of the future would be erroneous. A law prohibiting me from making decisions in these areas, if we considered no other aspect of the matter, would appear to be rational. In practice, of course, the costs must be offset against the advantages. Little can be said in general about this subject, but I doubt that the problem would be particularly difficult in any specific situation.

In the past, contracts of employment sometimes contained clauses under which the employee discharged his employer of liability in the case of injury to the employee. These clauses are now normally illegal. If we assume that an individual thinks that the risks are real, but also thinks that at the time he was about to be hired he might tend to estimate them differently than he does now, he would be sensible to favor such legislation. It is interesting that normally very dangerous activities are exempted. I cannot agree with my employer that he will not be liable for injuries I sustain as a lathe operator, but I can waive all claims for injuries received while driving a racing car. This would seem to support our line of reasoning since the risks of driving a racing car are less likely to be overdiscounted—they are too obvious.

Thus, it is possible to argue that numerous types of contracts should be prohibited. Again, costs are involved. Surely interest rates will be higher if bankruptcy is permitted and contracts calling for imprisonment for debt banned, and this may be a disadvantage that outweighs the gain. It will be more difficult for the man trying to get started in business, but failure will not be quite so final. These considerations must be weighed against each other in deciding which rule to choose. The conclusion in any given case is far from obvious, and it is fairly clear that different people could reach different conclusions, but this is a problem of judging likely future actions, not of principle.

Our discussion of contract law is now brought to a close. It has been lengthy, perhaps too lengthy, but it has hardly scratched the surface of the subject. What I have been trying to do is to demonstrate that it would be possible to draw up a law of contracts on the basis of our basic assumptions and without any ethical assumptions. From maxims of pure self-interest (in the sense that that term is understood by economists), we can deduce that a rather complex and detailed law of contracts, complete with enforcement agencies, is desirable. I think that I have carried the line of reasoning sufficiently far so that it is obvious that it could be used to formulate a complete law of contracts.

CHAPTER 4

ENFORCEMENT OF CONTRACTS

Chapter 3 ignored the problems of enforcement of a contract; these problems are discussed fully in this chapter. One point must be clarified at the outset—certain restrictions on freedom of contract in the existing law are discussed under the rubric of "lack of enforceability." We assume here that certain types of contract—involving enslavement or imprisonment for non-performance—are banned, and only discuss the enforcement of contracts that do not fall into these categories. Secondly, we do not explicitly discuss degrees of enforcement. It might, for example, be provided that the court would only enforce nine out of ten contracts brought before it or that it would not enforce contracts where the alleged defaulter was very poor or a clergyman or a member of the local aristocracy. It might also be that the measures taken in enforcement will vary according to the status of the defendant; the code of Hammurabi provides quite different penalties for persons of different status who have performed the same prohibited acts.

Enforcement of contracts can be divided into two grand divisions. Suppose that A alleges that he has a contract with B under which B has agreed to do act X. A further alleges that B has not done act X and asks enforcement. The first problem is deciding whether A's double allegation is correct, and the second is compelling B to perform. The second part, the actual application of compulsion, is not very interesting or complicated, and we need not linger over it.

The first problem in the other aspect of the problem of enforcement is the certainty of error. Any "judicial" system is certain to decide sometimes that B does not have to perform act X when he really should and decide sometimes that he should perform it, even though, in the eyes of God, he has no obligation to do so. In addition there are numerous cases in which it is most uncertain what "carrying out the contract" means. The intrinsic tendency to error can be reduced, but it cannot be completely eliminated and must be borne in mind in considering any judicial system. This fact, although perfectly obvious, tends to be ignored in most discussions of the problem. Theoretical discussion in which it is implicitly assumed that the court will always reach a correct decision are not at all uncommon. The view that appellate courts are less likely to err than courts of original jurisdiction is also widely held, although I have never seen any discussion of why this should be so.[1]

Our basic assumptions about human behavior do not directly help us in deciding what sort of judicial mechanism would be best. Clearly, individuals would normally prefer to be left a choice of judiciaries when they make their contracts. Such agreements would be subject to the restrictions outlined in Chapter 3, but the desirability of permitting individuals to freely contract and to include in their contract provisions for the enforcement of those contracts seems clear. This in itself, however, does not get us very far. Before trying to do more, let me diverge again from the main course of the argument to deal with an essentially false issue that might enter the minds of some readers. It is commonly stated that governments must have a monopoly on the legitimate use of force, and here we are discussing the establishment of a set of competing enforcement mechanisms, with the individuals who sign contracts deciding the ones they will patronize.

In fact, the problem is unreal. A government need not really have a "monopoly" on force. All that is necessary is that its forces be strong enough to enforce a reasonable degree of public order. I suspect that in New York City there are far more private policemen than publicly hired ones. Certainly the private guard forces are more conspicuous. Las Vegas, of course, is the extreme case in which the individual casino guard forces are larger than the city police force. Normally these private guard forces are nominally incorporated into the official government police force; all of the Las Vegas guards are deputy sheriffs, but this is mere lip service to the principle of governmental monopoly of force.

In any event, the physical enforcement of the contract—which is what is involved in the "monopoly of force"—is not our present subject. We are discussing who or what organization decides whether a man shall be compelled to perform a certain act. It is quite possible for this decision to be taken by some private citizen while the actual compulsion remains a governmental function. In much of the world, arbitration is a private "court" whose decision is enforced by the government. The jurisconsults, whose decisions shaped Roman law, were private citizens whose rulings were enforced by government officials. Whatever else one may think about these procedures, they clearly left "force" completely in government hands.

1. Appellate courts probably reduce the number of completely ridiculous decisions, since it is not likely that two different courts will have identical ridiculous ideas. The whole problem of appeal will be discussed in Chapter 10.

Thus, we return to our basic finding that the parties to contracts would wish to be permitted to choose the judicial mechanism that would enforce their contract. Can we say anything about the general characteristics of the judicial procedures that would be chosen? The answer to this question is "yes," but it requires a rather lengthy digression into high school algebra in order to make the issues clear. Assuming that we have some method of enforcing contracts, the payoff that an individual would obtain from entering into a symmetric contract is shown in Equation (4.1).

$$\begin{aligned} P_1 = B_{c_1}(1 - L_{b_1} - L_{b_2}) + L_{b_1} \{B_{b_1}L_{ns_1} + (1 - L_{ns_1}) \\ [B_{b_1}L_e + (1 - L_e)\, B_{c_1} - C_{c_1}]\} - L_{b_2} \{C_{b_1}L_{ns_2} + (1 - L_{ns_2}) \\ [C_{b_1}L_c - (1 - L_e)\, B_{c_1} + C_{c_1}]\} \end{aligned} \quad (4.1)$$

This equation requires some explanation in addition to the table of symbols, but I think I should begin by explaining what I mean by a symmetric contract. A symmetric contract is a contract in which each of the parties has about the same likelihood of breaching the contract as the other, and the benefits that each party will gain from the contract are the same. In other words, it is a contract for something to happen in the future with both parties making promises that they will perform in the future; both parties, therefore, are capable of breaching the contract. For the sake of simplicity I have made the symmetry perfect. We will shortly be dealing with asymmetric contracts.

P_1 is the net expected payoff to Party One. The benefit received by Party One from the contract continuing without any breach or attempted breach by either party multiplied by the probability that this will in fact occur is shown by the portion of the equation before the plus sign. The possible profit that Party One might obtain from breaking the contract himself or attempting to break it, which must be computed in terms of the probability he will do so, is shown by the portion of the equation within the first set of braces, together with the probability multiplier attached to it. If Party One chooses to breach the contract, he may obtain a profit from that breach, which is particularly likely if Party Two chooses not to sue him. Therefore, the probability of his not being sued is the first item inside the brace. However, if the other party sues him, he may nevertheless be in a better position than without having attempted to breach, and this is shown by the portion of the equation within the square brackets, together with its probability. If the other party chooses to sue, the court may erroneously decide in favor of Party One despite the face that he is in breach of contract; the probability of judicial error is shown at the beginning of the brace. On the other hand, the

TABLE OF SYMBOLS 4.1

B_{b_1} = Benefit obtained by Party One from successfully breaching the contract
B_{b_2} = Benefit obtained by Party Two from successfully breaching the contract
B_{c_1} = Benefit derived by Party One from the completion of the contract
B_{c_2} = Benefit derived by Party Two from the completion of the contract
C_{b_1} = Cost to Party One of the successful breach of contract by Party Two
C_{b_2} = Cost to Party Two of the successful breach of contract by Party One
C_c = Total court costs to both parties
C_{c_1} = Cost to Party One of court proceedings
C_{c_2} = Cost to Party Two of court proceedings
I = Insurance payment
L_e = Likelihood that court will make an erroneous decision
L_{b_1} = Likelihood Party One will attempt to breach the contract. Note this attempt may be successful, then again it may not
L_{b_2} = Likelihood Party Two will attempt to breach the contract. Note this attempt may be successful, then again it may not
L_{ns_1} = Likelihood that if Party One breaches the contract, Party Two will refrain from suing him
L_{ns_2} = Likelihood that if Party Two breaches the contract, Party One will refrain from suing him
P = Procedural function
P_1 = Payoff of contract to Party One
P_2 = Payoff of contract to Party Two
P_{b_1} = Payoff to Party One of breaching the contract
P_{b_2} = Payoff to Party Two of breaching the contract

---

court may decide in favor of Party Two, which would mean that the court is reaching a correct decision; again a probability is attached. In this event, the contract continues as if it had not originally been breached. In any event, if Party One does decide to break the contract and Party Two decides to sue him, Party One would incur a court cost, which is also shown within the brackets.

Although Party One may obtain advantages from the contract, he obviously can suffer losses if Party Two breaches the contract. These losses are shown in the second set of braces, together with the probability that they will happen, and they are basically the converse of the advantages that I have already described in connection with the first set of braces. In this symmetric case, all of the probabilities of Party One's doing something are the same as the probabilities of Party Two's doing it. Furthermore, the cost of a breach of contract to one party is the same as the benefit of the cost of that breach of contract to the other. This is not a necessary characteristic of the real world, and it is introduced here primarily to simplify the equation. As another simplification, I have left out negotiated settlements.

With these symmetries, Equation (4.1) simplifies to Equation (4.2) and, by collapsing the probabilities, to Equation (4.3).

$$P_1 = B_{c_1}(1 - L_{b_1} - L_{b_2}) - (L_{b_1} + L_{b_2})(1 - L_{ns_1} - L_{ns_2})\, C_{c_1} \qquad (4.2)$$

$$P_1 = B_{c_1}(1 - 2L_{b_1}) - 2L_{b_1}(1 - 2L_{ns_1})\, C_{c_1} \qquad (4.3)$$

Party One and, by symmetry, Party Two will enter into a contract only if the payoff is greater than zero. Note from Equation (4.3) that this amounts to saying that the benefit to be obtained from the contract, together with the probability that the contract will be carried out quietly—without lawsuits or threats of lawsuits—must exceed the cost of court action multiplied by its probability. In general, the lower the value of $2L_{b_1}(1 - 2L_{ns_1})\, C_{c_1}$, the greater the payoff will be. Furthermore, the lower the value of this expression, the lower is the benefit from the quiet continuation of the contract (B_{c_1}) while still making the contract profitable. We can thus tentatively draw the conclusion that the individual would prefer a system that minimized the value of $2L_{b_1}(1 - 2L_{ns_1})\, C_{c_1}$.

But why would anyone want to breach a contract? At the time of contracting, the parties, naturally, do not, but as time goes on, further information accumulates, and one party or the other may decide he would like to breach the contract. Suppose, for example, that one of the parties is a wholesaler who has contracted for the regular delivery of certain goods to a retailer for resale. After a period of time, the goods are no longer salable at the original price, and the retailer wants to stop future deliveries. Would he be wise to allege that the goods are substandard?

The payoff for the breach of the contract by Party One is shown by Equation (4.4).

$$P_{b_1} = B_{b_1}L_{ns} + (1 - L_{ns_1})\,[B_{b_1}L_e + (1 - L_e)\, B_c - C_{c_1}] \qquad (4.4)$$

If this expression (the right side of which is simply a portion of Equation (4.1)) is greater than zero, he will be well advised to breach the contract. One of the important things that he must determine in deciding whether or not to breach is the likelihood that Party Two will sue. The expression for the desirability of suing is shown in Inequality (4.5).

$$-C_{b_2} < (1 - L_e) B_{c_2} - C_{c_2} \qquad (4.5)$$

If the left side of the equation is less than the right side, then Party Two would be well advised to sue.

The decision whether to sue or not is greatly influenced by the probability of error. This in turn (Equation (4.6)) is a negative function of the investment of resources in court procedures that we consider as court costs and a variable called P that stands for the procedural routine of the court. This equation requires some explanation.

$$L_e = -f(C_c, P) \qquad (4.6)$$

When I say L is a negative function of something, I am using verbiage that I have invented myself, which simply means that, in general, as you increase each of the variables inside the parentheses it will reduce the likelihood of error. A negative function means that the thing to the left moves monotonically in the opposite direction from the things to the right. The fact that the percentage of errors would go down as resource investment is increased is not very surprising. It may be, however, that this reduction is very slow. For example, if both parties hire more expensive lawyers, the increase in the resources put into that trial is very substantial; but the reduction in the likelihood of error may be extremely small.

The procedural variable (P) is introduced because we have no reason to believe that our courts are operating at maximum efficiency. Normally, economists assume that any institution they are dealing with is efficient and, therefore, do not include a variable for its efficiency. We have no reason for this assumption with respect to courts. In fact, Chapter 5 presents an argument that the Anglo-Saxon tradition inherited from the Middle Ages is a highly inefficient method of organizing the courts. Thus, a change in procedure could significantly reduce the likelihood of error.

Our equations thus far will probably surprise no one, although they are perhaps more concrete than the usual discussion of the matter. We can, however, draw a most interesting conclusion from them. Let us suppose that we had a very great improvement in the efficiency of the courts in the sense that we were able to sharply reduce the court costs without changing the likelihood of error. The ironic result of the change is that the parties would more likely breach their contracts. In order to demonstrate this, let us first note that if the court costs were cut to zero, Inequality (4.5) would always be satisfied, and, therefore, Party Two would always sue if there were a breach. On the other hand, Equation (4.4), with court costs equal to zero, simplifies to Equation (4.7). Under these circumstances, the likelihood of a breach of contract would be very high. Whenever B_{b_1} became positive, there would be a breach. This may provide the best "social" justification for laws against barratry, i.e., "unauthorized" practice of law.

$$P_{b_1} = B_{b_1}L_e + (1 - L_e)\,B_c \tag{4.7}$$

Thus, court costs assume a new and rather surprising role. They are a basic reason why contracts are maintained. This does not mean, however, that we must compel parties to waste resources. If nothing else, a tax on the use of the courts could solve this problem.[2] Secondly, a reduction of legal error running *au pair* with a reduction in cost would be a more reasonable way of "using" improvements in efficiency. Note that, strictly speaking, the argument applies only on the assumption that only one party is willing to breach the contract. If the party who was injured by the breach would make a false claim against the party who had breached the contract, i.e., demand more than his true damages, and there were a finite chance of the judge's awarding this excess amount of damage, then there would still be some cost of breach, but probably less than the gain.

From our set of equations we can isolate the effect of the social control variables that are in essence the court proceedings themselves. By choosing between a more or less efficient procedural routine and reducing or increasing the amount of resources that are put into the court proceedings, parties can change the amount of legal error. Other things being equal, reducing legal error causes a reduction in the net waste in society. Thus, if I am setting up a contract, I have motives for choosing that court procedure that is least likely to make errors. There are essentially two types of errors a court can make in enforcing a contract—either a mistake in its interpretation of the contract or a mistake about the real world. We have already discussed writing

2. See my "Excess Benefit," *Water Resources Research* 3 (2d Quarter, 1967): 643–44.

contracts in order to obtain the optimal amount of error in court interpretation. Little else can be said about this in discussing court procedure except, of course, that on the whole the more intelligent the person who decides the outcome, the less likely he is to make such an error. Turning to the facts, however, the problem is essentially a new one.

The difficulty in determining what the facts are is that simple problems seldom turn up in court proceedings. Both parties will normally be arguing that what they have done is quite proper. In part, their arguments may depend upon interpretations of contract, but, in part, they involve statements about what has happened in the real world. For example, suppose that A is a retailer who has entered into a contract to purchase a certain quantity of goods each month from B, a wholesaler. A alleges that the goods delivered to him were not up to specifications and that, therefore, he is relieved from his obligation to purchase them. B, of course, says the goods were up to specifications. The court now is presented with the factual question of the quality of the goods. Furthermore, it is likely to be more interested in what the quality of the goods was at the time they were delivered to the party than now, several months later. In other words, it is attempting to make a historical reconstruction. The court is attempting to find out what happened in the past in order to apply the provisions of the contract to this version of the facts.

Such historical reconstruction is often extremely difficult. Furthermore, there is no reason to believe that the courts are much better at it than are the historians. We would normally hope that the courts would use those techniques that are most likely to produce the truth from any given resource investment, but let us temporarily leave that question aside. The use of specific procedural techniques and their relative efficiency is discussed in detail in a later chapter. Let us presently assume simply that the courts make efficient uses of the resources presented to them and discuss solely the problem of the amount of resources that should be invested.

In order to discuss this problem we require a little bit in the way of formal theory. In Figure 4.1, from right to left I have drawn in the amount of evidence that one finds against the defendant in various cases. All cases can be put on this axis in a location corresponding to the weight of the evidence. On the vertical axis, I have put the percentage of people in each evidence category who have, in fact, violated the contract. Thus, there will be many people at the far left who are accused of breach of contract but who are not so guilty. There will be some, also on the left, who have breached the contract but who do not have much evidence against them. As we move to the right and the evidence

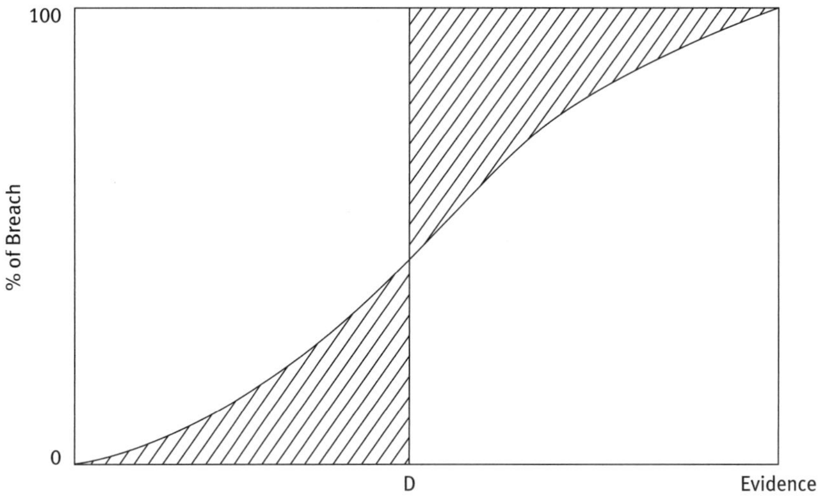

FIGURE 4.1
Evidence and decisions

against the person accused of breach of contract increases, the percentage of people who, in fact, have breached the contract will also increase. The court must make up its mind in terms of the evidence, not through some sort of absolute knowledge of who has breached the contract and who has not.

The court follows a simple rule. When the evidence is stronger for the plaintiff than for the defendant, it finds the defendant guilty of breach. When the evidence is stronger for the defendant than for the plaintiff, it finds the defendant not guilty of breach. This rule is represented by the vertical line (D) at the middle of our diagram. Naturally, there will be some miscarriages of justice (shaded in Figure 4.1). In some cases the evidence appears to indicate something that is not true. I have drawn in the curves showing this effect in a logistic form that seems reasonable.

Anything that increases the efficiency of the court in effect increases the accuracy of the evidence. Although we are now discussing the commitment of more resources, the point is perhaps easier to discuss if we consider an increase in scientific knowledge. Let us suppose that Puddin'head Wilson discovers that fingerprints are unique to each individual. The result of this would be that the S curve after this discovery would be somewhat steeper than before. This would occur because as the result of this improved knowledge, the amount of evidence against certain defendants would appear to be greater, and less against other defendants. This would shift the location of these cases on our horizontal axis, thus making the S curve somewhat steeper. Ideally, we would like to have the S curve actually merge with the vertical line, but we are not likely to reach this goal.

The court's efficiency in judging evidence and, hence, the steepness of the S curve in our figure is affected by the resources invested. Longer periods of time spent questioning the witnesses, seeking out less obvious witnesses, using additional technical methods—all take time and add to cost. Improving the quality of the personnel is also an expensive process. Every time the efficiency of the court is increased and every time we increase the investment of resources in this improvement and reduction of error, we reduce L_e. Presumably, however, investments in resources in improving courts would be subject to declining returns, as are all other resources. This would mean that if we compute the payoff of a given contract with a number of different amounts of resource invested in court activity, we would find a curve such as line A in Figure 4.2.

The parties would rationally choose the high point of this curve (D) as the optimum. Note that under some court arrangements they would not be interested in entering into the contract at all and there would be many court arrangements under which they would enter into the contract, but which they would not regard as optimal. Note also that as the total benefit of peaceful continuance of the contract ($B_{c_1} + B_{c_2}$) is reduced, the curve rotates

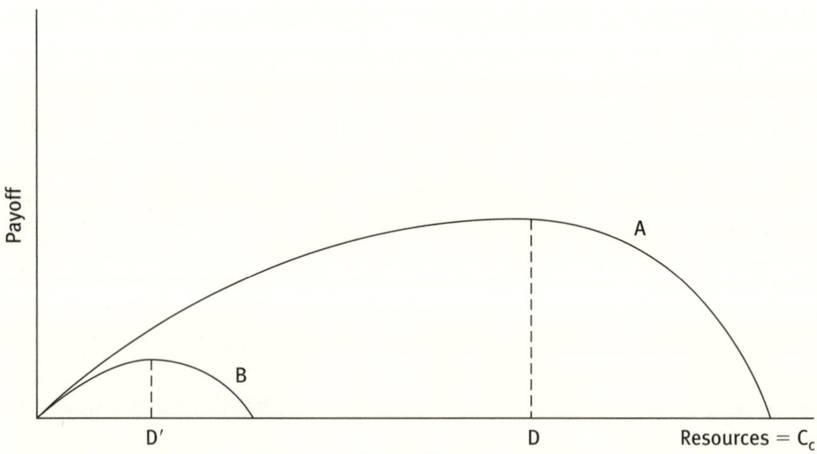

FIGURE 4.2
Optimal investment of resources

toward line B. As a consequence, the optimal amount of resources to be invested in court proceedings declines; D′ is optimal for the contract represented by B. This is, of course, what we observe in the real world. There are numerous quick and inexpensive judicial procedures that give low accuracy results for small claims. When we have a major issue at trial, however, we use elaborate procedures (normally including appeals) that we hope have a lower error content. Today people normally make decisions as to the court after the contract has been breached, although, of course, the small claims court is not available to everyone; but the parties would reach somewhat similar decisions if they were permitted to choose the courts beforehand.

In actual practice, in arbitration contracts there are sometimes arrangements for more complex arbitration if the problem is an expensive one than where the problem is minor. In any event, the arbitrators themselves are normally selected in such a way that the better ones are given the large cases and, for that matter, the larger fees, and the poorer ones take the small cases. In labor arbitration, for example, the Department of Labor keeps a list of arbitrators. Each arbitrator specifies his fee, and the parties to labor contracts simply select one from the list. All of this is in accord with our model and in accord, also, with common sense.

Risk aversion might have some effect on the calculation. If losing a lawsuit could be very expensive for the parties and the parties only very rarely are engaged in such lawsuits, they might be interested in “buying insurance” by putting more resources into court proceedings than otherwise. Conversely, if the parties are frequently engaged in litigation and each of the contracts that is litigated involves only a very small part of their resources, they might well be interested in minimizing court costs. A very interesting case is the situation in which one of the parties, let us say an insurance company, engages in a great deal of litigation about suits that are relatively minor to it, while the other party, perhaps a customer of the insurance company, is engaged in litigation very rarely and the amounts concerned are to him very major. This, one would anticipate, would lead to differential risk avoidance on the part of the two parties.

This is all that we can learn from the symmetric case—the case where the two parties are essentially identical. Let us now turn to the asymmetric case, and, in order to keep the discussion simple, let us go to a completely asymmetric example. Suppose that Party One lends Party Two money. The contract, then, is a contract by Party Two to repay Party One. Clearly, under these circumstances it is physically impossible for Party One to breach the contract, and all breaches must be breaches by Party Two. It is clear that we must have two equations—one for each party. Furthermore, these equations can be written easily as simplifications of Equation (4.1). In each case, one of the expressions in the braces vanishes because all the values in it are equal to zero. The two equations are presented as (4.8) and (4.9).

$$P_1 = B_{c_1}(1 - L_{b_2}) - L_{b_2}\{C_{b_1}L_{ns_2} + (1 - L_{ns_2})[C_{b_1}L_e - (1 - L_e)B_{c_1} + C_{c_1}]\} + I \quad (4.8)$$

$$P_2 = B_{c_2}(1 - L_{b_2}) + L_{b_2}\{B_{b_2}L_{ns_2} + (1 - L_{ns_2})[B_{b_2}L_e + (1 - L_e)B_{c_2} - C_{c_2}]\} - I \quad (4.9)$$

In Equations (4.8) and (4.9), however, I have added something—an insurance payment, I. With the possibility of breach entirely on one side, it is possible that one party may find it necessary to make a payment to the other party in order to induce him to enter into the contract. Needless to say, this is simply a possibility. Payment I could have a value of zero or even a negative value. Let us continue with our assumption that breaches of contract involve simple transfers from one party to another since any other assumption adds unnecessary elements of complication. Therefore, C_{b_1} is equal to B_{b_2}. For the contract to be entered into, it is necessary that both P_1 and P_2 be greater than zero. For this to be true, the double Inequality must also be true (4.10).

$$L_{b_2}[\ldots] - B_{c_1}(1 - L_{b_2}) < I < L_{b_2}[\ldots] + B_{c_2}(1 - L_{b_2}) \quad (4.10)$$

Certain limitations are placed on I, although these limitations are not necessarily very narrow. If, for example, $B_{c_1} + B_{c_2}$ were very large and L_{b_2} fairly small, I could well be a negative number.

It might seem that Party Two, the only person who can breach the contract, would have strong motives for favoring an inefficient court system. If it were not for the "insurance payment," this would clearly be true if Party Two could get Party One to enter into the contract with him. Note, however, that for Party Two to borrow the money from Party One, he must offer to Party One a positive value of P_1, which means that if the likelihood of legal error is high and, hence, L_{b_2} is great, the payment that Party Two must make to Party One under the insurance rubric is also large. There is, however, another matter. Let us suppose that we have a contract, which, in net, if it is quietly carried out, will produce a gain of \$5; that is, $B_{c_1} + B_{c_2} = \$5$. The cost of breach, however, might be much larger than that. If the loan were at 5 percent, nonrepayment inflicts \$100 cost on the lender. Thus, C_{b_1} and B_{b_2} might be as much as \$100. If, under these circumstances, L_{b_2} is greater than .05, I will necessarily be greater than \$5.

This would mean that the contract is impossible because Party Two cannot make enough by performing his obligations, no matter how much of the total gain he obtains, to make the payment to Party One that is necessary to induce Party One to enter into the contract. Party One, on the other hand, is unlikely to be willing to enter into the contract if he knows that the borrower will surely lose unless he succeeds in avoiding repayment.[3] Thus, if the courts are inefficient, there is no gain for Party One or Party Two. On the other hand, the more inefficient the courts and, hence, the higher the likelihood of error, the higher the net benefit of the contract must be before it becomes possible to enter into an agreement. In essence, the parties are charged a tax by the inefficiency of the courts, and this eliminates many agreements that would be desirable with a more efficient court system.

In the traditional Dupuit welfare diagram (Figure 4.3), all contracts are arranged on the horizontal axis in order of potential profitability. The ones with the highest net profit are at the left. The profits from various contracts are shown by the slanting line B_c. The horizontal line L_e represents the costs inflicted by a relatively inefficient court system. If we switch to a more efficient court system as represented by $L_{e'}$, not only do we pick up the traditional welfare triangle but the rectangle to the left of the welfare triangle is obtained by the parties through a reduction in waste, i.e., the inefficient court system. In both the symmetric and asymmetric cases, then, the parties have strong reasons for hoping that the courts will make relatively few errors and that the costs of legal proceedings will be relatively low. They have, of course, a motive for keeping the cost of legal proceedings always great enough so that the discounted value of the errors does not lead to continuous litigation, but this should be fairly simple to arrange.

I have used only the two rather pure cases for reasons of simplicity. We could easily extend our equation to five or six lines instead of the present two and obtain a general expression that would deal with varying degrees of asymmetry. We could similarly drop our assumption that the cost and benefits of a breach of contract involve simple transfers, where in the real world they probably normally do not, and produce an even more complicated equation—further "realistic" changes could be made. I do not think, however, this would

3. Special cases in which agreements of this sort are possible can be thought up. They have little or nothing to do with normal contractual situations, however.

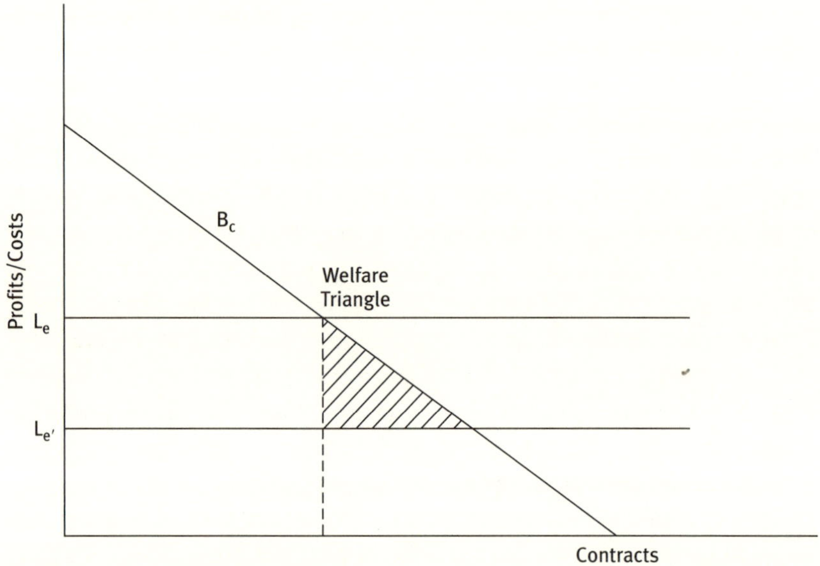

FIGURE 4.3
Gains from improved court procedures

give us any particular new information, and it would certainly make our exercise in high school algebra even more tedious.

Our conclusion that efficiency in the court decision process is desirable from the standpoint of all parties who are contemplating entrance into contracts would not be modified. Note, however, that this conclusion is an *ex ante* conclusion. Once I have entered into a contract with you, I have very strong motives to want that contract modified in my favor, and such modification may take the form of either injuring or improving the efficiency of the court's enforcement of the contract. Since most of us are likely to enter into far more contracts in the future than the number we are involved in now, it is likely that the value we obtain from generally efficient enforcement procedures is greater than the value we would obtain from making enforcement procedures less efficient.

As noted previously, a situation might arise in which one of the parties was engaged in a great deal of litigation and the other party was engaged in relatively little. In these cases the individual suit for the first party may be a relatively small matter, and for the second party, a relatively large matter. Since differential risk aversion would occur, it should, therefore, be possible to set

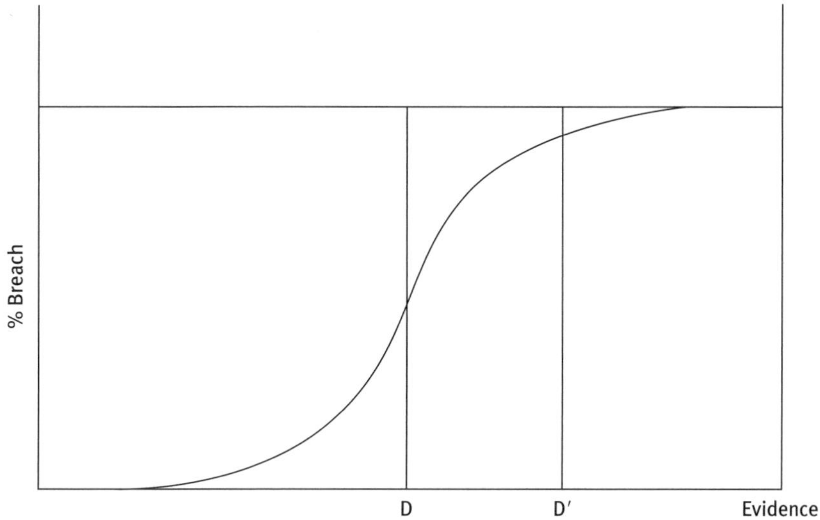

FIGURE 4.4
Biased court procedures

up an arrangement whereby one party pays the other a small fee for reducing his risk. If the risk is that the courts will decide incorrectly, then straightforward insurance against that risk is impossible. Since the courts are unlikely to admit that they are wrong in a given case, it would not be possible, if I lost a lawsuit, for me to successfully sue my insurance company alleging that I lost the suit unjustly. An insurance policy that insured me against the cost of losing lawsuits in all contracts would be equally difficult because I always have it in my power to simply breach the contract and, thus, put myself in a situation where I could profit. Thus, the moral risk would be overwhelming, and the insurance companies would not be willing to offer this type of insurance.

If, however, we cannot actually make a direct insurance contract of this sort, perhaps an arrangement between the two parties may serve something of the same end. Let us suppose that we have the situation shown in Figure 4.4, that the defendant is rarely likely to be involved in lawsuits, and these lawsuits are, for him, quite major. The plaintiff is in the opposite position with respect to these matters. For example, consider a bank that has a great many mortgages outstanding and an individual who will only undertake a few mortagages during his lifetime. Under these circumstances, we can provide something in the way of insurance for the potential defendant by biasing the proceedings. Instead of simply trying to follow the fair preponderance of the evidence and using decision rule D, the court might take the view that it will decide for the defendant unless the evidence is much stronger for the plaintiff as at the line D′. The number of errors the court makes, then, will be increased, but the number of errors against the defendant will be reduced. Individuals interested in risk reduction would presumably be willing to enter into contracts in which they paid a fee for this type of service. Similarly, the party on the other side would be willing to do this if the fee was large enough.

In the real world, a number of organizations do offer this kind of treatment to their customers. Insurance companies normally make quite a play in their advertisement and sales techniques of the generous way in which they settle claims against them by the people who have been insured.[4] Thus, it would appear that an insurance company sets up its own little court system—its claims adjustment office. This court system is under instruction to insure that any errors it makes are more likely to be against the insurance company than against the client. Needless to say, the cost of this bias is actuarially computable, and the insurance company adds the amount to its premiums. The net effect from the standpoint of the customer of the insurance company is that he is buying insurance in two different ways: he is buying insurance from the insurance company against fire by direct payment of premiums, and he is buying insurance from the insurance company against the contingency that the insurance company will erroneously refuse to pay him, again by paying a small premium to the insurance company. The same thing can be done by the courts. It is by no means obvious, however, that we would expect this phenomenon very often in a law of contracts. Later, when we turn to the criminal law, we will find it almost omnipresent.

We may pause profitably to briefly discuss out-of-court settlements. In Figure 4.5 we have a situation that confronts an attorney who is, let us say, representing one of the parties in a case at C. From the standpoint of the court that will reach eventual decisions, the outcome appears to be a simple application of a decision rule taking into account the amount of evidence. To the lawyer before the trial, it is not so simple. Firstly, he does not have access to all the evidence that will come out at the trial. Secondly, he cannot be

4. Note that in automobile accident cases the person who has the claim is not normally the insurance company's customer. He is someone who is threatening to sue the insurance company's customer. The insurance company's customer wishes to be protected against the suit, but he has no particular concern as to how this is done or how generously the insurance company pays off the person who is suing him.

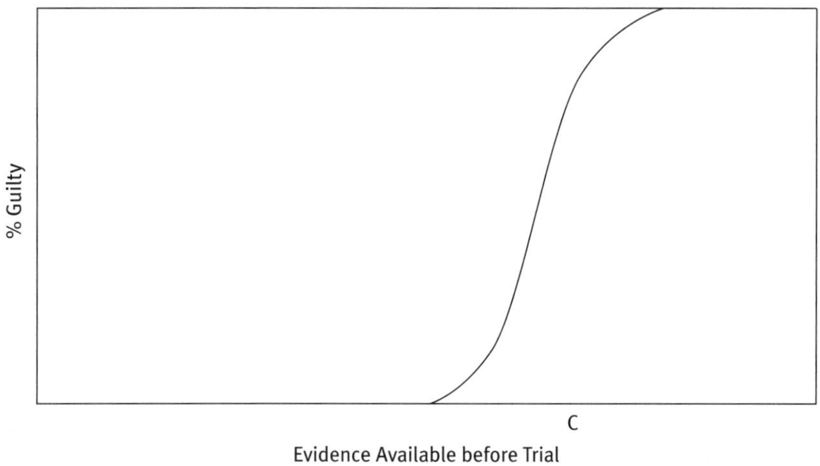

FIGURE 4.5
Negotiated settlements

certain exactly what will happen at the trial in such matters as good and bad impressions made by the witnesses. Thirdly, he cannot perfectly foretell the decision makers' reactions. Thus, the vertical line that is seen by the judge as describing his behavior appears as an S curve to the lawyers. In our case, from the standpoint of the lawyer, at point C the defendant has about three chances out of four of being found liable for breach of contract. If the attorneys for both sides are in general agreement as to these odds, then risk aversion would indicate that they should reach an agreement outside of court that properly discounts this predicted behavior of the court. If there is disagreement, which takes the form of the lawyer for the defendant's feeling that it is more likely that his client will be found guilty of breaching the contract than does the lawyer for the plaintiff, then again, an agreement is likely. If the lawyer for the plaintiff thinks that the decision of the court is more likely to go in his favor than does the lawyer for the defendant, then the matter will proceed to trial.

An element of bargaining and game theory, however, is involved in settlements, and occasionally the matter will go to trial even though a suitable bargain could be reached. This will occur in those cases in which the attorney on one side or the other (or, for that matter, the client on one side or the other) feels it important to develop a reputation for being tough. This raises no particular theoretical difficulty. Note that the question of whether the judge is simply attempting to determine what happened as accurately as possible or whether he is biased toward one party or the other makes no major change in the role of the attorneys. They simply attempt to predict his decision. The S curve drawn in Figure 4.5 would move to the right or to the left in terms of the degree of bias that the judge is believed to have. Bargaining, however, would still continue under approximately the same conditions.

CHAPTER 5

ANGLO-SAXON ENCUMBRANCES

We shall begin discussion of the procedure used in court and the problems of its efficiency by considering how information is brought before the court for decision. Obviously, the simplest method of obtaining information is to choose as the person to make the decisions someone who already knows this procedure. That is, of course, what is done. The judge is customarily an expert in the law, which is a technical matter. In those cases where the law is not known to the judge—foreign law, for example—it is normally "proved" as any other "fact." Where there is some doubt in the minds of the parties as to whether the judge does or does not know the law in any given area, the discussion of this matter is very similar to that of a factual question. Evidence in the form of written briefs and affidavits is presented and arguments are made by the attorneys.

It is not, by any means, necessary that the judge be a technical expert on this particular matter. In the formative period of Roman law, an outsider, the jurisconsult, was normally brought in as a technical expert to deal with any difficult problem of law. The jurisconsult who stated the law was not a judge—he was a private citizen. In our law when the jury is called upon to make ultimate decisions, it must also obtain information from the judge as to what the law is. Finally, in those innumerable cases in which the case proceeds to an arbitrator rather than a judge, the arbitrator may find it necessary to turn to an outside source of information on the law.

There is, however, no compelling reason why the special field of which the judge knows a great deal must be confined to the law or even be the law itself. In commercial arbitration, the arbitrator is very frequently an expert in some technical matter. If, for example, an importer alleges that a shipment of wool he receives is not up to the specified quality, the arbitrator selected for this matter will normally be a man who is capable of telling by inspection whether it is or is not up to that quality. Courts martial normally require that the officers on the court martial be as high or higher in rank than the person subject to court martial. The official explanation for this is that such persons will be able to understand, from their own experience, the problems confronting the officer under trial and, hence, can bring some knowledge with them.

It is an oddity of our law that although in many areas we attempt to see to it that the decision maker is already possessed of a good deal of information, in other areas we do just the opposite. There are efforts, for example, to see to it that jurymen know nothing whatsoever about the case before they enter the jury box. It is of some interest that the *raison d'être* of the jury has been completely reversed over the years. The original justification was that the twelve local men knew *more* than the circuit judge. It would seem, on the whole, that it is more sensible to follow the rule of selecting judges who know something about the subject than people who know nothing. This is, however, a subject on which two opinions are possible.

A second method of obtaining information for decisions in a court is to consult an expert who (himself) is not the judge. There are two ways of doing this: one is to have the judge select an expert; the other is to have the parties find (usually competing) experts who present their statements to the court. Once again, it would seem reasonable that the former is the better of the two procedures, and, of course, it is the procedure used in most of the world. We in the Anglo-Saxon world, however, have a rather provincial and unusual form of procedure in which the two parties themselves provide the experts.

Regardless of who provides the experts, there is the problem of obtaining them, which is normally done by offering them a fee. The parties to a contract, if they are interested in reducing L_e, would normally be willing to include provisions for such fees in the contract. If the court, for example, is to select its own experts, then one would anticipate that the parties would provide that it could, in cases of trial, draw the funds from the parties. The provisions could, of course, be arranged so that large fees would be available in major disputes and small fees in minor ones, and, hence, the experts would be much more expert for large contracts. Where the two parties provide the experts (as is the normal Anglo-Saxon practice), they, of course, pay them; but it is by no means obvious that this is a major defect in our procedure. The experts, after all, must protect their reputations.

The fourth category of information that may be important at a trial is documents and written papers. The text of the contract would do as an example. Our procedure, in general, descends from the Middle Ages, when illiteracy was common. It seems that this is the only available explanation for the fact that this procedure is primarily oral. It is frequently true that a written document, in order to be brought before a court in the United States or England, must be read aloud. In an attempt to be efficient in decision making, we would try to maximize the use of written rather than oral information. As much of the total volume of information as possible should be presented to the court in written form and should be circulated rather than compelling the parties to all get together at one time to receive it. This is, in general, the custom in commercial arbitration, although it must be said that in such cases the total volume of written documents may be small.

The fact that all the parties—the decision maker, the parties on both sides, the witnesses, and the attorneys—must all get together at the same time causes a great deal of waste in our present procedure. The use of written testimony, including the use of testimony taken before referees and then presented to the decision maker, would greatly reduce the total investment of time by various people waiting for other people. It would particularly be an improvement in the use of the time of the professional decision makers whom we call judges. Today they must spend most of their time hearing cases, and, as a consequence, sizable delays are imposed on other people who are waiting to have their issues decided. If judges could devote a greater part of their time to reading documents on cases, it would be possible to greatly improve the scheduling of that part of their time that is spent in hearing oral argument. There seems no reason why the formal speeches of the attorneys, for example, should not be replaced by written documents, or why a good deal of the testimony we now get should not be delivered in written form. Modern appellate procedure has moved in this direction.

It is, of course, true that under our present procedure the decision as to whether a witness is honest or not is made very largely by the technique of looking intently at his face while he testifies. This technique, in the present state of scientific knowledge, must be continued, and this does mean (at least to some extent) that witnesses must testify before the decision maker. Development of better ways of detecting lying would seem desirable. Such better methods will, in fact, be discussed later in this chapter, but for the time being we can note that a good many of the witnesses who appear in the average court case are not suspected of lying. The police photographer who appears for the purpose of identifying certain photographs that he took during the investigation of some crime, the fingerprint expert who simply testifies that certain fingerprints are the prints of a certain person, or the professor of comparative law who appears to testify as to the provisions of the German code of inheritance are all normally accepted by both parties as being completely honest witnesses. In those cases in which there is a question, of course, special arrangements should be made.

Thus far our problems with respect to obtaining information have been relatively easy. We now come to the difficult problems concerning evidence in the hands of people who would rather not present it to the court. The first and obvious case is found in the parties to the litigation themselves. A sues B for breach of contract. B would very much like to keep certain of his records out of the litigation because they will injure his case. Should he be compelled to produce them?

In the contract action we could, of course, simply provide an answer in the contract itself. It seems fairly certain that this would lead, in most cases, to a provision that both parties would be compelled (in the event of any dispute as to the enforcement of the contract) to present to whoever is to decide the dispute all the evidence in their possession. This would reduce L_e and, as we pointed out, would be to the advantage of both parties at the time the contract is entered into. The only exception would be cases whereby the presentation of this evidence might in and of itself be very expensive. We would, of course, weigh cost against benefit in this area, but it does not seem very likely that the cost would be sizable in many cases. The existing procedural law compels the parties to a litigation to produce their records; hence, it is unnecessary to include a special provision in the text of current agreements.

There is here, however, another problem. Suppose we are going to ask questions in court of the individual parties to the contract. They may well have strong motives to lie (or produce bogus documents). What should we do about this at the time we are drawing up the contract? If there were some perfect method of detecting lies, we could very easily incorporate the use of this method into the contract. Note that if we did so, there would be no need to place any particular restriction on lying when the matter came up for decision. The person who lied would normally find that (1) he prejudiced the decision maker against him; and (2) under some relatively ingenious questioning, his lies (each of which was properly detected) would, in fact, lead to the truth's being known to the decision maker. Unfortunately, we do not have such a certain method of determining whether or not people are telling the truth. The lie detector, which is discussed at somewhat greater length later, is an imperfect instrument. It is certainly better than staring at the man's face to detect lying, but that is feeble praise.

What then can we do? One procedure is to place a cost on lying. Thus, we can provide that, if one of the parties is called to testify and the decision maker thinks he is lying, some special cost will be imposed upon him. For example, suppose the contract provides that if Party A testifies falsely in a matter where the lie would profit him by the amount of \$100 (if his testimony were believed) and his falsehood is discovered, he will be required to pay a fine of \$500. If the probability of detection were greater than one in five, this would make lying unprofitable, and the parties would seldom resort to it. Here, clearly, we are coming very close to the criminal law of perjury, but note that the present line of reasoning would indicate that the parties would be inclined to include such provisions in their contracts if the law of perjury did not exist. We can, in fact, regard the legal provisions as a time-saver that makes it unnecessary for the parties to put such provisions into their contracts. A clause providing that testimony in any litigation arising out of a contract should not be under oath and, hence, not subject to prosecution for perjury would, I presume, be legally possible in present-day contracts. It seems unlikely that anyone will take advantage of this opportunity.

We now come, however, to the witness who is not directly concerned with the contract. It frequently happens that some factual information that would be of interest in determining whether or not a breach of contract has occurred is in the possession of an innocent bystander who is not a party to the contract or in any way connected with it. Note that what we are now discussing is not the expert witness. Expert witnesses are basically engaged in the competitive business of providing their expert knowledge for a fee. If one expert witness asks too much money for his services, the parties can turn to another. The individual who has seen something that is of importance to the trial, however, normally cannot easily be replaced.

Under these circumstances, if these outside witnesses (people not connected with the contract) are permitted to bargain for their fee, we can anticipate that they will attempt to extract the full economic value of their information in this bargaining process. Frequently, the economic value of their testimony is nearly as great as the total amount in dispute in the trial. Thus, permitting open bargaining would mean that the court costs would be so high that it would be very rare that contracts would be judicially enforced. This would be particularly true if there were several witnesses, each of whose evidence was of great importance to one or the other of the parties. Needless to say, the party against whom the witness was to testify would be willing to pay him not to testify. In Equation (4.5), $C_{b_2} - B_{c_2}$ would tend to equal C_{c_2}; hence, Party Two would not sue.

Obviously, since this type of witness is not a party to the contract, he cannot agree in advance to any specific treatment. Here all that can be done is to turn to broad social instrumentalities. Thus far, we have been able to discuss the law of contracts without any duties for the state. We have been able to demonstrate that agreements between the parties could lead to almost any outcome that was desired. The state has come in simply as the guardian of its own use of force and violence and as a labor-saving device providing certain facilities that the parties could otherwise provide for themselves. The problem of the essential witness who is not a signatory of the contract is impossible to solve by provisions in the contract. We are thus forced to turn to a purely governmental technique that we first describe simply and then with regard to its relationship to our fundamental assumptions.

Suppose that a law is enacted providing that in civil suits the parties or the judge (depending upon how we arrange the acquisition of information) may order any person they wish to testify. Let us further suppose that the law provides for payment for the witness's time. Unless the payment is excessive, this would be highly desirable from the standpoint of the parties to the contract. But would it be desirable to a person who is not, at the moment, involved in the contract under litigation? I think the answer is "yes." Firstly, a general law of this sort would make all future contracts that a person might wish to enter into much more readily enforced. *Ex ante*, it is a tremendous improvement in the efficiency of the contracting system. As we have pointed out, this is to the benefit of people who are thinking of entering into contracts, and we all are thinking of entering into contracts. There is, it might be said, an additional advantage to such a law. Not only are we ourselves interested in entering into contracts in the future, but the efficient functioning of our economy requires that it be possible for other people to do so as well. There is something similar to an externality involved in the contract process in that the existence of an efficient contract procedure makes it possible for the economy to function at a higher level than it otherwise would and, thus, raises all of our living standards.

We need not, however, depend upon this. Clearly, the present discounted value to me of a very sharp reduction in the cost of enforcing any contracts that I may enter into in the future is greater than the disutility I might suffer from not being permitted to bargain for a fee in those cases in the future in which I might become a witness to a breach of contract action. If the compensation that I would receive for testifying is such that I suffer no positive loss (only the loss of possible profits that I might make from bargaining), this is particularly clear. It is quite possible, however, that my present discounted value might be improved by compelling such testimony, even if witnesses were not paid at all. The payment of the witnesses really is important, less in terms of compensating them for their time (if we look at the matter *ex ante*) than providing an incentive for the court or the parties to be economical in the use of witnesses. In this case, we are eliminating an externality by imposing upon the parties to the litigation the cost of one of the resources they are using—the time of the witnesses.

Naturally, however, if we are going to compel people who are not parties to a contract to testify, we cannot permit the parties to the contract to set the conditions of this compulsion. In other words, we cannot permit the parties to a contract, when they choose their own method by which the contract is to be enforced, to also choose who is to compel the third-party witnesses and how much they are to be paid. For this purpose, we would need a social institution that represented the witnesses as much as it represented the parties to the contract. Thus, a court system that is established by the government would be necessary for this particular part of the process. Note that it would not be necessary for it to hear the witnesses; it could simply determine which witnesses should be called, what their compensation was to be, and the punishment (if any) if they were found to be lying in their testimony.[1]

This argument takes us back to the sets of possible institutions that benefit each person and their intersection discussed in Chapter 1. The present discounted value of compelling testimony with compensation is positive for everyone and, hence, would benefit all persons. Similarly, its abolition would injure all persons. It might, of course, be true that some person would be injured by being compelled to testify in a case tomorrow, but surely if we put the establishment of this institution off for several years and made it apply only to contracts entered into in the future, we would find no one who could reasonably object to it.

We now turn to the pure procedural variable (P) in our equation; that is, to a discussion of what types of procedure are most efficient in a court system. We have already noted that reducing the number of legal errors is extremely desirable. If we can do so in an essentially costless way (that is, by simply improving the efficiency of the organization of the court), this would obviously be sensible. It is my own opinion that this is quite readily possible in our present court system. The reader, however, may not agree with me. The remainder of this chapter, in any event, discusses improvements in our court system, mainly involving a radical change from the traditional Anglo-Saxon procedure that we have inherited from the Middle Ages. In a sense, the discussion is inconclusive. Here, as in so many other areas, a good deal of further research, particularly experimental research, is needed before one can have much confidence in the superiority of any given system. Thus, my arguments

1. The argument for putting a "price" on telling lies in court is just as strong for these witnesses as it is for other witnesses. Normally witnesses of this sort have much weaker motives for telling lies than the interested parties, and, therefore, perhaps it might be argued that we could get by with lower penalties.

for changes in our present system are really an attempt to demonstrate that there is a good case for a careful consideration of changes and extensive research in the area. Our present knowledge is simply not sufficient to permit placing any real confidence in our judgments of the efficiency of the various court systems.

I should like to begin by discussing two rather general issues that are, I think, normally the subject of a great deal of obscurantism and superstition. If we confine ourselves to the European legal tradition, we find two general ways of organizing legal procedure—the adversary and the inquisitorial system—and two methods of reaching ultimate decisions—judges and juries.[2] In both cases, the system used in the United States is the minority system. We use juries, whereas most Western countries use judges;[3] we use the adversary system, whereas most countries use the inquisitorial system. Since there are cases in which the inquisitorial system of organizing the courts is combined with juries,[4] and the adversary system of organization is also not infrequently combined with judicial decision making,[5] we can regard these as two independent variables and discuss them separately. As a further word of warning to the readers, I agree with the foreigners. Patriots who strongly favor retaining our sacred institutions will be annoyed by my analysis.

Three valid arguments for the peculiar institution of the use of juries are: it makes tyranny impossible, it makes corruption difficult, and it makes it likely that the results of judicial proceedings will be in accord with the "popular will" regardless of the law in the matter. The first argument was, perhaps, of historic importance. With the jury system, kings simply could not plan on

2. A number of European countries use an interesting system that combines the jury and the judge system. Under this system, a group of people are appointed to decide cases, but some, and usually a majority of them, have had no legal training. Furthermore, these nonlawyer members of the "judiciary" are not permanently assigned to this duty, but are periodically returned to the nonjudicial jobs and replaced by new untrained persons. The courts martial of most Western armies operate on somewhat the same basis, although in these cases the legally trained personnel are normally reduced to an advisory status.

3. During the period of the French Revolution, most European countries adopted the jury. Basically, they have now abandoned it, but a few remnants remain. See Harry Kalven, Jr., and Hans Zeisel, *The American Jury* (Boston: Little, Brown and Company, 1966), especially footnote 3 on pages 13–14.

4. For a few types of cases in Switzerland, for example.

5. All chancery cases in the traditional common law and the bulk of all cases now tried in the United States under either chancery or common law rubrics are examples.

imprisoning anyone. The juries were not necessarily favorable to rebels or opponents of the crown, but they were unreliable. Furthermore, if the king chose to follow a policy that was genuinely unpopular, the jury might follow popular feeling and not the law when it came to trial. Thus, an unpopular law might not be enforced.

It is probable, although not certain, that our traditional devotion to "the right of trial by jury" is derived from these considerations. I have always wondered why it should be such a privilege to be tried by a group of complete amateurs who have not been specially trained. In any event, the protection against despotism by the use of juries particularly concerns the criminal law. It is difficult to see any great danger to liberty in permitting contracts to be litigated before judges. In England—the home of our jury system—juries have been largely abolished for civil trials since about 1870.

A second argument for jury trials is that it is fairly easy to control juries so that bribery is unlikely. With reasonable care, it will be impossible for the parties to a litigation to know before the jury is finally impanelled who is going to be on it. Furthermore, once the jury is impanelled, it can quite easily be kept from any contact with potential bribers. Thus, if one fears corruption, the jury is more readily protected against bribery than is a judge. It should be noted, however, that if we are convinced by this particular argument, then a reform that has recently been much mooted in England would be desirable. The English noted that the unanimity requirement that is necessary in most cases in England, although not in Scotland, meant that only one person must be bribed in order to hang a jury. Therefore, they proposed reducing the requirement from unanimity to ten out of twelve, which would make it necessary to bribe three jurors and thus make it much more difficult to corrupt the jury. In any event, this entire argument of corruption, like that of the tyranny of the government, depends largely on other matters than the court procedure itself. It surely is not impossible to arrange things in such a way that the bribing of judges is extremely unlikely. If the likelihood of the corruption of judges is very low, then the argument for a jury under this head would be correspondingly weak.

The third argument for juries is "democracy." A judge is likely to follow the law a good deal more than a jury. Firstly, the jury does not know what the law is in any detail (and is likely to be confused by the highly technical "directions" on the law that the judge is required to give them). In addition, the jury is likely to ignore the law if it "doesn't seem right." Judges do this, also, but to a considerably lesser extent. Since the juries are an average group of people, this means that the mores and moral ideas, the emotions and sentiments of the average man are closely reflected in their judgments. Whether it is more "democratic" to have the cases decided in accord with rules which have been selected by democratic procedures, or to have them directly decided by a small random sample of the people, is clearly an open question. Arguments for the latter procedure can be made, however, and they are clearly arguments for the use of juries.

Before turning to the arguments against the use of juries for the enforcement of contract, I should like to point out that I am not suggesting that jury trials for this purpose be outlawed. In terms of our initial assumptions, we should favor the widest field of choice, which would mean permitting the contracting parties to choose their own form of enforcement. If they chose a jury, that would be their prerogative. I am opposed to our present law, which makes it extremely difficult or impossible to draw a contract in such a way that a jury may not be involved in its enforcement. My basic argument, however, is that contracting parties should be given greater freedom than they now have, not that their "right" of jury trial should be taken away.

Under our present procedure, in contract actions, there will be no jury if the matter falls within the completely arbitrary limits of a "chancery" action. If, on the other hand, the litigation is a "law" action, the parties decide at the time of the litigation whether there will be a jury. Normally either party may ask for one, and a provision in the original contract that barred a request for a jury would probably be void. The situation of the two parties at the time of litigation is quite different from that at the time the contract was originally signed. In particular, the party whose case is weaker is likely to feel that he would prefer to have the case heard by a group of untrained people of only average intelligence to having it heard by a trained expert on contract law who is of above average intelligence.

As evidence of real preferences, we can consider the real world situation in those contracts in which the parties are permitted to choose their own procedure. Those contracts in which the decision on enforcement will not be made by the regular courts are unusual in the United States, somewhat less so in England. Normally they are called "arbitration" contracts, but the word should not mislead us. They involve a private procedure for deciding who has broken the contract in the event of a dispute. In no case is this procedure the selection of a group of average and completely unqualified citizens who are then allowed to decide. In most cases an individual who is thought to be particularly well qualified is selected as the "judge" of the dispute, in some cases a board of such "judges" is established, or sometimes there is an arrangement for the automatic selection of such a "judge" at the time of the dispute.

It seems likely that granting a general permission to individuals who enter into contracts to select their own method of enforcement would lead to the expansion of the methods now used in cases where this freedom exists. The nonuse of the jury system by people who have a choice at the time they write their contracts would appear to be strong evidence that juries are not something that contracting parties value highly. In any event, the experiment should be tried. Permitting people to choose judges to enforce their contracts instead of juries would surely not be likely to lead to despotism, particularly if they are also permitted a freedom in deciding which judge they will "hire."

The advantage that judges have over juries is fairly obvious. On one side is training and selection, on the other a tiny random sample. The random sample is a good way of finding out the characteristics of the universe from which it is drawn, but it is not a good way of attaining superior performance. In any event, the variance of a sample of twelve is great. The judge, even the rather poor judges that we often have in the United States, is likely to be considerably above average intelligence. Even if his background has been basically political rather than legal (and that is the case with many of our federal judges, particularly those on the appellate and supreme courts), he will quickly pick up at least some expertise by hearing large numbers of cases. If we selected and trained our judges more carefully, these arguments would apply with even more force. An obvious improvement in our judicial system would be simply raising the level of the personnel on the bench; permitting the parties to contract for their judge (or arbitrator) in advance would probably lead to such an improvement.

Not only is the judge more intelligent and better trained than the jury, the lawyers who appear before him are aware of this fact. Skill in influencing the common man, so well known on Madison Avenue and at 1600 Pennsylvania Avenue, is also the secret of the success of any good trial lawyer. The experienced pleader before a jury knows that many of the jurors are not able to follow difficult lines of reasoning; he knows that the jury is likely to forget the details of the case, so he can rely on such convenient lapses of memory; he knows that the jury will either simply accept an expert's view or follow some vague idea of its own. With this idea of the average juror's ability, the jury lawyer does not make any real effort to present his case in a logical or coherent manner. He searches for slogans, simplifications, and emotional appeals.

Since his opponent is doing the same thing, the presentation of the case is not likely to be highly coherent.[6]

The contrast between the attitude taken by lawyers toward juries and that taken toward judges is sharp. Of course, judges have emotions, and the lawyers try to appeal to them. Furthermore, some members of the bench are not intelligent or have prejudices that are known to and played upon by the lawyers. Nevertheless, the intellectual level of judge trials is normally higher. The judge normally can follow involved lines of reasoning, so lawyers are willing to present them if they are relevant and serve their interests. The judge can understand the contract even if it is complicated. He has heard technical evidence before and probably has at least some idea of what it is about. Consequently, the attorneys present their case to the judge on a much higher level, and the outcome is likely to be a better decision, not only because the judge is better qualified than the jury to make a decision, but also because the attorneys, knowing that he is not as easily influenced by Madison Avenue techniques, make less use of them.

As a final matter, we might consider whether a single judge is better than a board of judges. A simple fact must be taken into account here. For a given amount of money, you can hire a single man of very high quality, three men of less quality, or five of even still less quality. Thus, in general, the board of judges will be individually less qualified than the single judge. This fact is not necessarily decisive, but it should always be remembered. Other than that, I do not think that we can say very much about the question of whether an individual judge is better than a board of judges. I, myself, tend to prefer the individual judge, but this may be simple prejudice. In continental Europe, boards of judges are used. The issue should receive further study, and any

6. These strictures are of considerably greater importance in the United States than they are in England. Under the English procedure, juries are drawn from the upper class, and the judge closes the case with a long, careful discussion of the case addressed to the jury. Since the juries are likely to be very heavily influenced by this performance on the part of the judge, the attorneys are almost as much concerned with influencing the judge as the jury. This leads to a more intellectual approach to the case. The reader who wishes to have an idea of the usual situation in the United States can do no better than to read *The Reader's Digest Murder Case*. This is very close to a verbatim record of the proceedings in a New York murder case that involved two employees of *The Reader's Digest* as victims. A reading of the opening and final statements of the attorneys involved is quite revealing. J. Fulton Oursler, *The Reader's Digest Murder Case* (New York: Collier Books, 1962).

definitive outcome would probably be applicable to fields far outside that of jurisprudence.

Our second general problem is the choice between the adversary system of procedure and the inquisitorial system. The latter system has had very bad press in the United States and England, possibly because of the resemblance between its name and that of the Inquisition. In fact, again, we are the ones who have a peculiar and unusual system, whereas the inquisitorial system is the norm of the Western world. Such countries as Sweden, Denmark, Switzerland, and the Netherlands all use the inquisitorial system; surely no one will argue that this results in any great loss in freedom for their citizens. The actual cause of the difference in procedure in the Anglo-Saxon world and in the continental countries is an accident of history. The Roman law used an inquisitorial procedure. When the German tribes conquered the Western empire, they replaced the Roman system with judicial chaos. In England, however, this chaos gradually developed into the distinctive Anglo-Saxon judicial procedure, while on the continent there was a return to the Roman system. It should be noted that the judicial systems used in the non-European world are also mainly of an inquisitorial nature, although in many of them the courts should not be regarded as models.

Even in English procedure there are elements of inquisitorial proceedings. In particular, Chancery, or "equity," with its close connections to canon law and through it to the Roman legal system, has a number of inquisitorial features. Even in strict "law" cases, the British judge has a much freer hand with the witnesses than does the United States judge. Thus, the British original, from which we copied our system, is somewhat closer to the inquisitorial procedure than we are.

Basically, the difference between the two systems is simply a matter of who dominates the procedure, the lawyers or the judge.[7] In the inquisitorial system, the judge or judges institute an inquiry into the matter. They call such witnesses and ask them such questions as they think desirable. The parties, either in person or through their attorneys, are permitted to ask such further questions and call such additional witnesses as they wish, but the basic procedure consists of an inquiry into the matter by the judge or judges. In the Anglo-Saxon system, the judge plays little role in the actual presentation of

7. This is true even in those cases in which inquisitorial procedures are combined with a jury as the ultimate trier of the facts.

the case.[8] The two lawyers dominate the proceedings. Normally the plaintiff's attorney first presents his case, and the defendant's attorney tries to break it down. The judge may ask questions himself, but this is frowned upon in the United States. The argument offered for the Anglo-Saxon procedure is that the judge is more likely to be impartial if he plays little or no role in the case except as an auditor.

This argument has never been completely clear to me, but what I think it means is that the judge, when he begins asking questions, must have at least some "theory." As the philosophers of science are so fond of pointing out, no investigator can start out with a completely empty mind. He requires at least some elementary theories in order to ask his questions. The judge is in the same position. Thus, he will start out with an idea, however faint, of what the investigation is likely to produce. It is the nub of the argument against the inquisitorial procedure that he is likely to stick to this initial theory even if the evidence does not support it. Or, in a milder form, he will stick to his initial theory unless the evidence against it is substantially greater than the evidence for it. This argument is not completely without merit; some such tendency might well exist. The problem is whether this particular disadvantage of the inquisitorial system outweighs the disadvantage of the adversary system.

If the judge simply sits and listens to the two attorneys, clearly he is less likely to be personally involved with any particular theory of the case. On the other hand, the greater importance of the lawyers means that the relative excellence of those hired by the two parties is of much greater importance. If the judge decides on the basic order form of the witnesses and asks 90 percent of the questions, the man who happens to have the poorer lawyer is obviously at less of a disadvantage than if the lawyers decide the order of the witnesses and ask almost all of the questions. Since a case in which the two lawyers are of exactly equal ability must be very rare, it would seem that the inaccuracy introduced by this factor alone would more than offset the possible inaccuracy resulting from giving the judge the dominant role.

A further advantage of the inquisitorial system is a reduction of the importance of courtroom strategy. As anyone who has had much contact with lawyers knows, strategy and tactics are very important to them, and lawsuits come to be thought of as contests between the lawyers. Given this attitude and the complex maneuvering that accompanies it, the smaller the role played

8. Again, this is much more true of the American court system than of the British. The English judge plays a much more active role than does his American opposite number.

by the lawyers, the more likely it is that the outcome will be in accord with the facts. The inquisitorial system does not, however, eliminate courtroom strategy, but it greatly reduces its importance.

If we turn from the Anglo-Saxon court system and inquire as to what system is used for other types of investigation in England and America, we find that the adversary system is almost never adopted. In the United States, if we wish to find out the facts about something, practically regardless of what it is, we do not appoint a judge and then have two attorneys present cases to him. We appoint an individual or a board to investigate, and we expect that the appointed individual will conduct the investigation himself. This is so even if the appointee is a judge. The Pearl Harbor investigation by a justice of the Supreme Court was completely inquisitorial in nature. The recent inquiries instituted in England into certain security problems were conducted by a judge, but his procedure was not "adversary." Even the advocates of the adversary system do not use it when they wish to find out something for themselves. Altogether, it does not seem likely that the adversary system would long survive competition if individuals were permitted to choose their own procedural rules.

We must now turn to another peculiarity of Anglo-Saxon law, one to which we are so accustomed that most of us do not realize how odd it is. In most courts in the world there are few, if any, restrictions on what evidence can be presented. The judge, it is assumed, is capable of weighing the evidence and gives unimportant evidence little or no weight even if it does get into the record. Although there are some exceptions to this rule, which are mainly of an administrative nature, basically the law of evidence is of little or no importance outside the area of the common law. In Anglo-Saxon areas, however, an elaborate "law of evidence" prohibits the courts from even hearing much potential evidence. This peculiar local institution to which we have become so thoroughly accustomed can be roughly divided into three general categories.

The first, although the last one to arrive on the scene, is essentially technical. An example is the rule that blood tests may be used to disprove paternity but may not be presented to prove paternity. This rule is basically a restatement of the scientific conditions surrounding the test and, as such, is completely unexceptionable. Why we should have a separate rule of this sort instead of leaving the entire matter to the experts, I do not know; but as long as the rules are in accord with science, they certainly do no harm. The rules in the second category are essentially ethical rules. The privilege against self-incrimination, for example, is normally considered part of the laws of evidence. Other examples are the rule that a wife cannot testify against her husband and that evidence obtained by improper means cannot be used by the prosecution in a criminal case.

The final category, and the most voluminous, is a vast collection of rules that prohibits the use of odd bits and pieces of evidence on the grounds that they are not very good evidence. When I took courses on evidence in law school, the explanation given for this giant collection of rules was simply that juries were stupid. It was thought by the early judges, who set the precedents, that the juries were simple people not used to complex reasoning and easily led astray. Certain types of evidence were particularly likely to mislead the juries and, hence, were banned. Odd though it may seem, this does appear to be the only explanation for the development of this branch of the law, and it is one more argument for not using the jury system. The Anglo-Saxon law paradoxically also applies the law of evidence in those cases (Chancery, for example) in which a judge rules without the assistance of a jury.

The most widely known of these rules is that against hearsay. Suppose that A is accused of murdering B. In fact, he was playing chess with C at the time, but C has since been killed in an automobile accident. It happens, however, that the chess game was a particularly interesting one, and on numerous occasions before the accident, C had talked about it to his friends, discussing the fine points of his strategy and how he had won. In these discussions, he had emphasized that the game was so interesting that neither player had moved from the table from 10:00 until 1:00; this three-hour period covers the time of the murder. Can A call these friends of C to testify as to what C had said? No, this is hearsay. In France, this testimony would be heard. In Switzerland, Denmark, and Japan it could be brought in; in the United States and England, it could not be.

Obviously, hearsay evidence is worth less than direct evidence. B's testimony that he had heard A say that Z was true is less convincing than A's testimony. Firstly, we have two potential liars involved instead of one. A may have been lying when he originally said it, or B may be lying in saying that he heard A say it. Furthermore, A was not under oath at the time he made the statement nor was he under any great pressure to be particularly careful in his statements. Most witnesses think their testimony over fairly carefully, simply because the courtroom drama convinces them of its importance. The same cannot be said of a man making a casual remark in the course of a conversation. As a last point, if all we have is B's testimony, then A cannot be cross-examined on his reasons for saying that Z was true. Altogether, hearsay is less valuable than direct testimony and the judge who weighed direct and hearsay testimony equally would be incompetent. This is not to say, however, that completely eliminating hearsay evidence is wise. The trier of the fact should have as much information as possible, and hearsay is information, even if it is not as good as direct testimony. Clearly A should be asked to testify if he is available, and the hearsay should be resorted to only if he cannot testify. Clearly, also, the hearsay should not be weighed as strongly as direct testimony, but equally clearly, hearsay should not be given a weight of zero.

The argumentation against admission of hearsay, heard again and again, is: "Would you like to be convicted on hearsay?" This is clearly unfair. What you object to is being convicted. The evidence used for that purpose is irrelevant except that, possibly, innocent people convicted unjustly may feel worse about it than guilty people. In any event, the hearsay rule is as hard on the defense as it is on the prosecution. "Would you like to be convicted because evidence in your favor was ruled inadmissable because it was hearsay?" Most courts accept all sorts of evidence, including hearsay, and weigh it appropriately in making their decisions. A small minority of courts, including our own, simply rule out certain types of evidence, which amounts to giving this evidence a weight of zero and can hardly improve the quality of their decisions. Surely the sensible thing to do is to present as much evidence as is available—poor evidence as well as good—and then let the judge weigh it all. This, as I have remarked, is what almost all of the world's judicial systems do.

I have discussed the hearsay rule because it is perhaps the best known of the rules of evidence. It is also typical in being based on historical precedents that have never really been thought out and in eliminating from consideration certain evidence that could be of assistance to the court. Other rules are equally silly. A witness, for example, may have taken voluminous notes at the time of the occurrence that he is asked to describe.[9] The sensible procedure, surely, would be to examine the notes and then to question the witness in order to get a cross-check and to see if there are any details that are not in the notes. Since a sizable gap in time frequently occurs between the event and the trial, the notes would normally be more reliable than human memory.[10] Needless to say, this is not the law of evidence. The witness is required to pretend that he is relying upon his memory. He may look at his notes, but only to "refresh his memory." Obviously, this is a most inelegant procedure,

9. Police officers quite regularly do this.

10. But not always.

and equally obviously, it is vastly inferior to considering both the notes and the memory.

The law of evidence is further responsible for most of the procedural quibbling that takes up so much time in American and British courts. Most of the lengthy debates as to whether a lawyer may ask a witness a particular question would be eliminated if the laws of evidence were abolished. This would not only shorten trials, but it would considerably improve their accuracy. Surely these debates tend to interrupt the train of thought of the judge and the jury and, hence, make it harder for them to appreciate the relevance of the testimony of the witnesses. When we add the fact that the laws of evidence frequently rule out the best evidence for a point, the arguments for their abolition appear overwhelming.

When I was attending law school, one member of the faculty was Max Rheinstein, a leading authority on European law (particularly German law). He was hired to testify, as an expert witness, on a point of German law. Unfortunately, he did not discover exactly what they wanted him to testify to until he got to the courthouse. He telephoned his secretary who had a good command of German. At his instruction, she looked up the relevant article in the code and read it to him over the phone. Unfortunately for Rheinstein, a court attaché happened to overhear his end of the conversation and told the opposing lawyer. The lawyer, not regarding the rules against hearsay as applying to him, objected to Rheinstein's testimony on the ground that he did not know what the code said of his own knowledge. The upshot was that Rheinstein returned to the university, personally read the article in the code, and then returned to court to testify. All of this resulted in his wasting a good deal of time, but that is not my reason for bringing up the matter. Surely the best evidence as to the German law was the German law itself. This, in fact, is what Rheinstein depended upon. The rational first step, if one wishes to know German law, is to obtain a copy of the law (with a translation if necessary). It may be necessary to hire an expert to explain it, but the law itself is clearly the best possible evidence. The law of evidence takes a contrary view.

But this discussion of the existing Anglo-Saxon law of evidence is but a preliminary to a consideration of the problem of detecting witnesses who are lying. The entire problem of dishonest testimony and its prevention bristles with difficulties. The basic problem, of course, is that we are not very good at telling when people are lying. Even if we had some perfect method of detecting lies, there would still be many reasons why decisions might be incorrect. The human memory is fallible; most people are poor observers, and the judges, of course, make their own errors. Still, eliminating lying testimony would be a gigantic improvement. The major method of detecting lies now in use is to look intently at the witness's face in the hope that his expression will indicate that he is lying. As a method it is not very good, although there is no real evidence as to exactly how bad it is. Experiments in which a number of observers tried to guess whether various witnesses were lying or not, with statistics collected and analyzed, would appear to be both easily performed and of considerable significance. Unfortunately, I have been able to find none.

The easiest way to detect a lie is simply to have contrary evidence. The witness says that he saw the defendant commit the murder by the light of the moon, but an astronomer says that there was no moon that night. There are two problems here: one is that the astronomer may either be lying or mistaken (having made a careless mistake in his calculations), and the other problem is that the witness may be mistaken about this, but not about the rest of his testimony. What do we do when the witness says, "Oh, yes, now I remember; I saw it in the light thrown by the headlights of a passing car"? Perhaps the commonest thing for a judge or juror at this point is to simply decide that the witness is a proven liar and his testimony on other points should thus be ignored.

This is not necessarily correct. The average individual is not a good observer, a fact that has been proven by innumerable experiments, and may well be mistaken on part of his evidence simply because he observed badly. Our witness, for example, might have just looked out the window for an instant when the murder was committed and assumed the light was moonlight when it was from headlights. Last, but not least, the average man is not a quick or terribly logical thinker. A skilled cross-examination may create various apparent inconsistencies in his testimony. Nevertheless, the rule that a witness who lies in one thing will probably lie in others is surely not irrational. If we emphasize that it is "probably" and not "certainly," we are fairly safe. In fact, human testimony tends to be less reliable than "circumstantial evidence" simply because of these natural defects of the human mind. The objective material evidences are normally more to be relied upon than human memory. Unfortunately, it is rare that we find a case in which there is enough objective evidence so that we do not mainly depend on the vagaries of the human memory.

If objective evidence that contradicts the testimony of a witness normally indicates that he is lying, what about contradiction by another witness or witnesses? Clearly someone is lying, but who?[11] An obvious rule, which is unfortunately completely wrong, is simply to count the witnesses on both sides. If this rule were followed, and it must be admitted that it is followed by some juries and judges (it is actually part of patent law), then criminals could live a life of crime with complete impunity provided only that they banded together so that there would always be more of them to deny that they had committed a crime than witnesses to aver it. If you propose to make your living by robbing individuals, then you should team up with a friend so that there will always be the word of two against the word of one. Needless to say, you should only commit your robberies when there are no witnesses, but this is a sensible precaution in any event. Criminals planning to undertake crimes where there are likely to be a number of witnesses, bank robbery for example, would be well advised to organize themselves in quite large groups so that they will always outnumber the witnesses.

All of this is absurd, yet it is the likely result of simply counting witnesses. In fact, our courts do nothing so foolish. Rape is a particularly good crime to illustrate the fallacy of simply counting witnesses. Normally the case will take the form of the girl who testifies that she was raped and the man (or men) maintaining that she consented. Any system of merely counting the witnesses on the two sides, when combined with the "reasonable doubt" criterion, would mean that convictions for rape would be impossible. In fact, of course, the judge and juries do not depend upon this simple-minded criterion. They try to decide who is lying by carefully looking at faces, listening to voices, and observing who is most confused on cross-examination.

The denials of the accused are, in any event, not normally weighted very heavily. Perhaps the oldest test for truth is the Roman "*cui bono?*" Who gains? If two people give conflicting testimony and one would obviously have a motive for lying while the other would not, then we are likely to believe the disinterested witness. Since the defendant in a criminal trial has an obvious and strong motive for lying if he is guilty, his statement that he is not guilty is normally given little importance. The rule, however, has a much wider application. The disinterested witness is obviously more to be trusted than the one who would have a motive to lie. Even more to be trusted is the man whose testimony is against his own interest. If A testifies to certain things and this testimony will obviously hurt A, then we are likely to assume that he is an

11. Perhaps not. Humans are very poor observers, and differences of opinion on what appear to be the simplest matters of fact may result from honest mistakes rather than lies.

honest man who tells the truth even if it hurts him. In any event, his testimony on these matters will normally be given great weight. The problem raised by these fairly obvious rules for weighing evidence, of course, is that we may not know the real situation of the witness. He may have a good motive for lying that is not obvious. He may make a lying statement that is apparently against his interest because the truth is even more likely to injure him. Still, the basic good sense of these rules is evident.

Cross-examination is also supposed to be a test for the lying witness, although whether it is or not seems to me an open question. It may, in fact, convince the jury that a perfectly honest witness is lying. A good lawyer can usually confuse the average man who is testifying on a fairly complicated event without much difficulty. In any event, under the adversary system, cross-examination serves another important function. The lawyer who calls a witness would prefer, normally, to ask the witness only for that information that will help the lawyer's case. Witnesses frequently have information that will help both sides. The fact that the witness will later be cross-examined by the attorney for the other side means that the additional evidence will eventually appear. The original lawyer, in fact, may anticipate its production on cross-examination by bringing it out himself. Without cross-examination, this information might be completely lost. Thus, under the adversary system cross-examination is necessary, even if it does not help much in uncovering lying.

But all of these methods of detecting lying are obviously inefficient. Furthermore, all of them are merely supplementary to looking at the witness's face and guessing from that whether he is telling the truth. The weakness of this method as a way of detecting lying is patent, and the only reason we have used it is that until very recently it was the only known method. Today we have better ways of telling whether people are lying, although no one would regard them as being very good. Falling under the general (and somewhat misleading) heading of "lie-detectors," they are the subject of a great deal of emotion, but not much real thought. In the first place, these machines do not detect lies, they simply improve our observational abilities. In addition to looking carefully at the man's face, we can measure his blood pressure, watch the electrical conductivity of his skin, as well as several other phenomena that are not visible to the naked eye. Experience indicates that watching these things is a better, although still far from perfect, way of guessing whether the witness is lying than is scrutinizing his countenance. It is, of course, quite possible to combine the two methods. There is no reason why one cannot watch both the witness's face and the measurement of his blood pressure.[12]

Normally, however, these devices for displaying certain changes in the physiology of the witness are not used alone; an expert is used in conjunction with them. Furthermore, this technician does not confine himself to keeping the machines in repair and seeing that they are properly connected to the witness; he regards these as the least of his duties. He is an expert, in his own opinion, in telling whether the witness is or is not lying. He will normally take the witness to a specially prepared room, ask him a set of questions that he prepared while the "lie detector" makes a continuous record of various physiological variables, and then emerge with an opinion as to whether the witness is or is not telling the truth. The procedure obviously raises different issues from simply improving the methods available for judging whether the witness is telling the truth. It must be admitted that the lie-detector operators are, as a group, the best detectors of lies we have. Their opinion as to whether a man is lying or not is usually better than that of any judge who has simply looked intently at the witness's face while he testifies. Nevertheless, the lie detector operator is in a quite different class from the ordinary expert witness.

The present technique of using lie detectors takes into account only the reactions of the witness and obviously is an inferior process. The sensible procedure is to take all of the evidence, including the blood pressure of the witness, into account at the same time. This is impossible under our present method of using these devices, but there is nothing preordained about our present procedures. There is no reason why the devices that show a witness's blood pressure should not be arranged so that the judge and the opposing attorneys can see their dials.[13] The judge can then take the information he receives from these instruments into account in assessing the weight to give to the evidence of each witness.

Note that I have referred to the judge throughout. The procedure suggested would be impossible, at least with our present techniques, if a jury

12. The present machines are not designed with the objective of making this easy. In this, as in many other respects, the "lie detectors" are suffering from a lack of research and development.

13. Current "lie detectors" do not register their results on dials, but there is no reason why they could not. In fact, it seems likely that methods of displaying the physiological changes of the witness in very compact and easy to understand ways would be available in these days of electronic computers.

were trying the case. In my opinion, this is a further argument against juries. Present-day judges would also be unable to use the information provided by the "lie detectors" because they do not have the necessary training. This, however, can be remedied.

Before turning to the arguments against the use of these instruments, it should be mentioned that there are some other psychological procedures that might also be helpful. To mention but a single example, reading the witness a long, carefully chosen list of words and then watching his reactions to some of them can be very informative. This procedure could only be undertaken if the inquisitorial type of procedure were used, but, again, in my opinion that is simply an argument for this type of procedure.

The objections to the use of the lie detector are seldom articulated with any degree of clarity. Basically, I think they boil down to the fact that it is new and, thus, suspect. Most of these arguments implicitly assume that the lie detector is to be used only in criminal proceedings, that only the defendant will be subjected to it, and that, somehow, it prejudices the position of innocent defendants. Since we are now talking about a civil suit to enforce a contract, these assumptions are largely irrelevant. It is generally unwise, however, to use "lie detectors" on only one witness. It may happen that there is only one witness, but normally there are more. Since a sizable possibility of error exists, we should put much less weight on indications in the blood pressure of one witness that he may be lying, than in readings from several witnesses that confirm each other.[14] Thus, if A avers that M is the case while B says $\overline{\text{M}}$, an examination of A's blood pressure that shows indications of lying is of value, but we could be much more confident if B's blood pressure showed no signs of dishonesty. If we have inaccuracy in this case, it is likely to show up as an inconsistent result—both A and B telling the truth or both lying—which would put us back in the same position as if we had not used the "lie detectors." It is possible, of course, that the errors would be arranged symmetrically so as to present a consistent but wrong picture, but the odds are against it. Furthermore, the more witnesses tested, the less likely is such a symmetric mistake.

The only remaining argument against the use of the "lie detectors" is simply that they are occasionally inaccurate. Since we make use of a great amount of evidence whose accuracy may be poor in trials, it is difficult to imagine why

14. Actually, the readings of the physiological instruments are like judgments of expression in that they do not give simple unambiguous indications of truth or lying. For purposes of discussion, however, I have somewhat simplified the situation.

this is an argument at all. Judging whether a man is lying by looking at his face is even less accurate than making the same judgment by looking at his blood pressure. Should we then put a screen between the witness and the judge so that the judge cannot be misled by this inaccurate information? It may be, of course, that the people who use this argument are thinking of jury trials and feel that juries, being stupid, will be unduly influenced by lie detector evidence. Thus, the dull jurors, in spite of being warned that lie detectors may lie, will assume that they are always correct and reach incorrect conclusions. Assuming that this estimate of the reactions of the jurors is correct, it seems to me an argument against the use of juries, not against the use of a recording sphygmomanometer. In any event, it is hard to believe that contracting parties would object to a provision for all witnesses being questioned under the most favorable conditions for detecting lies.

It should be noted that our present criminal procedure in fact makes use of the lie detector in a very important way, one that probably leads to much more error than the procedure I have suggested. In a great many jurisdictions it is the custom to give the defendant the option of taking a lie detector test. If the test shows him to be innocent, he is normally released without trial. If he refuses to take the test or if the test shows him to be guilty, he will be tried. Granted the inaccuracy of present-day lie detectors, these decisions by the expert must themselves sometimes be erroneous. This procedure was undoubtedly adopted in an effort to protect innocent defendants, but it must be noted that it is likely to prejudice the case of those people who have been erroneously found guilty by the lie detector operator.

It is well known to the judges and juries in most of these jurisdictions that the police and prosecuting attorney use this procedure. It is not at all infrequent for the outcome of the test to be printed in the newspapers before the trial. In any event, a regular rule such as that used in New York City to release the defendants who "pass" the lie detector test clearly should prejudice the judges and juries against those defendants who appear before them. The judges and juries know that the defendant who appears before them has either failed the lie detector test or refused to take one. It seems far more rational to permit the judge and jury to examine the results of the lie detector test along with other evidence than to use the lie detector in this way. Furthermore, it should be noted that when the lie detector is used in this way, only the defendant is tested. Those other witnesses in the case whose lying may be just as important to the outcome as the defendant's are not given the lie detector test. Thus, in many ways, this very widespread practice in our criminal law amounts to a less than optimal use of the lie detector. A conscious adoption of the lie detector as part of the regular trial proceedings could hardly help but improve matters.

Let us summarize. Using the basic assumptions outlined in Chapters 1 and 2, we have demonstrated in Chapter 4 that individuals would choose to be given freedom in the choice of courts to enforce their contracts. We have also been able to specify an "efficiency function" for courts. Chapter 5 is necessarily concerned with less clearly logical arguments. For deciding what type of court would maximize our efficiency function, we need judgments about the real world, and I have offered mine. If, however, the reader will try to think about the matter without simply relying on the customs and practices that have grown up over the years in England and the United States, I think he will find that he agrees with me. In any event, my position is that the suit to enforce the contract should be decided by a man who is specially selected and trained for that task, not a group of randomly selected, untrained men. The man selected to make the decision should take the primary role in the actual proceedings and not be reduced to the passive role of the judge of a debate. He should be given access to any evidence that he thinks is important and not restricted by the customs developed many years ago to prevent illiterate juries from making mistakes. Lastly, he should be allowed every aid that science can give.

CHAPTER 6

ACCIDENTS

Most laymen have a fairly clear idea of what they mean by accidents. Normally this idea itself is clear only because the layman does not understand the difficult ontological problems involved. Nevertheless, I should like to begin this chapter by accepting the layman's idea of what an accident is and only turn to the problem of defining it later. For simplicity, let us take as our example a common motor vehicle collision. In this case, the difference between the layman's definition of the term "accident" and the definitions that might be used by more sophisticated persons are of very little importance. What should the law on such accidents be? Chapter 8 discusses the issue of what type of state regulations we should impose with the idea of reducing such accidents, and we will here concern ourselves solely with the issue normally dealt with in the law of torts—the payment or nonpayment of reparations to persons injured in such an accident.[1]

The first aspect to note about compensation in these terms is that it makes very little difference to the final outcome what the law is. Our present law provides that, in accidents in which one party is "to blame," that party may be compelled to pay for the other party's injuries. Since we normally carry insurance to cover this liability, in practice this means that the first party's insurance company makes the payment. Let us suppose this law were drastically changed so that if a person reports to a court that he has been badly injured in an automobile accident through someone else's fault, the court will not hear him. We can be more extreme and assume that if I report to the court that I have been injured in an automobile accident caused by Smith, the court as an automatic routine requires me to pay for all damages that Smith may have suffered. The only effect of this would be to compel me to purchase a different type of insurance. There is no reason why I cannot carry an insurance policy against injuries

1. I have been greatly helped in preparing this chapter by a book by Walter Blum and Harry Kalven, Jr., *Public Law Perspectives on a Private Law Problem* (Toronto: Little, Brown and Company, 1965). Although my conclusions are not entirely theirs, it seems to me that this study greatly clarifies the basic issues and is decidedly more sophisticated than anything else in the field. In addition to this book, I was assisted by Alfred E. Connard, James M. Morgan, Robert W. Pratt, Jr., Charles L. Voltz, and Robert L. Bombaugh, *Accidents, Costs, and Payments* (Ann Arbor: University of Michigan Press, 1964). A recent and important book in this field is Guido Calabresi, *The Costs of Accidents* (New Haven: Yale University Press, 1970).

that I suffer, regardless of their source.[2] There is also no reason why I cannot purchase insurance against the risk that someone will cause injury to me and to himself by causing an accident, and that I (the innocent party) will be compelled by a particularly wild law to pay his costs. The major effect of law in this area is to identify the person who must purchase the insurance.

Let us consider the results of a radical change in our present institutional structure. If the law of torts for cases of pure accident of the sort we are now discussing were repealed, the individual who claimed that someone injured him in an automobile accident would receive sympathy from the courts, but nothing more. This proposal will shock many people, but it is not at all obvious that it would cause anyone any particular disadvantage once the new insurance policies had been obtained. Under these circumstances, I would insure myself against accidental injury. This insurance presumably would take the form of a policy that provided me with various specific amounts of money compensation for various particular types of injury. Policies now commercially available may, in the case of total disability, provide substantial pensions for life.

Note that I am not suggesting that the state set up a board to make payments to those injured in automobile accidents. The reason why one should have a state board for this purpose is unclear to me. Surely our experience with the workmen's compensation boards has not been very encouraging, and extending this type of apparatus to other areas would probably lead to the same results.[3] Furtheremore, there seems no significant reason why people who do not want to be covered by insurance should be required to purchase it (which the state procedure would, in essence, entail) or why people who want a higher coverage should not be permitted to purchase it. If, however, it is thought for some reason (presumably ethical) that it is necessary to make certain that everybody has some minimum amount of coverage, there is no reason why a law could not be enacted requiring people to purchase it.[4] We already have laws requiring the purchase of another type of insurance as a condition for driving an automobile.

2. This must normally rule out self-inflicted injuries, although in some cases these, too, can be covered. The problem of moral risks is discussed later in the chapter.

3. Blum and Kalven, *Public Law Perspectives*, pp. 24–27.

4. Note that our present law does not provide this guarantee of minimum coverage. I must carry insurance giving some minimum protection for people whom I injure. If, however, I am injured in an accident in which no one is to blame or in which I am to some extent at fault, there is no provision for any coverage. The current laws, of course, require me to buy insurance that

If it is thought that very poor people might not be able to afford the insurance premiums, we could presumably arrange to supplement their incomes for this purpose. It is notable that we do not legally excuse very poor people from buying liability insurance under our present system. Returning, however, to our proposal to eliminate present laws of damage to permit people to purchase insurance against injury to themselves, there are several obvious advantages. The statistics indicate that the costs of collection for people injured under present circumstances are extremely high, as much as 25 percent of the amount collected. In addition, for people who are seriously injured, the amount that they obtain under the present mechanism normally covers only a small part of their injuries. Finally, payment is normally very much delayed—occurring not at the time that the person needs the money most, but perhaps two or three years thereafter.[5] In all these areas, a direct insurance policy would gravely reduce the economic costs.

If I have an insurance policy providing for payments to me of certain amounts for certain specified injuries, I would normally be able to obtain the money from the insurance company with little more than a letter. The threat of lawsuit, which is a necessary part of our present procedure, would be unnecessary. Occasionally an insurance company would suspect fraud and, therefore, resist payment, but this would be an exceptional rather than a routine event. In addition, the money would be immediately available as it normally is with insurance. Most insurance companies make a fetish of giving fast treatment to claims by their policyholders because they feel that this improves their sales. Thirdly, I could obtain any amount of coverage I wished, which would make it easier to match economic loss with "damages."

It must be noted that, although insurance coverage of the type I have described is a relatively new phenomenon, the Michigan study shows that payments from such direct "reparation" and from various government programs that simply help people who are injured is now becoming a significant part of total "reparation" for people injured in accidents. There seems no obvious reason why these could not be our sole dependence. The number of lawyers who would lose profitable portions of their practice is large, but this is a clear social gain. Furthermore, it would greatly reduce the present burden on our courts. Lastly, but by no means least, it would eliminate what is essentially a

---

will protect other people. In other words, they are an effort to eliminate an externality. The law that I am now talking about would not have this feature, but it might still be argued for on ethical grounds.

5. Connard, Morgan, Pratt, Voltz, and Bombaugh, *Accidents, Costs, and Payments*.

completely irrelevant issue. Under present circumstances, an accident, if it is a pure accident (that is, if it is nobody's fault at all), should (if we believe in the law) result in no liability for anyone. In practice, this does not often happen, because judges and juries normally find that somebody has caused the accident. Still, the fact that they do make erroneous findings of facts in some cases is not an argument for requiring "fault."

Surely we should have arrangements by means of which an individual who is severely injured in a pure accident may be compensated for his injuries. At the moment, if I am involved in an accident, the court could find that the accident was a pure accident and that neither I nor the man whom I ran into was at fault. In this case, there will be no tort reparation. The court could likewise find that I was not the cause of the accident, but that the man with whom I collided was at fault. This would mean that his insurance company would be compelled to make some kind of settlement to cover my injuries. The Michigan study indicates that if my injuries were severe, this settlement would normally be comparatively modest. He himself would not in any way be compensated, even if he were severely injured. Finally, under the present law, if both of us were at fault, neither of us could be compensated.

Decisions on the factual question of fault are extremely difficult to make for a wide variety of reasons, and there is no obvious reason to believe that juries are good at performing this task. But even if they were, this is an essentially irrelevant question. There is no reason why I (as a person who has not caused an accident) should find my "reparation" dependent on the question of whether the other man with whom I had my collision was or was not at fault. If the person who has not caused an accident should be compensated for his injuries, this compensation should not be dependent upon the essentially accidental fact of whether or not somebody else had done something regarded as culpable.

The dragging of culpability into tort actions seems to be an accidental consequence of the latter's historical connection with criminal law. In a sense, we are punishing a man who has committed a sort of minor crime (being a little careless in driving) by putting liability upon his insurance company. There is, of course, no reason why we should not punish people through private suits rather than governmental action, but in this area there seems no reason why we should. The seriousness of the violation of the driving codes would be a better measure of the size of the fine placed on the violator than the essentially accidental measure of how much injury happened to occur as the result of the violation.

Repealing the present law of torts for automobile accidents would cause a certain amount of transitional problems. It would take some time for people to adjust from the present circumstances in which they carry insurance against the contingency that they injure someone else through their own fault, to insurance against the contingency that they are injured in an automobile accident regardless of fault. Transitional arrangements presumably could be made, however, and I do not think they would be terribly difficult.

In order to continue this discussion, it is necessary to examine the economics of insurance. Under our present assumptions, we have no particular reason why there should be any special provisions in the law differentiating insurance contracts from other contracts. In the real world, the former are severely and often ineptly regulated by a variety of commissions, but we need not discuss this now. Later, when we turn to the law of fraud, we will see that there may be reasons for restricting the contracts an insurance company can issue, but for the moment we can set this issue aside. We can think of insurance contracts as simply being drawn by the insurance companies according to their needs. In practice, this is generally what happens, except that it normally takes some time to get any technological innovation through the regulating commissions.

For simplicity, let us consider fire insurance rather than automobile insurance.[6] On Figure 6.1, the horizontal axis shows the present discounted value of potential fires in the future to a structure that I own. On the vertical axis I have plotted the expenditures that I might make in reducing the probability of fire—installing a sprinkler system, for example. The "risk production function" shows the present discounted value of fire with each possible investment of resources in methods of reducing the likelihood (or damage) of fire.

Assuming that fire insurance is not available, I would choose the combination of risk and expenditures on avoidance of risk in which the production function of risk is tangent to my highest indifference curve.[7] Given the production function for risk that I have drawn on this diagram, this leads me to point A-F. At this point, I would be expending AO resources on things such as sprinkler systems while taking a risk of my building being burned down, which is equivalent to FO. Equation (6.1) shows this situation.

$$AO + FO \cdot R = C \tag{6.1}$$

I have AO in protection costs, and FO is the discounted present value of a fire. If I attach to this second factor "R" as cost of risk, then the situation is

6. A very similar analysis of health insurance is found in Mark V. Pauly, "Efficiency in Public Provision of Medical Care," Ph.D. dissertation, University of Virginia, 1967.

7. Note that the indifference curves are concave to the origin.

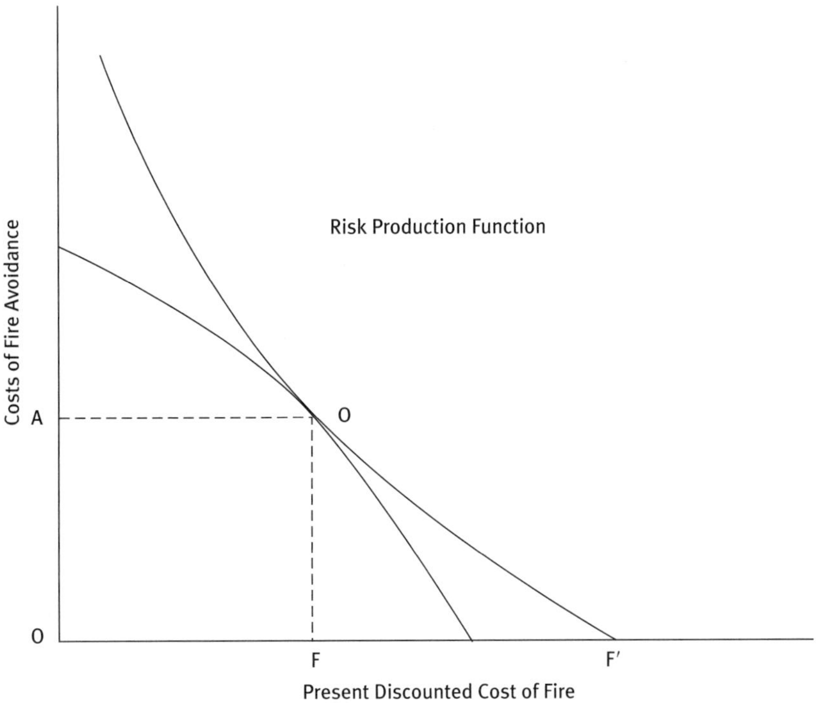

FIGURE 6.1
Fire insurance

as shown. It is generally assumed in discussions of insurance that individuals are risk avoiders and, therefore, that the situation is capable of improvement by transferring this risk to someone else. This transfer is not as easy as you might think. Equation (6.2) shows the insurance company's cost.

$$FO = C_i \tag{6.2}$$

For the insurance company, of course, the number of insurance policies is so large that risk aversion is of little consequence. At first glance, then, the cost to the insurance company appears to be less than the cost to me, and a bargain should be possible.

However, this is an oversimplification. In the first place, if I purchase the insurance, I would be rational to discontinue my risk avoidance activities. I will not bother to keep the sprinkler system in good working order. Most people who have used equations such as Equation (6.2) seem to have implicitly assumed that AO would remain unchanged, but this assumes that the individual does not respond to a change in the circumstances facing him. A more rational assumption would be that the individual stops trying to protect against fire. Samuel Colt refused to purchase fire insurance on his factory. He argued that it was his duty as a Christian master of property to protect it and that his attention to this matter would be reduced if he had insurance. Note that this applies only if the fire insurance is genuinely complete. Most fire insurance policies, for reasons discussed later, do not actually cover all of the cost of the fire.

For the man who has complete insurance coverage, the present discounted value of a fire occurring in the future is zero. Therefore, he would normally be unwilling to invest any of his resources to prevent it. Granted this, the cost to the insurance company of selling the insurance to the owner of the factory is not FO but rather F′O, the present discounted value of the likelihood of a fire in the event that the owner takes no precautions to prevent it. Risk aversion by and of itself is a necessary but not a sufficient condition for insurance. It is by no means obvious that Inequality (6.3) will be true, and that is the necessary condition for insurance.

$$AO + FO \cdot R \geq F'O \tag{6.3}$$

In the very early days of insurance, the insurance companies may have been ignorant of these matters, but they are now very well informed about them. As a consequence, they try to design their insurance contracts in such a way that the person who purchases the insurance still has some incentive for taking precautions against fires. One method of accomplishing this goal as shown on Figure 6.2 is to vary the size of the premium according to the precautions taken.

The insurance company has a number of different rate classes depending upon whether there is a sprinkler system or whether there is a fire station nearby. Note that it is not possible for the insurance company to perfectly fit this premium incentive system to the risk production function. Firstly, the insurance company cannot afford to put unlimited resources into supervising the companies insured; it does not have continuing day-to-day direct contact with the problem. This, insofar as I can tell, is what Samuel Colt had in mind when he argued that insurance increased the risk of fire.

Another and more sophisticated reason why the insurance companies cannot make their premiums perfectly fit the risk production function is that the insurance company requires actuarial computations in order to produce its premium rates. These actuarial computations require rather large samples in each of the rate classes. Thus, of necessity, the premiums will vary in a discontinuous manner in order to bring a large enough number of "risks"

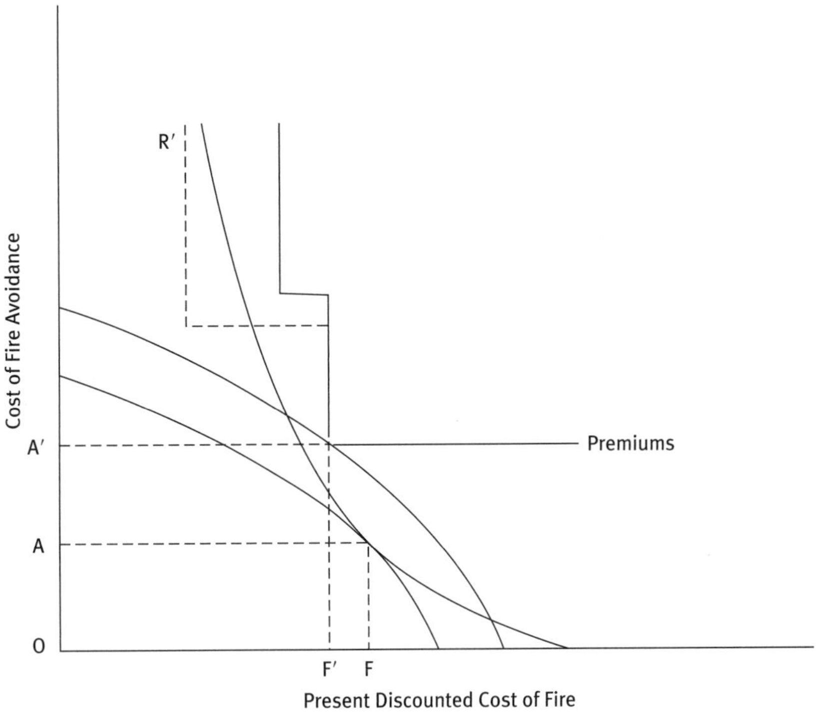

FIGURE 6.2
Fire insurance with varying premiums

into each class. Without this, the actuary would be unable to compute the proper rate.[8]

The potential purchaser of insurance, then, faces the risk production function of his particular plant and a premium schedule such as the one shown. Let us assume that without insurance, he would adjust to point AF with AO + FO · R as his cost. An insurance company appears, however, with the rate schedule shown, and he adjusts to point A′F′. Note that, on the figure, he is actually on a lower indifference curve than he was before because Figure 6.2 does not show his risk aversion. If we had a three-dimensional diagram that also showed risk aversion, he would be on a higher indifference surface. Nevertheless, with respect to just the two variables shown on Figure 6.2, he is in a somewhat worse state of adjustment than he was before. He is

8. In theory, it would be possible for the actuary to produce not a series of specific rates but a continuing premium rate. It is not inconceivable that in the future this particular problem will be solved.

purchasing risk reduction by making an inferior adjustment in these two variables.

It happens in this particular diagram that he is spending more resources on fire prevention than he would have if he had been left without insurance. This is mere coincidence, and no general principle is involved. Note one point, however; the purchaser of insurance will almost always find himself most satisfied if he adjusts the amount of insurance and the physical protection of his plant in such a way that he is at one of the lower left corners of the stair function of the premium structure. This means that the insurance company must keep the entire premium rate system outside the risk production function. If a mistake in calculating is made and part of the premium structure follows the shape shown by the dotted line in the upper part of Figure 6.2, then many of the insured would choose to be at the inner corner of the dotted line. The premiums would not pay for the losses, and the insurance company would be driven into bankruptcy.

In the real world, the step-function of the premiums actually will not be neatly adjusted to hit the risk production function at every level as I have drawn it. It will, in fact, be somewhat to the right. We need not worry much about this. The basic question remains: is the risk reduction from the purchase of insurance greater than the reduction in the efficiency of the adjustment of resources in other ways? Once again, the simple existence of risk aversion does not by and of itself explain insurance. The risk aversion must be large enough to cover losses that insurance causes by leading people to change their behavior.

Another method by which an insurance company can to some extent control the behavior of its clients and, hence, offer them lower premiums is shown in Figure 6.3.

If the insurance does not cover the entire loss, then the insured will still be motivated to engage in fire avoidance activities. In Figure 6.3, line R shows the risk production function, and I assume that the insurance covers half the losses in the event of a fire. Thus, the insured faces line R′ as the risk production function for himself. This leads him to move from point AF to point A′F′ and to continue to use his resources in fire avoidance. Note that the premium is the present value of the loss faced by the insurance company F″O. Although the insured faces a discounted cost of fire of F′O, his reduction in resources spent on fire avoidance moves the "social" risk to F″. He should insure if the following occurs. Once again we cannot say from the simple fact of risk aversion whether he should purchase insurance.

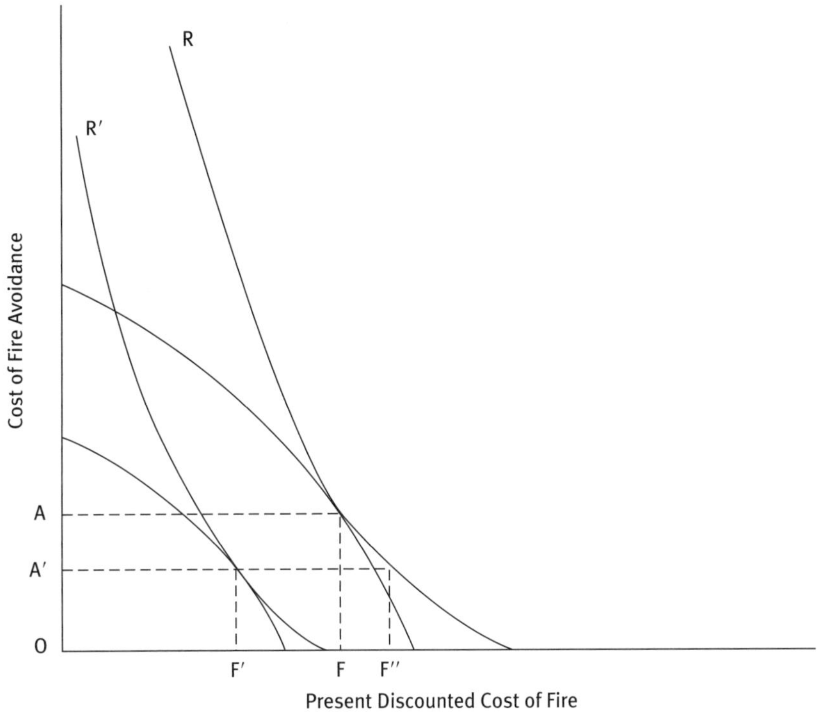

FIGURE 6.3
Fire insurance with a minimum

$$AO + FO \cdot R > A'O + F'O \cdot R' + F'F'' \tag{6.4}$$

One particular technique is to require the insured to pay the initial portion of the loss. This also has the effect of causing the insured to take some precautions against the loss. Naturally, all three of these techniques for controlling the behavior of the insured can be combined, and all three of them will permit lower premiums, although they reduce the advantage of the insurance to some extent.

There is, however, a rather important result of declining returns on risk avoidance—that is a higher payoff in risk avoidance from the first dollar of investment in insurance than from the later dollars. Thus, as more and more of the risk is covered by insurance, each additional reduction in risk has a heavier premium cost. This heavier cost in the first instance falls on the insurance company, but through increased premiums it eventually is transferred to the insured. Thus, one would anticipate an effective declining marginal return on

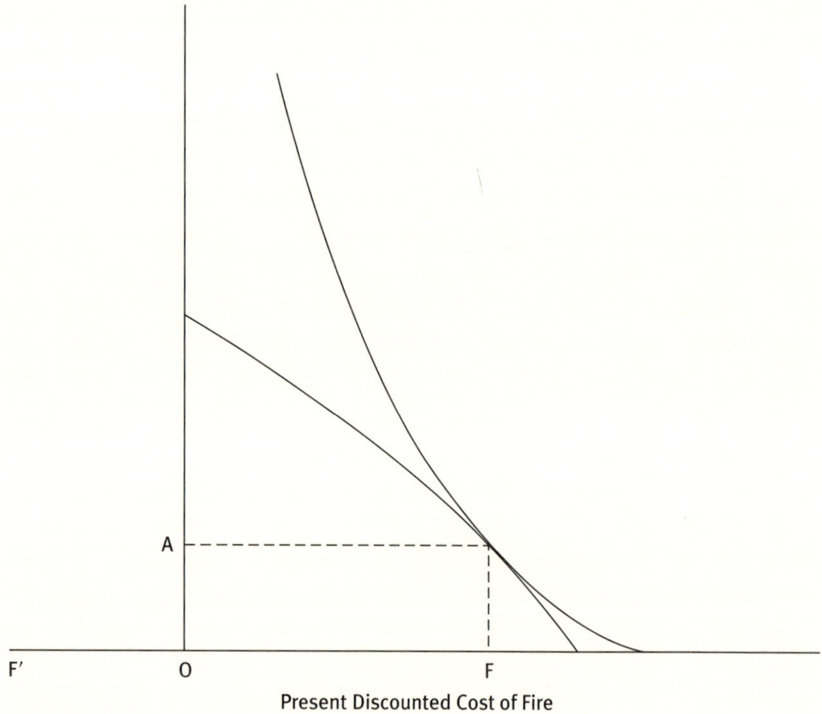

FIGURE 6.4
Incentives for arson

reduction of risk not because individuals are less averse to a small risk than to a large one, although this may well be true, but rather because the reduction of risk to smaller and smaller amounts leads to greater and greater costs in the risk avoidance measures. The result is that most people find it undesirable to purchase enough insurance to eliminate all risk.

A special case in which the existence of insurance changes the behavior of the insured is one in which the insurance payment is more than the actual cost of the fire, as shown in Figure 6.4. The insured facing a given risk production function without insurance settles on point AF. He is, however, given an opportunity by a foolish insurance company to insure his factory for considerably more than it is worth. As a result, the effect of a fire on him is not a cost but a gain, which on our present axes means that its present discounted value would be to the left of the vertical axis at F′. Under these circumstances, far from investing resources to reduce the likelihood of fire, the insured is well advised to invest resources in increasing it. The simplest method of doing this, of course, is to start a fire yourself, and thus insurance companies worry a good deal about this possibility.

The easiest protection against this situation is simply to make certain that the insurance is never large enough so that the insured will actually gain from a fire. Insurance companies, in fact, make great efforts in this direction, but they are not always successful. They also engage in a great deal of talk about what they call the "moral risk." As one could deduce from the use of the word "moral," this discussion is largely an ethical denunciation of people who act in a manner to increase their risk. The insurance companies seldom seem to realize that any adjustment to the existence of insurance, such as we have been discussing, is essentially the same kind of thing. It should, however, still be regarded as a "moral risk," if by "moral risk" we mean that people will behave differently with insurance than without it. Surely people will act differently, and they would be irrational if they did not. The problem facing the insurance company is to so design its policy that such behavior on the part of its customers does not unreasonably increase its premium rate.

The insurance men also place another problem under the rubric "moral risk." Let us suppose that I purchase insurance against my medical expenses in the event that I become ill and that the insurance company (misguidedly) has agreed to pay all of my medical expenses. The probability that I will become ill is actuarily computable.[9] However, the amount of medical attention I have after becoming ill is not in any way limited. I am sure that if I so desired, I could have a $10,000 expenditure out of the treatment for a common cold. One of the best-known treatments for a cold is to spend some time on the Jamaican beaches. My decision as to how much to spend on treatments if I am ill is affected very sharply by how much it will cost me to spend that amount. If any and all treatments are free for me, then I may be expected to spend a good deal more than if I faced a real cost.

As a consequence of this rather obvious fact, all schemes of medical insurance contain some kind of limitation on the freedom of the patient. The particular type of insurance that I carry, "major medical," pays only 80 percent of my expenses and has a deductible first segment. This clearly will put some restraint on my desire to spend money on medical treatment. More commonly,

9. Apparently the probability that I will become ill is very strongly positively connected with the likelihood that I will be injured by becoming ill. Arrangements under which people who are not working because they are ill are paid their full salary normally lead to considerably more illness than would occur without these arrangements.

Blue Cross simply provides flat medical fees for various specified diseases. In places such as England, where large-scale public health is provided, treatment is administratively rationed, and there are long lines of people waiting for treatment."[10] In those parts of the United States where contract medicine is available, we normally find that the suppliers who combine an insurance policy with the actual provision of medical service have rather stringent standards as to exactly what shall be done in specified cases.[11] This is, in fact, a highly efficient way of operating medical insurance.

It should be noted that this problem is as important for government-sponsored insurance schemes as it is for private insurance. Recently it has been suggested that the government reimburse people who are victims of crimes. This would be a deliberate move into a situation of this sort. The present insurance company sells an insurance policy against (let us say) burglary, but obtains a statement of the value of the property at the time it sells the policy. It is free to send out an appraiser to examine this property and calculates the premium based on that value. If the value of the property stolen is to be reported to a governmental agency after it has been stolen, one can fairly predict that very high evaluations will be normal. Requiring persons wishing this type of protection to make statements about the value of their property before the occurrence of the robbery would help, but not a great deal. As long as overestimates of the value of their property cost them nothing, they would be motivated to make them. An insurance system under which the individual is charged a premium based on the value he puts on the property seems to be the optimal arrangement.[12]

There is another reason why insurance companies charge different premiums to different people. A male driver under the age of twenty-five pays markedly more for automobile insurance than one over twenty-five. Clearly this rate structure does not lead to the investment of resources in efforts to change one's age. The insurance company is simply classifying people into rate categories according to the probability of their being involved in an accident without making any effort to affect their behavior. This should be distinguished from the efforts to control the behavior of the insured.

10. See James M. Buchanan, *The Inconsistencies of the National Health Service*, Occasional Paper No. 7 (London: Institute of Economic Affairs, 1965).

11. It is not possible in most places because of the opposition of the American Medical Association.

12. Those who feel that such activity should be governmental rather than private can, of course, argue for a governmental agency that sells people this kind of insurance.

If we regard risk as something that does not exist for society as a whole, then we can demonstrate from our previous discussion that insurance is an undesirable institution. I myself do not believe that one should deal with it in this manner, but the argument is worth developing since it does have some applications in certain areas. Let us then assume that we are simply trying to maximize a measured value of the national income and that we do not regard risk avoidance as part of that measured value because insured risks, looked at from the standpoint of a nation, are minimal. On the basis of these assumptions, insurance is a basically inefficient institution. It always moves people to a location on the risk-production frontier that they would not otherwise choose and, hence, leads to a lower amount of "utility." In this sense we can obtain higher efficiency if we abolish insurance.

The argument, however, is based on the assumption that individual preferences should be maximized when they are obtained from one type of service and not from another. Thus, I myself may obtain utility from reducing the risk I face, and, in fact, most people do. The fact that obtaining this utility reduces the amount of utility I get from other activities is no doubt unfortunate, but we usually have to pay for things in this world. If we sum utility over the entire society, assuming that this operation is somehow possible, we would find that the society with insurance would have a higher total than one without. We should, then, permit insurance in spite of the fact that it causes somewhat poorer adjustment of resources in other areas. Assuming that we are modern welfare economists and do not believe in an interpersonal comparison of utilities, the same conclusion follows.

This digression into the economics of insurance has been necessary as a background to a discussion of the second possible effect of our present accident laws. The first possible reason for a law dealing with accidents is to provide compensation for the person who is injured. If we confine ourselves to this objective, it seems clear that the simplest mechanism is to abolish the law of torts and to depend on each individual to insure himself. The second reason for a law of accidental injury, however, is the existence of externalities.

Suppose that I am a manufacturer of dynamite. I can reduce the cost of operating my dynamite factory by building it on a small area of ground instead of on a very large acreage. Then, in the event of an explosion, my neighbors will bear part of the cost. We need not go through a welfare economics discussion of the externalities involved in this case, since it is perfectly clear to everyone that part of the costs from potential accidents are actually borne by other people. The situation can be shown once again by our Figure 6.3.

The dynamite manufacturer faces the risk-production function shown as R′ because some of the damage an explosion causes will fall on other people. The true risk-production function is R, and we can predict, under these circumstances, that the neighbors of the dynamite manufacturer would be willing to pay him a sizable amount of money to stop him from operating in their neighborhood. In the event that they were unable to organize for such a payment, the value of their property would fall.

Under these circumstances, private bargains may well develop to eliminate the externalities. The standard justification for governmental actions is that the transaction costs are so great that it is not possible to eliminate the externality by private negotiations alone. A law requiring the dynamite manufacturer to pay for the damage to his neighbors in the event of an explosion would lead to an adjustment of resources equivalent to that which would arise from free contract if the transaction costs were zero. The government thus acts to improve the market by supplementing it. It may be the cheapest way of obtaining an economically sensible end.

It would also be possible for the government to place a tax on the manufacturer of dynamite in an inhabited area and not in an uninhabited area. Needless to say, the government normally does not make perfect computations, and the adjustment of the world is seldom optimal. Nevertheless, the costs of governmental activity in such an area frequently would be less than the cost of private activities. We are here comparing two imperfect instrumentalities, and there is no *a priori* reason for feeling that one is better than the other. We need in each case a careful analysis of the factual situation.

Consider an airline; under present circumstances, when an aircraft crashes, the airline suffers the loss of the plane and, in addition, is compelled to make some relatively minor payments to the passengers. The bulk of the protection for the passengers (i.e., the protection of their heirs), however, is the result of the insurance that the passengers themselves carry. Most of the passengers have regular life insurance policies, and a great many of them will have taken out special trip insurance just before the flight.[13] This means, once again, that we are in a situation shown on Figure 6.3. The airline faces a loss in the event of a crash shown by R′, and the total loss is shown by R. The airline would

13. There are, of course, a number of people who do not carry insurance at all. Being a bachelor, with no relatives dependent upon me, I carry no insurance except for a small policy that I receive as a fringe benefit from my university. Other people carry differing amounts of insurance, depending upon their comparison of the likely effects of their death on their relatives and the amount of premium. It should be noted, however, that in a sense life insurance is not a full reparation for the injury inflicted by death—the insured himself is not compensated.

thus be motivated to invest less than the optimum amount of resources in crash avoidance.[14]

Under these circumstances, it should be possible for the airline itself to sell insurance to its passengers, thus moving its own risk production function up to R and producing a somewhat higher investment of resources in crash avoidance. This should be a mutually profitable operation, with the airline being able to sell the insurance at a lower price than the insurance companies, which are not in a position to improve the crash ratio by an investment of resources in safety. Note that if the airline is to bear the full cost of the crash and face the true social risk production function, it should also reimburse the insurance companies for the payments that they make in the event of a crash. This could be done very simply by selling to the insurance companies an actuarily computed policy covering this particular contingency.

It may well be that the airline companies already are investing very large amounts of their resources in crash avoidance because of the bad publicity they receive from such crashes. I think that this would have been true twenty years ago, but I am by no means certain that it is true now. Air travel has become fairly well accepted, and the occasional crashes that do occur are not normally blamed on the particular airline involved.

The argument thus far has assumed that the airline company carries the risk itself and does not purchase insurance from anyone else. For very large airlines this would, of course, be the rational thing to do. They could anticipate a certain number of crashes and would need insurance only against "clusters" of accidents. Naturally not all airlines, and perhaps not any of them, are in this enviable position. Here we return to our discussions of forcing risks upon people in order to improve efficiency. It is arguable, although I think that the argument is not very persuasive, that airlines should be prohibited from purchasing insurance.[15] Note that the owners of the airline stock could reduce their risk to any degree they wished by suitable diversification of their portfolios. Nevertheless, it seems to me that this possible restriction on airlines' insurance would not be good policy.

14. Note that this carries with it an implicit assumption that the airline is solely responsible for avoiding crashes. Probably this is not true. The Federal Aeronautics Administration apparently causes a fair number of crashes. I say apparently because the Federal Aeronautics Administration also investigates crashes and is reluctant to find itself guilty.

15. Airlines should be prohibited from purchasing insurance *except* disaster insurance to cover the contingency that crash claims exceeded their current assets. A deductible insurance policy with the deductible amount equivalent to the full current value of their assets would, under this argument, be optimal.

Why do the airlines not sell insurance? One rather obvious explanation is the elaborate, detailed, tradition-bound, unimaginative, and highly decentralized regulation to which the insurance industry is now subjected. If United Airlines decided to offer this type of insurance to its passengers and to the insurance companies who have policies on its customers, it would immediately find itself in a tremendously complicated legal controversy both with the insurance companies and with the rate-setting commission, to say nothing of the Civil Aeronautics Board. It may be that this regulatory structure, in and of itself, is the reason why this type of insurance scheme has not developed.

Surely the technical problems of the sale of insurance are not insurmountable. The airlines could announce their rates and have the amount of the insurance purchased written on the tickets, the cost being collected when the ticket was sold. (The travel agency at which I buy airline tickets also sells trip insurance.) This would add another item of cost reduction in that it would not be necessary to buy insurance for a full day against all causes of death, but simply a policy for death or injury caused by a crash while you are on the plane.[16]

It is also possible, however, that the basic reason why this type of insurance has not yet been developed is not the noxious effect of inept regulation, but that transaction costs would be high. Any airline company, when it first offered this type of insurance, would find its own behavior only marginally affected and, therefore, probably could not offer markedly lower premiums than do the present insurance companies.[17] If, however, the transaction costs would be high in this case, we might again turn to governmental activity as a method of reducing them. The government could legally provide an "agreement" between the parties that is not greatly different from what they themselves would reach if they were not impeded by high transaction costs.[18]

16. It is by no means obvious that it is rational for people to purchase these short-term coverages for special risk situations. The subject was very well discussed in Robert H. Strotz and Robert Eisner, "Flight Insurance and a Theory of Choice," *Journal of Political Economy* 69 (August 1961): 355–68. It might well be that individuals should not purchase this type of insurance and should depend upon their insurance companies for general coverage. If so, the insurance companies could buy reinsurance from the airlines.

17. The possibility of offering insurance just for the time on the aircraft might, of course, permit much lower premiums and, therefore, make it possible to get this type of insurance started.

18. Note that none of the numerous nationalized airlines in the world offers this type of insurance.

In the particular case of airline trip insurance, the arguments for private agreement being impossible because of high transaction costs are rather weaker than those arguments would be in many other areas. Consider, for example, a restaurant. The efficient way of passing the costs of the possible injury onto the restaurant keeper, which he may inflict upon his customer through accidental poisoning, would be an insurance policy sold with each meal. Clearly, this is a case where the transaction costs would be vastly greater than the actual improvement in efficiency derived from such insurance. Here some type of governmentally imposed institutional arrangement could greatly reduce the transaction costs and, therefore, improve efficiency. There are, of course, more extreme cases. In many situations a person's activity may injure others who have had no previous connection with him at all. A careless construction company, for example, may cause injury to casual passersby. It would be substantially impossible for the construction company and these accidental victims to get together on an insurance contract. Here again governmental action could improve the efficiency of the economy.

The simplest set of institutions that would lead to reasonable efficiency under these circumstances is simply to place liability on the creator of the risk—the airline, the restaurant owner, or the construction company—for the injuries that it creates. By putting the risk on the person who is in a position to invest his resources to reduce it, we will normally improve the efficiency with which the particular risk-avoiding and -producing activities are carried out. Since all of us are both risk producers and victims of risks produced by other people, the net effect of this should be beneficial for each and every one of us.[19] This line of reasoning can be carried further into an area outside the law of torts. It is possible that I will pick up tuberculosis from eating tubercular meat. It would be impossible for me to collect damages, because I could probably not prove where I had caught the disease. Normally, it takes several months for the disease to manifest itself, and, in this case, the damage mechanism we have been describing would not work.[20] Under these circumstances, I would be presumably willing to pay the restaurant keeper to provide meat free from tuberculosis. Here again, however, the transaction costs would be extremely high for individual agreements. Social institutions can

19. This, of course, is only *ex ante. Ex post* the individual might find himself happier if this institutional structure did not exist.

20. Roger W. Weiss, "The Case for Federal Meat Inspection Examined," *Journal of Law and Economics* 7 (October 1964): 107–20.

once again provide for some kind of inspection system, thus reducing the transaction costs.

We do, of course, have such meat inspection in the United States, and other types of inspection are quite widespread in our economy. I do not wish to argue that every single case meets the standards presented in this chapter. Nevertheless, it is at least possible that many of them do. It should be noted that a good deal of this sort of inspection is actually carried on privately rather than by the government. The optimally efficient arrangement in any given case is a matter for empirical investigation, and I have nothing to say about it here.

Let me recapitulate. Accidents raise two problems. The first is to compensate the victim of the accident, and the second is to attempt to adjust compensation for individual injuries so that the costs of these injuries fall on those responsible for them, thus improving the general efficiency of the economy. It will be noted that thus far my argument could be taken as simply justifying the existing institutions. I have argued that, in the case of automobile accidents, we would be best off not to use our present liability system, but to depend upon private insurance, a radical change from the status quo. However, the criticism of our present method of assessing damages in automobile accidents is so widespread that it is practically orthodox.[21] My position on other types of accidental injury is not only generally speaking in accord with the law as it exists, but also generally speaking in accord with fashionable points of view.

The reader, however, may still wonder why I distinguish between automobile injuries, which make up 99 percent of all accidental injuries in the United States, and the other types of injuries, and give them different types of treatment. The basic reason is that, in the case of the automobile, the individual has very strong motives to drive carefully because he does not want to be injured himself. It is true that carelessness on the part of the individual driver creates an externality and endangers other drivers. Our experience, however, would seem to indicate that putting this externality on the driver does not materially affect his driving behavior. This may be simply because our methods of determining responsibility are so inaccurate that the individual is not motivated to avoid liability. It also may be because of the fact that the individual customarily carries insurance, and the insurance companies cannot make perfect adjustments in their rate classes. More likely than any of these reasons, however, is the fact that, for most drivers, the great disadvantage in automobile accidents

21. For a summary, see Blum and Kalven, *Public Law Perspectives*.

is the danger of agonizing pain and/or death to themselves. The prospect of being forced to pay damages to some other person is a relatively small factor. Thus, a driver's behavior is not much affected by whether or not his insurance company must pay for the damages to others.

The other types of accidental injury are mostly injuries in which the danger is relatively one-sided. A, through carelessness, is not likely to injure himself but someone else, namely B. In this case, forcing liability on A should have a significant effect on his behavior, and, hence, in these cases it is rational to do so. Thus, the standard welfare arguments connected with externalities would imply liability in both cases. However, it would appear that the externality in the case of the automobile accident situation is of much less importance. Furthermore, for various reasons, courts face a more difficult problem in the automobile accident case and, hence, probably reach less efficient conclusions.

If, thus far, I have been rationalizing the status quo (including the intellectual status quo of criticism of the present automobile liability provisions), I would now like to offer some suggestions for reforms aimed at reducing legal costs that would, of course, not cover automobile injury cases. It is possible to make considerable cuts in legal costs in this area without having any significant reduction in efficiency. In fact, we would obtain a somewhat better adjustment of our damage and liability institutions to the real world at the same time we made these cuts.

In the ordinary case in which A sues B for damages, alleging that B has injured him in some way, there are two issues: (1) Was B in fact responsible for A's injury? (2) Granting B's responsibility, how much compensation should A receive for that injury? If we are dealing with the type of injury that people may suffer as a result of some type of business activity, we can eliminate the first problem from most lawsuits if we simply make proprietors of business activities fully and strictly liable for any accidental injuries that anyone suffers while on their property. The issue of fact normally becomes a very simple one—where was the man when he was injured? There would be a further rule for such people as the dynamite manufacturer in which one simply proves that the explosion had caused the injury to some person and not inquire as to the reason for the explosion. It will be noted that, in this case, the owner of the property would be given the appropriate motives for adjusting his resource use on the property in such a way as to minimize the total social cost—that is, the sum of the present discounted value of the risk and the resources used to avoid risk. It would also be true, of course, that the owner would find himself paying damages for a number of injuries that he could not have prevented. These additional damages would be actuarily computable, and, therefore, he could insure against them. As a result, there would be a small transfer of income from the owner of the property to accident victims by way of an insurance company.

It will be noted that this suggestion is very close to the present law in many areas, and, in workmen's compensation cases, it is the law. In general, it is only necessary to prove that a given worker was employed by a specified individual and was injured in the course of that employment in order for him to obtain workmen's compensation. It is unfortunately true that the workmen's compensation boards have developed a web of complex and tedious laws that has made collection much less easy than it otherwise could be; but, as we shall see, there is a way around this problem. It is unfortunate that judges and lawyers trained in the Anglo-Saxon tradition tend to elaborate things far beyond the efficient point.

There is, however, one significant element of inefficiency in the proposal I have just made. It may well happen that if Smith goes on Jones' property, Smith should be investing resources to avoid injury to himself. If Jones is totally liable, Smith may underinvest resources in this objective. I may say that I doubt that this factor is of much importance, because Smith presumably is worried about being injured even if he does feel that he will be compensated for it. Still, it should have some effect. My argument here is simply that the reduction in the court costs, which comes from foreclosing the issue of fault, will more than compensate for this small inefficiency in the allocation of resources in risk avoidance.

The second problem that faces the court if a person has been injured is the monetary reparation for the injury. If we are in agreement that A must pay B damages for an injury, the value of that injury is likely to be something about which A and B disagree. A will normally think that only a small payment should be made, and B will claim that a gigantic payment is necessary. One way of dealing with this problem, as is done in many of the law codes of the world, is simply to establish a table of payments for each type of injury as part of the basic law. This, however, ignores the fact that the same injury may be of much greater importance to one person than to another. Our law does neither of these things; although, in the case of workmen's compensation, fixed payments for particular types of injuries are quite common.

Note, however, that the disagreement between A and B as to the value of this "injury" could be completely eliminated if A purchased an insurance policy covering this particular type of injury before the accident occurred. If we are considering, let us say, the loss of a leg, after the leg has been lost, the person who must pay for the loss and the person who receives the payment have radically opposed interests. If, on the other hand, the person who is to pay for it is an insurance company and we are considering the purchase of insurance on the leg some time before the accident occurs, there is no difference of interest between the two parties.

The insurance company, in fact, would like to have its client insure the leg for as much as they can talk him into (subject, of course, to the problem of moral risk). The client, under these circumstances, can himself decide how much insurance he would like to carry, that is, how much value he is willing to put on his leg. Thus, we very seldom see lawsuits between people who have insurance policies providing for a given payment, if an injury occurs to them, and their insurance companies in which the amount of payment is in debate. If we were willing to accept in all injury claims the value of the insurance carried by the injured person as the value of the tort claim against the person upon whom the responsibility of the injury has been placed, we would eliminate this very difficult legal question from most tort cases. The problem that we face at the moment with this suggested legal reform is that most people do not carry insurance that provides specific payments for various injuries. Very likely the situation will change over a period of time, but it might be wise to undertake institutional changes that would accelerate this change.

The present situation puts considerable unnecessary costs on this type of insurance. Let us suppose that I have an insurance policy that pays me $10,000 if I lose a leg, and I lose a leg under circumstances such that Smith would normally have to compensate me. Will that $10,000 be taken into account by a jury computing the damages which Smith will have to pay me? There is no clear and definite answer to this question in the United States today, but it does seem fairly certain that *ex ante* my probable collection in a tort action is lower if I have an insurance policy that has already reimbursed me than if I do not. Thus, when I buy an insurance policy, I make certain that I will receive the $10,000 if my leg is lost even if no one is at fault; but, at the same time, I reduce my probable collections in a tort action if I lose my leg under appropriate tort conditions. Suppose that I have a 1 in 1,000 chance of losing my leg, and if I do, the chances are 1 in 2 that I would be able to collect tort damages of $10,000. If I have a $10,000 insurance policy against this contingency, then I still have a 1 in 2 chance of collecting tort damages, but I will probably receive only $5,000. The value to me of the insurance policy is $7.50, but its cost will be $10.00.[22] Risk aversion may lead me to buy this policy, but clearly I would buy more if the price were $7.50.

This overcharge would not be of any significance if the insurance company were capable of suing in my name to recover the amount of money it had paid me. Most insurance companies put a clause subrogating it for me in any damage action involving their policies. It would appear, however, that the insurance companies anticipate unsympathetic treatment from the courts and, therefore, do not normally attempt to recover from the person who caused the accident the damages they have paid out to the victim. If they did regularly succeed in recovering damages in these cases, they could charge markedly lower premiums and, hence, this type of insurance would become more widespread. The first institutional change that would seem desirable would be to make it fairly simple for insurance companies to collect in these cases. Thus, it should be possible for insurance companies to sue the person who causes injury or death to one of their clients and to collect damages that are equivalent to the payment they themselves have made. The further step of providing that recovery would be measured by the amount of insurance would (if given sufficient publicity) probably lead to substantially universal coverage.[23] It should be noted that, in a way, the proposals I have been making would lead to a slight overestimation of the value of injuries. If the individual would always collect from other people if he is injured on their property, then he would be charged somewhat less than the right amount for his own insurance. Thus, presumably he would, to some extent, underevaluate the injuries to him. It does not seem to me, however, that this would be a major disadvantage.

With these institutional changes, we would have the following situation. Firstly, most people would carry insurance against injuries regardless of the cause. In the event of an accident, they would collect damages from their own insurance company. Since insurance companies that wish to remain in business have strong motives to make certain that claim adjustment is relatively quick and involves relatively little red tape, this would normally be a speedy and fairly simple process. Occasionally litigation would occur between an

22. In this, as in my other computations, I exclude sales and administrative costs.

23. For those people who feel that certain parts of the population cannot be trusted to manage their own affairs, a compulsory rule requiring them to carry a certain amount of insurance would seem sensible. This, however, is an ethical problem, and we cannot discuss it on our present set of assumptions.

insurance company and one of its clients, but litigation would be much rarer than current tort litigation to obtain reparation for injuries.

Secondly, if an individual were injured in an accident not involving an automobile, the insurance company that had paid him damages for his injuries would normally seek reparation from the person who, under our rather simple law code, would be liable for that injury. Normally no lawsuit would be necessary, because of the simplicity of the liability system we have proposed. Once again, an occasional suit would occur. In many cases, the transaction would involve only the two insurance companies. The system would do a reasonably good job of adjusting the amount of resources invested in accident avoidance. It would not, it is true, provide for a perfect arrangement of resources, but it seems likely that the saving in court proceedings would more than compensate for the imperfection in the allocation of resources.

We must now, however, turn to a problem that was discussed at the beginning of this chapter, only to be set aside; what is an accident? In ordinary speech, we assume that we know the difference between an accidental injury and a deliberate injury; but, as we have seen, individual choice of behavior is involved in accidents. Suppose I am the owner of an industrial installation. The type of investment that I undertake in avoiding accidents will have a considerable effect on the number of accidents that occur. To say that it is an accident if my investments are over a certain amount and not an accident if they are under a certain amount is drawing an essentially arbitrary line. There seems no reason, then, why we should choose any particular degree of precaution or nonprecaution as the boundary.

We can, however, distinguish a special set of cases in which individuals quite definitely decide to cause injuries. If I deliberately decide to beat someone up, this would be an example. It should be noted, however, that in some cases in which our courts now assume that people deliberately cause injury, they actually do not. These are generally cases in which the individual has gone into a business (such as bank robbery) in which there is a very high potential for causing injury. Clearly, the individuals holding up a bank who, in the process, kill someone are in really somewhat the same situation as a man who is building a bridge and, in the process, kills someone. We have tended over the years to consider these two things differently. In particular, since we want to prevent people from holding up banks, and want to help people to build bridges, we have tended to make the responsibility for injuries different. But in both cases, increased investment in risk avoidance could reduce the likelihood of people being killed.

However, if it is a little difficult to draw this distinction, there is no reason why we need it in discussing the question of reparation for injury. There is no reason why an individual who is injured by someone else should have his right to reparation in any way affected by the intent of the person who committed the injury. Thus, my wish to beat someone up is a clear case of an externality, and compelling me to pay in full the cost of that beating is a good way of getting optimal allocation of resources in society.[24] In our present law, some types of crimes do not normally lead to civil suits. Clearly this is a mistake. If a man is murdered, his family and his insurance company should have causes of action against the murderer. The fact that we are not going to rest content with giving them this cause of action has nothing to do with the question of whether they should or should not have it. Clearly they have been injured by the act, clearly this injury is an externality, and clearly we should impose the cost of that externality on the person whose activities caused the injury. This will improve the allocation of resources in society, although in this particular case we seldom think of the problem as being one of improved allocation.

This chapter concludes with a brief discussion of two points. The first of these is what type of court would we choose to deal with cases in this field. We should first begin by noting that in most cases it will not be possible for the parties to enter into an agreement in advance. This is because in most accidents the parties are strangers before the accident. After the accident has occurred, it is unlikely that we could obtain agreement among the parties as to the choice of court. Presumably one of them would like to have the decision indefinitely deferred and, if forced to go to court, would like to have the court as inefficient as possible. His opponent, on the other hand, would want quick justice and a high degree of efficiency. Requiring an agreement on the court would give great advantages to the party at fault.

This, then, is a clear case for social contrivance, and we have such a contrivance in our society known as the regular court system. If the government provides a set of courts that is available for dealing with the case and that all parties are compelled to accept unless they reach agreement on another court, then this problem will not arise. It is true that we will not obtain quite

24. As we shall see later, such private suits are not (in and of themselves) completely suitable in the area of crime. They must be supplemented by further action not undertaken by the victim of the crime. This does not mean, of course, that such private suits should be prohibited, but simply that we should not rely entirely upon them.

as accurate an adjustment of the court to the needs of the parties as if we could somehow permit them to reach agreement, but it is better than the available alternatives. In general, the individual should anticipate that the establishment of such a court would improve the future discounted value of his income stream. It should be noted that the considerations for the choice of an optimal court developed in the last chapter would, in general, also apply here. In particular, there is no reason why the parties should not reach agreement to move their case from the court provided by the government to some other court.

In general, we would anticipate that this would rarely happen, but the possibility of its happening should be left open. There is one particular case in which it might very well happen; that is, a controversy between two insurance companies over who is responsible for a particular injury. In this case, ironically, the insurance companies might consider the court provided by the government to be too good for their needs. An insurance company annually facing 10,000 cases of litigation of this sort would be interested in the general pattern of the outcome, not in the decision in any given case. Therefore, some cheap judicial process with a high random error would be quite attractive to the insurance company, provided that it could be sure the error was not biased. One would anticipate that the insurance companies would enter into arrangements among themselves under which this type of case was dealt with in some inexpensive and relatively inaccurate way. There is no reason why we should have any objection to this process that would surely reduce the costs of insurance.

The final question with which this chapter must deal is what the considerations we have been discussing have to do with our basic assumptions about human behavior. In general, if this system is established, it will increase the efficiency with which resources are allocated in society with respect to risk avoidance—in other words, it will internalize certain externalities and it will lead to individuals' having their personal risks reduced. The present discounted value of the future income stream of individuals increases in utility terms, and thus the line of reasoning can be justified on the assumptions of Chapter 2.

CHAPTER 7

STATUS

This chapter, our final discussion of the civil law, deals with a set of miscellaneous matters, all of them having to do with personal status. Sir Henry Maine, writing during the nineteenth century, argued that the law had seen a gradual movement from a status system to a system of contract. He obviously regarded this movement as progress. He saw the situation in his day as the beginning of a retrogression. When I studied law in the 1930's, the retrogression had clearly accelerated. Furthermore, my teachers (or at least some of them) seemed to regard this as a desirable change. Since that date, movements toward a basically status system of law have continued, although it must be said that status is still a minor part of our law. Special groups do have, however, all sorts of special privileges (and, in some cases, special responsibilities) as a result of their status in society. As a college professor, perhaps I should begin by discussing the specialized status of college professors. First is something called educational freedom, which as far as I can see, simply means that a college professor should not be fired unless he has committed a common crime.

Since I have dealt with this problem in *The Organization of Inquiry*, I will not discuss it in detail now.[1] The point to be noted, however, is that this special set of privileges for people who hold one particular status is representative of a vastly larger group of similar privileges. In fact, the special privileges granted college professors by virtue of their status are relatively modest compared with those granted to people such as barbers, beauticians, undertakers, and doctors. We professors have substantially no monopoly on status, and it is not likely that the income of college professors is markedly higher than it would be if "educational freedom" did not exist. It may even be less. The income of the other groups I have mentioned is, however, higher because of their legally established special status.

One of the significant developments of recent years has been the widespread development of specialized guild legislation. Under this legislation, some special activity (beauty culture, haircutting, or medicine) is declared to require special governmental control. All persons engaged in it at the time the

1. Gordon Tullock, *The Organization of Inquiry* (Durham, N.C.: Duke University Press, 1966), pp. 210–19.

new law is enacted are then declared eligible to continue with the activity, but new entrants are to be carefully selected in order to protect the public. The criteria for selection are turned over to a board, which is, needless to say, composed of present members of the profession. This board then uses its monopoly power to raise the economic returns in this particular field.[2]

Looking at this development from the standpoint of this book, it is clear that any individual who is a member of a group having a good political possibility of getting the state to give that group a legally protected monopoly should favor the obtaining of the monopoly. This will clearly improve his personal ability to make choices in the future by increasing the income he can spend. By the same token, however, he should be opposed to all attempts by people in other walks of life to obtain the same type of protected monopoly. It might be wise for him to enter into some kind of bargain under which his particular activity and a small number of other activities are protected. But, in general, granted the large number of guilds that have been set up by special legislation, it is probable that most people are, on balance, actually injured by the sum total of all legally granted monopolies even though they may gain from one such monopoly.

Here we have a case in which each individual group can gain from obtaining governmental aid, but where if all obtain such aid, all would be worse off. It is similar in this respect to a tariff. Like the tariff, the gains cannot be generalized. It is not possible for everyone to gain if everyone sets up a local monopoly. The individual should attempt to protect his own monopoly, or establish one if he does not have it, and to destroy the others. If there are a very large number of such monopolies, it is probable that the individual (if given the choice between having all of them or having none) would be well advised to choose to have no monopoly. This, however, is only a probability, and in each case it will be necessary to make detailed calculations. Personally, perhaps as a bias, I am strongly opposed to this development of status and guild in our modern society. I agree with Sir Henry Maine that the movement from status to contract was a movement toward progress. The present movement in the opposite direction is reactionary.

As a general rule we can say that most people are better off if, in most matters, they choose what they want themselves. It is very dubious that my knowledge of what will please you is better than yours (although it may well

2. See Milton Friedman, *Capitalism and Freedom* (Chicago: University of Chicago Press, 1962), pp. 137–60.

be that in some cases this could be so). It has never actually been proven that some individuals are not well equipped to choose for other people. It may well be that you would be better off if I ran your life through a set of detailed regulations. Personally, I doubt this, but I must admit that I cannot disprove the proposition. Those scholars who feel that individual preferences are not the ultimate data, and that they themselves can tell other people how to be better off, have never been disproved. Perhaps the strongest argument against this type of attitude is simply to ask the person who is posing the view that individual preference orderings are not the ultimate data whether he is willing to let you run his life.[3]

Although we normally permit people to make their own choices, all societies have a certain number of individuals among them who are not given this privilege. The most obvious examples, of course, are children. The insane and certain other cases (for example, people who are temporarily incapacitated for some reason or other) are also in this category. Obviously what we require is a way of distinguishing between people who are capable of looking after their own affairs and those who are not. The problem is particularly difficult because it is highly likely that we do not have two separate categories of the population, one composed of competents and the other composed of incompetents; rather we have a spectrum. Furthermore, probably the "incompetents" are perfectly capable of carrying on much of their daily life without supervision.

When we find people whom we decide are incompetent, our usual procedure is to try to get some person to manage their affairs. Normally, however, we do not completely trust these other persons, and some procedure is established to ensure that they do not abuse their position. Again, the most obvious cases are children. In our society the child is under the control of his parents. In general, this works very well, but we do not leave the parents' discretion completely uncontrolled. There are various laws restricting what parents can do, and provisions are available for removing children from the control of the parents when warranted. Our methods of dealing with insane adults are similar, but, in this case, we are more likely to give the guardian closer supervision.

Thus far, I have been describing in general terms what we now do, and have said very little about what we should do. Strictly speaking, it is impossible to apply the line of reasoning used in this book to our dealings with children,

3. I regret to say that in at least one case in which I tried this the man replied, "Yes."

because the decision makers are not now children and are not likely to be children in the future. If you are reading this book, you are presumably already in full control of your own affairs and will never again be a child. Any provisions for dealing with children will not directly affect you. You would be interested only insofar as a particular child, or perhaps children in general, have attracted your emotional concern. With respect to the insane, we all have some finite probability of becoming insane and, therefore, presumably should to some extent be interested in the treatment of the insane, but I find that very few people are very much concerned with this probability.

It would appear that basically we can do little about this subject, using the reasoning upon which this book is founded. It may be, however, that intermediate stages between our present competents and incompetents could be developed. Thomas S. Szasz has argued that a great many of the insane require no confinement or special treatment.[4] He may very well be right. It seems probable that a good many of the insane would require some kind of special guardianship with respect to certain things, but could be left free to handle other aspects of their lives by themselves.

Here, unfortunately, we are dependent upon what amounts to a purely technical, medical decision in areas in which medical knowledge at the moment is very slight. It should, perhaps, be noted that as one of the results of Russian economic planning, the facilities for the care of lunatics were gravely neglected. In view of the resulting shortage of facilities, the Russians introduced a special degree of lunacy for people who were insane but not dangerous. Such people were not incarcerated. Valarie Tarshish, the anti-Communist author, in fact was actually given an exit permit, although he was officially classified in this category. The United States is wealthy enough to maintain large and luxurious insane asylums (even if we do not do so), but it still might be wise for us to take a lead from the Russian experience in this matter. Perhaps an intermediate category, or even several intermediate categories, would not be impractical or particularly difficult. The "halfway house" is a step in this direction.

In practice, our methods of raising children amount to giving the child more and more responsibility as he grows older. Our criminal law, in practice, acts this way, although in theory it does not. In theory there are certain

4. He has made this argument so many times that citation may seem superfluous. For a particularly concise statement of his views, see his "Address at the International and Comparative Conference on Mental Illness and the State," Northwestern University School of Law.

young people who cannot commit a crime because the law considers them too young, certain young people who, if they commit a crime, are juvenile delinquents, and other young people who are considered adults when they commit a crime. In practice, however, the courts take into account the age of the younger person involved in the commission of a crime in a gradual way, with heavier sentences usually being imposed on the older juvenile offenders. This would appear to be a sensible proceeding. The basic problem, however (when does a person become a responsible adult?), is one on which we can offer no enlightenment. It may well be that it would be sensible to give some kind of examination and consider all people who did not pass it, regardless of their calendar age, as juveniles.

Another problem that raises very severe difficulties is marriage. Indeed, all problems of "family law" are difficult, and our analysis does not permit us to say much here. It may be possible to consider marriage as simply a contract and permit people to make what agreements they wish, but it must be admitted that few, if any, experiments in this direction have been made. It may be that this absence of experimentation reflects simple conservatism, but it may also be that there are good reasons why marital relations should be regulated.

So far in this chapter we have dealt mainly with areas in which there is very little we can say. We can conclude by dealing with several problems where definite conclusions can be reached. The first of these is "corporation law." If a number of people wish to jointly undertake an enterprise, their decision in this regard raises two issues. The first of these issues is simply whether they shall be permitted to engage in legal actions of various sorts (signing contracts, being sued, suing other persons) as a group or shall be compelled always to take this action in the name of all of them individually. As far as I know, no one objects to permitting any group of people to act as a group.

Lawyers say that the corporation is a legal person. The question of whether a corporation should be considered as a person or not has even been the subject of considerable metaphysical debate. If we look at it simply as a question of whether the group of people who own United States Steel may appoint someone to undertake legal action or sign contracts, in their name, or whether they must always sign their own names individually to all agreements, I presume no one would really raise any questions as to which would be more convenient. Saying that the corporation is a legal person is a rather unwieldly way of expressing this. Whether United States Steel has constitutional protection as a person is of really very little significance. Clearly its stockholders are persons and they have a right to constitutional protection. The only result of denying similar constitutional protection to United States Steel would be to make it necessary for the stockholders to undertake individual legal actions.

The second problem raised by corporation law is the limitation of liability. Here, again, there is no real issue. There is no reason why I, entering into a contract with someone else, cannot put into the contract a provision limiting my liability in the event that I default. Such contractual clauses are not common, but they are clearly legal. For example, if I borrow the money to build a house on a mortgage, normally the mortgage will provide that if I am in default, not only can the bank or insurance company seize the house, but they can also sue me for the difference between its value and the face value of the mortgage. There is nothing, however, to prevent us from agreeing that in the event that I default on the mortgage, the bank's ability to collect is limited to the building itself.

In practice in present-day situations most limited liability contracts are entered into through a corporation rather than individually. This, however, simply reflects present practice and does not raise any fundamental issues. If a group of people desire to get together to engage in the manufacture of steel, there is no reason why they should not put into their contracts with each of their suppliers a statement saying that collection on these contracts will be limited to the assets now involved in the manufacture of steel. Instead of this, they form a corporation.[5]

Clearly, this is merely a matter of convenience. I regret to say that the simplicity of the actual subject matter of this paragraph has escaped most legal scholars, and there is a great deal of discussion of the importance of the corporation as a way of limiting liability. As a matter of history, the limitation of liability did come in very largely with the corporation; but, if we are concerned not with how our present institution developed but whether they are desirable institutions, the concept of limited liability is only coincidentally related to the corporation. One can readily imagine corporations without limited liability, and one can equally readily imagine limited liability without corporations. Furthermore, under our present law it is perfectly possible to enter into contracts in which liability is limited; it is also perfectly possible to organize corporations with unlimited liability.[6]

5. My discussion of the corporation has benefited greatly from the work of Henry Manne.

6. We might have to use some other word in the title.

Our final area is the "status" of a dead man. Our present law provides that when a man dies (if he has any significant amount of property) a person known as executor is appointed to act as the "personal representative of the deceased"; in fact the man who is dead in a legal sense continues to exist until the estate is settled. This procedure, which is the mainstay of many legal practices and an entire set of courts, has normally been regarded as onerous by the common man.[7] A large number of techniques have been developed that make it possible to avoid probate. The most important of these are trusts and joint checking accounts.

In this case it would seem that the common man is right, and the law is a "fool and an ass." The historical reasons for the development of our present law of inheritance are reasonably clear, but it is by no means obvious that we should retain it. Essentially there are two different theories of "testimentary disposition." Under the first theory, I may make a particular form of gift of any property I own to other people. This gift is conditional upon my death—i.e., I retain complete use of my property until I die. If this theory is adopted (and it is the one I favor), we obtain for the individual owner of property the maximum control over that property.

The second theory of testimentary disposition is based not on the desire to give the present owner of property full control over the property (including the right to make a gift of it at the time of his death), but on a feeling that society has an interest in the disposition of the property.[8] Occasionally egalitarian ideas get involved in the law of testamentary disposition, but clearly this is a mistake. Requiring a wealthy father to divide his money equally among his children, for example, does indeed increase the equality with which the different children are treated, but its effect on the total wealth distribution in society is substantially nil. Equitable ideas as to the "duties" that individuals owe to different relatives may also be involved in some laws in this area. Such equitable ideas cannot be deduced from our basic assumptions and, hence, are foreign to this book.

7. At the time of this writing, one of the best sellers is *How to Avoid Probate*, by Norman F. Dacey.

8. There are perhaps arguments for seeing to it that certain people, e.g., widows, who might otherwise become objects of public charity, are taken care of in the disposition of an estate. This, however, simply may be a recognition of a wife's contribution in accumulating this estate. In many parts of the United States the wife already owns half of her husband's property even while he is alive.

In practice, in most of the United States the statement that the person who owns property may leave it to substantially anyone he wishes is fairly well descriptive of our law.[9] The only serious limitations are taxes on the estate. There are no reasons why taxes on this particular subject raise any special issues. In fact, as we shall see, one tax on inheritance is better than any other tax.

Granted that people are in general permitted to leave their money any way they wish, the law concerning inheritance falls into two categories. One, a tremendously complex and, to a large extent, unnecessary probate procedure; two, provisions for disposition if the deceased has left no will. Turning first to the latter situation, Jeremy Bentham suggested that a person who had left no will had indicated that he had no very strong preferences about what happened to his money, and, therefore, the state should use it for governmental expenditures. This is, as any economist can see immediately, an ideal tax. There is no perceptible excess burden, since the only thing that anyone needs to do in order to avoid it is to prepare a will.

Presumably, if this institution were adopted very few people would die intestate. In those cases where people died intestate, the existence of this particular form of taxation would not affect their behavior before their death, since they could avoid the taxation if they wished, and, hence, the only people who would "suffer" would be the occasional individuals who failed to obtain a gift. Although it seems to me this idea of Bentham's is simple, elegant, and obviously sensible, it shocks most people. They talk about people whose wills are lost, who had inadvertently destroyed their wills, and so on. It is clear that a person who wishes to avoid this tax on his estate would not only have to draw up a will, but would have to see to it that it was kept safe. There does not, however, seem to be any great difficulty in this. I think the real motive behind the objection is simple conservatism. What Bentham proposed, and what I am now endorsing, is indeed a radical change; and most people do not like radical changes.

There is, however, an argument of sorts for having a general law of intestacy. It might be argued that a great many people would rather not bother with drawing up a will, and a standard provision in the law would permit some people to avoid this task. Thus, for example, if the law provides that if a man dies intestate half of his estate goes in life tenancy to his wife and the remainder of his estate is immediately (and the half in his wife's possession on her death) divided equally among the children, it might save trouble in that

9. With some exceptions for a widow.

most people (who on the whole were planning on leaving their estate in that form anyway) would not have to bother with drawing up a will. There is something in this argument, but not a great deal. It is unlikely that very many of the people who refrain from drawing up wills have even bothered to find out what the provisions for intestacy are, and, hence, there is no strong reason to believe that these legal provisions would in fact carry out their desires.

In any event, it seems likely that the actual provisions for the disposition of an estate in the event of intestacy did not originate from the kind of reasoning I have outlined in the last paragraph. Originally the state felt that it had a very strong interest in the disposition of estates. This interest was expressed by requiring them to be left in certain ways. As time went by and more liberal ideas developed, individuals were permitted to avoid the rules if they wished. The rules remain, however, as a sort of residuum for those cases in which the individual has not made any specific disposition. They are, thus, interesting relics from the past rather than rationally conceived results of social engineering.

The basic problems in the field of testamentary disposition, however, are not the rules for intestacy but the probate procedure that so complicates and delays present-day transfer of property upon death. As I have mentioned, there is a recent best seller advising people how to avoid these provisions. While I was writing this section, *Reader's Digest* featured an article on joint tenancy as a method of avoiding probate.[10] The same end can be attained more certainly with the aid of expensive attorneys. The wealthy are interested in minimizing their inheritance tax as well as simplifying the procedure of transmission, and, hence, the devices that they use are frequently extremely complex and of very little general value. For the purposes of the rest of this chapter, we will ignore these legal devices, as well as changes in the inheritance tax.[11] Probate procedure, like the laws of intestacy, is actually a heritage from earlier times. Unlike the laws providing for intestacy, it is not of minor importance; the total costs are very great. Further, there seems absolutely no reason for these costs.

Let us consider a radically different system; assume that when a man dies, if a document called a will is found, it is regarded as simply a deed of gift. Currently, gifts by living people normally raise no particular problem. We do not have any special set of courts for them. It is, of course, true that on occasions ordinary deeds of gift will lead to lawsuits, but they are tried in the

10. October, 1967, p. 163.

11. There is no great difficulty in collecting inheritance taxes without probate procedure, and, in fact, inheritance taxes are frequently collected on property that did not go through probate.

ordinary courts; there does not seem to be any reason why special courts should exist for them. In fact, lawsuits concerning inheritance are relatively uncommon, and there seems to be no reason why a special court system should be set up to deal only with all inheritance matters so that the small minority of the inheritances that do lead to lawsuits may be determined by that court.

Given our present customs, the institution I have just described would raise a serious difficulty having to do with the debts of the deceased person. If the person died owing money to some people but having property that was left by deed of gift to other people, at first glance it would appear that the debtors would lose. If we observe the real world, we note that this is (generally speaking) not true with respect to gifts; gifts to prevent the repayment of debt are normally held invalid. However, there is no reason why we would need to worry about the problem. If the law were changed in the manner that I have been suggesting, then one can assume that people lending money or entering business deals with others would simply put special provisions into their contracts. Most loans, after all, are made on security; in these cases very few problems arise. For unsecured loans, a provision in the contract providing that if the person who borrowed the money dies, the loan immediately becomes a lien on his property, would be very simple and would involve no special problems.

The new procedure might cause some difficulty when it was first inaugurated. In fact, it would probably be desirable to provide a delay between the period in which the new procedure was enacted and its coming into effect, so that people could make appropriate changes in their contracts. Nevertheless, the change would appear to eliminate much waste. The lawyers would be injured by the change and, of course, the personnel of specialized probate courts; but everyone else would gain, and the gain would be large enough to compensate the losers. No doubt, the lawyers will be able to invent technical objections to it and will have the strongest possible motives to do so; but there seems to be no reason why we should pay attention to this type of sophism. From the standpoint of those who are thinking of leaving money to others and (although there is no need to pay much attention to this group) those who expect to eventually receive bequests, a reduction in the costs of transmission of property at death would be advantageous. Even if we consider economic efficiency in the old-fashioned Adam Smith sense, there is improvement. The long period in which wealth is tied up through probate would be abolished, and this would improve the efficiency with which property is used.

In this particular case, the suggestion that I have made superficially appears quite radical (although it is hard to find anything very serious in the way of an argument against it). In practice, however, the suggestion is not all that extreme. The common man is more and more turning to nonprobate methods of transmitting property to his heirs. The methods now available for this purpose (specialized trusts, joint accounts, joint tenancies of all sorts) have significant disadvantages attached to them. Permitting a similarly probate-free disposition of property by will would simplify matters, and it is very hard to see who would be hurt by the change other than the members of the probate bar.

PART 3

CRIMINAL LAW

CHAPTER 8

MOTOR VEHICLE OFFENSES AND TAX EVASION[1]

We now begin our discussion of the criminal law, a branch of the law that many people feel is clearly the most important. We begin with a discussion of motor vehicle offenses and later turn to a discussion of tax evasion. This may seem to be an eccentric way of beginning a consideration of the criminal law, but it seems a good idea to introduce the subject with a discussion of those branches with which the reader is personally familiar. Everyone who reads this book probably has committed a motor vehicle offense, and some may have even been arrested at one time or another for violating the motor vehicle code.

The average man feels not the slightest discomfort if he observes a policeman while walking down the street. If, on the other hand, we are driving, all of us feel a start of apprehension when we see a police car. Few professional criminals have had as much experience with their particular type of crime as the average man has had with motor vehicle violations. The average man also has a great deal of experience with the results of motor vehicle violations. All of us have seen such violations by other people; all of us have had our lives endangered at some time or other by these violations, and almost all of us have seen the really appalling injuries that a serious automobile accident can cause. Thus we are not only experienced in violating this law, we have a clear idea in our own minds of the consequences of such violation.

After completing our discussion of motor vehicle violations, we turn to tax evasion, where the average man's knowledge and experience are, on the whole, less than that of violations of the traffic code. Still most of us have at least contemplated padding our expenses on the income tax return, and we find very little difficulty in understanding why other people do it regularly. In addition, we are all fairly well aware of the consequences of large-scale tax evasion. We all know that the basic taxation rates would have to be higher or our total expenditures would have to be lower if tax evasion were permitted.

1. This chapter, in a slightly modified form, was printed in the *Social Science Quarterly* 50 (June 1969): 59–71, under the title "An Economic Approach to Crime." The orthodox point of view was presented in a comment on my article by Walter Firey, "Limits to Economy in Crime and Punishment," *Social Science Quarterly* 50 (June 1969): 72–78.

Another advantage in beginning our discussion of the criminal law with motor vehicle offenses and tax evasion is the fact that the customary element in such laws is extremely small. Most of our laws on crime evolved from antiquity and hence contain all sorts of quaint nooks and crannies. The motor vehicle law is almost entirely a creation of the twentieth century and is periodically revised extensively. The income tax code similarly is largely a recent development and is continuously being changed both by legislative enactment and by various administrative bodies. Thus we do not have to deal with the weight of immemorial tradition when we turn to these problems.

The most common and simplest of all violations of the law is illegal parking. This is a new problem. In the days of yore, there were not enough idle vehicles to raise any great difficulty. When, however, common men began to buy automobiles, the number of vehicles was such that simply permitting people to park where they wished along the side of the street led to very serious congestion. The number of spaces was limited, and rationing on a first come, first served basis seems to have been felt to be unsatisfactory.[2] Exactly why it was thought to be unsatisfactory is not at all clear. In any event, the proper governmental bodies decided that there should be a "fairer" distribution of parking space, and it was decided that individuals should vacate spaces at some specified time, frequently one hour, after they occupied them. Again, there is some difficulty in understanding why this remedy was chosen. The governments could have provided adequate free parking space, as the operators of shopping centers do, opened parking lots on a fee basis, or simply let the problem solve itself by private provision of fee parking space.

Nevertheless, the "remedy" chosen was to have people occupy parking spaces only for limited periods of time. The question then arose as to how to ensure compliance. The method chosen was to attach a penalty for noncompliance. The police were instructed to "ticket" cars that parked beyond the time limit, and the owners of the ticketed cars were then fined a small sum, say $10, by a court. Thus, the individual could choose between removing his car within the prescribed period or leaving it and running some chance of being forced to pay $10. Obviously, the size of the fine and the likelihood that any given car owner would be caught would largely determine how much overparking was done. The individual would, in effect, be confronted with a "price

2. We are now discussing the early development of parking regulations. The relatively recent invention of the parking meter has changed the situation drastically and will be discussed later.

list" for overparking and would normally do so only if the inconvenience of moving his car were greater than the properly discounted cost of the fine.[3]

Not all overparking is the result of a deliberate decision; a good deal of it comes from absentmindedness, and part is the result of factors not very thoroughly under the control of the car owner. Nevertheless, we do not generally feel that the fine should be remitted. The absence of a criminal intent, or indeed, of any intent at all, is not regarded as an excuse. When I was working in the Department of State in Washington, I served under a man who incurred several parking tickets a week. All of these violations occurred without any conscious intent on his part. He would get involved in some project and forget that he was supposed to move his car. The city of Washington was levying what amounted to a tax on him for being absentminded. The Washington police force was not particularly annoyed with my superior; apparently, they thought that the revenue derived paid for the inconvenience of issuing tickets and occasionally towing his car away. Suppose, however, they had wanted to make him stop violating the parking laws. It seems highly probable that an increase in the fines would have been sufficient. Absentmindedness about $10 does not necessarily imply absentmindedness about $100 or even $1,000. With higher fines, he would have felt more pressure to remember to avoid parking on the public streets as much as possible and to arrange with his secretary to remind him. Thus the fact that he was not engaging in any calculations at all when he committed these "crimes" does not indicate that he would not respond to higher penalties by ceasing to commit them.

Thus far, we have simply assumed that the objective is to enforce a particular law against parking. The question of whether this law is sensible, or how much effort should be put into enforcing it, has not been discussed. In metered parking areas the government, in essence, is renting out space for parking to people who want to use it. It may not be using a market-clearing price, because it may have some objectives other than simply providing the service at a profit, but this does not seriously alter the problem. The government should maximize the net benefit obtained from the operation. For simplicity, let us assume that it is charging market-clearing prices. It would then attempt to maximize total revenue, including the revenue from fines and the revenue from the coins inserted in the parking meters minus the cost of the

3. I am indebted to Alexander Kafka for the "price list" analogy. He insists, following his own professor, that the entire criminal code is simply a price list for various acts.

enforcement system. We need not here produce an equation or attempt to solve the problem, but clearly it is a perfectly ordinary problem in operations research, and there is no reason to anticipate any great difficulty in solving it.

But parking is a very minor problem; in fact, it was chosen for discussion simply because it is so easy. In essence, there is very little here except a calculation of exactly the same sort that is undertaken every day by businessmen. For a slightly more complicated problem, let us consider another traffic offense—speeding. The number of deaths from automobile accidents, the extent of personal injuries, and the material damage are generally all functions of the speed at which cars travel.[4] By enforcing a legal maximum speed, we can reduce all of these. On the other hand, a legal maximum speed will surely inconvenience at least some people, and may inconvenience a great many.

The material costs of lowering maximum speed are easily approximated by computing the additional time spent in traveling, and multiplying this by the hourly earning power of an average member of the population. This is, of course, only an approximation, leaving out such factors as the pleasure some people get out of driving at high speeds, and the diversion of economic activity that would result from the slowing down of traffic. Nevertheless, we could use this approximation and the costs of deaths, injuries, and material damage from automobile accidents to work out the optimal speed limit that would be simply the limit that minimized total costs.[5] The computation would be made in "social" terms because the data would be collected for the entire population. Individuals, however, could regard these figures as approximations for their personal optima.

To the best of my knowledge, no one has ever performed these calculations. Presumably the reason for this omission is an unwillingness to openly put a value on deaths and injuries. When I point out to people that the death toll from highway accidents could be reduced by simply lowering the speed limit (and improving enforcement), they normally show great reluctance to give any consideration to the subject. They sometimes try to convince themselves that the reduction would not have the predicted effect, but more commonly

4. Recently this relationship has been somewhat obscured by the publication of Ralph Nader's *Unsafe at Any Speed*. This is a misunderstanding. It is undoubtedly true that cars can be designed to reduce accidents. Recent discoveries on methods of reducing skidding by improved highway surfaces probably indicate that there is more potential in highway improvement than in car redesign. Nevertheless, for a given car and highway, speed kills.

5. For those who object to approximation, more elaborate research, taking into account much more of the costs of slowing down traffic, could be undertaken.

they simply quickly shift to another subject. For reasons of convenience, they oppose a substantial lowering of the speed limit, but they do not like to consciously balance convenience against deaths. Nevertheless, this is the real reasoning behind the speed limits. We count the costs of being forced to drive slowly and the costs of accidents and choose the speed limit that gives us the best outcome. Since we are unwilling to do this consciously, we probably do a bad job of computing. If we were willing to look at the matter in the open, consciously placing a value on human life, we could no doubt get better results.

As an example of this reluctance to think about the valuation we are willing to place upon deaths and injury, a colleague of mine undertook a study of the methods used by the Virginia Highway Commission in deciding upon road improvement. He found that they were under legislative orders to consider speed, beauty, and safety. The beauty was taken care of by simply earmarking a fixed part of the appropriations for roadside parks. For speed, they engaged in elaborate research on highway use and had statistical techniques for predicting the net savings in time that could be derived from various possible improvements. It was the possibility of improving these techniques that had led them to invite my colleague to make his study. For safety, on the other hand, they had no system at all.

It was clear that they did take safety into account in designing roads and spent quite a bit of money on reducing the likelihood of accidents. They did not, however, have any formula or rule for deciding either how much should be spent on safety or in what specific projects it should be invested. Clearly the money spent on safety could not be spent on increasing speed of travel or beauty.[6] They must have had some trade-off. This rule, however, remained buried in their subconscious even though they used fairly elaborate and advanced techniques for other problems. This is particularly remarkable when it is remembered that, given any exchange value, the computations of the amount to be spent on safety would be fairly easy. If, for example, it is decided that we will count one fatal automobile accident as "worth" $500,000 in inconvenience to drivers (measured in increased travel time), then with statistics on accidents and the volume of traffic, it would be possible to work out how much should be spent on safety and where.

6. In some cases the same improvement may increase both speed and safety, a cloverleaf, for example. In general, however, although speed, safety, and beauty may sometimes be joint products, more of one will reduce the supply of the others.

Since the highway commission did not spend all of its money on safety, some such "price" for accidents must have existed, but the rather sophisticated engineers were unwilling to admit, probably even to themselves, that this was so. Perhaps more surprising, my colleague fully approved of their attitude. Basically a "scientific" type, with a great interest in statistical decision theory, he felt that here was one place where careful reasoning was undesirable. He did not want to consider the ratio between deaths and convenience himself, did not want the people who designed the highways on which he drove to consciously consider it, and did not want to discuss the subject with me.

But even if we do not like to critically examine the process, clearly the decision as to the speed limit is made by balancing the inconveniences of a low limit against the deaths and injuries to be expected from a high one. The fact that we are not willing to engage in conscious thought on the problem is doubly unfortunate, because it is difficult enough so that it is unlikely that we can reach optimal decisions by any but the most careful and scientific procedures. The problem is stochastic on both sides since driving at a given speed does not certainly cause an accident; it only creates the probability of an accident. Similarly, our convenience is not always best served by exceeding the speed limit, so we have only a stochastic probability of being inconvenienced. There will also be some problems of gathering data that we do not now have (mainly because we have not thought clearly about the problem) and making reasonable estimates of certain parameters. In order to solve the problem, a table of probabilities is needed.[7] Obviously, with Table 8.1, and one more thing, a conversion factor for deaths and delay, we could calculate the speed limit that would optimize the "cost" of using the road. Equally obviously, no direct calculation of this sort is now being undertaken. Our speed limits are, however, set by weighing accident prevention against inconvenience. The only difference between our present methods and the ones I have outlined is that we are so frightened of admitting that we use a conversion ratio in which lives are counted as worth only some finite amount that we refuse to make the computations at a conscious level, and, hence, deny ourselves the use of modern statistical methods.

7. Note that I am ignoring all consequences of accidents except deaths, and that I am assuming that the speed limit is the only variable. These are, of course, simplifying assumptions introduced in order to make my table simple and the explanation easy. If any attempt were made to explicitly utilize the methods I suggest, much more complex methods would be needed.

TABLE 8.1

SPEED LIMIT	DEATHS PER 100,000,000 CAR MILES	COSTS OF DELAY PER 100,000,000 CAR MILES
10 MPH	1	$50,000,000,000.00
20 MPH	2	35,000,000,000.00
30 MPH	4	22,500,000,000.00
40 MPH	8	15,500,000,000.00
50 MPH	16	5,000,000,000.00
60 MPH	32	2,000,000,000.00
70 MPH	64	500,000,000.00

Having set a speed limit, we now turn to its enforcement. If, for example, the limit is fifty MPH, it does not then follow that people who drive over that speed will automatically be involved in accidents, nor does it follow that driving at fifty-one MPH is very much more likely to lead to an accident than at fifty MPH. The use of a simple limit law is dictated by the problems of enforcement. If we had some way of charging people for the use of the streets, with the amount per mile varying with the speed, this would permit a better adjustment than a simple speed limit.[8] In practice the police and courts do something rather like this by charging much higher fines for people who greatly exceed the speed limit. Let us, however, confine ourselves to the simple case of a single speed limit. Our method of enforcing this law is in some ways most peculiar. In the first place, if a citizen sees someone violating this law and reports it, the police will normally refuse to do anything about it. With an exception that we turn to in a moment, you cannot be penalized for speeding unless a policeman sees you do it. Think what burglars would give for a similar police practice in their field of endeavor.

A second peculiarity is that the penalty assessed is unconnected with the attitude of mind of the person who violated the speed limit.[9] Driving at seventy MPH may get you a fine of $100 or a ten-year sentence, depending upon the occurrence of events over which you have no control. Suppose, for

8. Needless to say, the cost of driving fifty MPH in a built up area would be higher than in the open countryside.

9. For certain special cases, a partial and imperfect exception to this may be made. The man who speeds to get his wife to the hospital before the birth of their child is perhaps the one that

example, two drivers: each takes a curve at seventy MPH. The first finds a police car on the other side, gets a ticket, and pays a fine. The second encounters a tractor driving down his side of the road and a column of cars on the other side. In the resulting crash, the tractor driver is killed, and the result may be a ten-year sentence for manslaughter.[10] We can assume both men exceeded the speed limit for the same motives, but the second had bad luck. Normally, we like to have penalties depend upon what the defendant did, and not on circumstances beyond his control.

The peculiarity of this procedure is emphasized when it is remembered that the man sent up for ten years for killing someone in an accident almost certainly had no intent to do so. He was driving at a high speed in order to get somewhere in a hurry, an act that normally leads to a moderate fine when detected. The heavy sentence comes not from the "wickedness" of his act but from the fact that he drew an unlucky number in a lottery. The situation is even clearer in those cases in which the accident arises not from a conscious violation of the law but from incompetence or emotional stress (losing one's head). In ordinary driving we frequently encounter situations whereby a small error in judgment causes deaths. A man who has no intent to drive carelessly may simply be a bad judge of distance and try to pass a truck when there is insufficient room. An excitable person may "freeze" when an emergency arises with a resulting accident. Both of these cases might well lead to long prison terms in spite of the complete lack of "criminal intent" on the part of the defendant. Our laws, in essence, provide that lack of skill or mental stability may, under certain circumstances, be serious crimes.

As game theory teaches, a mixed strategy may pay off better than a pure strategy. It may be, therefore, that the combination of three different treatments is better than a simpler rule providing a single and fairly heavy penalty for speeding, regardless of whether you hit anyone or happen to encounter a

---

gets the most newspaper attention. The general view, however, was well stated by the British Court of Criminal Appeal: "If a driver in fact adopts a manner of driving which the jury thinks was dangerous to other road users . . . then on the issue of guilt it matters not whether he was deliberately reckless, careless, momentarily inattentive or even doing his incompetent best." Regina v. Evans (1963) 1 Q.B. 412, p. 418.

10. Note that the rule that a traffic offense is prosecuted only if seen by a police officer is not followed in the event of a serious accident. A third driver may be imagined who took the curve at the same speed and met neither the police nor the tractor. He would, of course, go free even if his offense were reported to the police.

policeman while engaged in the criminal act. Although we must admit this possibility, it seems more likely that a single penalty based on the intent of the individual would work better in preventing speeding. The probable reason for the rather peculiar set of rules I have outlined is simply the incompetence of the court system. If someone who disliked me alleged that he had seen me speeding, and I denied it, the court would have to decide who was lying without much to go on except the expressions on our faces. Since "dishonesty can lie honesty out of countenance any day of the week if there is anything to be gained by it," this is clearly an uncertain guide. Under our present court system, permitting individuals to initiate prosecutions for speeding would almost certainly mean that innumerable spite cases would be brought before the courts, and that the courts would make many mistakes in dealing with them.

The use of two sets of penalties for speeding, depending upon factors not under the defendant's control, similarly, is probably the result of judicial inefficiency. The more rational course of a heavy fine or a brief imprisonment for every speeding conviction would very likely not be enforced by judges who do not really think speeding is very serious unless it kills somebody. That this is the restriction cannot strictly be proved, but at least some evidence can be provided for it. In Virginia, as in many states, multiple convictions for traffic offenses can result in the suspension of driving licenses. The state has encountered real difficulty in getting its judges to carry out this provision. Under the conditions of modern life, the deprivation of a driver's license is a real hardship, and judges apparently do not like to impose it for, say, a speeding offense, simply because the offender has already been twice convicted. Similarly, the courts are unlikely to inflict a very heavy penalty on the man who drives after his license is suspended if he avoids killing.[11] With more efficient courts, we might be able to make our laws more rational.

It is probable that judicial inefficiency accounts for another peculiarity of the motor traffic code: that it is almost impossible for an individual to defend himself against the accusation of a violation of that code. Normally the

11. Possibly, given the difficulties of enforcement, a restriction of the license rather than a removal might be wise. Restricting the license of a multiple offender to a limited area, including his home, a couple of shopping centers, and his place of employment, together with a low speed limit, say thirty MPH, might appeal to judges who would be unwilling to remove the license totally. Judges might also be more inclined to give heavy sentences to people who violated such restrictions than to people who continue to drive to work in spite of the lack of a license.

police officer's testimony in court is accepted regardless of other evidence. Furthermore, in general, the penalty exacted for a minor violation of the code is small if the defendant does not defend himself, but high if he does. Parking offenses, for example, may commonly be settled for $1 or $2 on a guilty plea, but cost $10 to $20 if you choose to plead not guilty. This amounts to paying the defendant to plead guilty. Most of the people who get tickets are indeed guilty, but those who are not guilty normally plead guilty anyway because of this system of enforcement. A similar procedure is used in connection with other crimes, and since it is of more importance in these other areas, we will defer its discussion.

Obviously, we could apply the same line of reasoning to deal with other parts of the traffic code. The problem is essentially a technological one. By the use of evidence obtained from statistical and other sources, we could compute a complete traffic code that would optimize some objective function. In practice we do not do this, because of our reluctance to specify an exchange value for life. Nevertheless, we get much the same result, albeit with less accuracy and precision.

Turning now to the income tax law as a sample of tax laws in general, we must begin by noting that our first assumption does not seem to fit here.[12] Apparently, almost anyone can get special treatment under the income tax law. The laws and regulations are a solid mass of special rules for special groups of people. In apparently innumerable cases some particular wealthy man or large corporation has succeeded in obtaining special tax treatment. Under these circumstances, I can hardly recommend that people favor a tax code that does not have special privileges for themselves. Nevertheless, we can consider how a tax code, once it is set up, should be enforced.

Unfortunately, here again, our first general assumption may not apply. A great many people (special classes that readily come to mind are doctors, waitresses, and farmers) have special facilities for evading the income tax because they are often paid in cash. It is widely believed that these individuals make very good use of their special opportunities. Whether this is true or not, I am certainly not in a position to advise them to refrain from taking advantage of their situation. Furthermore, it is quite widely believed that certain groups (the farmers in particular) have been able to make use of their

12. See J. Randolph Norsworthy, "A Theory of Taxpayer Behaviour: Evasion of the Personal Income Tax" (Ph.D. dissertation, University of Virginia, 1966), for a more exhaustive discussion.

political power to see to it that the Internal Revenue Service does not devote as many resources to detecting evasion by them as by other groups. Once again, I cannot, on the basis of my present assumptions, recommend that the individual refrain from taking advantage of these opportunities. The tax code contains within it both a set of special privileges for individuals and instructions for evasion that apply only to certain classes. The true tax law is a residual after we have knocked all these holes into what was, in 1912, a rather simple piece of legislation.

There are further difficulties. The individual presumably is interested in the taxes being collected from other people, because he wants the government services that will be purchased by them. He would prefer to be left free of tax himself, but this is unfortunately not possible. He, therefore, trades the tax on his own income for the benefits that he obtains from the purchase of government services by the entire community. It is by no means clear that the present amount of governmental services is optimal for everyone. If I believed that the level of governmental services being purchased today was too high (i.e., that lower tax rates and lower levels of service were desirable), I would presumably feel relatively happy about systematic evasion of a tax law on the part of everyone. On the other hand, if I felt that the present level of governmental services was too low and that the taxes should be higher, I might conceivably feel that "overenforcement" is desirable.

Even if I were happy with the present level of governmental expenditures, it is by no means obvious that I should favor efficient enforcement of the revenue code. I might favor a revenue code that set rates relatively high combined with an enforcement procedure that permitted a great deal of evasion to lower rates and better enforcement procedures. Surely I would prefer the former if I would be particularly able to evade payment at the higher rates. But even if I assume that everyone will have about the same ability to evade payment (which is, in essence, our first general assumption), I might still prefer the higher rates and higher level of evasion. Nevertheless, it seems to me that most people would prefer the lowest possible level of tax for a given net return. I have been unable to prove that this is optimal, but it does seem to be reasonable that this would be the appropriate social goal.[13] In any event, that is the assumption upon which our further calculations are built. It would be relatively easy to adjust these calculations to any other assumption on this particular matter.

13. I sincerely hope that some of my readers may be able to repair this admission.

TABLE OF SYMBOLS 8.2

C_p = Private cost of enforcement (includes cost of incorrect tax penalties)
C_R = Cost of revenue protection service
I = Income
I' = Some part of income
L_C = Likelihood of compliance
L_d = Likelihood of detection of evasion
N = Social return on tax (excess burden not subtracted)
P = Penal rate for detected noncompliers
R = Tax rate
T_r = Tax revenue (net of direct enforcement costs)

Under these circumstances and on these assumptions the return in taxation to the government for various levels of enforcement can be seen by Equation (8.1):

$$T_r = L_C \cdot R \cdot I + (1 - L_C) \cdot I' \cdot L_d \cdot P - C_R \tag{8.1}$$

Once again we have a fairly difficult-looking equation that is actually quite simple. The first term listed in Table 8.2 is the likelihood that individuals will fully comply with the tax laws multiplied by the tax rate and income. Note that this is deliberately somewhat ambiguous. It could be taken as any individual's tax payments or the payments for the economy as a whole, depending upon which definition we choose for income. We add to this the probability that an individual will attempt to evade payment of taxes on all or part of his income, multiplied by the probability of detection, multiplied by the penalty he will be compelled to pay on a detected evasion. This gives us the total return that the community will receive. There is, of course, the cost of maintaining the inspection and revenue collection system that is subtracted from this output in the final term C_R.

In Equation (8.2) we see the conditions for an individual's decision as to whether or not he should attempt to evade the tax payment on a particular portion of his income.

$$L_d \cdot P \cdot I' < R \cdot I' \tag{8.2}$$

It indicates that if the likelihood of detection multiplied by the penalty he must pay on being detected is less than the standard rate, he would be wise to attempt evasion. It will be noted that both in this inequality and in the previous equation there is an implicit assumption that the individual will be able to pay a fine if he is found to have evaded the tax and that this fine will settle the matter. This is not a bad approximation of the situation in tax law. In other parts of the law, this is normally not true, and, hence, there is a very great difference between tax law and the law of burglary. The reason that the individual is normally able to pay a fine is simply that, in general, in order to get into income tax difficulties, you have to be well off. No one plans to have zero assets in order to avoid the necessity of paying income tax fines.

Nevertheless, although this is a very good approximation, it is not entirely accurate. The income tax authorities do sometimes attempt to put people in prison for tax evasion. In general, the Internal Revenue Service has a dual system. If you make a "tax saving" that is relatively easy for them to detect, they will normally "adjust" your return and charge you a relatively modest fine. If, on the other hand, you do something that is quite difficult to detect (normally a directly dishonest rather than a somewhat misleading statement), they assess a much heavier penalty. No doubt this is a sensible way of minimizing enforcement costs.

There is another peculiarity of the income tax policing process. The policeman himself (i.e., the internal revenue man) normally simply assesses a deficiency on the face of the form. This is usually the only legal proceeding. In minor cases the individual normally pays, although he may complain. It is highly probable that in this matter, as in other small-claims litigation, there is a great deal of inaccuracy. Since these are small matters, the use of a relatively inaccurate procedure is optimal. For major matters, however, very elaborate legal proceedings may be undertaken. These proceed at first through the administrative channels of the Internal Revenue Service, and, only if all administrative methods are exhausted, turn to the regular courts.

Returning, however, to our basic equations, it will be noted that the likelihood of quiet compliance (i.e., the likelihood of the income tax payer making no effort to evade) is a function of the likelihood of detection of evasion as shown in Equation (8.3).

$$L_C = +fL_d \tag{8.3}$$

The likelihood of detection of evasion in turn is a function of two things as shown in Equation (8.4).

$$L_d = +f(C_R) + f'(C_p) \tag{8.4}$$

The first of these, of course, is simply the amount of resources that we put into the revenue service. The second, however, is the quantity of resources that we force the taxpayer to put into keeping records and filling returns and doing other things that make it easier to enforce the tax. Thus Equation (8.1) is socially incomplete. Equation (8.5) shows the net social benefit or loss from the tax, including the factor C_p.

$$N = L_C \cdot R \cdot I + (1 - L_C) \cdot I \cdot L_d \cdot P - C_R - C_p \tag{8.5}$$

It will be noted that these computations ignore the problems of excess burden.

C_p is an interesting and very comprehensive term. It not only includes the trouble of filling out the income tax forms but also the necessity of keeping our accounts in a form such that the Internal Revenue Service may survey them. It includes the possibility that we will be audited even if we have not violated the law. It does not include any penalty that we might incur if we have violated the law, because that is included under P. It also includes a number of other things that are somewhat less obvious. For example, it includes the inconvenience we may occasionally suffer when the Internal Revenue Service is investigating a potential violation of the internal revenue code by someone other than ourselves. We might for some reason have some evidence that the Internal Revenue Service wants and be compelled to furnish it. It also includes the possibility that the Internal Revenue Service will wrongly suspect us and will assess an incorrect fine upon us. Lastly, of course, it includes legal expenses involved in all of those mentioned. Thus it is by no means a small figure. When we turn to other types of crime, we will find it necessary to divide the equivalent of this figure up into a large number of components, and this will make our analysis much more complex.

Still, under our present circumstances, the problem is relatively easy. We could simply maximize N. An examination of this equation indicates some mildly paradoxical consequences. We could, for example, be in favor of increasing enforcement even though we know it is likely to raise our own payments. It will be noted that nowhere in the equation is the assumption that we will obey the law while others will not. If we really believe that the government's money is being spent for something worthwhile, we then make a gain of some nature from increasing N. It is true that the N in our equation very crudely represents this gain since it takes a total figure rather than a marginal figure, but we need not worry about it. Once again, when we turn to other crimes we will produce more elaborate and more complex equations.

It should be noted that we might feel it desirable to include a risk aversion factor. If the penalty for evasion of the tax is quite large, say twenty-five times the tax that is evaded, and if we feel that there is a fair probability of the Internal Revenue Service's going wrong in assessing such penalties, then our term C_p would be large.

These are refinements, however. Basically, we could calculate an optimum tax enforcement policy from a set of equations such as those given. If the reader considers his own reactions, he will realize that his attitude toward the income tax authorities is based upon something like this reasoning. He does, of course, hope that the income tax authorities will give him special treatment and does his best to obtain it. Insofar as this special treatment has already been taken into account, his behavior would be appropriately described by Equation (8.2). His behavior with respect to general social policy in this period would then be described more or less by a desire to maximize N in Equation (8.5). There may be people who have strong moral feelings about their own payments under the income tax, but I have never run into them.

In this chapter we have discussed two areas of the law with which the reader is likely to have fairly heavy personal experience. We have demonstrated in both cases that very simple computational tools permit defining an "optimum law." Application of these computational tools would, it is true, require the development of certain empirical information we do not now have, but they are nevertheless suitable guides to further work. In addition, our computational tools in this respect are simply formalizations of the thought processes now used by most people in dealing with these matters. When we turn to other crimes, we will find that somewhat more complex tools are necessary. Nevertheless, the basic line of reasoning will be very similar to that which we have employed in this chapter.

CHAPTER 9

JURISPRUDENCE

SOME MYTHS DISPELLED

Most Americans feel that the commission of a crime is likely to be followed by imprisonment, that people who are in prison are there as the result of a trial, and that in the United States people are not kept in prison by administrative decisions. These beliefs are mythological. Most crimes are not simply the preliminary to punishment for the criminals, most people who are in prison have not had anything that we would recognize as a trial, and administrative decisions keep people in prison and (in effect) extend their sentence. There are, in fact, a good many people in prison who have actually been put there by an administrative decision. Having said so much, however, I would add that I am by no means convinced that it is undesirable that these myths are false. Chapter 9 is devoted to dissipating a set of myths, but should not be regarded as necessarily critical of our present judicial system. It is not obvious that we would be better off if our judiciary functioned in closer accord with popular mythology.

In order to see how unlikely it will be for crime to be followed by punishment, we need look no further than that high point of establishment opinion, namely, *The Challenge of Crime in a Free Society, A Report by the President's Commission on Law Enforcement and the Administration of Justice*.[1] As part of this study, the commission undertook some statistical investigations of crime. Although this statistical information is not ideal, it is the best we have.

The first thing to note is that many crimes never even get reported to the police. It is not known how large a percentage of crimes are unreported or at least unrecorded, but the commission hired the National Opinion Research Center to investigate this problem by asking individuals whether they had been victims of crimes. This research design is not ideal, but it should produce reasonably good data. It is a commentary on the state of our law enforcement statistics that such a research project should be needed. According to the results in this survey (which is reproduced herewith as Table 9.1), only about one-half of all serious crimes are contained in police statistics (the uniform

1. *The Challenge of Crime in a Free Society, A Report by the President's Commission on Law Enforcement and the Administration of Justice* (Washington, D.C.: U.S. Government Printing Office, 1967). A large number of task force reports are also available from the Printing Office.

TABLE 9.1 ***Comparison of Survey and UCR Rates (Per 100,000 population)***

INDEX CRIMES	NORC SURVEY 1956–1966	UCR RATE FOR INDIVIDUALS 1965	UCR RATE FOR INDIVIDUALS AND ORGANIZATIONS 1965
Willful homicide	3.0	5.1	5.1
Forcible rape	42.5	11.6	11.6
Robbery	94.0	61.4	61.4
Aggravated assault	218.3	106.6	106.6
Burglary	949.1	299.6	605.3
Larceny ($50 and over)	606.5	267.4	393.3
Motor vehicle theft	206.2	226.0	251.0
Total violence	357.8	184.7	184.7
Total property	1,761.8	793.0	1,249.6

SOURCE: *Uniform Crime Reports for the U.S.*, issued by J. Edgar Hoover, Director, FBI, 1965, pp. 21 and 51. The UCR national totals do not distinguish crimes committed against individuals or households from those committed against businesses or other organizations. The UCR rate for individuals is the published national rate adjusted to eliminate burglaries, larcenies, and vehicle thefts not committed against individuals or households. No adjustment was made for robbery.

crime reports); presumably this means that only about one-half of such crimes are even reported to the police. Probably the ones that are not reported are less important on the whole than those that are reported, but it is still clear that a great many serious crimes are not reported.

The flowchart reproduced from the President's Commission report (Figure 9.1) shows the outcome of crimes that have been reported to the police. Approximately 2.75 million significant crimes were reported in 1965, the base year, which means that at least 5.5 million crimes were actually committed, the remainder not being reported. The number of arrests resulting from this 5.5 million crimes was 727,000 or about one arrest for every seven crimes. Of the arrested, approximately one-third were juveniles who were removed from the remainder of the flowchart. The number of people under detention after conviction of a crime among adults is 362,000 and among juveniles only 62,000, as shown by Table 9.2. The percentage of juveniles who are actually imprisoned is lower than that of adults. Nevertheless, let us assume the juveniles committed one-third of the crimes and that two-thirds of the crimes committed were committed by adults. With this

FIGURE 9.1

Criminal justice system model, figure 5, with estimates of flow of offenders and direct operating costs for index crimes in the United States in 1965

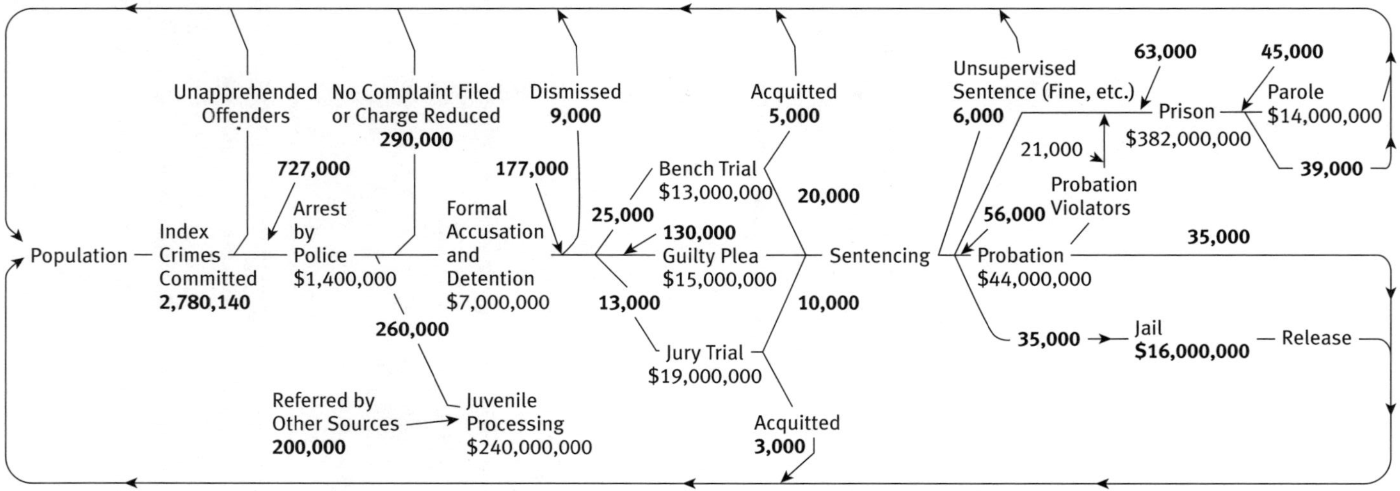

SOURCE: *The Challenge of Crime in a Free Society: A Report by the President's Commission on Law Enforcement and Administration of Justice* (Washington, D.C.: U.S. Government Printing Office, 1967), pp. 262–63.

Numbers in boldface indicate estimated flow of persons arrested for index crimes.

Numbers in regular type indicate estimated costs incurred at processing stages.

TABLE 9.2 ***Daily Average Number of Inmates in American Correctional Institutions in 1965***

Institutions primarily for adults:	
Federal prisons	20,377
State prisons	201,220
Local jails and workhouses	141,303
Total	362,900
Institutions primarily for juveniles:	
Public training schools	43,636[a]
Local juvenile institutions	6,024
Detention homes	13,113
Total	62,772
Grand total	425,673

SOURCES: National Survey of Corrections and U.S. Department of Justice, Bureau of Prisons, "Statistical Tables, Fiscal Year 1965," pp. 2 and 172.

[a]Includes 1,247 juvenile and youthful offenders in Federal Bureau of Prisons institutions.

conservative assumption the imprisonment figures at the right end of the chart are the result of the commission of approximately 3.5 million crimes.[2] It will be noted that only 63,000 people were sent directly to prison as a result of these crimes, which works out to about one person sent to prison for every sixty crimes committed. Of course, another 35,000 persons were sent to jail (which means a short sentence), and there was another group of people who received "unsupervised sentence, fine, etc.," some of whom were fined. The fact remains, not however, that the danger of imprisonment if you commit a crime in the United States is quite low.

The statement that crime does not pay is frequently made. Surely the statistics shown offer no supporting evidence for this maxim. Indeed, in the United States, the people who are involved in what is known as "organized crime" apparently make a very good thing out of it. The President's Commission special report on organized crime makes this clear.[3] Even if we do not concern ourselves with "the Mafia" and confine ourselves instead to

2. The people who were actually sent to prison in 1965 no doubt frequently had committed their crimes in 1964 or even earlier. In the absence of any evidence that there has been a sharp change in the flow through the process however, the use of the imprisonment and the number of crimes as being directly related will cause no great error.

3. *Task Force Report: Organized Crime* (Washington, D.C.: U.S. Government Printing Office, 1967), especially pp. 2–4.

crimes such as burglary, assault, and robbery, it may well be that the present discounted value of these crimes is positive. We cannot be sure that this is true without further data, and it is indicative of the general level of criminological research that the President's Commission did not look into the matter.[4]

It is certainly possible that crime is an attractive profession in the United States for the person who is not much concerned by scruples and who is willing to take rather large risks. This is particularly likely since the criminals who are captured have a low average intelligence. The usual explanation for this phenomenon is that criminals are stupid. Actually, the evidence simply indicates that criminals who are captured are stupid; they may not be a random sample of the total population of criminals. It is quite possible that an intelligent man entering into this profession could expect a much lower rate of capture and hence would have a much higher payoff on his career than the stupid people who make up the bulk of the population in our penitentiaries. This is, however, only a possibility. The characteristics of criminals who are not caught are unknown, and the characteristics of the criminals who are seldom caught are hard to deduce from our present data. Although we cannot prove it, it would seem probable that one of the major causes of the high crime rate in the United States is the fairly low detection rate that a careful criminal would face. If stealing $1,000 gives you a fifty-fifty chance of going to jail for two years, you are less likely to take up the profession of burglary than if a similar crime gives you a 1-in-100 chance of going to jail for two months.

Furthermore, the figures collected by the President's Commission in a sense overstate the likelihood of conviction for the professional criminal. In the first place, surely some of the people who have been convicted are innocent; subtracting these would give a lower probability of being convicted for a person who commits a crime. Secondly, "crimes of passion" make up about 10 percent of the total number of crimes committed in the United States. The conviction rate for such crimes is markedly higher than for crimes calculated for material gain, for the simple reason that a crime of passion is normally not committed with any care. Some rather rough manipulation of the uniform crime report data indicates that the conviction rate for crimes of passion must be at least three times as high as that for crimes of calculation.[5] We must, of

4. I am engaged in an effort to produce the necessary data.

5. These data are compiled from the 1962 issue of the *Uniform Crime Reports*, Table 11, p. 87. I reasoned that murder, rape, and aggravated assault would all contain a considerable

course, keep in mind that many of the criminals are convicted of more than one crime at a time. Thus a burglar who is caught committing a burglary may be tried for three or four burglaries, possibly because some of the loot from the other burglaries was found in his home.

Let us now proceed along the flowchart provided by the President's Commission from the arrest to the trial period (Figure 9.1). In the first place, it will be noted that the number of cases in which no complaint is filed or the charge is reduced is considerably greater than the number in which there is a formal accusation and detention for trial.

Furthermore, there is a small group of persons whose case is dismissed after they have been formally indicted. The decisions here are purely administrative, and, considering the number of people involved, perhaps more important than those of the trials themselves. However, few readers will object to the police and the district attorney having the right to refuse to proceed to trial when they feel that this is desirable.

When we reach the disposition level, three possibilities are shown: bench trial, jury trial, and guilty plea. It will be noted that "guilty plea" is listed in contrast to "trial." This is correct; there is no trial in these cases. Let us, however, begin by discussing the two forms of trial. About two out of three of the accused who choose to go to trial select a trial by a judge, rather than a trial by a jury. This is in spite of the slightly higher likelihood of conviction in the bench trial. The number of accused persons acquitted by judges is about 20 percent of those who choose the bench trial, and the number acquitted in jury trials is about 25 percent. The accused is permitted to choose between a judge trial or a jury trial, and presumably chooses the one that he thinks has the best present discounted value for him.[6]

Approximately 39 percent of the people convicted of serious crimes in the United States are sent to prison, about 22 percent are sent to jail, about 35 percent are given probation, and the remaining 6 percent receive unsupervised sentences. The people who take the risk of a trial and are convicted have a higher probability of going to prison than those who plead

---

number of crimes of passion and that the other types of crimes would not. Needless to say, this is far from a definitive calculation, but poor figures are sometimes better than none at all.

6. See Harry Kalven, Jr., and Hans Zeisel, *The American Jury* (Boston: Little, Brown, 1966), especially pp. 17–22, for a discussion of the factors that may lead the defendant to choose a judge or a jury.

guilty. The basic reason for pleading guilty is the promise of a reduced punishment. Thus, if you plead guilty, you have considerably less than a 39 percent chance of going to prison. In fact, as we shall see in our later discussion of the confession process, the accused normally knows exactly what sentence he will get at the time he makes his plea. Thus if committing a crime in the United States is not a particularly dangerous activity, even confessing to it is not tremendously risky.

The reason for giving a lighter sentence to someone who has confessed than to someone who has been found guilty as a result of a trial is not obvious. The custom, however, is part of the judicial practice in practically every legal system. There seem to be two main reasons for this practice. The first is to spare the state the expense of the trial. Actually, however, the costs of the trial are not very great when compared with the costs that both the state and society undergo when a man is imprisoned, so this would normally not call for a very large reduction in return for a confession. The second, and more important, reason for giving a man who confesses a lower sentence is simply to reward confessions. Assume you are accused of a crime. If you go through the trial, there is at least some chance that you will be acquitted. It is true that you will have to undergo the cost of the trial, and in the case of a wealthy man, this may be a large cost, but it probably would pay you to do so unless the evidence is extraordinarily strong. Trials sometimes have the most unlikely outcomes. If you confess, you are certain to be punished. If you do not confess, you have a finite chance of getting off. If the punishment will be the same whether you confess or not, confession would be irrational.

Let us turn to the way in which confessions are normally obtained. For this purpose, let us re-examine the figure showing the amount of evidence and degree of likelihood of guilt that we used in the chapter on contracts. There the likelihood that the plaintiff should prevail was shown on the vertical axis; in this case the vertical axis shows the likelihood that the accused is guilty. Again, the amount of evidence is shown on the horizontal axis. In criminal cases, we deliberately introduce an element of bias. The reasons for this bias and a discussion of its probable rationality are deferred to another chapter. For the time being, let us accept the fact that bias does exist. Thus the decision line has been drawn on the diagram not to minimize total errors, but to reduce the number of errors that involve convictions of people who should not be convicted. It is not possible, short of refusing to convict anyone, to completely eliminate convictions of innocent people, but we can

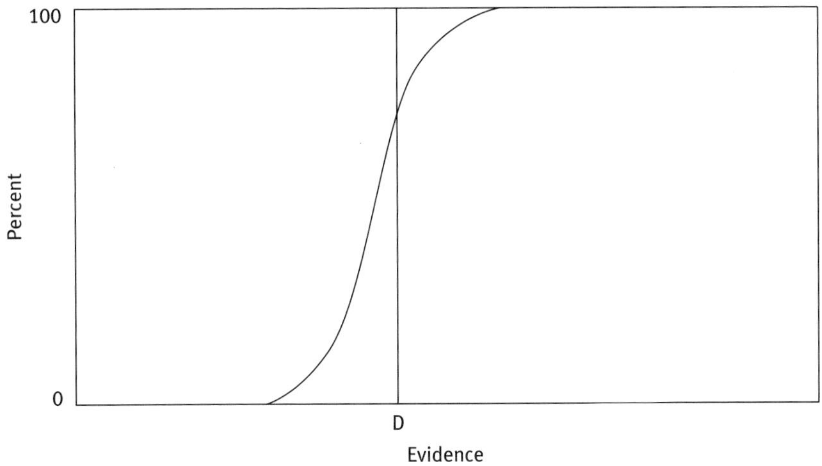

FIGURE 9.2
Evidence and outcome in a criminal proceeding

make the erroneous findings of innocence more common than the erroneous conviction of an innocent person. The line D, which shows the amount of evidence necessary for conviction, has been drawn in Figure 9.2 to introduce this type of bias.

Figure 9.2 looks at the matter from a standpoint of whoever is to make the ultimate decision, the judge or the jury. Figure 9.3 shows the same problem from a standpoint of an attorney considering the situation before a trial. He is unable to perfectly forecast the behavior of the judge or jury, and from his standpoint, therefore, their behavior is not shown by a vertical line, but by another S curve such as D in Figure 9.3. Note that D on Figure 9.2 and D on Figure 9.3 are really the same thing, from different points of view. In both cases, they represent the behavior of the judge and/or the jury.

The skilled attorney confronting this line makes estimates of the likelihood of conviction of his client in terms of the evidence. I have drawn in three such likelihoods as three vertical lines, one showing a three-quarter probability of conviction, one showing an even probability of conviction, and one showing a one-quarter probability of conviction. If the probable sentence after trial and conviction is ten years, and the defense attorney feels that his client has a three-quarter chance of conviction, the defense attorney would be willing to make a deal with the prosecuting attorney for a

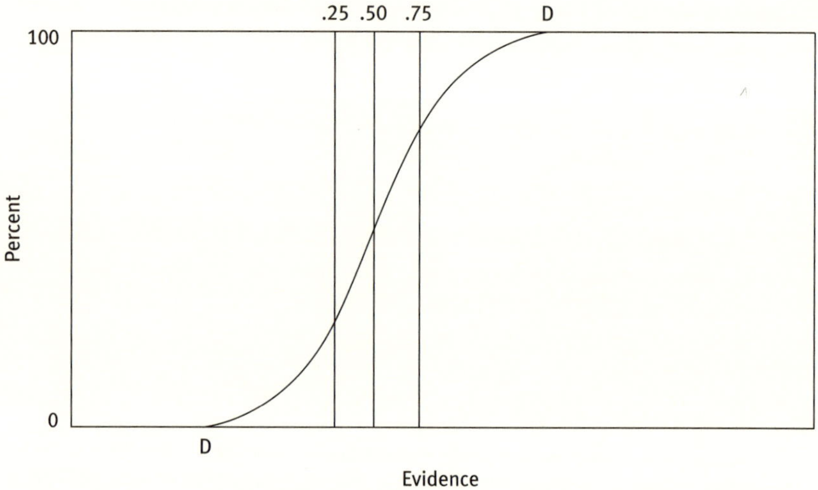

FIGURE 9.3
Negotiated pleas in criminal proceedings

confession in return for a reduction in the length of sentence that exceeds one-quarter.[7]

The district attorney may be delighted to make such an arrangement. The district attorney does not have sufficient staff to make it possible for him to try all cases. This, of course, is known to the defense attorney. Again, the district attorney normally wants to have a high conviction rate on those cases that he does try. Frank Hogan of New York, for example, is very displeased if any case is brought to trial without a conviction.[8] As a predictable consequence, his assistants would be willing to make deals with defense attorneys in which very substantial reductions in sentences are exchanged for confessions. Most cases in New York are handled by confession. The federal courts are another area in which a high percentage of cases are handled by confes-

7. In practice the decision as to what sentence properly discounts a risk of three-quarters or one-half is a little difficult because the sentence will occur in the future. Therefore, it is necessary to use a rather complex discounting formula to reach an accurate present value. I have not done so here mainly for simplicity, but it is likely that my desire for simplicity in this case parallels that of the attorneys making the decision.

8. Martin Mayer, "Hogan's Office Is a Kind of Ministry of Justice," *New York Times Magazine*, 23 July 1967, p. 7.

TABLE OF SYMBOLS 9.3

C_c = Court costs
C_l = Cost of lying
D_c = Disgrace resulting from confession
D_t = Disgrace resulting from conviction at trial
E = Evidence
L_c = Likelihood of conviction
P_c = Punishment resulting from confession
P_t = Punishment resulting from conviction at trial
P_u = Publicity case has received (if high, prosecutor may have to proceed despite high Q_d)
Q_d = Quality of defense
Q_j = Quality of trial system
R = Risk aversion factor
R' = Prosecutor's aversion to low conviction ratio

---

sion; as a matter of fact, 90 percent. In courts in which a very high percentage of the cases are handled by confession, one can feel fairly confident that the prosecutor is offering quite favorable terms to the defense attorneys.

Let us once again turn to high school algebra in order to put the matter more precisely. The conditions for confession are shown by inequalities 9.1 and 9.2, respectively (the variations of which are shown in Table 9.3), for the guilty individual and the innocent individual. Once again, these equations are somewhat formidably appearing but are actually very simple.

$$R \cdot L_c(P_t + D_t) + C_c + C_l > P_c + D_c \tag{9.1}$$

$$R \cdot L_c(P_t + D_t) + C_c > P_c + D_c + C_t \tag{9.2}$$

In each case the costs of standing trial are on the left side of the inequality, and the costs of confession on the right. The inequalities are, with the exception of one factor, identical. Basically, the punishment that is likely to result from conviction at a trial added to the disgrace that results from conviction at trial is multiplied by the likelihood of such conviction and risk factor. To this is added the court costs. On the right side we find the punishment that would result from a confession and the disgrace that would result from a confession. Another item that may or may not be of any significance is the cost of lying, which simply represents the fact that some people at least dislike lying and, therefore, will take this dislike into account. For the guilty person, the cost of lying is on the left side of the inequality because he lies by saying that he is not guilty; for the innocent person, it is on the right because he lies by pleading guilty.

The cost of lying might seem a way of sneaking ethics in through the back door in this equation. My impression is that it would be a rather small factor for most defendants in a serious criminal case. In any event, I should like to defer further discussion of this factor until later. It is, of course, clear that the difference between P_t and P_c is the control variable available to the prosecutor. He has no control over the individual person's risk preference and very little control over L_c, so if he wishes to induce confessions, he must offer a punishment after confession that is sufficiently less than the punishment if there were a trial and conviction to counterbalance $L_c \cdot R$. If he makes such an offer, then the defendant should accept.

The conditions for the prosecutor are shown in Equation (9.3). Note the risk premium.

Prosecutor

$$\begin{aligned} R' \cdot L_c P_t - C_c &> P_c \\ L_c &= f(E, Q_d, Q_j) \\ R' &= -f(P_u) \end{aligned} \tag{9.3}$$

This risk premium is rather unusual in form; in fact it might better be called "loss aversion." The prosecutor, of course, has many cases and is not unduly concerned with any one of them. He is, however, interested in maintaining a fairly high level of convictions. As we have noted, the prosecutors, in fact, obtain convictions in three-quarters or more of the cases they try. What the prosecutor has, therefore, strictly speaking, is not a risk-aversion factor but a desire to have a certain percentage of convictions. This means that he is unlikely to go to trial unless L_c is at least .75. The defendants know this and take it into account. Thus the R′ that shows risk aversion actually varies with different values of L_c. Otherwise the equation is fairly simple. It points out that if the likelihood of conviction multiplied by punishment minus the court costs is less than the punishment to be given if confession is obtained, then the prosecutor would be willing to accept the confession. The principal difference between this equation and that of the defendant is the switch of the court costs from one side to the other, together with the disgrace factor in the defendant's calculus.

This desire on the part of the prosecuting attorney to have a good record of convictions plays an interesting role. On the whole it means that unless the evidence against the defendant is quite good he will not be prosecuted. In the mythology, there is a great deal of talk about the court procedure itself being biased in the direction of the defendant. There seems to be little if any empirical evidence that our procedure is in fact so biased. There are a few parts of the rules of evidence and a few parts of our procedural rules that might give the defendant an advantage. In general, however, our procedural rules and the laws of evidence are about as much of a handicap to the defendant as they are to the prosecutor. It may be that the verbal formula of "reasonable doubt" is in itself a protection for the accused. It would be interesting to have empirical evidence on this point.

Whatever one can say about the bias of the trial procedure, toward or against the defendant, it is clear that the prosecutor's desire to have a good percentage of the cases he tries end in convictions leads to some protection of those defendants against whom the evidence is weak. Assuming that the courts have no bias at all and do not give the defendant the benefit of the doubt, the prosecutor, as we have noted, only undertakes those cases in which he feels he has at least a three out of four chance of conviction, so many people against whom the evidence is relatively weak would not even be tried. Note that if this attitude on the part of the prosecutor is combined with a similar bias on the part of the court, it might make a very great amount of evidence necessary for conviction. It should also be noted, however, that if the courts happen to be biased against the accused, then this practice on the part of the prosecutor would not necessarily mean that only those against whom the evidence was overwhelming were convicted.

As we have noted, most judicial systems arrange a reward for the person who confesses; he is normally given a lighter sentence than the person who does not confess. If I feel that I have about an 80 percent likelihood of conviction if I stand trial, and there is a provision in the law that says that any person who confesses is given a sentence 75 percent of the sentence of the person who is convicted after a trial, I would be wise to confess. From the standpoint of the government, this proposal provides some saving, i.e., the saving involved in not holding a trial, and little loss. Out of a collection of trials, they would end up with only a slightly smaller number of years of imprisonment imposed on the people tried than they would have had if they had gone to trial in each case. If they are trying to prevent the commission of crimes by making the present discount value of the crime negative, a high probability of a somewhat low sentence is as good as a low probability of a high sentence.

In discussing confession, I have said nothing about the guilt or innocence of the accused. There is no real reason why this should have any major bearing on the matter. A person who feels that the evidence is such that he has a certain probability of conviction will, if he is rational, confess if he is given a suitable reduction in sentence. If he is a typical middle-class American, it may be that the disgrace of confessing to a crime is so great that the reduction would have to be extremely large in order to overcome it. In talking to various middle-class people, I have found that they say that no one who is innocent would confess to a crime, regardless of what he was paid for doing so. I suspect this reflects naïveté. In any event, most people who are accused of crimes are very decidedly lower-class people, who frequently have already been found guilty of committing another crime. In general there is no reason to believe that they have an extreme aversion to confessing to a crime they did not commit.

In this connection, I found it rather interesting that most of my friends were unwilling to discuss whether they would confess to a crime of which they were guilty. Nevertheless, they are, in essence, alleging that human beings are so constituted that they will confess to crimes of which they are guilty and not confess to crimes of which they are innocent. Although I think they exaggerate its importance, there can be no doubt that some such tendency exists. It is surely so that most guilty persons will have at least a little less reluctance to confess than innocent persons. How large this difference is will, of course, vary greatly from person to person and according to circumstances. Basically, however, the reason for confession is that the evidence seems to indicate that you are better off if you confess than if you don't. Whether you are guilty or not is in most cases of less importance, unless the calculation of other factors is very close.

One of the interesting characteristics of the literature on negotiated pleas is the lack of an open and thorough discussion of the likelihood that innocent defendants may find it wiser to plead guilty. The only direct discussion of the matter that I have been able to find, and it is a very brief one, is provided in Appendix A to the *Task Force Report* on the courts by the President's Commission on Law Enforcement and Administration of Justice.[9] This contains the single sentence, "Even counsel may see the occasional practical wisdom of pleading an innocent man guilty."[10] There follows a short and inconclusive discussion. Indirectly, the same subject is dealt with in a number of places including the President's Commission report itself, the *Task Force Report* on

9. Arnold Enker, "Perspectives on Plea Bargaining," in *Task Force Report: The Courts* (Washington, D.C.: U.S. Government Printing Office, 1967).

10. Ibid., p. 114.

the courts, and Donald J. Newman's book *Conviction*.[11] In all of these sources, however, instead of discussing the possibility that an innocent defendant may be led to plead guilty, the point discussed is the desirability of minor precautions.

These precautions, which are normally suggested as reforms rather than as descriptions of actual practice, are usually limited to an investigation by the judge to find out whether or not there is a *prima facie* case against the defendant. This avoids the main issue. Unless there is fairly good evidence against the defendant, he is unlikely to plead guilty. The plea bargaining process should normally eliminate people against whom there is no *prima facie* case. It would seem certain, however, that some innocent persons confess because it is the best alternative available to them.

There is, furthermore, no obvious reason why we should find this undesirable. People would only confess to a crime of which they are innocent if the evidence against them is strong enough so that they feel there is a reasonable probability of conviction. The sentence to be given to them in return for their confession would be appropriately discounted in terms of the evidence against them. Thus if all innocent persons chose to go to trial rather than confess, one would anticipate that the erroneous outcomes of the trials would lead to about as many net years of imprisonment among these innocent persons as would the plea-bargaining process. The distribution of prison sentences would, of course, be different.

There is, however, one aspect of the present plea-bargaining process that is decidedly objectionable. It is, in general, necessary to go through a little ceremony in which everyone concerned denies that negotiations have taken place and maintains that the plea of guilty is not the result of a threat or promise (Table 9.4).[12] This hypocritical ceremony should be abolished, and the agreement between the prosecuting attorney and the defendant's counsel should be treated in exactly the same way as any other out-of-court settlement. Judicial supervision here is not more important than it is in a large automobile damage suit.

Thus far, I have been discussing the plea-bargaining process in what one might call a Utopian manner. In actual practice, it is unlikely that either

11. Donald J. Newman, *Conviction* (Boston: Little, Brown and Company, 1966).

12. See the President's Commission Report on Law Enforcement and Administration of Justice, *Task Force Report: The Courts* (Washington, D.C.: U.S. Government Printing Office), p. 9.

TABLE 9.4 ***Negotiated Guilty Pleas***

STATE (1964 STATISTICS UNLESS OTHERWISE INDICATED)	TOTAL CONVICTIONS	GUILTY PLEAS NUMBER	GUILTY PLEAS PERCENT OF TOTAL
California (1965)	30,840	22,317	74.0
Connecticut	1,596	1,494	93.9
District of Columbia (year ending June 30, 1964)	1,115	817	73.3
Hawaii	393	360	91.5
Illinois	5,591	4,768	85.2
Kansas	3,025	2,727	90.2
Massachusetts (1963)	7,790	6,642	85.2
Minnesota (1965)	1,567	1,437	91.7
New York	17,249	16,464	95.5
Pennsylvania (1960)	25,632	17,108	66.8
U.S. District Courts	29,170	26,273	90.2
Average (excluding Pennsylvania)[a]			87.0

SOURCE: The President's Commission on Law Enforcement and Administration of Justice, *Task Force Report: The Courts* (Washington, D.C.: U.S. Government Printing Office, 1967), p. 9.

[a] The Pennsylvania figures have been excluded from the average because they were from an earlier year, and the types of cases included did not appear fully comparable with the others.

the defendant or the prosecuting attorney would engage in such subtle calculations as we have described. As Herbert J. Simon is fond of pointing out, when you have a complicated problem, the usual human reaction is to resort to simple rules of thumb. We do have complex cases. The case cited by Jerome H. Skolnick in *Justice Without Trial* in which two burglars who had committed (between them) at least 500 burglaries got off with almost no sentence at all is an extreme case, but good bargaining can lead to very great gains on the part of the defendant.[13]

Normally, however, we find a rather rough system under which precise and difficult calculations are not made.[14] Still this rather rough set of rules of

13. Jerome H. Skolnick, *Justice Without Trial* (New York: John Wiley & Sons, 1966), p. 178. It may be argued that I have oversimplified this case in which other factors were involved. The reader is referred to the actual text of Skolnick's book for a more complete description of the matter.

14. This rather rough system is described in considerable detail in Donald J. Newman, *Conviction*.

thumb approximates our sophisticated calculations. Once again, I would reiterate that I am not criticizing the institutions described. I am simply pointing out that what happens is not what the common man thinks happens. The procedure merely means that different people who are convicted of the same crime receive different sentences depending upon the strength of the evidence. A person against whom the evidence is weak may receive, not a discharge, but a light sentence. If there were no negotiated confessions, he would get a trial at which he would have a small chance of getting a heavy sentence and a large chance of getting no sentence at all. Since he has a voluntary choice of going to trial, presumably he prefers the confession, but there is no reason why we should object. We can, after all, simply raise the average sentence a little bit.

The principal argument against the negotiated confession would seem to be that the attorneys are not likely to be quite as well informed about the evidence at the time they engage in negotiations as the judge and jury would be after the trial. Things do come out at the trial, and time does indeed sometimes bring out new evidence. Furthermore, the two attorneys are unlikely to be completely candid with each other. Basically each will try to convince the other that he has more evidence than he really does, and each will discount his opponent's statements, whether appropriately or not. Furthermore, in some cases one attorney or the other will prefer to withhold evidence until the trial rather than mention it to his opponent. Also, the principal purpose of the negotiating process looked at from the standpoint of the attorneys is the saving of time, and therefore *ipso facto* they spend less time on negotiating than they would on the trial itself. For all of these reasons the negotiation of confessions probably introduces a certain amount of random noise into the judicial process. It is not obvious, however, that this is undesirable. It also reduces the social resources invested in trials, and this may balance the random errors introduced.

Let us now consider the administrative routes to prison. We begin with the fact that both the police and the district attorney have administrative discretion as to whether or not to proceed with the case. The police must first investigate the crime and decide who they think is guilty; they are privileged to stop at any time if they think their resources could be better invested elsewhere. The district attorney, furthermore, can then refuse to proceed with the case.[15] Most people would agree that these two types of

15. In Newburgh, New York, this type of discretion has substantially abolished the law against simple assault. See James Q. Wilson, *The Varieties of Police Behavior* (Cambridge, Mass.: Harvard University Press, 1968), p. 136.

administrative discretion are completely acceptable. As a result of this discretion, there is, as previously pointed out, an interesting modification of our traditional criminal law in most jurisdictions. It is not constitutionally possible to compel the defendant to take a lie detector test or even to ask him to take a lie detector test and then use his refusal against him on trial. A great many jurisdictions, however, routinely give the defendant a lie detector test. If he passes it, he is released in most cases. An example of this may be taken from New York City, where the district attorney's office as a regular routine permits any defendant to take a lie detector test, and if the lie detector test is in his favor normally drops prosecution.[16]

As a bit of administrative discretion, this procedure is not open to criticism (although it should be noted that it is not the best way of making use of the lie detector). Nevertheless, the fact that it is done and that all the judges and a certain number of jurymen know that it is done means that a defendant facing trial is normally believed by those people who make the ultimate decision for or against him either to have flunked a lie detector test or to have failed to take this opportunity to clear himself. Thus, in practice, the lie detector has been brought into our procedure although it is not mentioned in court.

It will be noticed in the chart in the President's Commission report that of the people who are convicted of crimes, 56,000 are put on probation, and of these, 21,000 are eventually sent to prison for violation of their probation. The process of sending someone to prison for a violation of probation is essentially an administrative one. The probation officer usually makes the decision. He normally has to make a routine report to the judge, and the defendant may find it possible to protest, but in practice the probation officer's decision is final. Thus 21,000 people a year are sent to prison by essentially administrative decisions, usually for rather minor matters. Most probation violations involve something that is not a crime—changing one's address, for example. Furthermore, it seems in some cases that the "probation violation" is in fact an accusation of another crime. Smith is found guilty of robbery and placed on probation, but two months later his probation officer sends him to prison, and the probation violation is an alleged second robbery—a robbery for which he is never given any formal trial. But again there is no reason to believe that this is improper; it is simply different from the myth.

16. Martin Mayer, "Hogan's Office."

In fact, the probation official and his administrative discretion are important in the actual sentencing of a man who has been convicted by a genuine trial. The President's Commission recommends that the probation report be made use of for, in essence, convicting people for a newly invented crime.[17] If their recommendation is carried out, a person who is reported by the probation officer to be a member of the administrative hierarchy of the Mafia will receive a very severe penalty. The decision as to whether he is a senior member of the Mafia will be made by the judge in chambers as a result of a confidential report by the probation officer. Clearly this is administrative justice with a vengeance.[18]

In the prison itself administrative justice has always been an ordinary part of administration. Today there is a "good-time" system, under which a prisoner who does not cause significant difficulty for the prison administration is given a reduction in his sentence. Normally this is one day off his sentence for every four days in which he behaves himself. If he never gets into trouble, he will get off with a 20 percent reduction in his sentence. If he gets into trouble, the "good time" that he had accumulated before will be lost to him and he must begin accumulating again. The decision as to whether he will receive "good time" or not is entirely an administrative matter for the prison authorities.

We see here an example of word magic. If the law provided that the guards might add 25 percent to the sentence of any prisoner who they thought was not behaving himself, there would be a terrible scandal. Giving them the power to cut 20 percent off the sentence, mathematically the same thing, however, does not seem to be a matter of much note. In actual practice, of course, the two are identical. Most sentences are given by judges who are aware of this custom, and surely if the law were changed to permit 25 percent addition to sentences instead of 20 percent reduction, they would reduce their sentences accordingly. The only difference between the present law that permits a reduction in sentences and a law that permitted guards to increase the sentence is in the form of words used. It is a telling indication of the importance of word magic that no one, insofar as I know, has ever complained about the present system.

17. *The Challenge of Crime in a Free Society, A Report by the President's Commission*, p. 203.

18. The *Washington Post* has recently been urging the denial of bail to some accused if the judge thinks that they are dangerous.

The use of the "good-time" system by prison administrators and the absence of any objection to it on the part of prison "reformers" also indicates that the people who are in prison can be influenced in their behavior by the traditional techniques of the carrot and the stick. This seems obvious, but unfortunately a great many of the specialists in criminology deny that criminals are deterred by punishment. Why they think that a man's decision to rob a bank is not influenced by the penalty that he will receive for doing so, but that his decision as to whether or not to join a prison riot will be, is something that I do not understand. Furthermore, in my cautious interrogation of criminologists upon the point I have never received a coherent explanation.

The carrot and stick technique is used to keep prisons orderly in another way. Most prisons have disciplinary arrangements under which prisoners who have in some way transgressed the rules, or who are at least thought to have done so by the guards, are administratively confined in much more stringent and strict conditions. In a sense, they are moved to a special prison called "solitary," which is as much more unpleasant than the regular prison as the regular prison is than outside life. Again this imposition of a very considerable punishment on prisoners by administrative orders does not seem to cause any concern among reform groups.

In any event, many prisoners at any given time are in prison because the guards have taken away their "good time" by administrative decree. Another administrative board capable of doing the same thing is the parole board. Here, again, we have a case in which word magic is important. A provision that a board could triple the sentence would surely cause great indignation. The present situation in which it can slash the sentence to one-third does not cause any indignation. Substantially, the two are identical. The judge in deciding on the sentence takes into consideration the fact that the convict is only certain to serve the first third of it, and that whether he serves the remaining two-thirds depends upon the discretion of an administrative board.

Under present circumstances, if the judge sentences a man to prison for six years, he feels that he should be kept in prison two years and perhaps four years more at the discretion of a board.[19] If there was a board that was permitted to triple sentences, the judge would probably give a two-year sentence. The additional sentence that a prisoner may receive by annoying the parole board or, for that matter, by simply making it administratively

19. I am here ignoring "good time."

difficult for them to parole him, is very large. As a general rule, such minor matters as the ambition and work habits of members of the parole board have considerable effect on the period of time a prisoner spends in prison. Thus, again, we have an administrative body determining whether or not people will be in prison. Furthermore, once a man is paroled he can be sent back to prison again by a purely administrative decision, normally by his parole officer.

Altogether, although there do not seem to be any statistics on the point, it seems fairly certain that at least two-thirds, and perhaps three-quarters, of all prisoners in the United States at any given time are in prison because a parole board, a guard, or a probation officer decided that they should be. In all cases, of course, they have appeared at some time before a judge, mostly to register a guilty plea. Nevertheless, the relevant decision, the decision that keeps them in prison, is an administrative one.

A final feature of the parole process must be mentioned. Parole boards are more likely to release people who (they feel) have repented of their crimes. This is a natural consequence of their efforts to determine whether or not prospective parolees are likely to commit further crimes. Quite naturally, the parole board does not feel that people have repented of their crime unless they say that they have. They are, in fact, very dubious of the repentance even when it is expressed.

This puts the innocent man who has been convicted after a trial in a difficult position. It is not absolutely certain that he will not receive a parole if he does not confess to his crime and express repentance, but the odds are against it. In consequence, a large percentage of prisoners who are convicted through regular trials later confess in order to obtain a parole. This makes it very difficult to measure the accuracy of our judicial process. A confession sends about 90 percent of all federal prisoners to prison. Of the 10 percent who don't confess before they go to prison, the great majority confess in order to obtain a parole. In all cases they are being paid very heavily in the form of sentence remission to confess, and, therefore, their confessions are suspect.

This is merely a statement that the present system makes life difficult for researchers, not that it is a bad system in itself. To repeat a statement that I made at the beginning of this chapter, its point has been to dispel certain myths that are widely held. This chapter is not intended to criticize our present judicial institutions. I do not know whether the institutions that I have been discussing are desirable or undesirable. The fact that they do not operate in accord with publicly held myths is no evidence one way or the other. There is no reason why we should regard ill-informed popular opinion or the views of men who about 200 years ago adopted our present judicial procedures as scientific evidence. If I do not criticize the system, however, at least the reader should realize what it is. Our discussion of the law should not be based upon myth nor should we confine ourselves to pointing out that reality does not fit the myth and from that fact arguing that reality should be changed. Perhaps it is the myth that should be changed.

CHAPTER 10

JURISPRUDENCE

SOME GENERAL PROBLEMS

Chapter 9 was devoted to dissipating certain myths about our criminal procedure. This chapter is devoted to a discussion of certain truths that almost everyone already knows but that for some reason are not mentioned in most books on law. The first of these truths: that which we normally call the "criminal law" is only a small and arbitrarily selected segment of the total activity of the state in repressing criminal activity. Whether justice is done in some particular case may be as much, or even more, affected by how many detectives are assigned to that case as by what happens in court. Inadequate investigation may lead to very serious mistakes in the judicial proceedings.

Furthermore, if we look over the world in general, we observe that the very rigid Anglo-Saxon distinction between the court and the preliminary proceedings that lead to a person's being brought into court is not widely copied. In many countries the court and the police force are melded into one organizational body. This was true in the early days of the Communist regime in Russia and it is true of the present Communist regime in China, although the matter is somewhat disguised, and at the bottom level—the traffic court—it is true in the United States. As a general rule, people accused of traffic offenses never have any contact with anyone except employees of the police department or, in a few cases, of the revenue department, which collects on the tickets.

In fact, if we look around the world, we frequently find a melding of police and judicial activities in which the judicial power is the superior of the police power. In the Old West, the district judge was in essence the chief of police. He had supervisory control over the United States marshals who were the principal police force of the area. Arrangements of this sort are not uncommon. It was the early system from which the modern English police force developed. In addition, the continental institution of *juge d'instruction* is similar. It is a matter of definition whether this official is a policeman or part of the judiciary. The entire tradition of Mohammedan law is based upon a mixture of administrative and judicial activities in the same person. Under the old system in China, the magistrate was simultaneously the chief judge in his own court, the chief of police, and the prosecuting attorney.

In the United States we normally have different personnel sitting as judges in trials and engaging in bringing the person to trial. I am not criticizing this custom, but I would point out that much that is of importance occurs at the pretrial level. Viewed from the standpoint of a criminal, the government must surmount a set of hurdles if he is to be convicted. First, the police must decide that he committed the crime and arrest him. The police fail to do this, as we have seen, in 90 percent of all crimes. Second, the district attorney must decide that he should stand trial. Third, the judge or the jury must convict him. And finally, if he decides to appeal, the conviction must be upheld on appeal. Failure of process for suppression may occur at any one of these four levels. It is just as much of a failure if the police fail to discover who committed a crime as if the Supreme Court of the United States releases a criminal. The only difference is that the police failures receive less publicity. Still it is at the police level that the largest opportunities for improvement now exist. If the police could double their detection level, this would have a much greater effect upon our total crime rate than would almost any change in the judiciary. If we assume (and I see no reason not to assume it) that the percentage of criminals convicted would not change, then the probability of a prison sentence for a criminal would almost double.

This is, however, largely a matter of administration and technique in the police area. I have very little to say about this except that I believe that there are prospects for very great progress in this area. The government has gravely underinvested in criminological research. Furthermore, it has refused, for various reasons, to make use of more efficient techniques in many areas. Changes in these matters would not be dramatic and might not appear to be policy decisions. Nevertheless, they could work a very great improvement in the way we treat criminals and, for that matter, the way we treat innocent persons who are suspected of crimes.

Proceeding forward from police activity, a person who has been arrested by the police is normally held pending trial or released on bail. In their present form both of these practices date back to the Middle Ages, and it seems to me that drastic reform is desirable. Let us consider first a man who, for one reason or another, cannot post bail. He is in prison sometimes for very long periods of time awaiting trial. Clearly this is hard on a man who has not been found guilty of any crime. The reason for holding him is that he might run away. As I hope to demonstrate in a moment, this is not necessarily an insoluble problem, but let us temporarily assume that there is a good reason for holding the person in prison. No doubt there would be at least some persons who would have to be held in prison awaiting trial.

The question then arises, if the federal government or the state government needs to keep the person in prison, why does it not compensate him for his time? The only argument I can see against this is simply tradition. In the late Middle Ages, a person who was in prison not only was not paid but he had to pay the jailer for his food. If he was later found innocent, he could not be released until he paid these bills. We have abandoned this barbarous practice, but we have retained the equally barbarous practice of keeping him in jail without compensation. Assume that it is necessary for the enforcement of criminal law to keep a certain number of people under detention for varying periods of time before trial. If we do not compensate them, we are placing a special tax upon them, and there seems to be no reason why such a special tax is desirable.

Paying a person who is in prison awaiting trial the fair value of his services, together with a reasonable amount for the general inconvenience of living in an uncomfortable jail, would be a considerable improvement in what Aristotle called distributive equity.[1] Furthermore, from the standpoint of most of us, the prospect of having to pay slightly higher taxes if we are not accused of the commission of a crime, in return for a guarantee that if we are so accused we will be fully compensated for our time spent in a cell awaiting trial, would appear a good bargain. There is, however, another advantage in requiring the police to pay people awaiting trial the opportunity cost of their imprisonment. It would lead to a very great administrative interest in methods of reducing the number of people so imprisoned and the amount of time that they are imprisoned.[2] If we assume that the police and other administrative authorities are interested in reducing the amount of time that people spend in prison awaiting trial, these techniques are not hard to find. Bail is an old and almost barbarous technique, but there is no reason why a simple modification of the law should not permit most accused to be freed to await trial without having to post bail. If failing to appear for trial, after having been formally informed of the trial date, is made a serious crime, it is reasonably certain that very few people would fail to turn up.[3]

There are many other areas in which what are regarded as difficult constitutional problems could quite easily be settled by simply paying people for things that we now take from them by force. As an example, consider the

1. If the prisoners were paid a fee that included the inconvenience of living in a jail, one could assume that jails would very rapidly be improved so that this inconvenience (and the fee) was reduced.

2. It should be noted that *some* people are in prison more or less voluntarily. For various reasons they are deliberately delaying their trial. There is no obvious reason why people who are imprisoned under these circumstances should be compensated.

3. Arrangements would have to be made to prevent defendants from avoiding being formally informed.

present-day search procedure in the United States. The police may not enter upon my property in order to search it without first having obtained a warrant from the magistrate. Exactly why this is supposed to do me very much good if my property is searched is unclear. The police, in practice, normally evade these requirements in any event.[4]

If we substituted for this a law providing that the police may at their discretion search any person's property, subject, however, to putting everything back in the same order they found it before they began the search and paying a reasonable fee for the intrusion, I would predict that the entire problem would vanish. In fact, I would predict that a number of people would attempt to get the police to search their property because it would be a convenient way of obtaining a little extra cash. Noncriminals, in general, are somewhat put out by having their property searched but not enough that a rather small fee would not completely assuage the hurt.

The present situation is quite to the contrary. The police search and are not required to put things back the way they were found, although frequently out of good manners they will do so, and do not make compensation for their searches. An extreme example may be found in the case of the three civil-rights workers who were murdered in Mississippi. The FBI obtained information as to where the bodies were buried by the payment of approximately $30,000 to an informer. They then went to a dam that was being built by a private person on his property and destroyed it in the process of searching for the bodies buried in it. Suppose, however, they had, with their perfectly valid search warrant, destroyed the dam looking for the bodies and not found them. Under our present law, they would be under no obligation to restore the dam to its previous condition. Clearly this is not a desirable state of affairs. Our law on this matter is largely held over from a previous and barbarous state in England in the late Middle Ages, a time when most governments were impecunious and harsh, and the English government was more impecunious and harsh than most. The restraints put upon the king were perhaps rational, granted the nature of the royal government at that time, but they are quite irrational under modern circumstances.

We can think of further areas, many of them in fact, in which the present system of permitting the police to do something or prohibiting them from

4. Their methods are numerous and complicated. See Lawrence P. Tiffany, Donald M. McIntyre, Jr., and Daniel L. Rotenberg, *Detection of Crime* (Boston: Little, Brown and Company, 1967), pp. 99–207.

doing it should rationally be replaced by simply requiring them to pay for doing it. In some cases this is very difficult. Suppose, for example, the police become curious about me and arrange to have me followed by a man who (whenever possible) sneaks up close to me and listens to my conversation. This is perfectly legal in the United States today. It would be very hard to arrange a system of payments for me for the inconvenience that this may or, then again, may not cause me, because obviously the police do not want me to know it is happening. It nevertheless might be possible, even in this case, for the police to make suitable payments after the event. This same rule might be applied to such things as telephone tapping and bugging. Once again, if a rule providing for reasonable payments were made, I suspect that the real problem would not be a police desire to spend large parts of their budget on unnecessary and undesirable searches, seizures, and wire tappings, but a desire on the part of the private citizens to get themselves searched, bugged, or wire tapped in order to obtain these fees.

Payment as part of police activities is what is normally meant by "scientific police methods" in English discussions. The Bow Street runners, when they first brought "scientific methods" to England, actually depended very largely on simple straightforward payments of money for evidence. This is still the English tradition, although it is perhaps disappearing now. In the United States, we have been very reluctant to use this system, even though, as I mentioned before, the FBI has purchased information at a very high price upon various occasions. Our courts have tended to feel that purchased testimony is unreliable, and there is much to be said for this point of view. It certainly is true, however, that purchased information that is confirmable is desirable information. The case of the location of the civil-rights workers' bodies is a good example. The money was paid, and the bodies were then found. If the bodies had not been found, clearly no innocent person could have been convicted.

Unfortunately, in the United States the fact that we restrict payments for evidence or other information has led to the use of "stool pigeons" that in many ways is much worse. Under this system, various minor criminals are given a "license" to continue their minor criminal activities providing only that they inform police officers of the minor criminal activities of other people.[5] This system in many ways combines the worst of both worlds. The information obtained is paid for, and the method of payment protects some

5. See Jerome H. Skolnick, *Justice Without Trial* (New York: John Wiley & Sons, 1966), pp. 126–32.

people engaged in the commission of minor crimes. Switching to a system of direct monetary payments would be an improvement.

It must, however, be remembered that paying witnesses is a risky business because of the possibility of false testimony. This is, of course, a possibility in any court system, but particularly so if you pay witnesses. In general, a witness who has been paid for producing his evidence should be regarded as somewhat less reliable than a witness who has not been paid, and this testimony should not be given great weight unless it can be corroborated. In most cases, of course, the witness, if he is genuinely reporting a crime, will have some information that the police do not already have and can be checked after he has told the police. Corroboration, therefore, is normally not too difficult.

Still, this type of testimony is inferior to voluntary testimony. The reason for desiring that it be added to our present system is simply that it is more evidence. Our present witnesses would not be driven away, and we would obtain further witnesses. Furthermore, large payments to people who turn in their friends and colleagues make it very hard for criminal organizations to retain their internal coherence. Criminals, after all, are criminals, and they are as likely to commit "immoral" acts against their confederates as anyone else when there is much to be gained. Thus, the undermining of criminal morale and the cohesion of criminal organizations will be a secondary consequence of large payments for information. Once again, however, great care must be used in dealing with such evidence. We have here another place to use the polygraph.

Once the police have made up their minds as to who they think committed the crime and feel they have enough evidence to proceed, they then take the matter to an attorney. In England this attorney is usually a barrister who is hired by the police for the individual case. In the United States he is a permanent official of the government. It is probable that the English system leads to a somewhat more even match of the attorneys on the two sides. In cases where the police anticipate that the defense will be in the hands of an exceptionally competent attorney, they hire an exceptionally competent one themselves. On the other hand, in cases where they feel that the defense will be poorly handled, they don't waste their money on a first-rate man. In the United States, the district attorney is a relatively constant quantity, which means that a defendant who can afford first-class counsel will normally be better represented than the government, and the average defendant normally has a poorer attorney than the government. In any event, the attorney decides whether to continue with the case. There is little to be said about the decision to give the prosecutor this discretion. In the United States, we have another preliminary procedure—a grand jury or, in some states, a special judicial proceeding. Insofar as it has any rationale at all, it makes it difficult to persecute individuals by initiating prosecutions on obviously inadequate evidence. It probably, however, has very little effect on anything. Certainly we find no need of a similar process in the civil courts.

Turning to the court itself, we should begin by noting that the function of the court is largely to find out what happened at some time in the past. In *most* cases the legal situation is fairly straightforward. Smith did or did not shoot his wife. Once we know what happened, we have little or no difficulty in determining what the legal consequences of that act are. There will, of course, be cases in which we do not find the legal situation quite that simple, but these are decidedly the exceptional ones. Furthermore, in most cases under the criminal law, where there is a real question as to the law, it makes little difference. There are cases in which there is real doubt as to which of two legal rules applies, and consequently there are cases where at the time the act was committed it was uncertain what the law was. In consequence, although a decision as to the legal consequence of the act will have to be made, in terms of deterrence, it makes relatively little difference what that decision is. Anyone who gets himself in a situation in which the law is unclear is taking a risk, a risk proportional to the lack of clarity.

The fact that courts are predominantly engaged in finding out what happened in the past is obvious to any outside observer, but would not necessarily be obvious to anyone who studied Anglo-American law in law school. In these schools, almost no attention is paid to the problems of fact finding, that is, determining what really happened, and a vast amount of attention is given to a study of the minutiae of the law. The presumed reason for this phenomenon is that the proceedings of the courts are recorded in the words of the judges themselves. The judges normally state what they think happened and then discuss at some length its legal consequences. As a result of this method of teaching law the difficult problems of guessing what happened tend to be slurred over and are largely omitted from the training of legal personnel.

Training fact-finding organizations, the courts, in the procedures of application of the law with very little attention being given to the facts and technicalities of evidence seems odd. How we got into this is a problem of history that will not be discussed here. It does seem clear, however, that steps should be taken to remedy the situation. Judges should be given training in such things as fingerprint analysis and the scientific aspects of real evidence. In addition, if it is possible to tell whether a witness is lying by any method, the judges should be given training in this field. Of course, it may be that nothing much can be done about detecting lying. It is of some interest that Continental legal training does include some attention to the facts and does not deal entirely in the law as does ours. This may have something to do with the fact that Continental law is a great deal simpler than ours.

Turning to the trial process: there are three general methods of selecting the people who will determine the facts. In a number of cases in Anglo-Saxon countries, people are selected at random and instructed to make a unanimous decision as to the facts. In the cases in which this method is used, this decision is, in theory and, to a considerable extent, in practice, subject to no appeal. Appeals in the American system and, to a large extent, in the English system are, in theory, only possible on the legal consequences of the finding of facts or on the legal details of the proceedings of the courts. They do not deal with the factual matters determined by the jury.

The second basic procedure for selecting people to make decisions in court is to choose an individual. This method was the basic procedure in Roman law and, oddly enough, is the most common method in modern British and American law. As we have seen in criminal trials, judge trial is more common than jury trial. Minor cases are uniformly tried by single magistrates. Juvenile cases are also tried before one person as are all cases in equity. In the United States, those civil cases that are "law" cases are tried by a single judge if the parties decide to waive a jury. In England juries have been largely unavailable in civil cases since the beginning of the century. On the Continent, on the other hand, a great many cases are tried by a board of judges. As a general rule, these judges are legally trained individuals, although as we have noticed, Continental legal training involves a certain amount of schooling in interpreting facts. In some cases, however, certain laymen have been introduced into the court.

The appointment of a single official as a judge raises relatively few issues unless we contrast it with the board of judges. At first glance it might appear that the Continental system of having several judges at most trials is clearly superior to the old-fashioned Roman or modern American and British procedure of having only one. Surely the American court systems in which all appellate courts consist of more than one person could be evidenced as supporting this view. In general, in the United States, the higher the appellate court, the larger the number of judges sitting on it. All of this would seem to indicate that in judicial numbers there is strength.

The arguments for the use of a board of judges instead of a single judge are, however, by no means completely convincing. Resources are inherently limited. If we assume that the people who appoint judges are capable of selecting better judges over worse judges (and without that assumption we can hardly argue for the selection of judges at all), they should be able to obtain a better single judge than the average of five members of a board. It is not even that simple. Clearly we could afford to pay a single judge five times as much as we could afford to pay the average judge on a board of five. Perhaps we could pay even more because the board of five would probably spend more time on each case than would a single judge. Thus it should be possible to obtain very materially better personnel by using the single judge system rather than the board of judges. In practice we appear to feel that a single judge is suitable for the actual case but that for appeals we need a board. It is hard to say anything definite about the desirability of a single judge as opposed to a board of judges, but this would seem to be an empirical problem that could be solved by suitably designed experiments. Lacking such experiments, I simply note that there are these two different techniques and proceed to discuss other matters.

A somewhat similar issue is raised by the appeal process. As we have already noted, the most important decisions made by a court (the decisions as to fact) are, at least in theory, not appealable. The reason for not permitting an appeal of factual matters is simple tradition. However, a rationalization, and not a bad one, has developed. This rationalization is that the people at the trial see the witnesses and are able to judge to some extent whether they are telling the truth or not or whether they are reliable people. This, however, points to a peculiar characteristic of our appeal process. It is not a rerunning of the trial in an effort to use better personnel and reach a better conclusion. On the contrary, it is simply an examination of the record compiled at the trial, and as this rationalization I have just given indicates, this record is far from complete. There seems to be no reason why a judge might not be just as readily mistaken in his judgment of a witness's veracity as in his judgment of other matters. Prohibiting any rectification of such errors on appeal is hard to understand.

Another argument for permitting an appeal on the law is that it is thought desirable to have a law that is uniform within a particular jurisdiction. This argument will be dealt with at some length later. At this point, we will only say that uniformity should mean that equals are treated equally. Inequality can come as easily from a misapprehension of the fact as from a misapprehension of the law. Furthermore, uniformity is not an infinite good, and we should not be willing to pay an infinite price for it.

Before proceeding with the discussion of uniformity, let us first consider the appeal process in itself. As we have already noticed, in Anglo-Saxon law, a good deal of the work in any court is not subject to appeal. The findings of the jury, the chancellor, or the judge is supposed to be final on a great many matters. Other court systems have permitted no appeal at all, the most notable of which is the Mohammedan system that seems to have worked well over a long period of time depending upon summary proceedings with a total absence of appeal. When the Communists seized power in Russia, they actually set up a court system that was in many ways copied from the Mohammedan system. As a general rule, the arbitration courts that have been voluntarily established to deal with contract problems also function without appeal. It is thus by no means obvious that an appeal system is desirable.

What then are the arguments for providing appeal? The first and most naïve is that the court of the first instance may make errors and that it is desirable to have someone to correct them. The problem with this argument is that the appellate court may also make errors and therefore, if the initial court has reached a correct decision, the decision by the higher court overruling it may put the law in a worse situation than it would have been had the original decision been left unappealed. In order for the higher courts with appellate authority to have an effect of reducing the number of errors in the law, there must be some reason to believe that they themselves make fewer errors than the lower court whose decision they reconsider. In general, appellate courts are somewhat more highly paid and somewhat more carefully selected than the lower courts. Furthermore, in the United States, at any event, the lower court is usually one man and the upper court is usually a board that may, or then again may not, give the upper court the advantage.

Still, it is by no means obvious that the higher courts will indeed make fewer errors than the lower courts, particularly when the higher courts are denied access to certain information, such as the appearance of the witnesses. We can, however, assume for the sake of argument that in a well-organized appellate court system the higher court would make fewer errors on the law than the lower court, and therefore the possibility of appeal to the higher court would lead to fewer errors. Immediately two questions are raised. Who appeals, and why not simply make the entire court system as accurate as the appeal court? Taking these questions in reverse order: if all cases are appealed, then it would require as many (or perhaps more) judges in the appellate courts as in the trial courts. Thus, abolishing the findings of the trial court judges and letting the supposedly superior judges of the appellate courts sit on the original trial of the case would seem to be a good idea. This logic seems invulnerable as long as we assume that all cases may be appealed. When we realize that for one reason or another only a rather small number of cases are actually appealed, we see the possibility of improving court functioning by using the appellate system.

The first obvious reason for only a few cases being appealed is that in a great many criminal cases the defendant is represented by a public defender who seldom takes appeals. In many other cases, the financial resources of the defendant are limited, and he cannot appeal. Similarly, in civil cases the amount in question may be small enough so that an appeal is not sensible. Although there are some restrictions on the right of appeal, it does seem that financial resources are really the basic reason why some cases are appealed and others are not. The lawyers, of course, also take into account the likelihood of winning, but this is something of a gamble in any case, and there certainly will be considerable delay on appeal that normally benefits whichever side has lost the first round. Thus, in a sense, the appeal process permits the more important members of the community to have two or even three goes at their cases, whereas the less influential individuals are only given one. It may well be that this is an excellent idea in terms of limiting social tension. It may also be that the cases that are appealed are the most important and, therefore, the ones in which correct decisions are most important.

There are, however, less naïve explanations for the appeal process. The first of these would be that it provides a desirable discipline on the trial judge. The knowledge that he may have his decision reversed and have his superiors make public statements that he is not quite bright surely will put pressure on him to be careful. In this respect it is unfortunate that a similar pressure is not put on him to be careful about the facts. The Swedes go further and permit disappointed litigants to sue the judge, alleging he has brought in a wrong decision. It should be noted that the judge, in general, will be able to guess fairly accurately which cases are to be appealed and which are not. He need pay little attention to the prospects of appeal if the defense is by a public defender. Similarly, if it is a civil suit and the amount involved is small, he can safely assume that there will be no appeal. Still it would not be wise to rule this particular factor out. It may work a small improvement in the behavior of the trial courts, but it is an improvement.

The second non-naïve argument for the use of appellate courts is the maintenance of the uniformity in the law. People offering this argument will say that they do not wish the law to vary from judicial district to judicial district. This naturally brings up the whole question of the uniformity of law. Most people seem to be convinced that the law ought to be uniform, but the reasons given for this preference are not terribly convincing. It is not necessary, for example, that the law be uniform in order to be predictable. We could have a highly nonuniform law that was nevertheless extremely predictable. It could, for example, provide that your punishment in the event that you committed murder depended on the first letter in your last name. This would be nonuniform but highly predictable.

The genuine arguments for uniformity are twofold. First, it makes it easier for individuals to "know" the law if the law is the same over a large number of cases; and second, if we believe that the law represents some desirable standard, presumably the best standard is the same everywhere. Elaborating upon the first argument, I can devote less time to learning the law if it is the same in Athens as in Chicago. In those cases in which I might be concerned with the law in Athens, I could simply apply my knowledge of the law in the United States. As Bruno Leoni has pointed out, this line of argument would also indicate that it is desirable that the law be uniform over time, i.e., that it not be changed, or be changed very slowly. The need for people who move from one area to another to learn new law is paralleled by the need to learn new law if the law is changed. Most people, however, will not accept uniformity as having an absolute value. They are in favor of the law being fairly simple and fairly easy to understand, but they do not feel it is an infringement on their rights that Greece has a different law from their state or, for that matter, that their state has a different law from the next state. Similarly, they do not object terribly to changes in the law. Still it must be admitted that the argument does have some validity. The wider the range in time and space of any given law, the less resources need be invested in relearning the law.

The second argument, that the law is an ideal standard, and that that standard should be the same everywhere, is basically an ethical one. It is, of course, true that if we had some reason to believe that our law of contracts was the best of all possible laws, then we would be doing other people a favor by forcing it down their throats. But in practice most differences between law codes do not involve a clear-cut superiority on one side. There is, in fact, an excellent reason for not having uniformity if we are really interested in working toward a good legal system. Empirical investigation will be necessary to produce an ideal legal system. Clearly this will involve the use of the experimental method. For this purpose we must establish some method by which a proposed change in the law can be compared with other or older provisions of the law. The method, of course, is simple and well established in science—it is the method of controls. Thus, if Texas changes its law of burglary and Illinois does not, and we observe the two states in action through a period of fifteen to twenty years, we should be able to obtain at least some idea of the effects of the new law. It would be even better if we arranged a formal experiment. Kalven, Zeisel, and Buchholz recommend this very highly.[6]

It will be noted that the arguments for an appeal system are not overwhelmingly strong. Our present appellate system is supported more from custom than from careful thought. The implicit assumption that the higher courts correct the errors of the lower courts and commit no errors of their own may also be involved. If we are to have appeal, however, it would appear desirable that the lower courts be unable to predict in advance what aspect of their behavior will be examined and which case will be appealed. A possible procedure would be to arrange for a random sample of cases to be automatically surveyed with great care by a superior court. This should fulfill most of the duties of the appellate system and could do so in a much more efficient manner.

This suggestion may seem extremely radical, but in practice it is not too different from the military court system. In this system all convictions by court martial are automatically reviewed in Washington. This is a very old and traditional system that has recently been supplemented by a more conventional appellate court system.

The appeal court system, particularly since the foundation of the United States and the development by our court system of the modern version of *stare decisis*, has not only served to review trials but has actually created new law. It frequently happens that some matter comes up that is not clearly and obviously covered by the law. The court is forced to make a decision, and the tradition at the moment is that, if it is a higher court, this decision is regarded as the law for all future similar cases. It is not exactly obvious why this should be the custom. It was not so in the original common law or in the jurisconsult law of Rome, which so closely resembles the common law. In both of these systems, a judicial decision, although final for a given case, was not regarded as binding on future cases until much the same case had come up several times and had been considered by several different authorities. The rigid rule of the single precedent seems to have come out of the practice of the

6. See Harry Kalven, Jr., Hans Zeisel, and Bernard Buchholz, *Delay in Court* (Boston: Little, Brown and Company, 1959), pp. 241–50.

American Supreme Court in its early years and does not seem to have been carefully thought out.

It should be noted that the filling in of the gaps in the law by court decisions does not necessarily reduce the uncertainty of the law. Each little piece of patchwork may simply move the zone of uncertainty a little bit without reducing its size. In any event, it is impossible to make the law fit all possible future cases, and we should not attempt to do so. The Continental system, with a fairly brief law code and the courts not absolutely bound to follow previous decisions in every case, provides a simple system and does not seem to have any other great disadvantage. If we assume, as all of the arguments for judge-made law must assume, that the legislature will not keep the law up to date, then we must also accept something like the common law. There is, however, no reason why individual courts trying individual cases should be the authority that supplements the inadequate legislature. The French administrative court that produces an authoritative interpretation of the law in general terms rather than with respect to individual cases does as well. Thus, we could have the law itself and a gloss on it made by a selected group of judges. It would not be necessary to wade through thousands and thousands of judicial decisions in order to determine the rights of a party to a dispute.

We now turn to the situation that arises after the courts have reached a final decision. If the matter is a civil suit, most people would agree that the court should proceed to enforce its decision. It should seize the property of the defendant, if it is decided that the defendant owes money to the plaintiff and does not make the payment, or in some cases it may put him in prison. Admittedly, the enforcement of the decision will work considerable inconvenience on the person against whom the decision is made, and some of the decisions will be wrong. Nevertheless, we must accept the fact that the courts are sometimes wrong, and the unfortunate man who is wrongfully compelled to pay $50,000, perhaps losing his house and business, is indeed unfortunate, and nothing can be done about it.

If, however, the defendant is found guilty on a criminal charge, we customarily turn to some other procedure to deal with him. It is true that if the defendant is to be fined, we treat him like the defendant in a civil suit who has lost, and similar procedures are undertaken to collect the money. In most cases, however, the defendant in a criminal case either is indigent and cannot pay the fine or is not given the alternative of a fine but is subject to other penalties. It is these other penalties, in particular imprisonment, to which we now turn. A reading of the literature on penology will quickly convince any student that he is dealing with one of the most confused areas in modern thought. Exactly why this should be so, I do not know; but in fact it is so.

In general, a discussion of penology is conducted as a sort of debate between two schools of thought that I shall call the "curative" and "punitive" schools. As a matter of fact, this debate is about little, since one normally finds that the two parties to the debate are in general (although not detailed) agreement about many practical matters, and their basic philosophical positions are not logically inconsistent. It is possible to apply both curative and punitive measures simultaneously. Normally, the people who argue for a curative type of approach to prisoners are strongly in favor of various forms of education and vocational training for prisoners, and frequently are also in favor of psychiatric treatment for them. One will also normally find, however, that they feel (even though they don't say very much about it) that more serious crimes should be followed by longer imprisonments than less serious crimes, and that discipline in the prison can best be kept by the imposition of punishments for violations.

The advocates of punishment, on the other hand, will normally talk a great deal about the need to make prison life a true punishment and are sometimes (in England) in favor of flogging. Normally, however, they also favor the prisoners being put to work while in prison. I have never run into one who feels that those prisoners who are in need of psychiatric attention should not receive it. Thus, the difference between these two "schools of thought" is largely a matter of verbiage and emphasis.[7] Unfortunately, much of the work in penology is, as I have mentioned, a debate between these two quite consistent positions.

My position is that potential criminals should not anticipate a positive present discounted value from the acts of the crime that they are contemplating. This would mean that a criminal faces a possibility of suffering some amount of unpleasantness, which, suitably discounted, is greater than the benefit obtained from the crime. Since, however, we normally imprison people for this purpose, it seems only sensible that they be occupied at something, and there

7. Richard Wagner, on reading the original draft of this book, pointed out that the two approaches lead to a different procedure for varying lengths of sentence. The advocates of punishment, if they were consistent, would have the period of time spent in prison a simple function of the crimes committed by the criminal. The curative people, on the other hand, would want it to be the function of "response to treatment." Logically, I cannot disagree with Wagner, but my reading of the literature indicates that the advocates of the two sides are not as logical as he.

surely is no reason why they should not be occupied at learning a useful occupation. If there were some danger, and in practice there is not, that the learning of a useful trade in prison might be a positive incentive to commit crimes, then this could be offset by appropriately increasing the length of the prison sentence or the unpleasantness of the prison.

The present-day prisons are unpleasant places to live (some more unpleasant than others) which offer very little in the way of training or treatment to their inmates. In some institutions for juveniles, this is not necessarily true, but in general it applies to almost all prisons. Whether it is possible to convert prisons into educational or curative institutions is a question to which I have very little to contribute. The difficulties are immense. Thus far, what controlled experiments have been made have been mostly unsuccessful. It is probable that if our prisons have any desirable effect on their inmates, it is solely because they are unpleasant, and people having once been in them do not wish to be sent back. It seems likely that the major educational effect is counterproductive. The individual is thrown into an environment in which his most important social contacts are with fellow prisoners. Among these fellow prisoners the major criminals seem to have a dominant role. Thus, the major real educational effect of our present-day prisons may well be the training of the individual in improved techniques of crime and equipping him with a network of connections that can later be used in a life of crime. Clearly, changing prisons from educational institutions of this sort is highly desirable. Nor do I think this is beyond the ingenuity of man.

CHAPTER 11

THEFT AND ROBBERY[1]

Perhaps the easiest way to make a living, and certainly one of the oldest, is to take another's property. I might take your money, not for my material gain but because the thought of your starving filled me with joy. In this case, the motive would be the inflicting of injury on the person robbed, and we shall leave its discussion to Chapter 13 and concentrate in this chapter on those cases in which the motive for taking another's property is material gain.

The system of private property (or state property, in a Communist system) requires that property be kept in the hands of its owner (which may, of course, be the state). This is so obvious that it is often said that even professional thieves would favor laws against thievery. This protection could theoretically be provided by the owners, but this is an extremely inefficient system.[2] Each individual would have to devote a considerable amount of his time and energy to standing guard over his possessions. In addition, the weaker members of the population could not guard their possessions even if they tried. Note that you could not hire protection without at least some rudimentary capacity of self-defense, because the people capable of being guards could help themselves to your property without the tedium of standing guard. This line of reasoning is so obvious that it might be thought that no one could possibly doubt it, but the anarchists do.

Turning once again to our high school algebra, Equation (11.1), the symbols for which are presented in Table 11.1, shows the payoff obtained from the various possible institutions for dealing with theft.

$$P = L_s[D_t(1 - L_d) - L_d(C_c + L_cP_u) - C_o] - P_c - I_c - L_{fc}P_u - C_rC_t - P_r \quad (11.1)$$

Once again it is an extremely complex-looking equation that has relatively little in the way of mathematical content. For any given level of enforcement of laws against theft—and this level may be zero—the individual will have a particular likelihood of committing that particular crime. This is shown by the L_s. The area within the square brackets is the payoff to be expected from

1. See Gary Becker, "Crime and Punishment: An Economic Approach," *Journal of Political Economy* 76 (March–April 1968): 167, for an essentially similar treatment of the problem.

2. See my "The Welfare Costs of Tariffs, Monopoly, and Theft," *Western Economic Journal* 5, No. 3 (June 1967): 234.

TABLE OF SYMBOLS 11.1

C_c = Court cost
C_o = Conscience cost
C_r = Crime rate, likelihood individual will be victim of crime
C_t = Cost of being victim of crime
D_t = Direct profit of crime
I_c = Cost to individual of investigation of crimes that he did not commit
L_c = Likelihood of conviction
L_d = Likelihood of detection
L_{fc} = Likelihood individual will be falsely convicted for crime he did not commit
L_s = Likelihood individual will commit crime
P = Payoff (may be negative)
P_c = Cost of maintaining police, prisons, and courts
P_r = Private cost of protection against theft. Includes nonproduction
P_u = Punishment
R = Risk aversion factor

---

such a crime. It consists of the profit to be made from the undetected crime less the likelihood of the crime's being detected together with the penalty that results from being detected. Note that if you are detected some type of legal costs will certainly fall upon you (assuming, of course, that we have a law against the crime), but being sent to prison is a matter of probability rather than certainty. Finally, there is a cost of conscience for the person who feels that theft is wrong.

A number of additional costs then are associated with the existence of theft and measures to combat them are shown in the factors that follow the square bracket. Note that the payoff from the institution of theft is a negative number; i.e., the average individual would prefer that the institution not exist. Note also that if we do not have laws against theft, a good part of Equation (11.1) vanishes, and we get Equation (11.2), which is almost certain to be a much larger negative number than is Equation (11.1). Thus, the individual is likely to feel that laws against theft are desirable, and the problem is, in essence, optimizing Equation (11.1) rather than making up one's mind between Equation (11.1) and Equation (11.2).

$$P = L_s D_t + L_s C_o - P_r - C_r C_t \qquad (11.2)$$

I must, however, digress about the cost of conscience in the equation. My real reason for putting it in is to simplify the presentation in the last chapter of this book, my return to ethics. A full discussion of the matter is deferred until then. We should, however, note that people do in fact have such conscience costs that affect their behavior. It should, perhaps, be noted also that the person who has the strongest conscience is most inhibited from stealing and, therefore, is disadvantaged by the institution. This is particularly true if there is no (or very weak) legal protection against the crime. A man who had a very strong aversion to committing theft would be under a disastrous disadvantage if he lived in a society described by Equation (11.2). But I must leave further discussion of the conscience problem until later. For the present I should like to have the reader consider conscience as existing but not being a major part of our main chain of reasoning at this stage. He can perhaps consider that he is dealing with Justice Holmes' "wicked man," who had no conscience problems at all, and for whom C_o would be zero.[3]

In passing, we may note that a great many people apparently assume that for themselves C_o has such a high value that they would never commit a crime. This may be true, or then again it may not. For a person who feels this way, however, the principal effects of the institution of theft are costs with no gain anywhere. The individual who is never going to commit a crime himself may be the victim of a crime, may find himself unjustly imprisoned as a result of a false charge of crime, and certainly will end up paying taxes to support the police and court apparatus. He is likely to be interested in reducing these three factors and perhaps in making trade-offs among them. A very large part of the public discussion of crime is confined to these three areas. This probably reflects the opinion of most of the people involved in the discussion that, for them, the possibility of their committing a crime is zero.

Putting the problem in its most general form, however, and assuming that we do have some institutions for the repression of theft and robbery, then an individual considering whether or not to commit such a crime would make his decision on the basis of Inequality (11.3).

$$D_t(1 - L_d) > R \cdot L_d(C_c + L_c P_u) + C_o - I_c - L_{fc} P_u \qquad (11.3)$$

The profits of the crime, together with the probability that it will go undetected, are on the left side of the inequality figure, and the costs, together with a risk aversion figure, are on the right. Note that costs are opportunity

3. Oliver Wendell Holmes, *The Common Law* (London: Macmillan & Company, 1881).

costs. If he does not commit a crime, there is some finite possibility that he will nevertheless be sent to prison for it and some finite possibility that he will be inconvenienced by the investigation. These factors therefore should be off-set against the costs of the crime. For most of my readers, these items are small, but in some slum neighborhoods exists a significant probability of people being unjustly convicted of a crime. For people in this environment, it is likely that the cost of crime is lower than for the intellectuals reading this book.

Inequality (11.3) is roughly approximated by Equation (11.4).

$$\frac{D_t(1 - L_d)}{R} = L_d \cdot L_c \cdot P_u \tag{11.4}$$

Equation (11.4) might be said to be (roughly speaking) the social control equation. If we can increase any of the terms on the right, we can reduce the crime rate. All of these factors are under control of the government.

$$L_c = {}_f(C_c \cdot I_c) \tag{11.5}$$

Equation (11.5) indicates that L_c, the likelihood of conviction, is a positive function of court costs and, in a much more minor way, the cost to individuals of being involved in an investigation of crimes that they did not commit. The appearance of I_c here simply indicates that, in general, if we increase our prevention and police activity, we are likely to inconvenience innocent bystanders. It is, of course, a very minor cost. It should be noted that in Equation (11.6) the likelihood of false conviction is a negative function of the same two factors.

$$L_{fc} = {}_{-f}(C_c \cdot I_c) \tag{11.6}$$

Increased investments in police, courts, and the bothering of witnesses will both increase the number of criminals who are convicted and reduce the number of innocent persons who are unjustly convicted.

Equation (11.7) indicates that the likelihood of initial detection of the criminal is once again the result of police costs and the bothering of individual persons who are not directly involved in the crime.

$$L_d = {}_f(P_c \cdot I_c) \tag{11.7}$$

It will be noted that we can lower the crime rate by increasing either L_d, L_c, or P_u. In Equation (11.8) a number of things that could be expected to deter criminals are collected on the right side.

$$C_r = -f[(L_c - L_{fc}), (C_c - I_c), L_d \cdot L_c P_u, C_o] \tag{11.8}$$

Note that the improved detection of criminals permits a reduction in punishment without increasing the crime rate. If we can raise either the rate of detection or the rate of conviction, this permits us to reduce the sentence we give to the convicted criminal while obtaining the same "deterrence."

As a general rule, people who are in favor of "tougher" police and court procedures are also in favor of longer sentences. On the other hand, the people who favor giving criminals shorter sentences are also normally great enthusiasts for various procedural techniques that make it less likely that conviction will be obtained. Although there is no direct logical contradiction in either of these positions (we might have either too heavy or too light a net $L_d \cdot L_c \cdot P_u$ in our society), it would seem more sensible to favor either a tougher court procedure with lighter sentences or more safeguards in the court procedure with heavier sentences.

Before we discuss the institutions that will give the best payoff for Equation (11.1), let us examine the range of institutional structures that might be established with respect to theft. Under the common law, two quite different procedures were available. Firstly, as part of the law of torts, the individual whose property had been stolen could proceed against the thief in a civil suit. If he was successful, he could either get his property back or force the thief to pay him its value as assessed by the court. This particular approach to thievery is not used much in practice. In fact, suits in conversion or for return of property normally do not involve anything that we would recognize as theft.[4] The reason, of course, is that cases of genuine theft normally lead to criminal prosecutions. Nevertheless, the law is clear, if someone steals my car, I can sue him in conversion and make him pay me for it.

Even though civil suits play almost no role in the present day, let us consider them at some length. Suppose that the standard remedy for theft were a suit for the return of the stolen property, and, for simplicity, let us assume that in such cases the police and courts never make mistakes. If you steal my car, there is no chance of the police failing to catch you or of the court deciding that

4. They sometimes involve embezzlement.

it was your car in the first place. This procedure would make the stealing of cars useless as a business, for you obviously couldn't sell something you were going to have to return, but you could go through life using other people's cars.[5] You steal my car, and while the suit is pending you drive it. When you have to return it, you simply steal somebody else's, and so on.

The remedy for this state of affairs is simple enough: make the thief pay a fair rent for the period in which he held the property plus, probably, a few dollars for the inconvenience to which he put the true owner by taking the car without permission. This would, I think, be a most superior state of the law. It would mean that no one would ever take anyone else's property, except in emergencies. If, however, I had a very great need of a car immediately, I could simply take any that I saw, subject to later payment. I would, of course, run the risk that the owner would also need the car for emergency purposes, in which case the payment for his inconvenience might be extremely high.[6] On the whole, however, this system would give a high degree of flexibility to the property system in times of emergency. It is indeed unfortunate that we cannot use it.

The problem, of course, is that we may not know who has stolen the car. Private suits would require that the thieves be identified. Today we depend upon the police to find the person who stole our property, and the thief is then prosecuted. Let us divide these two steps and assume that the police still locate the thief, but that once he is located the owner also sues. It would seem reasonable in this case that the police also sue for their expenses in hunting down the thief. Thus a citizen who took a car in an emergency could promptly inform the police and limit his liability, while the man attempting to make a career of crime would try to keep his theft a secret and pay more if he was caught. Let us retain our assumption that the courts make no mistakes, and, therefore, there is no prospect of a miscarriage of justice. If the accused took the car, the court will so rule; and if he did not, he will be given a judgment accordingly.

If the police caught the thief every time, then there is no obvious reason why this system would not work reasonably well. Under those circumstances, thieves might be largely paupers who could not pay damage judgments, but let us put off a discussion of this problem until later. The police, however, will not catch every thief. Consider, for example, the situation if

5. If sale at an assessed value was the remedy rather than return, the assessed value would then almost certainly be high enough so that there would be no profit.

6. Assuming, of course, that there is no other car about for him to take.

they caught every other thief.[7] Suppose that the average car is worth $2,000 and that the police normally expend $500 in investigating each missing car. If I steal twenty cars a year, I will have to return ten of them and pay the police "finding fees" of $5,000, but I will net $15,000 for relatively little effort. Clearly, this would be an excellent career for an ambitious young man. Unfortunately, as in all businesses where the profits are supernormal, competition would be attracted. Shortly there would be so many thieves that ownership of a car would become almost an empty form. It probably would even become impossible for the thieves to sell their loot at reasonable prices.[8]

Suppose, however, that the rate of police successes is taken into account, and the man whose car has been stolen is given the right to sue for twice its value in damages. The average thief would then lose $500 (police fees) for each pair of cars he steals. Clearly, this would not be profitable. Car owners who were not thieves would face a fifty-fifty chance of double or nothing in the event that their cars were stolen. Presumably, insurance companies would be willing to sell them "insurance" under which the car owners would be compensated whenever their cars were stolen, but would surrender the right to recover from the thief to the insurance company. Although this system would work out all right for the police, the insurance company, and the car owner, it would not necessarily be "fair" to the thief.[9] Different thieves would have different degrees of skill. There would be newcomers to the business who were caught practically every time, and highly skilled craftsmen who were caught only once every twenty or so times. The first group would pay a disproportionate part of the damage suits. Our objective in setting up this system, however, is not to enforce some sort of implied contract between the thief and his victims but to protect people against having their cars stolen.

Looked at from this point of view, the system would surely reduce the

7. No existing police force even approximates such a favorable performance.

8. It was mentioned earlier that even thieves would favor laws against theft. Here, they would favor strengthening the law.

9. Not necessarily to the police. Placing the cost of the police services on the thief who is caught has some rather complicated implications. The more thieves that are caught, the larger the police budget, and hence the less likely you are to get away with stealing a car. A fall off in thievery, however, would lead to a decline in the takings of the police and hence to a cut in the police budget. This would then make stealing safer and lead to an increase. The problem is similar to the carnivore problem in population ecology.

number of cars stolen and would probably weed out all but the most skillful of thieves. It would, however, permit a good deal of thievery by skilled and intelligent criminals. With this change in the ability of the average thief, the effectiveness of the police might well fall. Perhaps they would only catch the thief in every fourth robbery.[10] An obvious remedy for this situation would be to raise the possible damages to four times the cost of the car. This, in turn, would surely force more criminals, the moderately skilled ones, to seek another line of endeavor. The process could be continued. Presumably, there is some ratio, say damages of $200,000 per car stolen, at which no one, no matter how skilled and lucky, would be interested in stealing cars.

Would we really want to put a damage claim for $200,000 on the man caught stealing a car, particularly since the person might be caught while stealing his first car? Most readers will probably think this is a silly problem; they may have felt that our whole discussion of damage claims as a way of preventing theft is simply foolish. In fact, we are considering issues fundamental to the theory of crime, but in a radically different context from that normally used. The "change of scene" will, I hope, improve our understanding of these issues. Another, obviously correct, objection to the question that begins this paragraph is that it is based upon other premises than those outlined in the first two chapters. Although this is true, let me at least ask the question.

Let us make just one change in the radically simplified model of the last few pages. A large number of real-life criminals are insolvent and could not pay damage claims. Furthermore, if the result of being caught stealing a car were merely a damage claim, then it would be sensible for car thieves to plan to be perpetually poor in capital goods, like merchants who continuously skirt bankruptcy. They might have large incomes, but they would have no property. They would live in expensive furnished apartments and drive rented Cadillacs. Although they would be able to continue in their profession, they would be driven into bankruptcy periodically by large damage judgments that they could not pay. Thus it would be impossible to compensate the owners of stolen cars out of collections in damage suits; the owners must buy insurance or take precautions against theft. The damage mechanism also had a second effect. It made the business of car stealing an unprofitable one, and hence one that did not attract many entrepreneurs. The fact that many criminals are insolvent, and all of them can become insolvent if they wish, makes it impossible

10. This is, in fact, the rate maintained by the very efficient London police force for all crimes. (C. B. Norton, "Letter to the Editor," *London Times*, 20 August 1963, p. 9.)

to pay owners of stolen cars out of the receipts from damage suits. Can we nevertheless impose costs on the criminals so that car stealing is not a suitable way of making a living?

All known societies have answered this question "yes" and have had methods of imposing costs on the thief. These costs cannot, by the very nature of the problem, take the form of monetary collections.[11] They involve, therefore, the direct infliction of costs upon the thief, whether in the form of branding, ear clipping, hanging, or imprisonment. Thus, the individual thinking of taking up theft as an occupation must weigh the profits against the likelihood that, say, for every tenth car he steals he will be caught and sentenced to five years in prison. Our discussion of the amount of damages, thus, becomes relevant. As Equation (11.3) showed, the "cost" to be imposed is a function of the efficiency of the enforcement mechanism. If anyone stealing a car could be immediately caught, the most minor punishment would be sufficient—a $5 fine, for example. If police only caught every other thief, then a punishment equivalent to a fine of about $4,000 would be necessary.

Similarly, the differential skills of the thieves would mean that a level of punishment that would keep the incompetent out of the business would still leave it a good racket for the well-trained specialist. The highly skilled criminals who operate the "gangs" of our large cities apparently feel more than amply compensated for their occasional prison sentences. Although we do not have much data on which to make a judgment, they are probably right.

Again, as in the damage suit case, raising the cost of getting caught would, presumably, eventually make even the most skilled operators move out of the business. But here the question of how much of a punishment we wish to impose, raised in connection with the damage suits, becomes relevant. Most people do not believe in death sentences for automobile theft.[12]

Looking at the matter rationally, the crime rate is a function of a number of things, among which the likelihood of getting caught and the likely punishment are important. If we hold the likelihood of getting caught constant, then the crime rate will decline as the punishment goes up. A one in ten

11. Although this is frequently provided as an alternative in the event the thief can pay the fine.

12. The Communists, of course, do sentence people to death who have stolen or embezzled property, or sometimes people who have merely "speculated." Since they announce such executions in the newspapers, it must be assumed that they are proud of them, and that, therefore, at least some people follow the line of reasoning we have outlined to its ultimate, rational conclusion.

chance of getting a slap on the wrist is quite a different thing from a one in ten chance of being executed. There can be no doubt that the Communists are correct in their belief that death penalties for economic crimes will deter them. If the punishment is to serve this purpose, however, it must be known to the potential criminal, which means that you must give it publicity. It might, in fact, be sensible to exaggerate its unpleasantness. Thus, when a new prison is put up, the authorities might well make statements to the press to the effect that it would be an awful place in which to be confined, instead of pointing out its "humane" features.

In law school I learned that judges and juries were reluctant to impose severe penalties, which meant that raising the punishment for a given crime automatically lowered the likelihood of the criminal's being punished at all. Thus, for example, the "four-time loser" laws, which provide life imprisonment on the fourth conviction for a felony, amount to giving three-time losers a license to commit petty crimes. Juries, my professor said, will not send a man to prison for life on a minor charge. The odds of conviction are, in this view, a declining function of the punishment imposed. Since a one in four chance of a year in prison may be a better deterrent than a one in one hundred chance of a ten-year term, the milder punishment may work better than the more severe one. The problem would appear to be largely one of control over the courts. If the courts can be organized in such a way that they carry out the law as it is given to them, this problem would not arise. If, on the other hand, the courts followed their own ethical system instead of the law, or mixed the two together, then this fact must be taken into account when drawing up the basic law.

We have, however, tried to keep ethics out of the discussion insofar as possible. Let us, therefore, assume that the courts will carry out the law as it is given to them and will not impose their own personal ethical system upon it. This permits us to ignore the effect of the severity of the punishment on the likelihood of conviction. We can simply select a suitable punishment in view of a given likelihood of the criminal's being caught. The situation in which the punishment also affects the likelihood of conviction is more complicated and will normally not permit as satisfactory a solution, but in the real world we may be in this suboptimal situation. For the purposes of our study, this complication will be ignored.

Is there, then, any rational reason why we should not follow the Communists' example and impose the death penalty for minor crimes? Surely this would reduce the crime rate. For the rational man, it would appear to be all gain with no loss. He would himself make rational calculations and, hence, never commit a crime for which the discounted value of the punishment exceeded the probable profit. The system would give him the maximum protection from crimes committed by others, since the deterrent effect would surely reduce the crime rate even if the criminals weren't highly rational. The only offset would appear to be the possibility of erroneous conviction. Since the courts are clearly not always right, each individual will always have the possibility of being convicted of a crime that he did not commit. Such things are unpredictable, and no one can really protect himself. The raising of the penalty on a crime is, thus, a straightforward increase in the cost of an erroneous conviction. Surely this is a factor that should be taken into account, although the weight it is given will depend upon the efficiency of the courts and the police. In well-functioning systems it should, I imagine, be a very minor item in determining punishments. In situations where false convictions are fairly frequent, on the other hand, it could be a major factor.

The problem can be dealt with a little more rigorously, although it is by no means sure what actual explanation is dominant. Presumably as the punishment for a given criminal act is increased, the likelihood that anyone will commit that crime declines. Normally, however, there will be at least some occasions on which the crime would be committed in spite of high penalties, because there would be some opportunities to commit the crime under circumstances when detection seemed extremely unlikely. In general, one would anticipate, however, that the number of crimes committed would decline as the severity of punishment increased. If we assume the opportunity for committing crimes with different probabilities of detection is distributed normally, however, the "payoff" in terms of reduction in number of crimes as the penalty was increased would steadily decline. Further, individuals might regard this as a declining return investment in terms of utility, as well as in terms of technology. Under the circumstances, the marginal return to the individual from an increase in the penalty rate on some crime would be a declining function.

The cost to an individual of raising the punishment rate would mainly take the form of the possibility of his being unjustly convicted under the new punishment scale. Presumably, as the punishment is increased and the total number of crimes committed is reduced, the likelihood of incorrect convictions also goes down proportionately. Thus, an increase in the penalty which reduced the total number of crimes might leave the objectively calculated present discounted cost of possible unjust conviction not much changed. If, however, people have an aversion to risk which increases as the size of the risk goes up (which seems likely), they would face an increasing marginal cost on this side of the balance sheet. Thus, the marginal benefits from increasing the weight of the sentences is subject to declining marginal returns, and the cost is subject to increasing marginal weight. Under the circumstances, the optimal punishment would not be infinite and might be fairly low.

But how about the "natural sympathies" of Adam Smith? Certainly the man who gives money to orphanages on Christmas may feel that he should be equally charitable to convicted criminals. The decision that a robber should be given four years instead of five years may be taken on exactly the same set of motives as the decision to make a gift to the American Cancer Society. Since this involves preferences, we cannot in our present state of knowledge make any judgment upon it. Presumably, there is some sort of exchange between security from theft and the pleasures obtained from not making the punishment for thieves heavy, but we have no idea of the ratio. Furthermore, it seems likely that it varies greatly from individual to individual. Thus, all we can say at this point is that people are likely to be at least a little charitable to convicted criminals. If we had exact statistics on the effect of changes in the extent of punishment upon the crime rate, the individual's judgment would no doubt be more informed than it is now, but there is no reason to believe that it would be identical from man to man. Under the circumstances, we can only regard the charitable motive as, to some extent, offsetting the purely practical considerations.

Our present law distinguishes between theft and robbery, the latter being marked by force or the threat of force in removing the property, whereas the former normally involves stealthy removal. For our present purposes we can ignore this distinction. Everything we have said about theft would also apply to robbery. In addition, although robbery is normally thought to be worse than theft, particularly if there is actual violence, this is essentially a moral judgment that we need not follow. Robbery with violence, in fact, is likely to be easier for the police to handle, since the victims normally have seen the robber. With the resulting higher conviction rate, a somewhat lower penalty would be sufficient to deter robbery as a profession.

This contention, that robbery should (if anything) be punished less severely than theft, will strike most readers (and certainly most police officers) as extreme. Uniformly the use of violence in a crime is penalized heavily. Similar crimes without violence are punished more lightly. It seems to me that this may be a mistake. Acts of violence that occur as by-products of an effort to obtain someone else's property can be prevented if you make the obtaining of the other person's property in and of itself an activity that has a negative present discounted value. The only murder trial that I ever attended concerned a murder in which the victim had been killed for $5. I once shocked a group of intellectuals, all of whom generally believed in much lighter punishment of criminals than I did, by suggesting that if in the jurisdiction in which it was committed, thefts of $5 were detected approximately one time out of five, a suitable penalty for committing such a crime would be $27 or $28. The discounted value of the punishment would have exceeded the potential gain.

The concentration of police resources on violent crimes, and the severe sentences on criminals who commit such crimes, may be taken as an attempt to change the type of crime committed. But surely this is not a very high priority social goal. In a sense, our present behavior in this field, as in so much of the law, is simply a hangover from the Middle Ages. We have not carefully thought the matter through and, therefore, do not realize that we can prevent the use of certain production methods by preventing the production.

Let us now, however, turn to the question of the court that should try cases in this area by considering courts trying any kind of criminal case, since the analysis will be identical for any other crime. In our current mythology, it is always said that the court system should be biased against conviction; i.e., instead of attempting to convict when the evidence is stronger for conviction and acquit when the evidence is stronger for acquittal, the courts should only convict when the evidence is stronger than a fair preponderance. Various magical phrases such as "beyond a reasonable doubt" are used to describe this system. As was mentioned before, there seems to be a lack of convincing empirical evidence that our courts actually behave this way, but the myth says they do and we can now inquire whether they should.

In Figure 11.1, I have plotted evidence and percentage of defendants found guilty in the manner to which you have by now become accustomed. If the courts attempted to decide according to the fair preponderance of the evidence, they would use the rule indicated by line A. If, on the other hand, they are biased in favor of the accused, they would follow the rule represented by line B. Note that if they follow the rule represented by line B, there will be few cases of erroneous findings of guilt and many cases of erroneous findings of innocence. If we return to Equation (11.1), which shows the payoff on various types of institutions in dealing with theft, we will note that change from line A to line B will make two changes. The likelihood of conviction (L_c) and the likelihood of false conviction (L_{fc}) will both go down. In order to avoid an increase in the crime rate, we would have to increase the punishment

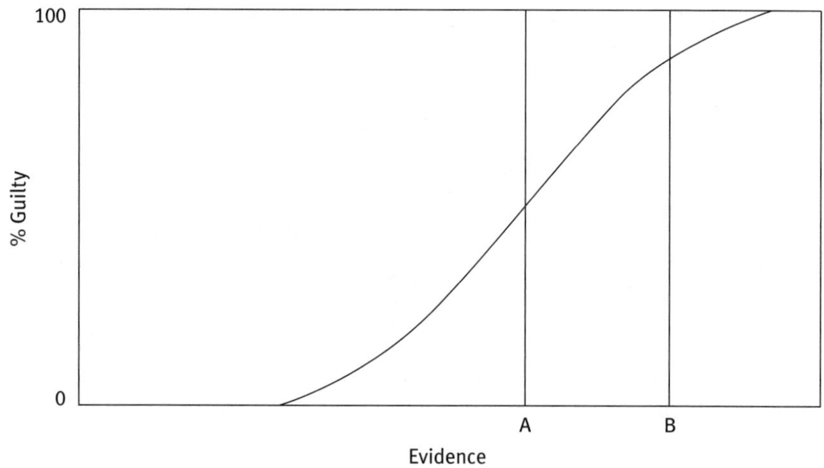

FIGURE 11.1
Bias in criminal proceedings

(P_u). It is by no means certain that this change would benefit people who are erroneously accused. It is possible that they would find that the combination of a new lower probability of being unjustly convicted with the higher penalty if convicted makes them worse off than they were before. Still, this is only a possibility. It might well be that providing the highest payoff under Equation (11.1) (which, of course, means the smallest negative number for P) would involve some such bias. This is essentially a technological question and one that can only be dealt with when we have far more information about the nature of the enforcement process.

It is, of course, quite possible that the common view in this matter, that we should so bias our court proceedings as to make what we might call type 1 errors more likely than type 2 errors, is the correct policy. We cannot say. What we can say, however, from an inspection of our equation is that improvements in procedure will be helpful. If we can increase L_c, reduce L_{fc}, and leave C_c unchanged, then we would get an unambiguous gain. Here we have a *quasi-Paretian rule*. If we have a number of factors, the interaction of which we cannot now measure, it may nevertheless be possible to make unambiguous improvement in the real world by improving one of them without worsening any other. Thus costless improvements in the accuracy of the court process or the detection process will have an unambiguously positive payoff. Furthermore, these two improvements would reduce the product of L_{fc} and P_u.

Here again, we find that improved efficiency in our apparatus for finding out what actually happened (the "police" and "courts") would have a clear and decided benefit. In general, improvements in the accuracy of our system can come in either of two ways: increasing the resources devoted to it or adopting improved procedures. The first, of course, carries with it the cost of the resources invested. The second is essentially free. We should not permit customs that descend from the Middle Ages to bind us today. Improved procedure should be considered not in terms of sacred rules but as a matter of science and technique. Problems of innocence and guilt, of imprisonment and the crime rate are too important to leave to the judgment of men who died long ago.

CHAPTER 12

FRAUD AND INFORMATION CONTROL

It may surprise the reader to hear that some intelligent and well-informed people believe that fraud should be legal. These people are normally associated with the "Austrian school" of economics, and the arguments they offer against making fraud illegal are worthy of brief consideration. Although fraud, like robbery and theft, is an effort to obtain property that is not properly yours, it does raise rather different issues. In the first place, it is normally fairly easy to avoid being defrauded. A few simple precautions—such as not buying gold stock unless it is listed on an exchange—will usually be sufficient. Secondly, it is normally impossible for the person perpetrating the fraud to conceal his identity. This means that he will not be able to continue in a career of fraud unless he changes his environment fairly frequently.

These two factors mean that fraud is never likely to be a major influence upon the economy regardless of how lightly the law treats it. The small minority of economists who argue that there should be no laws against fraud point out that fraud is almost unknown in markets where the same sellers deal with the same buyers over long periods of time. In any event, legal restrictions on fraud are, from any point of view, less important than those on theft and robbery.

In practice, the laws against fraud take these arguments into account to some extent. The normal prosecution for fraud results from an inability to repay. If the person who has perpetrated the fraud is willing and able to repay, there will usually be no prosecution. This is not true with theft and robbery. The jury system, of course, makes prosecution for fraud particularly difficult. Many successful frauds are too complicated for the jury to understand, and, hence, successful prosecution against fraud defendants is difficult if not impossible. This is particularly true of that type of fraud called embezzlement. The record of prosecution of reasonably skilled embezzlers is so poor and the danger of suits for false arrests is so great if prosecution fails that few victimized firms and prosecuting attorneys are willing to take the risk. Normally, an embezzler who works out a complicated plan of embezzlement and who does not confess will find that he is simply fired when he is discovered.

Nevertheless, neither fraud nor embezzlement is likely to be a permanent career. Both require getting the confidence of someone, which is difficult to do if you are either a stranger or a man with the reputation of a defrauder.

Each fraud, however, either ruins your reputation and/or requires that you move; hence, continued fraud is unlikely.

It might be argued that the more intelligent part of the population would have a net gain from making fraud legal. They would be relatively immune from fraud themselves, and the legal situation would give them the right to defraud their less intelligent fellow citizens. It seems unlikely, however, that this would really work out to the advantage of even the most clever part of the population. The legalization of fraud would surely lead to a great proliferation of protections against it. Business deals would become much harder to negotiate if each party had to be continually on his guard. Fraud normally involves misinforming people, and any increase in the quantity of misinformation in a system will always reduce its efficiency. Altogether it seems likely that the less fraud is attempted, the higher the national income will be. It would be a small factor, but still worth some investment of resources.

The laws against fraud, although difficult to enforce if juries are depended upon, are easy to enforce if the court system is reasonably efficient. It is usually fairly obvious who is the guilty person. The man who sold you the gold stock may have suddenly left town, but at least you can recognize him. The man who works out a complicated plan of embezzlement may have covered his tracks so carefully that he is hard to pick out of the mass of other bookkeepers, but this is exceptional. Normally, once the embezzlement is discovered, it is fairly easy to tell who was responsible. The embezzler must, if he is to be successful, run a continuing fraud, and this is normally impossible. Most embezzlers get involved in embezzlement without much prior thought, perhaps as a result of a sudden need of money. By a single embezzlement, they may make enough money to retire, particularly given the difficulty of getting convictions, but they are unlikely to have the opportunity to do it twice.

In order to clarify the issue, let us once again turn to our high school algebra exercises. Equation (12.1), the variables for which are presented in Table 12.1, shows the payoff to an individual who plans fraud if there is no law against it.[1]

$$P = BLP_n - C_o - (1 - L)C_rL_r \qquad (12.1)$$

As usual, the equation is basically simple. The benefits to be obtained from successfully deceiving the person whom you are attempting to defraud

1. The following discussion is based largely on the author's "The Economics of Lying," *Toward a Mathematics of Politics* (Ann Arbor: University of Michigan Press, 1967), pp. 133–43.

TABLE OF SYMBOLS 12.1

B = Benefit expected to be derived by potential liar from the action being urged
C_{in} = Cost of information
C_o = Conscience, internal cost of lying
C_p = Costs of punishment
C_r = Injury to reputation through others' knowledge that an individual has lied
I_l = Injury suffered by victim from carrying out action urged by liar
L = Likelihood that lie will be believed
L_p = Likelihood of punishment if lie is not believed
L_r = Likelihood that injury to the reputation will occur if lie is not believed
P = Payoff
P_u = Persuasive effect of the lie: probability that the lie, if believed, will bring about the desired action

---

multiplied by the likelihood that your lie will have a persuasive effect, i.e., lead him to undertake the action you desire, are at the left. We subtract from this the conscience cost (which we discussed to some extent in the last chapter and will return to again in Chapter 14) and the probability that the lie will not be believed, together with the injury to the reputation of the individual that will be occasioned by the disbelief of the lie. Those persons who argue that fraud should not be illegal are, in essence, saying that the $C_r \cdot L_r$ is so large and L is so small that this equation would normally show P as a negative number.

Equation (12.2) shows the net payoff to the individual to whom the lie is addressed. The I_l in this case is the injury that he will suffer in the event that he believes the lie, and the lie has the desired persuasive effect. As a consequence, P is actually a negative quantity—an injury in all cases where it is not zero.

$$P = I_l \cdot L \cdot P_n \tag{12.2}$$

Even if I_l is equal to B, i.e., if it is a straightforward transfer of funds from one person to another—a fake sale of gold stock or something of that sort—it is clear that the benefit achieved by the potential confidence man is less than the injury suffered by the victim. In most cases, of course, there is no such simple transfer, and the benefit received by the confidence man is much less than the injury to his victim.

Note, then, that if it were possible, the potential victims of fraud would be willing to pay potential confidence men to desist. A bargain could theoretically be struck between these two groups. In practice, of course, no such bargain is possible, because the people who plan frauds must, of necessity, conceal that fact from their potential victims. Nevertheless, we may call this difficulty an extreme case of a transaction cost and, therefore, can say that such a payment would be a Pareto-optimal change. Here, as in many other cases, it may be possible to use the government to minimize transaction costs. In particular, a procedure under which resources are used to repress fraud may be a suitable procedure. Before turning to this matter, however, let us consider Equation (12.3) in which the potential victim invests resources in obtaining information in order to reduce the likelihood of fraud.

$$P = I_l \cdot L \cdot P_n + C_{in} \tag{12.3}$$

If we compare Equation (12.3) with Equation (12.1), it is once again clear that the net cost to the potential victim of fraud is greater than the net benefit to the person who might gain from the fraud. It is not true, of course, that the P in Equation (12.3) is necessarily lower (a larger negative number) than the P in Equation (12.2). Although in Equation (12.3) the potential victim of fraud is investing resources in obtaining information to protect himself against fraud, this would have the effect of reducing the value of L. If he has invested his resources rationally, the negative payoff from Equation (12.3) would be less than the negative payoff of Equation (12.2).

Let us now consider the situation if we have a law against fraud; i.e., some cost will be assessed on a person who is detected in committing or attempting to commit a fraud. Equation (12.4) shows the payoff for attempted fraud under these conditions.

$$P = B \cdot P_n \cdot L - C_o - (1 - L)(C_p L_p + C_r L_r) \tag{12.4}$$

Note that I have collapsed the likelihood of detection and likelihood of conviction terms of the equations in earlier chapters to simple costs of punishment and likelihood of punishment. This is merely for simplicity and does not change the argument. It is, of course, clear that the payoff under Equation (12.4) is lower than the payoff under Equation (12.1). Marginal individuals who are contemplating fraud under conditions given in Equation (12.1) would be dissuaded under the conditions given in Equation (12.4).

However, the cost of establishing the punishment system would be greater than the benefits to be obtained thereby. Looked at in terms of present discounted value, I would contemplate the possible benefits that I might obtain from being successful in committing fraud under Equation (12.1) less the possible injuries I might suffer from being the victim of fraud under the Equation (12.3), and weigh that against the situation that would occur if we were in the situation described by Equations (12.3) and (12.4). For the potential victims of fraud or for a professional confidence man (when he is not trying to defraud someone else), the principal difference between the two situations is the different value of C_{in}, which could be lower if there were laws against fraud, and of L, which would consequently also be lower. The first question would be whether the present discounted value to me of reducing these two factors in Equation (12.3) is greater than the injury I will suffer from the reduction in the payoff from any potential frauds I might undertake in Equation (12.4). It is reasonably certain that this calculation would favor the enacting of laws against fraud.

The sole problem remaining is whether there are major costs of enforcement in connection with the law against fraud. The only sizable cost that I can see is the real possibility of judicial error and consequent conviction of innocent persons. In many cases, the only witnesses to the act of fraud are the two parties involved. Since the successful confidence man is necessarily a plausible fellow, it is possible that he will be able to convince the jury that he is telling the truth and that the victim is not. If this is so, it will be possible for people to get out of contracts and place their partners in contract in prison by simply lying in court. It is probably the danger of this type of miscarriage of justice that led to the rules restricting oral testimony that would tend to alter a written contract. If we were confident of the court's ability to detect lies, we could relax these rules.

Nevertheless, the problem of prosecution for fraud does not seem to be overwhelmingly difficult. There is, in fact, one area in which the prosecution of fraud would seem to be remarkably easy. One way of committing fraud is to sell something to the public through false advertising. In this particular case, the proof that false claims have been made is ridiculously easy. The only problems in court would be whether the claims in fact were false and whether the businessman might not have, perhaps, believed them himself. The latter possible defense in this case could be eliminated if we had a rule that people engaging in large-scale advertising campaigns are required to assure themselves to some reasonable degree as to the accuracy of their statements.

It is an interesting fact that we have not, in general, turned to the standard law of fraud to deal with this problem. It is not obvious why this should be so. It is true that the development of nationwide advertising was rather quick and that an adjustment of the court system to this new type of crime may have been difficult. Nevertheless, it would seem that the easy way of dealing with this particular type of fraud would be to appoint special bunco squads and special divisions in the prosecuting attorney's office rather than to set up federal governmental agencies such as the Federal Trade Commission. This is particularly so since most of these federal administrative agencies do not have the full powers that are given to district attorneys and the courts. The penalty they can impose upon people who commit fraud is considerably lighter than the penalty imposed by regular courts.

Regular court procedures were not, however, the methods chosen, and we now have a number of special governmental bureaus engaged in dealing with dishonest advertising, which is not treated as simple fraud. Note that, in general, it is not possible for private persons to sue for damages in such cases. If you were to sell me a piece of land under conditions that the court would consider fraudulent, and you had sufficient funds, I could sue you and get the money back. But, in general, if you defraud me by engaging in a nationwide advertising campaign, and the amount of money that I personally lose through my believing your advertising is small, our court system provides no remedy.

Theoretically, there are two types of private suits that would be possible in this event. First, one would anticipate that the competitors of the company engaging in the fraudulent advertising would be able to sue for the damages that they suffered from the resulting loss of customers. Unfortunately, as the result of a rather peculiar legal decision made in the latter part of the nineteenth century, this type of suit is impossible. The courts refused to permit this kind of suit on the grounds that it would be hard to determine what the damages were. It is, of course, difficult to determine the proper amount of damages, but it does not seem that this would deter the courts. They are willing to decide the monetary damage of having a girl's nose bent slightly. It does not seem that it would be any harder to calculate damages against a man who had made false claims and, hence, injured his competitors. This would be particularly true since the major effect of permitting such suits would be to make it more unlikely that people would make false claims. Thus, the potential purchasers would be benefited even if the amount of damages was improperly computed.

This particular remedy has the fairly obvious advantage that a company's competitors are more likely to be both in a position to detect its false advertising claims and better motivated to take action against such claims than any other group in society. Thus, using these competitors as policemen would seem to be a rational policy. In the antitrust area, of course, we do use this technique. We permit private persons or companies who are injured by monopolies to sue for triple damages. It would be sensible to permit similar suits by competitors who were injured by false claims in advertising.

A second method of enforcing rules against false advertising would be to encourage the customers to sue in the form of a class suit. This is a rather unusual form of litigation. Essentially, a lawyer who is looking for business finds a large number of people who have each been injured slightly. He then collects three or more of these people, and they institute a class suit in the name of all of the others so injured. If the suit is successful, the defendant in the suit is compelled to make restitution to the large collection of people who have been injured, and the judge awards a standard percentage fee for the lawyer. Obviously, it is a very lucrative practice for lawyers; only our obsolete rules restricting entrepreneurial activity on the part of lawyers make it rare. Here, again, we have a method that could make false advertising claims extremely expensive.

Turning from direct fraud, there are also other areas in which control of information may be desirable. First, let us consider statements that, although not directly dishonest, are likely to deceive. We can include in this category things such as packaging which makes the contents appear larger than they are, and other methods that deceive the unwary but not the careful purchaser. By turning back to our equations, it is again obvious that the purchasers or potential purchasers would be willing to pay the potential sellers to desist from this kind of activity, because it will permit a reduced investment by the potential purchasers in obtaining information. Once again, it is not possible to have a direct agreement between the two parties in these matters because of the transaction costs, but governmental activity may reduce the transaction problems and, therefore, be desirable from everybody's standpoint. In this case, the traditional law of fraud is not (strictly speaking) applicable. The objective is to make it easier to purchase safely.

If legal restrictions on this type of activity are sensible under our welfare criteria, the question of organization is much more difficult. Specific laws requiring accuracy in the packaging or the labeling of commodities are difficult to draft. If the enacting of specific legislation is difficult in this field, the use of administrative agencies has also not been very successful. Apparently the type of information that seems useful to a governmental regulatory board is not the type that seems useful to actual purchasers. The Securities and Exchange Commission, for example, has required all new issues of securities to be accompanied by a thick disclosure booklet that meets its approval, but purchasers of securities seldom read these booklets.[2] It is perhaps significant that there is a debate currently going on in the economics profession as to whether the Securities and Exchange Commission has had any desirable effect at all.[3] The only effect that all parties to the debate are agreed on is that the cost of preparing these booklets is high enough so that it is no longer possible for small companies to go into the public issue market.

It may be, however, that these difficulties in making the actual sale nondeceptive simply indicate the ineptitude on the part of the specific regulators and are not a permanent characteristic of regulatory commissions. Surely we can hope so. This is an area in which experimentation and research might have a high payoff. The elimination of deceptive information from the total information stream would be a net improvement in efficiency. Requiring parties who have differential access to some type of information to provide it to people with whom they are dealing would, in most cases, be a net improvement. The only problems are practical questions of organization. These practical problems may be insoluble, and certainly the agencies now engaged in enforcing this type of regulation have made very little progress in solving them. But experiments aimed at their solution would be a rational investment of resources.

It should be noted that a great deal of supervision and enforcement of standards in the commercial area is undertaken not by the government but by private organizations. A particularly conspicuous example is the Howard Johnson Company, which enters into contracts with local restaurant owners under which they are required to provide a highly standardized set of services to their customers. The improved information flow that results from this has been vastly profitable to both Howard Johnson and most of the local owners. There are a great many other areas in which private persons commercially provide standardized and/or improved information.

Another special problem concerns contracts. If we consider the contract of insurance, for example, the average man never reads it and has small under-

2. The booklet is required by law to carry a false statement that it has not been approved by the Securities and Exchange Commission.

3. For a summary, see Henry G. Manne, ed., *Economic Policy and the Regulation of Corporate Securities* (Washington, D.C.: American Enterprise Institute, 1969).

standing of its contents. This has led a number of states to establish organizations that provide a standard contract (or, to be more exact, a wide range of standard contracts) that the insurance companies are compelled to use. In practice, this reform has not worked out very well, partly because the insurance companies have been able to influence the agencies in various undesirable ways and partly because the agencies themselves tend to be incompetent and resistant to new ideas. Nevertheless, in theory, one can argue for the provision of standardized contracts. Normally, one would want to permit the parties to make another contract if the standard contract did not meet their requirements, but the provision of standardized arrangements might be a way of simplifying the information flow.

There are other areas in which the establishment of standards would simplify the information problem for the buyers and sellers of a commodity. The grade labeling of meat would be an example, and surely does no harm as long as the people who benefit by it pay for it, and as long as it is possible for meat that is not grade labeled to be sold. The basic problem with grade labeling or setting standards is that most commodities can vary in a very large number of different ways. The establishment of standards involves a setting off of reductions in one attribute against improvements in another. It may well be that, for some people, the particular trade-off used by the governmental regulatory commission is not ideal. Thus, they would prefer a somewhat different set of qualities, and we should leave them free to obtain this different set in the market.

In addition to commercial problems, there are a number of other areas in which false or very careless statements are made—and their elimination would be desirable. The most obvious single area is also the area that is best known by the average man to be extremely dishonest. This is politics. Under present circumstances, except for very slight restrictions under the law of libel, false statements by politicians are completely and totally uncontrolled by law. It is only if the C_r portion of our equation seems to be particularly high for a given politician that he need worry about dishonesty. It is, I suppose, obvious that our previous reasoning would lead to the conclusion that making false statements in the course of a political campaign (or, for that matter, on the floor of Congress) should be severely punished. Unfortunately, here again we run into extremely difficult practical considerations.

The practical problem is not that it is difficult to detect this type of fraud but that the person who is successful is put in a position to protect himself against any governmental action.[4] Here again, however, it would seem that research and experimentation are called for. Perhaps some arrangement under which a reasonably impartial judiciary is supplemented by a prosecuting apparatus in the hands of the opposition might work. I would hesitate to make any specific recommendations, but it certainly is important and we should invest considerable resources in this area of research.

Turning to another area, a false statement by Smith about Jones that injures Jones is grounds for a suit for libel or slander. The arguments normally given for this depend upon what are essentially property rights on the part of Jones in his own reputation. This, of course, assumes that it is desirable that Jones have property rights in his reputation, and, as far as I know, no one has demonstrated this. It is, however, true that on the whole the average person would be better off if the number of false statements that he encounters in his daily life were reduced. This would mean that the information that he receives is somewhat more reliable and that he is required to invest less in checking statements that come to his attention. Permitting suits in libel and slander presumably has some effect in reducing the number of false statements with which the individual is bombarded.

It should be noted that our method of dealing with libel and slander is not the only possible one. The Brazilians, for example, do not permit libel suits against newspapers. They require, however, newspapers to permit a person who has been criticized to answer in the paper. There are some signs that a somewhat similar provision is being introduced into our radio and television law. Whether this is better or worse than libel actions is not clear.

Lastly, it seems reasonable that the reduction of the total amount of noise in the form of false statements that we obtain from the media would be desirable. It would permit us to have a given level of information with a reduced investment in checking. Thus, if a popular journal runs an article on, say, a small island off the coast of Australia that is romanticized to a considerable extent and reflects what they think their readers would like to think about the island rather than what actually exists, no one is obviously injured. Actions for fraud, libel, or slander would not lie. Yet the net effect of this article is that, in a real sense, society is somewhat less well informed than it was before.

4. Treason never prospers. What's the reason? When treason prospers, none dare call it treason. Sir John Harington, *The most elegant and wittie epigrams of Sir John Harington* (Princeton: Princeton University Press, 1916).

It, or at least some members of it, now believes things that are untrue, whereas before it had a zero information level. Furthermore, anyone who wanted to find out about this particular island might find this particular article; this surely would make his information-gathering activities somewhat more difficult and somewhat more hazardous in outcome than they otherwise would be.

Restrictions on this type of false information raise even more severe practical problems than the restrictions we have discussed thus far. It is unlikely that any private individual would be motivated to take action. Surely there is no one who could sue.[5] Furthermore, the danger in governmental restriction is extremely high. Once again, however, it seems that we should at least do some research.

In a sense, the first part of this chapter was devoted to laboring the obvious. We proved that fraud is a bad thing. Some of the later conclusions that are drawn from the same line of reasoning, however, will be regarded by many readers as not only nonobvious but absurd. I can only suggest that the line of reasoning that I have followed and that leads to these surprising results does not seem to have any serious defects. The proposals are largely proposals for experimental investment of resources. It does seem to me that we should look into the possibility of exercising more control over the dissemination of misinformation. The problem of instituting such controls without at the same time preventing dissemination of information that is for one reason or another objectionable to the government is extremely difficult. It may be insoluble, but I see no reason for accepting the status quo until we have thought much more about it.

5. Possibly the competing news media might be permitted to sue in this case. They would have at least some motive to bring such suits and might serve as policemen.

CHAPTER 13

CRIMES AGAINST THE PERSON

The usual distinction between crimes against property and crimes against the person is simple and straightforward and involves the nature of the crime. A more basic distinction would be between crimes that are intended to improve the material well-being of the criminal and crimes that are merely motivated by a desire to injure someone else and, thus, give the criminal utility. Crimes against the person falling in the first class can be dealt with by the reasoning given in Chapter 11. In discussing crimes motivated by a desire to injure, we should note that there are some crimes against property of a similar nature. It sometimes happens, particularly in family disputes, that a person will engage in, for example, arson, not because he anticipates any particular direct gain from it but because he wishes to injure the person whose property is burned down. This is a crime against property, but it is very similar to the crimes against the person to be discussed in this chapter.

Crimes that are not motivated by desire for material gain are actually much less common than materially motivated crimes. The commonest single example is injuring somebody in a fight—such as a barroom brawl. In such cases, the desire to inflict bodily injury is usually transitory. Less commonly, there are cases of the planned infliction of injury as a result of hatred or dislike of the person injured. This is sometimes the motive for murder. In other cases the crime of murder is committed primarily to get rid of the person murdered, but not to make a direct material gain or to satisfy hatred. Thus, for example, a man who would like to get rid of his wife may murder her without necessarily feeling any violent aversion to her personally. She is in his way, but is not a hated object.

Last, but by no means least, we have crimes in which violence is worked upon the victim for reasons of direct pleasure in the act by the perpetrator. The commonest example of this, of course, is rape. There seem, however, to be a number of other rather similar crimes, in particular some types of sex crimes in which children are the victims, and there have been cases in which sadists have obtained pleasure by torturing their victims. Usually, again, the victims are children, and usually some type of sexual assault is included. The last group of crimes are the result of severe mental derangement, and I shall not discuss them further.

In order to consider the simplest possible case of a crime committed for the purpose of inflicting injury, let us begin with a most rare crime—carefully calculated assault. Consider a person who has a desire to injure another person and is contemplating doing so. For present purposes, we need not inquire as to why he wishes to injure his victim. It may be that he is a sadist who likes to inflict pain; he may have a violent feeling of hatred toward the person who is to be injured; or the injury he is contemplating may be murder, and he may simply wish to get the person to be injured out of his way for one reason or another. In all of these cases, the criminal will gain satisfaction from his criminal act, and the victim will, we can safely assume, have his utility reduced.

If we wish to avoid interpersonal comparison of utilities, we could only say this and then inquire as to whether the victim would be willing to pay enough to the person planning the crime to stop him. This is the standard Paretian way of avoiding interpersonal comparison, and, with this type of crime, it is not particularly helpful. It would be possible, for example, to make a living by threatening violence and then collecting the payment made to avoid it. The contrary procedure—requiring the person contemplating violence to purchase from his victim the right to commit the violence—would have the disadvantage that in many cases it would eliminate the motive for the violence. If I am trying to injure a person and must actually make him slightly better off by giving him full compensation for any injury, obviously I cannot accomplish my goal.

We are, thus, in an area in which the standard welfare tools do not work very well. Most of us would simply engage in interpersonal comparison in this case, but without some kind of interpersonal comparison of utilities, we cannot say that laws prohibiting people from using force and violence against other persons solely for the purpose of working injury are undesirable. It will be recalled that we included among our assumptions the proposition that individuals did not get more pleasure out of inflicting pain on others than the pain they would receive from the same amount of injury upon themselves. With this assumption and risk aversion, it is easy to demonstrate that people would be opposed to making assault and battery and other crimes of violence legal. It should be noted in this connection that, although there would presumably be some strong, vigorous people who, in their youth, could anticipate inflicting far more injury on other people than they themselves would receive, all of us are going to become older. The youth of twenty who injured a number of other people might find that the latter part of his life was extremely uncomfortable. Thus, we can argue, on the base of this special assumption, that laws against force and violence are desirable.

It is possible that there are some people in society for which this assumption is not true; i.e., they obtain more pleasure from the inflicting of violence than the pain that they would suffer from receiving similar violence. If there are such persons, we could arrange a special "violence" club for them in which they would be able to inflict violence on each other. Granted the assumption, this would be a desirable institution from their standpoint, and there is no reason why anyone else should object to it. Historically, it is clear that there have been many cases in which people have gained positive pleasure from fighting. In fact, it is possible to argue that young males in general get a positive payoff out of fighting, and certainly many drunks act as if they do.

Whether this is something we should prohibit in terms of *our* judgment of their behavior is, of course, different from the question of whether it is Pareto optimal. If both parties to a fight, duel, or brawl obtain pleasure from it, there is no welfare reason why outsiders should interfere.[1] In any event, the rules prohibiting the use of violence on a person whose own personal preference function is not such that he gains more out of the chance of inflicting violence than he loses from having violence inflicted on him is clearly justifiable, as long as we leave people who have other preference functions free to commit violence upon each other.

Having decided that crimes against a person (outside the violence club) should be controlled by law, we are still left with a most difficult problem: what amount of punishment fits a crime of this sort? For theft the problem is easy. We can simply make the punishment heavy enough so that the present discounted value of the punishment is greater than the present discounted value of the loot, and the computation can be done in material terms because the object of the crime is material. In our present case, the object of the crime is to receive an immaterial satisfaction from the act itself. Computing the cost that will make it unlikely that people will undertake it is, therefore, much more difficult. I regret that I can offer nothing very impressive in the way of such computation. In fact, as we shall shortly see, the problem in real life is even more difficult. Nevertheless, we have here a case in which empirical tools would work. We could experiment with raising and

1. If the state has an institution that automatically provides payments to people who are crippled (and fighting of one sort or another is likely to lead to such crippling), then perhaps a suitable tax on the fighting to pay the full cost of this possible payment would be rational.

lowering the penalty for this type of crime and find out the effect on the number of such crimes.

It would, of course, be desirable to make clear to the potential criminals the size of the penalty they are risking and the likelihood that they will be caught. In the case of the carefully calculated crimes we are now discussing, the probability of punishment is high. Once again, it may be that our present methods greatly overemphasize the amount of deterrence that is necessary for this type of crime. Unfortunately, this type of crime is closely connected to the next type we are to discuss and may be practically indistinguishable from it. If so, it may be that the fairly light penalty that would be necessary to prevent carefully calculated crimes of violence will have to be replaced by the heavier punishment necessary for the next type of crime.

Most crimes of violence are not carefully calculated. They are either by-products of other crimes intended to improve the well-being of the criminal or a result of something such as a barroom brawl. The former case has already been discussed, but the latter case has not been touched upon. Up to this point we have been talking about what must be a very tiny category of crimes against the person—those crimes that are carefully thought out and are intended solely to injure someone.

All of the crimes discussed thus far are, if we except only some of the automobile offenses, crimes of calculation. This does not mean that the individual who commits the crime has done a lot of careful thought but that they are the type of crime that we can well imagine a person deciding to commit even after careful consideration. They could involve calculation even though in some cases they may not. Many of the crimes against a person, however, are not of this sort. They result from losses of temper. Sometimes they involve a desire to fight, particularly on the part of someone who is drunk. In a few cases, they involve a sudden strong emotional drive that the criminal does not or cannot resist.

At first glance, it might seem that this type of crime cannot be prevented by providing a penalty for committing it. Since the crime itself is not the result of much in the way of rational thought, we might assume that rational criteria would not stop people from committing such crimes. If, however, we think a little bit about our ordinary day-to-day behavior, we will realize that the degree to which we give in to our emotions is affected by the consequences. While preparing this chapter, I happened to be in England and came across an article in the *Daily Mail* in which the president of the football league remarked that English football had recently been disgraced by a number of acts of violence on the field. He proposed to deal with this problem by imposing very stiff penalties on the players who lost their tempers.[2]

One might think that such control would be impossible, but a little thought about the way people actually behave will indicate that it is not. Furthermore, no one wrote to the editor and said that the president was imbecilic in thinking that he could stop people from losing their temper by making it painful. In most walks of life we depend upon such controls. Parents will teach their children not to lose their temper by punishing them. The police are unkind to people who lose their temper on being arrested, and this also has an effect.

In this field, there seems to be a certain amount of doublethink in much popular discussion. Perhaps this can be illustrated best by a page from *Time* magazine. The issue of 3 September 1967 began with a long discussion of Negro rioting and remedies that could be used to prevent it. It was the theme of the discussion that police force would not stop the riots. The following article, however, dealt with Mace, which inflicts a great deal of pain and suffering on a rioter without much further damage to him. This article began by saying that Mace can do a great deal to prevent rioting. Clearly, the editors of *Time* did not realize that they were using two different criteria in their two successive articles. Regardless of the truth or falsity of the first approach to rioting, the second certainly will work. This does not, of course, indicate that it should be our sole dependence.

Most of the acts of violence that are not committed in the course of a crime aimed at improving the material well-being of a criminal are the result of a loss of temper or something of this sort. The category of calculated crimes of violence that we discussed at the beginning of this chapter is probably very small, and it is a difficult administrative problem to separate the two types. It may well be necessary to treat all crimes against the person as if they were the result of a loss of temper.

Determining the proper amount of punishment for such crimes is clearly

2. Len Shipman, *Daily Mail*, 25 August 1967, p. 14, Suspension of up to three months or half a season will have to be introduced for persistent offenders. Now is the time to act, particularly in the cases where players lose their tempers. I don't mind so much the cases where a player is sent off for tackling from behind, for instance.

"What has to be stamped out immediately is the incidence of players going berserk for a split second. I mean players who retaliate violently after they have been fouled and start kicking and lashing out. For men like that, we have to think of the stiffer punishments of up to half a season's suspension."

difficult. It seems likely that the probability of an individual's committing assault and battery late in the evening in a bar would depend upon a number of variables. One may be how much he had to drink, another the strength of his emotions at the time, and a third would be the probable consequences of the action. Considering the latter, which is the only variable we have available for social control, we could probably not totally prevent such assaults without extraordinarily cruel punishment. It is likely that if all bars were equipped with two husky policemen who would immediately pounce upon any individual engaging in any kind of violence and pop him into a kettle of boiling oil, acts of violence would not occur (at least not in bars). Furthermore, people who thought they might succumb to temptation to commit acts of violence would stay out of bars. Needless to say, I do not propose this method.

The fact that we can imagine ourselves committing such crimes is, perhaps, relevant. We would like to minimize the total suffering that might be imposed upon us through being victims of such crimes and also through being severely penalized for a possible loss of control of our emotions. In any event, the exact amount of punishment that should be handed out in such cases is a very difficult problem. I suspect that we would find a rather slow payoff to increases in the amount of punishment. That is, if we experimented by gradually raising the punishment for attacking a man in a bar from a fine of $25 to life imprisonment, we would find a relatively slow reduction in the number of assaults that were committed as the penalty was being raised. All that can be done in the present state of knowledge is to make some kind of rough-and-ready approximation of the correct penalty.

The lack of calculation in this type of crime is, of course, its distinguishing characteristic. Nevertheless, I think that we would be unwise to draw too firm a line of division between crimes of this sort and crimes such as theft or embezzlement. There, also, a lack of calculation may sometimes turn up; there, also, we have a spectrum from crimes that are carefully thought out to those crimes that in many ways result from the impulse of the moment. The so-called thoughtless act of violence also represents a somewhat similar spectrum, although probably the degree of advance thought is much less than in embezzlement, and the difficulty in deterring this type of crime by threat of imprisonment is correspondingly greater.

Thus far, I have deferred discussion of one very large category of crime; namely, sex crimes. This category is actually composed of two quite different types of acts. In the first group (prostitution, homosexuality, and a number of so-called deviations in which all the persons involved in the act give their consent) no one is directly injured. Laws against crimes of this sort, and statistically they are almost certainly among the commonest, are expression of moral disapprobation and not an example of the type of reasoning used thus far in this book. I may, perhaps, be annoyed by the musical review *Oh! Calcutta!* If this were so, there is an externality involved, and I am, in a sense, injured. But in this case, the externality and my injury come, in essence, from my moral feelings; this is something of which we have avoided discussion thus far. Thus, this type of behavior falls outside the scope of this book. The most significant legal reforms in English history—associated with the name of Bentham—included the legalization of prostitution that is still perfectly legal in England. There are, however, restrictions on the efficient economic organization of prostitution in England. Pimping is certainly a nasty occupation in the view of most people, but there is no obvious, nonmoral, reason why it should be illegal.

The professional criminal operating in an area where no one concerned in the crime is likely to complain to the police has found it a profitable and not particularly dangerous field of crime. Furthermore, the police have tended to feel that there is very little wrong with the activity and, hence, have been willing to accept bribes to permit it to continue. Thus, the repeal of laws against this type of activity (also gambling) would probably work a very great change in the structure of our criminal community.

There remains, however, a minority of sex crimes in which it cannot be said that all parties consent. Rape, of course, is an obvious example. It is probable, however, that the commonest example is exposure. Regardless of the details, in each case some person (usually a woman) is subjected to some kind of sexual behavior to which he or she objects. In many of the cases, it is very hard to explain the behavior of the person committing the crime except on grounds of mental derangement. It would appear still to be so, however, that the principal instrument of social control is the use of punishment as a deterrent, and these matters would not differ theoretically from assault committed in a bar. In this class of crimes, as indeed for most sex crimes, we should hope for medical progress that may eventually solve the problem. Meanwhile, we must continue to use the ordinary penal methods.

In some ways, the chapter we are now concluding is most unsatisfactory. To a very large extent, it deals with crimes that are undertaken for reasons that do not really lend themselves to careful calculation, either by potential criminals or by students. We cannot hope to have as simple a system for dealing with these crimes as for such obvious crimes of calculation as straightforward burglary. It is, nevertheless, true that these crimes are undertaken in order to maximize the preference function of the criminal and that by putting a penalty on the commission of the crime, we will affect behavior. The mother who punishes a child for having a tantrum is not behaving irrationally. Similarly, punishing someone for losing his temper and killing in a drunken rage is also not irrational. Unfortunately, it is unlikely to be as effective as similar punishment for burglary.

PART 4

ETHICS

CHAPTER 14

ETHICS

Traditional legal theory started with an ethical foundation and built a legal structure upon it. Thus far, we have largely avoided ethics and have used only utilitarian considerations. It is true that such words as "unjust" have occasionally occurred in the text, but primarily as a result of the limitations of the English language. If a law is enacted that provides for punishment for committing assault and battery, then it is clumsy to say, when the court procedure miscarries, that the outcome was contrary to the intent of the persons who drafted the law. The use of the phrase "unjust" in such a case seems to be an excusable simplification.

In this chapter, we finally turn to ethical considerations. Our approach, however, will be opposite to that of the usual legal treatise. We shall argue not that the law should be ethically correct but that our ethics should be in accord with the law. In a sense, our argument will be based on the work of John Wesley, the founder of Methodism. When discussing his preaching with the upper classes, Wesley always pointed out that his missionary activities reduced the crime rate, which in turn resulted in a reduction in the expenditures for such things as police and prisons. It is clear that this is a valid argument. The prevention of crime and enforcement of contracts by use of courts and police may be effective, but making this our sole reliance is probably not the least expensive way of dealing with these problems. One part of all educational systems is the indoctrination of children in a particular ethical code. If children are indoctrinated in this way and if the indoctrination is continued while they are adults, it is likely that it will be somewhat easier to enforce the law. This indoctrination will, however, make it harder to change the law when that seems desirable.

Perhaps my own interest in this aspect of the matter is greater than that of the average person because I spent some time in China. The Chinese approach to the law has been very largely an exercise in propaganda. Among the major duties of the state was propagandizing the law, and fairly large expenditures of resources were made to this end; much more, proportionately, than we use for similar activity.

A number of the equations that we have used to deal with specific crimes have contained the term C_o or "cost of conscience." When I first introduced this terminology, I apologized for its use, as it clearly carried ethical overtones.

It is now time to discuss these ethical overtones. If we can (by the indoctrination of children or of adults) put a sizable C_0 into the utility function of all individuals in society, then violation of the laws will become rare or indeed nonexistent. The question, of course, is whether this is a lower-cost method of reducing the crime rate than the use of policemen and prisons. This is an empirical problem on which no real research has been done. It would seem likely, however, that at least some resources should be employed in such indoctrination.

There is another part of our basic equation in which indoctrination may be helpful. The likelihood of detection L_d and the likelihood of conviction L_c are actually quite low in our society. If we could convince potential criminals that they were high, this would change their probability calculus and, hence, make their commission of crimes less likely. It is notable that this particular type of propaganda is a major part of the current approach to crime. Such phrases as "Murder will out" or "There is no perfect crime" are repeated endlessly. Their objective is to convince the average man that the danger in committing a crime is vastly higher than it actually is. Surely this must mean that our crime rate is lower than it would be if potential criminals had a more accurate view of the risks involved.[1]

These considerations are not entirely left out of the standard approach to law and ethics. One of the purposes of education is to give moral indoctrination to the children. Furthermore, a good deal of similar indoctrination is given to adults. It is no accident that on television criminals never succeed in the long run. In real life, of course, they do; but it is likely that the continuous repetition of crime stories in which the criminal eventually gets caught discourages crime. Last, but not least, the highly ethical content of a great deal of our literature probably leads people to a somewhat more ethical approach to many problems. All of these things should reduce the cost of enforcing the law. Note, however, that they simply reduce the cost; they do not mean that we can abandon the courts and the police. Our appropriations for courts and police may be lower with an active system of indoctrination than they would have to be without it, but they will still be positive.

Furthermore, reliance on indoctrination has the unfortunate characteristic that it gives the badly indoctrinated people a distinct advantage over the well indoctrinated. If we reduce our police activity, we reduce the real risk

1. No book that I have written has sold more than 10,000 copies. In view of these considerations, this is perhaps very fortunate.

that individuals will be punished for their crimes. Many people are poorly indoctrinated either because they are resistant to indoctrination or because there is some failure in the process. For them, this is a net advantage. If we relied solely on indoctrination, we could end up with a situation in which those people who are systematic violators of the social norms have a very great advantage over those who are not. Needless to say, this is only a theoretical possibility. No society has ever put its total reliance on indoctrination.

If we consider the source of our ethics, we will find that, to a large extent, they are simply something we were taught when we were children; possibly there has been some change since we became adults. Furthermore, in different countries and in different cultures, the ethical principles that are taught to children differ. For those who do not believe in the natural law, there is no reason why we would anticipate that ethics would be similar in different areas. For those who do believe in the natural law, and I suppose it will not escape the reader that the author of this book is not one of them, a uniform ethical code for the world as a whole would be expected. Among those friends of mine who do believe in the natural law, I find that this expectation has been formed and that they will allege that such a worldwide ethical code does in fact exist.

In order to avoid the empirical problems into which this view would lead them, they sometimes deny that people in foreign countries have somewhat different ethics than they themselves do. More commonly, they will not deny that foreign countries have different ethics than we, but will allege that, at the fundamental level, all ethical codes are identical and that the differences are superficial and not important. This is not the way that I read the anthropological literature. As far as I know, for example, the people who ran Stalin's concentration camps were not subject to any particular qualms of conscience. They honestly thought that disposing of the "enemies of the people" in a painful way was a desirable thing to do. In this case, the ethical indoctrination to which they were responding had been given them after they were adults, but cannibals normally receive their ethical training as children.

In any event, this book has been based upon the assumption that ethics are something we learn. If ethics are learned, then we can inquire what would be the best ethics to teach. Clearly, this would involve the ability to compare different ethical systems. An ethical system that led to efficient behavior in society would presumably be superior to those that led to inefficient behavior. The considerations that we have developed in this book with respect to the law would apply also to ethics. Thus, in a sense, what I am recommending in this book is that we first work out the most efficient legal system and then enforce it by use of the courts and police forces. But we should also indoctrinate a similar ethical code.

Under this system (which many readers will, no doubt, think paradoxical), the ethical system becomes subordinated to the law rather than *vice versa*. People who have been indoctrinated into a given ethical system differing from the system of law that we have developed in this book would normally regard my proposal as being very wicked, and, indeed, it would be in terms of the particular ethical code that they happen to believe in. If, however, we cannot change ethical systems, clearly we are stuck with a nonprogressive part of our society. It seems to me that progress might be made. The traditional methods of "research" in ethics have had very little success. It is not at all obvious that we are more knowledgeable in this field than was Aristotle or Epictetus. Under the circumstances, a radical change in research strategy would seem advisable. This book has been based upon such a radical revision. It may be the wrong type of radicalism, but I hope that it will be judged on its merits rather than condemned simply because it proposes drastic changes in a very conservative field of study.

APPENDIX A

EXCEPTIONS TO THE SOCIAL CONTRACT

In Chapter 2, I promised to demonstrate in this appendix that a society could include a certain number of people who had rather odd preferences without the general principles of the book being inapplicable. Since these preference orderings are unlikely, the demonstration is basically of little importance. It may, however, permit us to make a slight improvement in our society. It may be that a rearranging of our laws to provide for these unusual preference orderings would be an improvement in our polity. This improvement would come partly from those very rare people who actually did have these peculiar preference orderings finding their preference better fitted, but more importantly from the fact that a great many people would be given an open choice between accepting or rejecting certain institutions. A certain element of irrational discontent would thus be eliminated.

I have never met a person with a preference pattern in which being robbed had a high value, although I have met some anarchists who would argue that there should be no laws against robbery. Thus, to repeat, our demonstration is not about a matter of much importance. There are, however, some groups of people who are quite disenchanted with our present system of law. It might be desirable to permit these people to find out, by experience, whether their view of the world is correct. The most important of these groups are the pacifists, and I would like to proceed now to a modest proposal to change our institutional structure so as to make it possible for the pacifists to eschew all use of force and violence.

Pacifism has always posed a serious problem, both to the pacifist and to the nonpacifist. The nonpacifist, feeling "a pacifist is either a slave or a parasite on someone who will fight for his freedom," tends to resent being a host. The pacifist, on the other hand, does not wish to use force or to have it used for him by others. In a recent case, some pacifists who were pushed around by some drunken teenagers refused to prefer charges because they were not willing to even indirectly apply force. Having the police and courts use force or the threat of force on your behalf is as much a violation of nonviolence as using force directly. Furthermore, some pacifists not only object to the use of force by those parts of the social organization (police, courts, and the armed forces), which are built upon the premise that the use of force is necessary, but they also object to the very existence of these institutions of organized violence and would rather not pay taxes for their support. They will refuse to serve if drafted, which means that their share of the burden of military service is shifted to nonpacifists. Since the number of pacifists is small, this is, of course, a minor effect.

It would seem sensible to search for an institutional improvement—a change that from the standpoint of the pacifist and from the standpoint of the nonpacifist will appear to be desirable.[1] In part, this agreement would result from the somewhat different views of the nature of the world and of human nature held by the pacifist and the nonpacifist, and the enactment of the necessary changes would, in a sense, be an experiment of finding out which view of the world is correct. The scientific value of the experiment would be a further argument for the change.

The proposal, stated in the simplest terms, is to permit the pacifist to put his principles into practice by arranging to let him stop paying taxes to support the police and army, and, at the same time, see to it that these agencies do not use force to protect him.[2] Pacifists can be roughly divided into two classes: those who object to the use of force or the threat of force to protect them from foreign enemies, and those who object to the use of force or threats to protect them both from foreign and domestic enemies. The first group does not object to police forces, only to armies, and are much more numerous than the second. For simplicity, however, let us begin our discussion with the second group—those who also object to the use of force by the police.

The institutional arrangements would be fairly simple. Anyone who formally declared himself a pacifist of this sort would be immediately excused from paying that share of *future* taxes that went to support the organs of force and violence, the police and armed forces. He would be compelled, however, to wear a conspicuous symbol of his pacifism and to display a similar symbol on all of his property.[3] This would leave him with all of his rights as a citizen

1. Some of the people who call themselves pacifists are actually simply trying to evade the draft by lying. These people would not be benefited by the proposed changes.

2. Pacifists do not necessarily object to all of the activities of the police and armed forces. The police direct traffic and return lost children, and the army engineers engage in public works. The pacifist presumably would wish to continue paying that part of his taxes that supports these noncoercive activities and continue to benefit from them.

3. The converse possibility, having everyone except the pacifists wear and display a symbol of nonpacifism, would be more trouble in view of the disproportionate numbers involved, but there would be no other objection. In practice, keeping up-to-date lists of the pacifists and their property and making them available to anyone interested would, no doubt, be sufficient even without the symbols.

except the right to call on the organizations of force and violence to protect him, and would resemble the situation in some small towns where fire protection is provided only for those who pay subscriptions to the volunteer fire department.

If, for example, someone occupied the pacifist's house, he could go to court and get a judgment against the occupier that he could then display to the person wrongfully living in his house or put on a picket sign, but the sheriff would not remove the occupier. Similarly, if the occupier, tiring of the pacifist's picketing his house, came out with a club and inflicted severe injury upon him, this would be an illegal act, but the police would not use force to confine the assaulter or to stop him. It would be open to anyone, including, of course, the police, to expostulate with the illegal occupier of the pacifist's house and to point out to him the wicked nature of his activity, but no force or threat of any sort would be used to coerce him into the paths of virtue.[4]

The possibility of a private citizen's using force to protect pacifists would require special arrangements. Suppose, for example, Miss Smith, a registered pacifist, is being raped by an evil-doer. Jones, passing by, attacks the rapist. Clearly, Jones is violating the wishes both of Miss Smith, who does not want force used to protect her, and the rapist, who wishes to be undisturbed. Strictly speaking, he is committing an assault on the rapist. It would, however, not be necessary to arrest Jones in order to ensure Miss Smith against forcible protection. Jones could have the situation explained to him by the police and, if necessary, they could restrain him while the rape proceeded.[5]

Another complication would arise if one of the registered pacifists used force to defend himself. Richard Roe, for example, approaches pacifist Doe with the objective of taking his wallet and car key. Doe tries to prevent this by hitting or threatening to hit Roe. There are three possible explanations for his behavior. The first, that Doe is not really a pacifist, but only a man trying to fraudulently reduce his tax liabilities, raises no particular difficulties. He can be sent to prison for tax fraud. The second, that Doe has changed his

4. Since policemen normally wear uniforms that suggest the use of force in such situations, if they chose to chide the unlawful occupier, it would be advisable for them to make the situation clear to him in order to avoid his misunderstanding their words as containing a threat of force. Some form of words such as: "Your victim is a registered pacifist and, therefore, we police will not use any form of force or threat of force to stop you from beating him or to put you in prison or collect a fine from you, but I think what you are doing is wrong," would be suitable.

5. If Jones were the hot-tempered type, it might be wise to put him under peace bond in order to ensure that he does not assault the rapist the next time he sees him.

mind and wishes to cease to be a registered pacifist, also raises no particular difficulties. The rule should be that he can cease to be a pacifist at any time, subject only to the requirement that he proceed forthwith to the tax office in order to make arrangements to be put back on the tax rolls. If, however, Roe had got hold of the wallet before Doe ceased to be a pacifist, Doe would not be permitted to use force to reclaim it because that would be the use of force to protect a registered pacifist even though retroactively. It might also be wise to put Doe under a peace bond to make sure that he did not take his abandonment of pacifism too far.

The third possibility, that Doe is still a pacifist but has temporarily lost control of himself, raises more difficult problems. Clearly he has violated his own standards of morality and presumably wishes to be punished for his dereliction. He has also violated the law by using force to protect a pacifist—legally, he is assaulting Roe. It would seem clear that he should be imprisoned, but here it may be wiser to be merciful. After he has recovered himself, Roe could be allowed to proceed. If Doe has any doubt of his ability to stay true to his principles, the police could help him by, say, handcuffing him so that he will not be able to interfere with Roe even if he once again loses control.

So much for the total pacifists. The pacifists who object to the use of force against foreigners but not against domestic criminals can be dealt with in a very similar manner. They would be excused only that share of their taxes that went to the support of the armed forces and would receive normal police protection against depredation by their fellow citizens. If a citizen or agency of a foreign country, however, takes a pacifist's car or kidnaps him in order to put him to work in a slave labor camp, no force would be used to protect him. Presumably there would be a certain time lag between the institution of this special status for pacifists and the establishment by foreign businesses and governments of the necessary organizations to take advantage of the opportunity. With time, however, it would be fair to assume that various alien individuals, companies, and governments would establish offices in the United States for the purpose of exploiting the situation. The underdeveloped countries, with their shortage of technically qualified personnel, would probably be particularly active in acquiring selected pacifists. If the present king of Saudi Arabia is not successful in suppressing the slave trade in that kingdom, it should provide a ready market, particularly for young women.

The basic idea could be expanded to deal with other groups. In recent years there has been an upsurge of anarchism, and providing the anarchists with the right to refuse to pay all taxes in return for their agreement that they will receive no governmental services might be practical. In my own opinion, both the people who call themselves anarchists and those who claim pacifism would, if presented with the opportunity of putting their principles into practice, refuse. Furthermore, those who at first chose to abandon the protection of the organized use of violence by special organs of society would, I think, rapidly change their minds on experiencing the results.[6] But this is only my opinion. Making the institutional change I suggest would not only increase freedom by making a set of alternatives that is now barred open, it would also provide experimental evidence on what is now a debated point of social theory.

Pacifism and anarchism, however, are general social philosophies. The purpose of this book has been to deal with a large number of detailed problems of social policy. It is true that the use of force to compel people to carry out the policies decided upon has been implicit, and, hence, the argument is relevant. But, basically, we have been concerned with such mundane matters as whether theft and robbery would be illegal. The reasoning can be applied in many of these areas, as well. The social contract is not necessarily without exceptions. Let us suppose that Smith objects to laws against theft. There is no reason why we could not provide a modification of the law so that he is free to steal the property of his neighbors (subject, of course, to possible reaction on their part) and is not protected against theft of his own property. If a great many people took this option, it might cause serious economic difficulties; but if only a few did, there is no reason why it should raise any difficult problems.

Furthermore, it is highly probable that in practice no one would take advantage of the "privilege"; if a few people did, they would very rapidly decide to retract. We can think of a number of other parts of our law in which this is also true, the law against murder, the law against assault and battery, and the law against robbery. We could not, of course, permit people to suddenly move out from under the law of murder and then move back in again a few minutes later.

There are certain parts of the law where this option could not be offered because the "criminal" activity is not reciprocal. Rape is the obvious case, but automobile offenses are probably much more important. In general, the

6. Einstein, during his early life, was an active pacifist. During the later period of his life, he was an active proponent of preparedness and war. His experience with the Nazis was the cause of his remarkably rapid conversion.

individual who decides he does not wish to obey the speed limit would be endangering his own life and would be endangering other people's lives as well, but there is no way in which his desire not to obey the speed limit can directly react back on him in the same way as would his withdrawal from the law against theft. Thus, it would not be possible in this case to permit individuals to opt out.

Still, there does not seem any basic reason why we should not give individuals the right to opt out of a number of particular portions of the law. This, it must be admitted, would have very little practical effect; since it would be a complication, we might object to it on those grounds. Its principal advantages would be in making the mutually beneficial aspects of the law more obvious. If individuals were permitted to step outside some particular portion of the law anytime they wished, they would then be prevented from arguing that this law worked to their disadvantage. This is, however, a very modest advantage and this whole appendix is, in my opinion, a matter of very little importance. That, in fact, is the reason it is an appendix instead of part of the text of the book.

APPENDIX B

GENERAL TABLE OF SYMBOLS[1]

B = Benefit expected to be derived by potential liar from the action being urged
B_{b_1} = Benefit obtained by Party 1 from successfully breaching the contract
B_{b_2} = Benefit obtained by Party 2 from successfully breaching the contract
B_{c_1} = Benefit derived by Party 1 from the completion of the contract
B_{c_2} = Benefit derived by Party 2 from the completion of the contract
C_l = Cost of lying (conscience cost)
C_{b_1} = Cost to Party 1 of successful breach of contract by Party 2
C_{b_2} = Cost to Party 2 of successful breach of contract by Party 1
C_c = Total court costs to parties
C_{c_1} = Cost to Party 1 of court proceedings
C_{c_2} = Cost to Party 2 of court proceedings
C_{in} = Cost of information
C_o = Conscience cost
C_p = (Chap. 8) Private cost of enforcement (includes cost of incorrect tax penalties)
(Chap. 12) Costs of punishment
C_r = (Chap. 11) Crime rate, likelihood individual will be victim of crime
(Chap. 12) Injury to reputation through others' knowledge that an individual has lied
C_R = (Chap. 8) Cost of Revenue Protection Service
C_t = Cost of being victim of crime
D_c = Disgrace resulting from confession
D_t = (Chap. 9) Disgrace resulting from conviction at trial
(Chap. 11) Direct profit of crime
E = Evidence
I = (Chap. 4) Insurance payment
(Chap. 8) Income
I' = Some part of income

(cont.)

1. In some cases, the same symbol has been used to represent different things in different chapters.

GENERAL TABLE OF SYMBOLS *(cont.)*

I_c = Cost to individual of investigation by authorities of crimes that he did not commit

I_l = Injury suffered by victim from carrying out action urged by liar

L = Likelihood that the lie will be believed

L_{b_1} = Likelihood Party 1 will attempt to breach the contract

L_{b_2} = Likelihood Party 2 will attempt to breach the contract

L_C = Likelihood of compliance

L_c = Likelihood of conviction

L_d = Likelihood of detection of evasion

L_e = Likelihood that court will make erroneous decision

L_{fc} = Likelihood individual will be falsely convicted for crime he did not commit

L_{ns_1} = Likelihood that if Party 1 breaches the contract, Party 2 will refrain from suing him

L_{ns_2} = Likelihood that if Party 2 breaches the contract, Party 1 will refrain from suing him

L_p = Likelihood of punishment if lie is not believed

L_r = Likelihood that injury to the reputation will occur if lie is not believed

L_s = Likelihood individual will commit crime

N = Social return on tax (excess burden not subtracted)

P = (Chap. 4) Procedural function
(Chap. 8) Penal rate for detected noncompliers
(Chap. 11) Payoff (may be negative)
(Chap. 12) Persuasive effect of the lie: probability that the lie, if believed, will bring about the desired action

P_1 = Payoff of contract to Party 1

P_2 = Payoff of contract to Party 2

P_{b_1} = Payoff to 1 of breaching the contract

P_{b_2} = Payoff to 2 of breaching the contract

P_c = (Chap. 9) Punishment resulting from confession
(Chap. 11) Cost of maintaining police, prisons, courts

P_n = Persuasive effect of the lie: probability that the lie, if believed, will bring about the desired action

P_r = Private cost of protection against theft. Includes nonproduction

P_t = Punishment resulting from conviction at trial

P_u = (Chap. 9) Publicity case has received
(Chap. 11) Punishment
Q_d = Quality of defense
Q_j = Quality of trial system
R = (Chap. 8) Tax rate
(Chap. 9) Risk aversion factor
R' = Prosecutor's aversion to low conviction ratio
T_r = Tax revenue (net of direct enforcement costs)

The Economics of Legal Proceedings

THE "DEAD HAND" OF MONOPOLY

James M. Buchanan and Gordon Tullock

Introduction

There is apparently some sort of common agreement, one presumably based on observation, that firms possessing and exercising monopoly power in varying degrees do in fact exist in many local, regional, national, and international markets. And by analytical definition the exercise of such monopoly power violates the necessary conditions for optimum efficiency or, more technically, for Pareto-optimality in resource use. By inference, then, there must necessarily exist some unexploited gains-from-trade between the monopolist, on the one hand, and his consumer-customers, actual and potential, on the other. Why, then, do we not also observe, especially in localized markets, more efforts on the part of consumer-organized cooperatives to secure control of the monopoly firms through ordinary market purchase or acquisition? Casual observation suggests that such attempts are rare indeed.[1]

"EMERGING COMPETITION"—ORGANIZATION COSTS

This set of circumstances can be explained, of course, on either one of two familiar grounds. It can be argued, first, that the pervasiveness of emerging competition is such that monopoly power, where it exists, is *always on the way to being dissipated.* Thus, in this view, the dynamics of the competitive process itself are such that monopoly is not really a serious problem at all, and the absence of consumer-cooperative attempts at market control is merely evidence of this fact.

A second line of reasoning partially contradicts and partially supplements that first one. Monopoly power can, it is admitted here, be a serious problem, and major inefficiencies can and do exist because of those monopoly restrictions. However, consumers cannot be expected to organize to exploit the resulting gains-from-trade because of the *cost of organization.* Consumers of the

Reprinted from *Antitrust Law and Economics Review* 1 (summer 1968): 85–96. Copyright by *Antitrust Law and Economics Review*. Reprinted by permission of the copyright holder.

1. See John S. McGee, "Patent Exploitation: Some Economic and Legal Problems," *Journal of Law and Economics* 9 (October, 1966), page 148: "It *is* true that intelligent, self-coerced consumer organizations, if created at low cost—or [by] the state acting in their behalf—could outbid the monopolist, producing net benefits and yet paying off the inventor. But little has been said of this possibility in the reform literature."

monopoly firm's product are likely to be many, and any attempt on their part to secure joint action would run into prohibitively high cost barriers. Thus, even in the presence of a significant degree of monopoly exploitation, it still might not be feasible for consumers to organize themselves, or to submit to the activities of entrepreneurs seeking to organize them, and enter into market-like negotiations to buy out the monopolist.

MONOPOLY PROFITS

There is doubtless some measure of validity in both of these familiar arguments. But they nonetheless tend to gloss over and conceal an important aspect of the whole monopoly issue, namely, the fact that the *current* owners of monopoly firms may not in fact be earning more than a competitive return on *their* investment, that all present and future monopoly profits may have already been "capitalized" and removed by former owners of the firm. Thus we might still fail to observe such units being formed even in the presence of what seem to be really serious cases of monopoly power and even if the *costs* of organizing such effective consumers' cooperatives were absent or, say, fully subsidized from federal funds. In one sense, however, our analysis here can be incorporated into the "cost" argument, since we also demonstrate why individual consumers would be reluctant to enter into such arrangements.

The Welfare Triangle

CONSUMER GAIN—SOCIAL GAIN

Consider a single consumer of a monopolist's product, as, for example, the one depicted in Figure 1. For the sake of simplicity, assume that all of the many consumers of this product are identical and that the monopolist himself is secured in his position, i.e., freed from the threat of entry by potential competitors by, say, patent rights. The costs of producing the good, including a normal rate of return on market-valued assets, are known to be $1 per unit, and these are constant over a wide quantity range. The price charged by the monopolist is $1.50 per unit, at which price each of his consumer-customers purchases 5 units per period, for a total outlay of $7.50. At a price of $1 (the normal or "competitive" price), the consumer would purchase 10 units, for a total expenditure of $10. The measure of the gain that would accrue *to this consumer* by abolition of the monopoly is shown by the familiar triangle, shaded in Figure 1, *and* the profit rectangle to its left. Arithmetically,

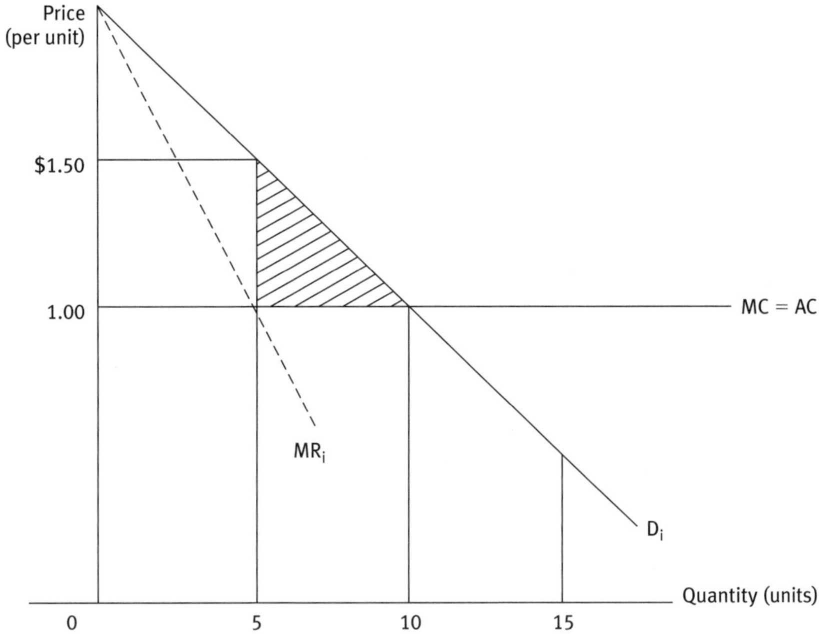

FIGURE 1

this amounts to $3.75 in this example, and, of course, $2.50 of this is a pure transfer. *The measure of the welfare gain to society would be $1.25 per buyer, i.e., $1.25 multiplied by the number of consumers of the product* (all of whom are assumed to be identical).

RECAPTURING THE "WELFARE TRIANGLE"

This simplified example suggests that the consumer should, rationally, stand willing to offer *up to $3.75* ($2.50 plus $1.25) for the privilege of being allowed to purchase freely at a normal or competitive price of $1. The monopolist should, on the other side of such a potential exchange, stand willing to provide the consumer with this privilege *at any sum over and above $2.50.*

Note that, if we confine the discussion to one customer, there seems to be no reason, at least in the conventional economic analysis of this problem, why the monopolist and the customer should not in fact make a mutually profitable arrangement here. The monopolist himself, for example, could form a discount club, one selling the right to buy the commodity for $1.00 to all customers willing to pay the present value of an income stream of, say, $2.90 per year. This would *recapture the welfare triangle ($1.25)* and thus benefit *both* the monopolist and the customers. (Under monopoly pricing, *neither* gets it.) And this opportunity for mutual profit would not appear, at least at first glance, to be confined to abstract models. If we consider only the traditional arguments, we should also expect such bargains to be struck in the real world, as can be readily demonstrated if we consider the problems of the real monopolist who wishes to maximize the *present* value of his *future* income stream. Clearly he could not sell the right to buy unlimited quantities at the competitive price, but putting limits on the quantities purchased should not pose any major problems for him. The prices charged for entry into the "discount club" could be a simple multiple of the number of units purchased in the year before it was organized.[2]

CAPITALIZED VALUE OF MONOPOLY FIRM

This scheme, it will be seen, immediately obviates one of the major reasons normally given for the absence of such efforts by customers to buy out monopolists. There is no need here for agreement among all the customers, although we might well expect all of them to buy into the discount club and hence eliminate the monopoly altogether. The real question, then, as noted, is the reason for the extreme shortage of such arrangements in the real world. (Dr. Ferdinand Levy has suggested that the sale of repair warranty contracts by manufacturers of consumer durables [e.g., automobiles] may be an example.) For this purpose, let us return to our earlier model, one in which all of the customers are equal, and consider the bargaining situation when a sequence of time periods is explicitly taken into account. Protected by a patent monopoly in this example, our monopolist will sell his right to exploit any customer for any sum above [$2.50/r], where *r* is the appropriate rate of discount (corrected to reflect risk premiums). Assuming consumers estimate the monopolist's risks to be the same as he estimates them, they should then be willing to pay for the whole operation any sum up to a maximum total of [$3.75/r]. Gains-from-trade continue to exist in terms of capitalized values.

CAPITALIZED VALUE OF "CONSUMER'S SURPLUS"

Consider, however, the position of the single consumer who may be asked to buy into this permanent discount club. Suppose that the monopolist has

2. Note that there is no effort here to obtain the consumer's surplus above the original monopoly price. Further, there is no need to get *all* of the customers to join the discount club. Membership could be offered on a non-discriminatory basis to anyone who wanted to pay for it.

set a selling price of [$3.00/r.] for membership. If the consumer expects his individual demand for the good to remain stable for a sufficiently long period of time, a subjective capitalization of a prospective consumer's surplus in subsequent periods may yield meaningfully high present values, and the consumer may, in this case, express a willingness to buy. Rarely, however, will the individual consumer actually expect his demand to remain stable over such long periods of time, and, even if this should be the case, the limitation on life spans would doubtless interfere to prevent the full capitalization of the consumer's surplus the above computation suggests.

This failure of the individual to capitalize fully his prospective consumer's surplus on his own account may not prevent his joining the club under certain conditions, however. Even if he expects his personal demand to be highly unstable and acts on the basis of a very limited time horizon, he may nevertheless express a willingness to buy in if, in exchange for his investment, he can secure a readily *marketable*, transferable asset. In the prospective exchange between the monopolist and the consumer, however, there is an asymmetry in that, for his part, the monopolist secures a currently liquid asset, while the consumer, on his part, secures the present value of an expectation only, his own expected consumer's surplus, an intangible that cannot so readily be transformed into current liquid assets.

Suppose, for example, that an exchange is made on the terms suggested and that, after a few time periods have elapsed, the consumer seeks to market his membership. It is possible, of course, to imagine several institutional arrangements that could make such a marketing of individual shares reasonably efficient, but these arrangements would in every case be costly in themselves. The individual who either enters the market or leaves it entirely can probably be taken care of without too much difficulty, but it is hard to see how the consumer who wishes to reduce his consumption (perhaps as a result of a change in technology) could get his capital back. If, for example, individual consumers (and/or the monopolist) could yearly buy and sell the right to purchase one unit, then the real cost per unit to the individual purchaser would return to what it was before the discount club was organized. The best alternative would probably be to sell the original memberships at a price that discounts not only the monopolist's view of changes in his market, but the individual consumer's view as to whether or not he will remain a part of that market. New customers could buy in, but old customers could not sell out; they would simply lose their capital when they moved out of the market. This would, of course, sharply reduce the desirability of entering the club in the first place, however, thus suggesting that the individual, as a consumer, might well be reluctant to capitalize his prospective consumer's surplus in such a highly uncertain world.

Monopoly Profits, "Deadweight" Debt, and "Future Generations"

THE "TIME-DIMENSION" PROBLEM

The difficulty in organizing exchanges where consumers can secure fully marketable assets stems, in turn, from the more fundamental problem raised by the *time dimensions* of the exchanges, a problem that is almost wholly ignored in orthodox analysis. The welfare gains that might possibly be secured from the elimination of monopoly output restrictions accrue largely to consumers in periods of time *subsequent* to that in which an institutional exchange of the sort discussed above might take place. Consumers in any *current* period may be reluctant to enter into such purchase agreements because of this feature alone, a fact that immediately suggests the analogy with the retirement of deadweight public debt. In this latter situation, current taxpayers may be very reluctant to retire outstanding issues of deadweight public debt for the simple reason that the *beneficiaries* of this action will be taxpayers living in time periods *subsequent* to the retirement operation, i.e., future generations. Only to the extent that they themselves expect to be members of such future taxpaying groups will current taxpayers willingly retire such deadweight public debt, and there are perhaps very few who will be sufficiently Ricardian in their outlook to carry out the full capitalization required to make such a decision wholly rational.[3]

"BURDEN" OF MONOPOLY

The suggestion here is that the burden of existing monopoly restrictions is similar to that involved in carrying public debt of this type. The latter consists in the *interest charges* on the debt and, within any single period of time, these charges may be small relative to some appropriate national output measure, e.g., gross national product (GNP). Similarly, the burden of monopoly,

3. For the theory of public debt upon which this discussion is based, see James M. Buchanan, *Public Principles of Public Debt* (Homewood: Richard D. Irwin, 1958); for subsequent discussions by both supporters and opponents, see James Ferguson (ed.), *Public Debt and Future Generations* (Chapel Hill: University of North Carolina Press, 1964).

a loss approximated by the welfare triangle, may be small relative to GNP in any single period, as indeed recent attempts at empirical measurement have tended to suggest.[4] Neither of these conclusions should imply, however, that major public benefits would not be produced by the elimination of the burden-producing debt instruments and monopolistic institutions. Effective retirement of outstanding deadweight debt would produce definite *present-value* benefits, the magnitude of these being measured by the capitalized annual interest charges. And elimination of monopoly restrictions would also produce substantial *present-value* benefits, the size of these being measured by the capitalized current welfare losses (approximated by the welfare triangle in Figure 1). It is these present-value *benefits* that must be placed alongside the *costs* of taking such action in any rational cost-benefit calculus.

MONOPOLY-CREATION "MODELS"

The analogy with deadweight public debt can be applied also to the *creation* of monopoly. The monopolization of an industry previously competitive in structure is, in the absence of technological change, analogous in effect to the issuance of public debt to finance *wholly worthless* public outlays. The net *wealth of the community is reduced* in either case, with wealth being properly measured to include present values for future tax liabilities, in the one case, and present values of foregone consumers' surplus, in the other.

As an alternative model, consider a monopoly that emerges coincident with a technological innovation, say, through a conferred patent right. The wealth of the community may well increase, and the monopolist's valuation of his patent right should be included in any measurement of national wealth. In addition, some consumers' surplus may also be produced, despite the prospects of monopoly restriction. (This is represented in Figure 1 by the *upper* triangle above the monopoly-profits area.) And conceptually, at least, the present value of *this* stream of prospective consumers' surplus should also be included in any measurement procedure. This latter monopoly model thus becomes partially analogous to an issue of public debt to finance a public project that is *more than marginally productive.* Here, net *national wealth is in fact increased* to some extent. The claims that public creditors, internal or external, have against the community in the form of the debt instruments is thus in some respects similar to the "claim" of the monopolist, as measured

4. See A. C. Harberger, "Monopoly and Resource Allocation," *American Economic Review* 44 (May, 1954), 77–87.

by his valuation of his patent right. The differences between the two cases here stem from the different *locations* of the wealth-creating activity. In the monopoly case, new wealth is presumably brought into being by the monopolist, this act of creation justifying or validating his "right" to a claim against the community. In the debt-issue case, new wealth is also presumably brought into being, but by an act of the community as a whole. The net worth of the creditors who lend funds for the activation of the new project is not changed; instead, the increase in net worth is distributed over all citizens in accordance with their expectations of "beneficiaries' surplus." Aside from this essentially distributional difference, the two cases differ also in that the proper valuation of the debt-financed project will include a full measure of prospective "beneficiaries' surplus," the whole of the area under the "demand curve," with no expected monopoly restriction. In other words, the welfare triangle will be included in this measure.

A third model of monopoly creation lies somewhere between these first two. The introduction of a technological innovation, for example, even if it causes or allows a previously competitive industry to become monopolized in the process, might well leave the country's net *national wealth unchanged.* In this instance, the monopoly output restriction might do no more than *just offset* the technological gains introduced. Hence the appropriate analogy in this case would be that of a public-debt issue employed to finance a project that is *just marginally productive.*

MONOPOLY PROFITS "CAPITALIZED" AT "MOMENT OF CREATION"

Attention to the various analogies between monopoly creation and public-debt issue produces what should be an obvious conclusion but one that, in our view, has not been sufficiently emphasized before. *The benefits of monopoly tend to be capitalized at the moment of creation*, at least to the extent that marketable assets (e.g., stocks) are brought into being. And insofar as such capitalization does in fact take place, future generations, in the aggregate, must bear the monopoly burden in terms of the offsetting losses in consumers' surplus.

Suppose that, in some base year t_0, an individual is granted a monopoly right to produce the good depicted in Figure 1. The present value of this right, over and above the market value of the assets used to produce it, is measured at [\$3.00n/r]. This is a marketable asset, and the individual monopolist enters this on the left-hand side of his balance sheet, offsetting it with a similar increase in net worth on the right-hand side. On the national balance sheet, therefore, there will appear an increment to or increase in the wealth of the economy. We assume that the capitalized value of consumers' surplus, measured by the upper triangle, is not computed.

Suppose now that, in a later period t_1, the individual who owns the monopoly right sells out to a purchaser at a price approximated by [\$3.00n/r]. To the purchaser, this investment must be roughly equal in yield to his alternative investment prospects. And, to the seller, competition among prospective purchasers will insure that the yield is equal to that on alternative investments of roughly the same risk. The purchaser of his monopoly right, in t_1, thus writes up this asset on his balance sheet and writes down some other asset. His net worth remains unchanged, save for the possibility of marginal adjustments. Having acquired the monopoly right, however, the net worth of the new owner *now depends on the continuation of the existing and expected monopoly output restrictions.* If through governmental action or otherwise, his monopoly right is now eliminated, he suffers a capital loss. *His* net worth is reduced, while the *net worth of the original monopolizer remains unchanged.* To make our example dramatic, we can allow the latter to die between t_1 and t_2, with the monopoly restriction eliminated only in the latter period, after his death.

NO MONOPOLY PROFITS FOR CURRENT OWNERS

Thus it may be quite literally true that existing monopoly restrictions do not differentially benefit *current* owners of monopoly firms, save in some opportunity-cost sense, but, rather, that these benefits have long since been capitalized by monopoly entrepreneurs of generations past. The evil of monopoly lies in the period of creation, and the ill-gotten gains may now be enjoyed by third-generation playboys who cruise the Riviera and live off giltedge coupons, quite beyond the reach of any antitrust order. These gains thus remain untouched by any efforts to break up and eliminate the monopolies existing at any particular moment in time, leaving the unfortunate current owners of the monopoly rights as the ones singled out for unjust public treatment.

It is, of course, widely recognized that monopoly restrictions do not necessarily imply monopoly profits. It is perhaps less widely acknowledged that the existence of monopoly profits, in the ordinary sense, do not imply that any current owner of a monopoly firm earns more than a normal rate of return on his own *personal* investment. The *physical* assets of the firm will be employed in such a way as to yield more than a normal return but the current owner, in *purchasing* these assets, may have transferred to the *former* owners the fully capitalized value of all expected *future* monopoly returns.

Implications for Public Policy

The monopoly problem is thus seen here as a blend of simple capitalization theory, simple accounting, and a recognition of the analogy with the problem of "deadweight" public debt. Once these separate elements of the analysis are seen, the general conclusions are fairly self-evident. Mention might be made here, however, of a number of practical policy suggestions presented by this analysis.

"PREVENTION" VERSUS "CURE"

Both equity and casual observation of the collective or political decision-making process suggests the importance of concentrating on the *prevention* of monopoly, rather than upon its elimination after it has already been created. The social "evil" of monopoly tends to be *concentrated in the moment of creation*, and, once this original sin is committed, the effects are capitalized or frozen into the system. And while it is, of course, true that monopoly creation can be, and probably is in many cases, a continuous process that grows over time, the more instantaneous phenomenon is nonetheless sufficiently real to warrant a shift of emphasis toward the prevention rather than the attempted cure of monopoly problems.

"COMPENSATION" FOR CURRENT MONOPOLY-OWNERS?

Equity considerations alone suggest the desirability of providing appropriate *compensation* to current stockholders when long-existing monopoly restrictions are eliminated by express governmental action. These restrictions having probably been long since capitalized by former owners, the *current* owners may well be realizing, as noted, no more than the normally expected gains from their individual investments. Simple norms of justice would thus suggest that those current owners of shares in monopoly firms be considered no more "guilty" than non-owners and hence that any monopoly-elimination without compensation would amount, in such cases, to a particularly discriminatory "tax" on current shareholders, one that, if placed on that group openly, might well fail to win legislative approval or even constitutional sanction by the judiciary.

"POLITICAL" BARRIERS TO "COMPENSATION"?

Despite these acknowledged equity considerations, however, even cursory attention to democratic decision-making processes suggests that public policy would rarely attempt to eliminate any existing monopoly positions if compensation *was* in fact tied to the elimination measures. To pay compensation requires an outlay of public funds, and it would doubtless be very difficult to persuade current-period taxpayers (as represented in legislative assemblies) that *they* should support such outlays today when the prospective beneficiaries of their sacrifice would be consumers of *future* periods. The policy solution is almost implied in the question, What is the best form of compensation to monopolists that the government is eliminating? The appropriate *method of financing* such compensation would be one involving the use of special issues of public debt instruments, a solution that would of course allow for an appropriate balancing-off, in a temporal sense, of anticipated costs and anticipated benefits, making the suggested outcome plausible for a rational democratic choice while at the same time securing reasonable equity in results.

Thus at least two specific applications of these principles come immediately to mind. First, if a collective decision should be made to shift a long-standing private monopoly to public or national ownership for the purpose of eliminating its monopoly output restrictions, this analysis clearly suggests that the funds to be used for compensating existing owners should be financed by debt issue, not by taxation.

PATENT POLICY—FREE LICENSING

Perhaps a more important practical application, however, lies in the realm of patent policy. If the award of monopoly rights is considered essential to insure the continuation of adequate incentives for invention, research, and development, this analysis suggests that many of the undesirable side effects of patent monopolies could be eliminated by a combination of the institutional devices noted here. Thus an individual or firm could be granted full patent rights on new products, but, once those rights were established at market values, public purchase (financed by debt issue) could be undertaken, accompanied by an arrangement for *free licensing*, a solution that would allow public purchase of the patent right without implying public purchase or ownership of producing assets.

DOES PUNISHMENT DETER CRIME?

Traditionally there have been three arguments for the punishment of criminals. The first of these is that punishment is morally required or, another way of putting the same thing, that it is necessary for the community to feel morally satisfied. I will not discuss this further. The two remaining explanations are that punishment deters crime and that it may rehabilitate the criminal. The rehabilitation argument was little used before about 1800, presumably because the punishments in vogue up to that time had little prospect of producing any positive effect upon the moral character of the criminal.[1]

But with the turn to imprisonment as the principal form of punishment—a movement which occurred in the latter part of the 18th and early part of the 19th century—the idea that the prison might "rehabilitate" the prisoner became more common. The word "penitentiary" was coined with the intent of describing a place where the prisoner has the time and the opportunity to repent of his sins and resolve to follow a more socially approved course of action after his release. The idea that prisons would rehabilitate the criminal and that this was their primary purpose gradually replaced the concept of deterrence as the principal publicly announced justification for the punishment system. I should like to defer discussing my views as to why this occurred until the latter part of this article, but here I should like to point out that whatever the motive or the reason for this change it certainly was not the result of careful scientific investigation.

So far as I have been able to discover, there were no efforts to test the deterrent effect of punishment scientifically until about 1950. At that time, several studies were made investigating the question of whether the death penalty deterred murder more effectively than life imprisonment. These studies showed that it did not, but they were extremely primitive statistically. This is not to criticize the scholars who made them. Computers were not then readily available, the modern statistical techniques based on the computer had not yet been fully developed, and, last but by no means least, the

Reprinted, with permission of the author, from *The Public Interest* 36 (summer 1974): 103–11.

1. Of course, they might prevent him from committing the crime by making it physically impossible. Cutting off both hands of a forger and hanging them about his neck probably had no effect on his desire to commit forgery, but certainly made it very hard to do.

scholars who undertook the work were not very good statisticians. Under the circumstances, we cannot blame them for the inadequacies of their work, but neither should we give much weight to their findings.

Moreover, even if it were the case that the death penalty did not deter murder, it would not automatically follow that deterrence does not work in general. The argument is frequently made that life imprisonment is actually a more severe punishment than the death penalty, and it might turn out to be true—at least in the eyes of potential murderers. If this were the case, then one would anticipate that life imprisonment would have a greater deterrent effect than would execution. But in any event, the findings obtained in these early studies were largely the result of their very primitive statistical techniques.

Statistically testing deterrence is not easy, because the prospect of punishment obviously is not the *only* thing that affects the frequency with which crimes are committed. The crime rate varies with the degree of urbanization, the demographic composition of the population, the distribution of wealth, and many other circumstances. Some statistical technique is necessary to take care of these factors—and such techniques are now available. Using multiple regression (or, in a few cases, a complicated variant on the chi-square test), it is possible to put figures on each of these variables into the same equation and to see how much they influence the dependent variable which, in this case, is the rate of a specific crime. Although there are difficulties, this procedure will give a set of numbers called coefficients that are measures of the effect of *each* of the purported causative factors on the rate of commission of the given crime. If punishment deters crime, it will show up in these figures as a coefficient that is both significant and negative. A number of other things in the equation may also show up as affecting the crime rate, but the purpose of this article is to discuss only whether *punishment* does or does not deter crime.

One of the basic problems with any kind of statistical research in the field of criminology is the appallingly poor quality of the data. Any study will have a great deal of what the statistician calls "random noise" in it. Most of the studies mentioned below use the FBI's *Uniform Crime Report* statistics, and almost all of the authors have made comments about how bad these statistics are. I am happy to say that the Law Enforcement Assistance Administration has begun a project aimed at a sharp improvement in crime statistics, and hence we can anticipate that such research will be a great deal easier in the future. All of the studies I will report are based on the earlier and poorer statistics, but in about a year or so there should be a new generation of studies drawing upon the much better data that will be available at that time.

The recent studies in deterrence come partly from economists and partly from sociologists. As an economist myself, I may be pardoned for starting with the economic studies, but I should say that owing to the long delay that intervenes between research and publication it is not at all obvious which discipline actually had priority.

Most economists who give serious thought to the problem of crime immediately come to the conclusion that punishment will indeed deter crime. The reason is perfectly simple: Demand curves slope downward. If you increase the cost of something, less will be consumed. Thus, if you increase the cost of committing a crime, there will be fewer crimes. The elasticity of the demand curve, of course, might be low, in which case the effect might be small; but there should be at least *some* effect.

Economists, of course, would not deny that there are other factors that affect the total number of crimes. Unemployment, for example, quite regularly raises the amount of crime, and, at least under modern conditions, changes in the age composition of the population seem to be closely tied to changes in the crime rate. The punishment variable, however, has the unique characteristic of being fairly easy to change by government action. Thus, if it does have an effect, we should take advantage of that fact.

The 19th-century utilitarians had drawn this conclusion, and when economists in the 1950's and early 1960's began turning their attention to the problem of deterrence, this rather simple application of economic theory was one of the first things that occurred to them.[2] The first econometric test of this theoretical deduction from economics was performed by one of Gary Becker's graduate students, Arleen Smigel Leibowitz, in her master's thesis.[3] The basic design of this research project was reasonably sophisticated, although, as can be seen below, it has been improved upon since then. Leibowitz used as her basic data the crime rate and the punishment for a number

2. See Gary Becker, "Crime and Punishment: An Economic Approach," *Journal of Political Economy* 76 (March/April, 1968): 169–217. See also Gordon Tullock, "The Welfare Costs of Tariffs, Monopolies, and Theft," *Western Economic Journal* 5 (June, 1967): 224–32; and "An Economic Approach to Crime," *Social Science Quarterly* 50 (June, 1969): 59–71.

3. Arleen Smigel Leibowitz, "Does Crime Pay: An Economic Analysis" (master's thesis, Columbia University, 1965).

of different crimes in each state in the United States. She took into account both the severity of punishment (i.e., the average prison sentence) and the probability that punishment will actually be imposed (i.e., the percentage of crimes whose perpetrators are caught and sent to prison). A number of essentially sociological factors that might affect the crime rate were also included in her multiple regressions. Leibowitz's findings revealed an unambiguous deterrence effect on each of the crimes studied—that is, when other factors were held constant, the states which had a higher level of punishment showed fewer crimes. Such crimes as rape and murder were deterred by punishment just as well as (indeed, perhaps better than) burglary and robbery.

Another of Becker's students, Isaac Ehrlich, in his doctoral dissertation went over much the same ground as Leibowitz but with a much more sophisticated and careful statistical methodology. The results, which are available in full text in his dissertation and in a somewhat abridged form in an article,[4] once again indicate that punishment does deter crime.

Further work along the same general lines was carried out by Llad Phillips, Harold L. Votey, Jr., and John Howell. In general, these scholars used the same basic data and analytical methods as Leibowitz and Ehrlich, and confirmed their findings. More recently, this group of scholars has used the same data and similar methods in an effort to produce more detailed and specific results.[5] These studies, which are of great interest in themselves, are relevant to our present purpose only in that, as a sort of by-product, they contain further confirmation of the basic finding that punishment does deter crime. Further, Phillips has run a time-series test using national data in his multiple regression to supplement the cross-sectional tests on state

4. Isaac Ehrlich, "Participation in Illegitimate Activities: An Economic Analysis" (Ph.D. dissertation, Columbia University, 1970); and "Participation in Illegitimate Activities: A Theoretical and Empirical Investigation," *Journal of Political Economy* (May/June, 1973): 521–65.

5. Harold L. Votey, Jr., and Llad Phillips, *Economic Crimes: Their Generation, Deterrence, and Control* (Springfield, Va.: U.S. Clearinghouse for Federal Scientific and Technical Information, 1969); Harold L. Votey, Jr., and Llad Phillips, "The Law Enforcement Production Function," *Journal of Legal Studies* 1 (June, 1972); Llad Phillips and Harold L. Votey, Jr., "An Economic Analysis of the Deterrent Effect of Law Enforcement on Criminal Activity," *Journal of Criminal Law, Criminology, and Police Science* 63 (September, 1972); and Llad Phillips and Harold L. Votey, Jr., "The Control of Criminal Activity: An Economic Analysis," in *Handbook of Criminology*, ed. Daniel Glaser (Chicago: Rand McNally & Co.), forthcoming.

data.[6] It also produced similar results. Last along this particular line, Morgan Reynolds, in his doctoral dissertation, has treated the same basic research design en route to some new results in another area.[7]

In addition to these studies using essentially the same data on crime and punishment in the 50 states, there are two important studies using different data. Michael Block compared the crime rates for Los Angeles police districts with the likelihood in each of these districts that offenders would be caught and sent to prison, and found a clear deterrence effect.[8] And R. A. Carr-Hill and N. H. Stern carried out a study using data drawn from England and Wales and, once again, determined that punishment does deter crime.[9]

Joseph Magaddino and Gregory Krohm, using California county data, have begun work which, from the results shown by their first regressions, apparently will lead to the same conclusion.[10] David Sjoquist and Phillips, Votey, and Donald Maxwell investigated somewhat different problems, but their statistical outcomes provide further support for the deterrence theory.[11]

Finally, some students under my direction attempted to make a cost-benefit analysis of certain property crimes, primarily burglary, from the standpoint of the criminal—that is, they looked into the question of whether crime does pay. The data were particularly bad in this area, as the reader can well imagine, but they supported the conclusion that most people who took up the profession of burglary had made a sensible career choice. They did not make very much from burglary, but they were not very high quality laborers and would have done as badly (or worse) if they had elected honest

6. Llad Phillips, "Crime Control: The Case for Deterrence," in *The Economics of Crime and Punishment*, ed. Simon Rottenberg (Washington, D.C.: American Enterprise Institute for Public Policy Research, 1973), 65–84.

7. Morgan Reynolds, "Crimes for Profit: The Economics of Theft" (Ph.D. dissertation, University of Wisconsin, 1971).

8. Michael Block, "An Econometric Approach to Theft" (Stanford University, mimeographed).

9. R. A. Carr-Hill and N. H. Stern, *An Econometric Model of the Supply and Control of Recorded Offenses in England and Wales*, rev. ed. (University of Sussex, School of Social Science, 1972).

10. Joseph P. Magaddino and Gregory C. Krohm (untitled paper, in progress).

11. See David L. Sjoquist, "Property Crime and Economic Behavior: Some Empirical Results," *American Economic Review* 83, no. 3 (1973): 439–46; and Llad Phillips, Harold L. Votey, Jr., Donald Maxwell, and John Howell, "Crime, Youth, and the Labor Market," *Journal of Political Economy* 80 (May/June, 1972): 491–504.

employment.[12] This is not of direct relevance to the deterrence hypothesis, but it does seem to indicate that at least some criminals make fairly rational decisions with respect to their careers and, hence, that raising the price of crime would presumably reduce the frequency with which it is committed.

Recently this point of view has been questioned by a short study by Michael Sesnowitz.[13] (The article was commented upon by Krohm and a reply was made by Sesnowitz.[14]) Following an approach rather similar to that used by my students, Sesnowitz found that burglary did not pay in Pennsylvania. Basically, the difference between Sesnowitz's results and those which I would have expected comes from the fact that there are no data on the amount of time served by burglars in Pennsylvania who are sentenced to jail rather than prison. Sesnowitz assumed that the average jail sentence was the same as the average prison sentence for burglary (43 months). But since it is illegal in Pennsylvania for anyone to spend more than 23 months in jail (as opposed to prison), it is most unlikely that this is so; and if adjustments for this discrepancy are made, the results wind up rather similar to those obtained by my students. Incidentally, Pennsylvania apparently does have an exceptionally high punishment level for burglars—and, correspondingly, an exceptionally low rate of burglaries, just as the deterrence hypothesis would predict.

So much for the economists; let us now turn to the sociologists. All the economists I have cited began their studies under the impression that punishment *would* deter crime. All the sociologists I am about to cite began under the impression that it *would not* and, indeed, took up their statistical tools with the intent of confirming what was then the conventional wisdom in their field—that crime cannot be deterred by punishment. When they found out they

12. William E. Cobb, "Theft and the Two Hypotheses," in *The Economics of Crime and Punishment*, ed. Simon Rottenberg (Washington, D.C.: American Enterprise Institute for Public Policy Research, 1973), 19–30; Gregory C. Krohm, "The Pecuniary Incentives of Property Crime," ibid., 31–34; and J. P. Gunning. Jr., "How Profitable Is Burglary," ibid., 35–38.

13. See Michael Sesnowitz and John Howell, "The Returns to Burglary," *Western Economic Journal* 10 (December, 1972): 177–81.

14. Gregory C. Krohm, "An Alternative View of the Returns to Burglary," *Western Economic Journal* 11 (September, 1973): 364–67; and Michael Sesnowitz, "The Returns to Burglary: An Alternative to the Alternative," *Western Economic Journal* 11 (September, 1973): 368–70.

were wrong, they quite honestly published their results, although they found it rather difficult to get their work accepted in the more conventional sociological journals.

The first of these sociologists was Jack Gibbs, who published a study in the *Social Science Quarterly* which indicated that punishment did indeed deter crime.[15] His statistical methods were basically rather different from those used by the economists—indeed, speaking as an economist, I would say they were more primitive; but the fact that the same conclusion comes from two different statistical techniques is further confirmation of its validity. The publication of this paper set off a spate of other papers by Louis Gray and David Martin, Frank Bean and Robert Cushing, and Charles Tittle.[16] All of these scholars took up their cudgels with the intention of demonstrating that Gibbs was wrong, and all ended up agreeing with him. In the process, they greatly expanded and improved upon his work. Moreover, they continued using statistical tools that were somewhat different from those that had been employed by the economists; hence, their work can be taken as an independent confirmation of the economists' approach.

The sociologists were very much interested in a problem that had also concerned the economists, but not so vitally. The question facing the criminal is whether the severity of the sentence or the likelihood that it will be imposed is more important in deterring crime. In my opinion, this is not a very important question. Suppose a potential criminal has a choice between two punishment systems: One gives each person who commits burglary a 1-in-100 chance of serving one year in prison;[17] in the other there is a 1-in-1,000 chance of serving 10 years. It is not obvious to me that burglars would be very differently affected by these two punishment systems, although in one case there is a heavy sentence with a low probability of conviction, and in the other a lighter sentence with a higher probability of conviction.

15. Jack Gibbs, "Crime, Punishment and Deterrence," *Social Science Quarterly* 48 (March, 1968): 515–30.

16. Louis N. Gray and J. David Martin, "Punishment and Deterrence: Another Analysis of Gibbs' Data," *Social Science Quarterly* 50 (September, 1969): 389–95; Frank D. Bean and Robert G. Cushing, "Criminal Homicide, Punishment, and Deterrence: Methodological and Substantive Reconsiderations," *Social Science Quarterly* 52 (September, 1971): 277–89; and Charles R. Tittle, "Crime Rates and Legal Sanctions," *Social Problems* 16 (Spring, 1969): 409–23.

17. This is actually somewhat higher than the risk that burglars now face in most parts of the United States.

I would suggest that the appropriate technique is simply to divide the average sentence by the frequency with which it is imposed, and to use that as the deterrent measure. Most of the sociologists and a good many of the economists mentioned above have attempted to determine which of these two variables is more important. Leaving aside my theoretical objections, I do not think the statistics are accurate enough for the results obtained from these tests to be of much value. Be that as it may, more often than not the researchers have found that the frequency with which the punishment is applied is of greater importance than its severity.

The first studies in this field, the ones I criticized at the beginning of my survey of the empirical literature, dealt with the death penalty. Recently Ehrlich has returned to this problem and, by using a much more sophisticated method, has demonstrated a very sizeable deterrence payoff to the death penalty for murder.[18] His figures indicate that each execution prevents between 8 and 20 murders. Unfortunately, the data available for this study were not what one would hope for, so not as much reliance can be put upon his results as one normally would give to work by such a sophisticated econometrician. Earlier, and using a quite different set of statistics and a different method, I arranged to have a graduate student do a preliminary study of the same issue; his results showed that each execution prevented two murders. Here again, however, the data were bad, and the methods were suitable only for a preliminary exploration.[19]

It should be emphasized that the question of whether the death penalty deters murder is a different one from the question of whether we wish to have the death penalty. One widespread minor crime is failure to return to the parking meter to put in a coin when the time expires. I take it that we could reduce the frequency with which this crime is committed by boiling all offenders in oil. I take it, also, that no one would favor this method of deterrence. *Thus, the fact that we can deter a crime by a particular punishment is not a sufficient argument for use of that punishment.*

18. Isaac Ehrlich, "The Deterrent Effect of Capital Punishment: A Question of Life and Death." This is to be published in the *American Economic Review*.

19. Since I cannot possibly claim to have read everything that has ever been written on the subject, I have been conducting part of my research in this area by asking people who hear my speeches or read my papers to tell me if they know of any other articles or books in which the effectiveness of deterrence has been tested in a reasonably scientific manner. I have never received a positive response to this question, but I repeat it here.

In discussing the concept of deterrence, I find that a great many people seem to feel that, although it would no doubt work with respect to burglary and other property crimes, it is unlikely to have much effect on crimes of impulse, such as rape and many murders. They reason that people who are about to kill their wives in a rage are totally incapable of making any calculations at all. But this is far from obvious. The prisoners in Nazi concentration camps must frequently have been in a state of well-justified rage against some of their guards; yet this almost never led to their using violence against the guards, because punishment—which, if they were lucky, would be instant death, but was more likely to be death by torture—was so obvious and so certain. Even in highly emotional situations, we retain some ability to reason, albeit presumably not so well as normally.

It would take much greater provocation to lead a man to kill his wife if he knew that, as in England in the 1930's, committing murder meant a 2-out-of-3 chance of meeting the public executioner within about two months than if—as is currently true in South Africa—there were only a 1-in-100 chance of being executed after about a year's delay.[20]

Another example can be drawn from the American South. Before about 1950, there was a great deal of violence among blacks, particularly on Saturday nights. The local authorities took the view that this was an inherent matter of black character, and hence were reluctant to punish it severely. It has been pointed out that the reluctance of the police to punish such "black" traits was probably the principal reason for their existence. A black who slashed another black's face with a razor on Saturday night would probably merely be reproved by the police and, at most, would get a short term in jail. A white who did the same thing to another white would probably get several years in prison. The difference between the statistical frequency with which blacks and whites performed this kind of act is thus explicable in terms of the deterrence effect of punishment as it was then administered.

It should be noted that thus far I have said nothing whatsoever about whether criminals or potential criminals are well informed as to the punishments for each crime in each state. For punishment to have a deterrent effect, potential criminals must have at least some information about its likely severity and frequency. Presumably, the effect of variations in punishment would be greater if criminals were well informed than if they were not. In practice,

20. These figures are for blacks killing blacks, not for blacks killing whites or, for that matter, for whites killing whites.

of course, potential criminals are not very well informed about these things, but they do have some information.

Reports of crimes and punishments are a major part of most newspapers. It is true that most intellectuals tend to skip over this part of the newspaper, but the average person is more likely to read it than some things that appeal to intellectuals. And an individual who is on the verge of committing a crime or has already taken up a career of crime is apt to be much more interested in crime stories than is the average man. He should have, therefore, a rough idea of the severity of punishments and of the probability that they will be imposed. This information should affect the likelihood that he will choose to commit a given crime.

Nevertheless, the information that he will have is likely to be quite rough. Undoubtedly, if we could somehow arrange for people to have accurate information on these matters, we would get much better coefficients on our multiple regression equations for the deterrence effect of punishment. But since governments have a motive to lie—that is, to pretend that punishment is more likely and more severe than it actually is—it is unlikely that we can do much about improving this information. Still, the empirical evidence is clear. Even granting the fact that most potential criminals have only a rough idea as to the frequency and severity of punishment, multiple regression studies show that increasing the frequency or severity of the punishment does reduce the likelihood that a given crime will be committed.

Finally, I should like to turn to the issue of why "rehabilitation" became the dominant rationale of our punishment system in the latter part of the 19th century and has remained so up to the present, in spite of the absence of any scientific support. The reasons, in my opinion, have to do with the fallacy, so common in the social sciences, that "all good things go together." If we have the choice between preventing crime by training the criminal to be good—that is, rehabilitating him—or deterring crime by imposing unpleasantness on criminals, the former is the one we would *like* to choose.

The Reverend Sydney Smith, a follower of the deterrence theory, said a prison should be "a place of punishment, from which men recoil with horror—a place of real suffering painful to the memory, terrible to the imagination . . . a place of sorrow and wailing, which should be entered with horror and quitted with earnest resolution never to return to such misery . . ."[21]

21. Sydney Smith, *On the Management of Prisons* (London: Warde Locke and Company, 1822), 226, 232.

This is an exaggeration. Our prisons do not have to be that bad; the deprivation of liberty in itself may be a sufficiently effective punishment. But in any case, deterrence necessarily involves the deliberate infliction of harm.

If, on the other hand, we can think of the prison as a kind of educational institution that rehabilitates criminals, we do not have to consciously think of ourselves as injuring people. It is clearly more appealing to think of solving the criminal problem by means that are themselves not particularly unpleasant than to think of solving it by methods that *are* unpleasant. But in this case we do not have the choice between a pleasant and an unpleasant method of dealing with crime. We have an unpleasant method—deterrence—that works, and a pleasant method—rehabilitation—that (at least so far) never has worked. Under the circumstances, we have to opt either for the deterrence method or for a higher crime rate.

TWO KINDS OF LEGAL EFFICIENCY

In discussing the efficiency of the law, there are two quite different problems. The first is whether the law itself is well designed to achieve goals that society regards as desirable. The second is whether the process of enforcing the law is efficient. To take an example from a totally different field, in the recent unpleasantness of Vietnam one could have made judgments as to the likelihood of the war accomplishing its proclaimed objectives independent of the question of whether the American military forces were fighting the war in an efficient manner. It would have been possible to say that the army was doing an excellent job in a war that we would have been better off not fighting in, or that the military was doing a poor job fighting a war for which a victory was important.

The problem is a bit more complicated in a legal context.[1] On one hand, there is the apparatus for enforcing the law, from policemen and sheriffs to courts, juries, and prisons. On the other hand, there is the law itself, which is what this apparatus is designed to implement. Efficiency or inefficiency in the law can refer to either of these two areas.

As far as I know, no one has ever questioned the desirability of efficiency in the process of law enforcement, though if a law itself is undesirable, poor enforcement may be preferable. If the Ministry of Interior in Moscow, for example, became hopelessly incompetent and, hence, could not carry out its duties of political surveillance, this could be considered a step in the right direction, because the law itself is undesirable. In most cases, however, although there is objection to a given law, enforcement of a few bad laws is a small price to pay for the efficiency of the legal system as a whole. Thus, attempts are made to change bad laws, but they are enforced until they can be changed.

Confining the discussion solely to process, as opposed to the law itself, one custom that is widely approved and that perhaps should be called an "inefficiency" is the deliberate biasing of process towards one side. For example, the law is frequently biased in favor of the accused in criminal actions. For reasons that are discussed both in *The Logic of the Law*[2] and *Trials*

Reprinted, with permission of the Hofstra Law Review Association, from *Hofstra Law Review* 8 (spring 1980): 659–69.

1. For a formal discussion of the problem, see A. Breton, *The Economic Theory of Representative Government* 20–26 (1974).

2. G. Tullock, *The Logic of the Law* 176–78 (1971).

on Trial: The Pure Theory of Legal Procedure,[3] this author is not convinced of the desirability of this institution. Assuming that such a bias is desirable, however, it could be simultaneously desirable and inefficient. The problem here is essentially verbal, depending upon the meaning given to "inefficiency" in a particular context. Since such bias would be a method of achieving a goal desired by its advocates, the average economist would say that it is not inefficient even if it does lead to less accuracy in courts. But if the reader wishes to regard this as falling within the rubric "inefficient," then this would be deemed an exception in which that inefficiency is desirable.

There are other areas where people sometimes argue for bias. For example, if it is said that the law should be used to benefit the poor, a lawsuit between a wealthy corporation and an impecunious person would be biased in favor of the impecunious person to obtain a better distribution of income. There are many people who believe that this "deep pockets" approach is a good idea, and it has sometimes achieved favor with judges and juries. It is clear, however, that this is an inefficient institution, and it is fairly easy to demonstrate that it is an unduly expensive way of reducing inequality in society.[4] Any desired amount of equality can be obtained by direct tax and payment methods at lower social cost than could be obtained by biasing legal proceedings.

There is, however, an argument for this kind of bias, which this author usually calls the "well-intentioned Machiavellianism" argument. There are those who feel that the voters would not vote for the appropriate amount of income redistribution directly, but that they can be tricked into providing more equality indirectly by a technique such as biasing legal procedures. The first thing to be said is that the individuals making this argument are putting their own views as to the proper amount of equality above those of the voters. If some people believe that their own judgment is better than that of other voters, it should be openly recognized that on the basis of this belief they are imposing their ideas on society. Second, and much more important, when one begins this indirect and covert type of egalitarian behavior, it is likely that other people will take advantage of it. The net effect is that some special interest group will get significant benefits and the poor will receive little or none.

In general, process efficiency in the law raises few problems. In this con-

3. G. Tullock, *Trials on Trial: The Pure Theory of Legal Procedure* (1980).

4. Accepting for the moment Learned Hand's justification for tort law—see *United States v. Carroll Towing Co.*, 159 F.2d 169, 173 (2d Cir. 1947)—it is immediately obvious that if the courts regularly bring in decisions against the wealthy and in favor of the poor, the wealthy will be led to too many resources in avoiding accidents and the poor too few.

text, efficiency clearly means the same as it does in manufacturing for example. If we say that the Chrysler plant in Altoona, Illinois, is highly efficient and the one in Brookhaven, Massachusetts, is inefficient, we know what we mean by the word. A similar notion is at stake in process efficiency in the law. Achieving this efficiency requires balancing two costs against each other. The first is the cost to society of the laws being badly enforced. If murderers go free we may expect more murders. On the other side, if the law is badly enforced, innocent people may go to prison, and people may be unjustly deprived of their property in civil suits. Weighed against these costs of bad enforcement are the costs of enforcing the law. Increasing the effectiveness of enforcement is presumably achieved by increasing the resources invested in it. The goal is to invest the resources in the most efficient way, which is possible by achieving the correct balance between the competing costs.[5] Most people would regard this goal as rather noncontroversial.

When we address the problem of whether the substantive law itself is efficient in its choice of goals, then matters are unfortunately more complicated, even in the purely technical sense. The problem is further confused because this part of the law has traditionally been discussed in ethical terms.[6] A minor digression will demonstrate the way in which inefficient institutions may sometimes develop out of moral principles. In late nineteenth-century Brazil there was a great debate as to whether or not corporations should be permitted to exist. The popular point of view[7] was that corporations are wicked because they permit people to avoid paying their debts. In other words, limited liability violates natural law. The progress of the Brazilian economy was set back for a number of years by this ethical argument, which most people today would regard as simply silly.[8]

As an empirical observation, there is fortunately little clash between ethical criteria and efficiency considerations. If we concern ourselves with the substantive law rather than with process, then the efficiency criterion leads to

5. There has been surprisingly little research on improving the efficiency of court procedure. I hope this will change and indeed my book *Trials on Trial: The Pure Theory of Legal Procedure* is intended as a step in this direction.

6. People are executed for murder, for example, because murder is wicked, and the guilty deserve death (an eye for an eye).

7. Apparently shared by W. S. Gilbert. See W. Gilbert, *Utopia, Limited* 30–32 (1893).

8. I do not wish here to argue against the use of ethical criteria, not because I believe in them, but because I have discovered that arguments with ethically minded people tend to be frustrating. The reader can imagine trying to explain to an Islamic leader that usury is

conclusions that are similar to those of most western law codes. There are occasional areas of conflict, but they are not generally very important.[9]

Basically, an efficient legal institution would be one that cannot be changed without making us worse off. This, of course, limits analysis to the present state of knowledge.[10] But all of this is based on the assumption that we can tell which of two states of nature makes us better off. In general, the question of "betterness" is not very difficult, although there are cases where that raises problems. The word "us," however, is difficult. Suppose some change is urged that will benefit some of us and injure others. This has been a problem for a long time, and this author proposes to solve it in much the same way other economists have.

First, in connection with the law it is frequently true that changes will not actually injure anyone, although they will benefit someone. The reason is simply that the improvement of some particular legal institution may not affect any interests now in being. It may, for example, provide that contracts drawn in the future may make use of a new opportunity that was not previ-

---

desirable even though the Koran prohibits it. Most of the people with whom I have discussed the law on ethical grounds have been, of course, much the same in cultural background to myself, and I presume the reader is as well.

9. Legal scholarship, including judicial decisions and legislative discussions, has always addressed efficiency considerations to some extent. While justice and equity are frequently involved as well, laws regarding credit instruments, mortgages, and nonrecourse notes, in particular, are normally discussed in terms of their effect on the future credit market, which is an efficiency consideration rather than a consideration of abstract justice.

As an example of the type of conflict that may occur between ethical and efficiency considerations, consider the ethical rule that the punishment should fit the crime. Almost anyone interested in designing an efficient legal system would argue that the punishment should be calculated by a function that takes into account both the benefit the criminal gets out of the crime and the likelihood that he or she in fact will be punished. On occasion I have had discussions with people with strong ethical feelings in this area who argue that this is simply wrong. They claim that the grievousness of crime is the only thing that should be considered and that this should be measured by the injury inflicted on society, not by the benefit to the criminal and certainly not by the probability that he or she will be caught.

Although I have on occasion, as I said, had arguments of this sort, I don't really think that most moralists would regard this as a major problem. Similarly, the other cases in which what I regard as an efficient law code deviates to some extent from conventional morality are not too important. Thus, although I do indeed think that efficiency considerations should be dominant, I do not anticipate great difficulty from moralists when I urge improvement in the law.

10. One of the points of this article is to urge that we increase our knowledge in these

ously in existence. The English, for example, have drastically changed their law on commercial arbitration to provide people who want commercial arbitration with more freedom in selecting procedures that meet their needs.[11] This is merely one of many examples; there are numerous cases in which efficient changes in the law do not injure anyone, because everybody can adjust to the new law.

Second, there are many changes in the law that will make everyone better off ex ante, although they will indeed make somebody better off and somebody worse off in the future. Suppose, for example, that the law of torts is changed and that it is possible to reliably predict that the change will reduce the total number of accidents without markedly increasing accident avoidance costs. As of now, since nobody knows when they will be in an accident or on which side they will be in the resulting lawsuit, the change is a net benefit for everyone. Once an accident occurs and the lawsuit begins, some of the parties may find that they are worse off than they would have been under the previous law. Still, ex ante everybody benefits, and rational persons would choose the improved law simply because it gives them a better gamble, even though as a matter of fact they may lose that gamble.

Lastly, however, and this is the most difficult problem, there may be changes in the law that benefit some yet directly injure others. The first thing to be said about such changes is that every effort should be made to minimize resulting injuries. The law might be drawn, for example, to take effect some time in the future so that people will have an opportunity to adjust and hence reduce their losses. Another simple way of lowering the cost to those injured is to compensate them.[12] If the people who will be injured cannot be identified beforehand, then everyone is only better off ex ante. If, however, it is possible to identify who will be injured, then there is no reason for com-

---

areas with the prospect that we will be able to make ourselves better off by changes. Such improvements in knowledge might also permit us to stave off ill-advised changes.

11. See Arbitration Act 1975, § 1, reprinted in 8 *Halsbury's Laws of England* ¶ 411 (4th ed. Supp. 1979).

12. Ideally, the cost of the compensation should be paid by the people who gain from the change in law. In practice this will be difficult or impossible to arrange in many cases. When it is not possible, spreading the cost over the entire population by paying compensation from a general tax fund seems sensible. Even here, however, it should be emphasized that we are unlikely to be able to exactly measure the cost and hence the compensation will be approximate at best.

pensating them, either with direct payments or by some other change in the law. Preferably this change should offer an improvement in efficiency, but in any event, it should be one that does not lower efficiency. If a law must necessarily injure some group of people, then the calculation is whether the benefits are great enough so that in theory those injured could be compensated. If so, then there is an improvement in efficiency, even though it will injure these people.

There is a great deal of debate in economics as to whether this kind of calculation is actually legitimate. However, if there are a very large number of changes, then it is possible to consider not whether the individual change benefits everyone, but whether the policy of making such changes would be ex ante beneficial. Suppose, for example, a policy is adopted of calculating the gains and losses from a potential change in the law, and the change is made if the gains exceed the losses. If this happens over a large number of specific changes in the future, then the odds that any individual will benefit more often than he or she loses are better than even. Thus, ex ante everyone is made better off by adopting this particular policy. It may, of course, be true that some people will have a long run of bad luck and will find themselves on the losing side for a very large number of these changes. However, because it is impossible to predict in advance what changes will be suggested in the future or what position any individual will be in with respect to these changes, everyone is better off ex ante.

The actual calculation of benefits and costs is an extremely difficult task, and there is every reason to believe that present techniques lead to errors. While existing measurement techniques need improvement, the fact remains that the ex ante paradigm developed here makes it possible to use imperfect methods. Suppose that careful studies of individual institutional changes have a reasonably good chance of producing the right decision on whether the benefit or loss is greater. Using the ex ante technique, making the changes that are recommended by such studies and refraining from making those that the studies indicate are undesirable would, over a long series of decisions, produce a net gain. In sum, although the calculations in this area are frequently difficult, it is possible to adopt policies that improve the law's efficiency.

Sometimes the problem of whether a given law is efficient is fairly easy and requires little in the way of research. Consider an example from *The Logic of the Law*:[13] Should the law against theft be repealed? This author's con-

13. G. Tullock, *supra* note 2, at 211–27.

clusion that the law should not be repealed is based on the following line of reasoning: Imagine a society in which there is no law against theft. There is a saving over our present society because the police force can be smaller, but there is a very sharp increase in cost in other areas. In such a society individuals would be forced to divide their time between producing real goods, attempting to steal others' goods, and protecting their own goods. It is clear that the effort invested in protecting your own property and attempting to steal others' does not add to the total wealth of society.[14] Thus, the total quantity of goods produced in society will be less and the individual well-being less on the average than in a society where there is a law against theft.

This line of reasoning is simple and straightforward, but note that it does require certain assumptions about the real world. The first is that the cost of maintaining a police force is relatively small compared with the effectiveness of that police force in preventing crimes. Consider, for example, the total cost under the system with a law against theft. First, there will still be some people putting part of their time into trying to steal things. Second, there will still be some effort put into protecting property. We all have locks on our doors. Indeed, unless the police are superefficient, it will always be sensible to retain at least some private protection instead of depending entirely on the police.

The question then is whether the net "waste" imposed on society by the institution of legalized theft is greater than the "waste" imposed by the laws against it. In the first case the wasteful activities are the time spent in attempting to steal and the time spent in private protection. In the second, there is, once again, the time spent in attempting to steal and on private protection plus the cost of the police. The conclusion that the costs are lower in the second society is essentially a technological judgment on the net cost of a police force in lowering the rate of crime as opposed to the net cost of private protection. It is a technological judgment that few people will disagree with, but there are some, for example the anarchists of the right, who would argue that this is simply wrong on moral grounds. The basic structure of the law appears to be efficient on much the same simple arguments as above. This appears to be true of the law of most countries insofar as it deals with such simple matters as theft and murder. Since these are the basic issues that moralists concern themselves with, the prospect of conflict between morality and efficiency in these areas is small.

14. It should be noted that one way of protecting your own property is not to acquire it, e.g., to consume that unstealable commodity, leisure.

The problem becomes much more difficult, however, when discussing the details of the law. A good deal of research is needed for each detailed provision to find out whether it is efficient and, if it is not, what improvements could be made. Apparently most of the decisions regarding the efficiency or inefficiency of detailed provisions of the law are normally made without much research. Let me illustrate with a fairly simple example drawn from Professor Richard Posner, a well-known proponent of the view that the common law is indeed efficient:

> Another common law rule was that a railroad owned [*sic*] no duty of care to people using the tracks as paths (except at crossings). The cost to these "trespassers" of using alternative paths would generally be small in comparison to the cost to the railroad of making the tracks safe for them. The railroad's right, however, was a qualified one: the railroad was required to keep a careful lookout for trespassing cattle. It would be very costly for farmers to erect fences that absolutely prevented cattle from straying, so we would expect that, if transactions between farmers and railroads were feasible, farmers would frequently pay railroads to keep a careful lookout for animals on the track.[15]

In truth, the least costly way of dealing with cattle on the track is by no means obvious. The cost of fencing, which is an important matter in farm areas, can be dealt with in many different ways. One possible approach is to put the entire burden on individuals who wish to keep cattle out of their crops. These farmers would be required to put up their own fences, while the cattle owners are not burdened with any duty to keep their animals from straying. An alternative approach is to require farmers to fence the northern and western sides of their land, with no responsibility for the eastern and southern sides except where the land is contiguous to a road. This approach makes certain that all land is fenced and allocates the responsibility unambiguously. Nevertheless, it requires individuals to put fences up to protect their neighbors' property as well as their own. The relative efficiencies of these institutions is a difficult empirical problem.

The allegation that the particular institution discussed by Professor Posner is efficient is based on a completely ad hoc view as to the costs, together with a statement about what bargain would be made if transaction costs were nil. Professor Posner may be perfectly correct, but it would be

15. R. Posner, Economic Analysis of Law § 3.4, at 37 (2d ed. 1977).

mere coincidence. Although I have not carefully examined his research methods, I feel confident in saying that Professor Posner has done no research whatsoever on the relative costs of the various ways of containing cattle near railroad tracks.

But there are other difficulties with Professor Posner's discussion. Let me pick another quotation:

> *Ploof* may be viewed as a special application of the "last clear chance" doctrine. A man is using the railroad track as a path. Since he is a trespasser, the railroad has no duty to keep a careful lookout for him. But if in fact the crew sees him, it must blow the train's whistle and take any other necessary and feasible precautions to avoid running him down. The economic rationale is that, even though the accident might be prevented at low cost if the trespasser simply stays off the track, at the moment when the train is bearing down upon him it is the engineer who can avoid an accident at least cost, and this cost is substantially less than the expected accident cost. Alternatively, the case may be viewed as one where, although the cost to the victim of preventing the accident is less than the accident cost, the cost to the injurer of preventing the accident is lower than the victim's accident prevention cost.[16]

Note that the apparently superior position of cattle over human beings given by the previous rule vanishes here. If the railroad crew is keeping a sharp lookout for cows they would surely see the man on the track. Indeed, I have great difficulty imagining an attorney arguing to a jury that the railroad is not liable for hitting the plaintiff because the engineer, drunk perhaps, was not watching where the train was going. Professor Posner's belief that the engineer has a positive duty to look out for stray cattle but not for stray human beings may be a good statement of the law in the way it is written, but it certainly is not a good statement of law as it is in fact applied. In fact, the last-clear-chance doctrine invalidates the basic efficiency argument normally offered for efficiency of the negligence–contributory negligence rule. The resources I would put into preventing an accident are clearly lessened if I know that my liability can be eliminated by way of the last-clear-chance rule. It might be possible for advocates of the efficiency argument used in *United States v. Caroll Towing Co.*[17] to demonstrate that the combination of both of

16. *Id.* § 6.7, at 129 (footnote omitted).
17. 159 F.2d 169, 173 (2d Cir. 1947).

these rules is efficient provided the original negligence–contributory negligence conditions are properly interpreted, but they have not done so.

This particular example, which in fact is merely the first one that I came across in rereading Professor Posner's book, is simply part of what is now a very large literature. Various common law rules are stated, sometimes incorrectly, and then the statement is made that because of transaction costs this particular rule is the most efficient. It may or may not be. The only way to tell is to engage in careful research, making an effort to measure all the costs and to figure out the most efficient way of accomplishing a stated goal. For example, Burrows, Rowley, and Owen examined the problem of cleaning oil tankers' crude-oil tanks without causing too much pollution.[18] The study was lengthy and detailed, and the authors reached the conclusion that the cheapest way of dealing with the problem was to wash the tanks in port.[19] Efforts to determine whether any law is efficient or to suggest improvements in existing laws require further research of this sort. Unfortunately it is difficult and requires fairly large applications of highly skilled labor.

As one other example: Burrows, Rowley, and Owen studied the Torrey Canyon disaster, and as a result of this study suggested that the basic law of marine salvage should be changed.[20] The authors suggest, rather than firmly recommend, because they did only a single case study. Nevertheless, they do offer strong arguments to indicate that a major research project on these lines should be undertaken. Simply speculating on whether or not the current law minimizes transaction costs will not do.

Conclusion

I hope by now I have convinced the reader that efficiency is indeed an important consideration in designing the law. I myself tend to feel that it is almost the only consideration we should take into account. For those people

18. Burrows, Rowley, and Owen, *Operational Dumping and the Pollution of the Sea by Oil: An Evaluation of Preventive Measures*, 1 *Journal of Environmental Economics and Management* 202 (1974).

19. *Id.* at 218. As an interesting sidelight, washing the tanks in port was not the technique preferred by the oil companies, and the oil companies had hired Burrows and company to carry out the research. This was a case in which the sponsorship did not control the outcome.

20. Burrows, Rowley, and Owen, *Torrey Canyon: A Case Study in Accidental Pollution*, 21 *Scottish Journal of Political Economy* 237 (1974).

who want to maintain moral principles as a foundation for the law, it is fortunate that the conflicts between efficiency and morals are not very great. In most cases where efficiency considerations dictate a change in the law, moral principles are either irrelevant or unimportant.

There remains the question of whether our present law code is efficient. Although I think the general outlines probably are, I also think that we should retain an open mind. Detailed research would either prove that the law is efficient or provide us with a number of opportunities for changing it to make it efficient. This research, even though lengthy and hard to do, should be given a high priority in any plans for social reform.

OPTIMAL PROCEDURE

So far I have developed only a very primitive idea of the objectives toward which courts should aim. Instead of beginning by setting down some function the courts are designed to maximize and then discussing how well or how badly the courts do, I have discussed court efficiency in terms of two very simple criteria—cost and accuracy. There has been an assumption that we want to lower cost and raise accuracy, but little or nothing has been said about how these two characteristics should be traded off against each other, or whether or not there are other things we want from the courts.

This somewhat unusual approach was chosen, quite simply, because I could hardly talk intelligibly about what the courts' objectives should be—the success indicator for a good court system—until I had covered the material in the previous four chapters. Efficiency in the courts involves understanding certain things which the average person would find paradoxical on first glance, and therefore I thought it desirable to discuss cost and errors before I began discussing true optimization.

I will now repair the omission and discuss the characteristics of a desirable court and the trade-offs between the various desirable characteristics. Of course, accuracy and low cost are among these characteristics and, indeed, by a wide margin the most important, but the social value of these two characteristics is rather indirect and its measurement not exactly simple.

Let us begin by assuming that the substantive law is socially desirable, or that the contract which is to be enforced is in fact desirable from the standpoint of the parties to the contract and with no negative externalities. In both cases, of course, these considerations are ex ante. By the time the matter comes to court, there most certainly is at least one person who would rather the law not be enforced.

These assumptions may be a little strong. All of us know at least some laws which are not in the social interest—indeed, they may be positively perverse—and foolish contracts are sometimes drawn up. Still, the point of procedure is to carry out policy decisions made in other areas, whether these other areas are the legislature or the salesroom in which an installment contract is made, not

Reprinted, with permission, from *Trials on Trial: The Pure Theory of Legal Procedure* (New York: Columbia University Press, 1980), 70–86.

to *create* these laws or contracts. Thus, I will leave aside the investigation of perverse laws and foolish contracts for some other time and place.

As pointed out in chapter 3, however, the defects of the court proceedings necessarily *do* have some effect on what is an optimal substantive law. Further, they clearly have an effect on which contracts should be made and the clauses thereof. The contract must be drawn up with knowledge of the efficiency or inefficiency of the procedure which will be used to enforce it, and some provisions will differ from those which would be chosen in a nirvana of perfect enforcement.

But this matter can be left for another book. An improvement in the efficiency of the court in general means that the law can be made substantively better and that contracts can be drawn up which lead to greater net gain to the two parties. We can simply regard these changes in the law and in the contracts as supplementary gains to the improvement in the efficiency of the courts.

Let us begin by considering, once again, the diagram used in the preceding chapters. As usual, in figure 1, line *P* shows the probability of judgment for the plaintiff, who in this particular case is in the right. Once again, the assumption that the plaintiff is in the right is only a convenience for purposes of exposition. Also, line *P* has been drawn not on the basis of empirical knowledge but on the basis of drafting convenience. We badly need good empirical research on the accuracy of the courts, but, with the present ignorance in the area, it seems sensible to try to draw diagrams so that they are readable.

As is usual, the costs are shown by lines P_c and D_c. I am assuming for this diagram that each party pays his own legal costs, simply because that approximates the way we normally do it in the United States. Anyone who wishes can fairly easily adjust the diagram to show some other way to handle the costs. Thus the line D_c shows the expected cost for the defendant, and the line P_c shows the expected gain for the plaintiff.

The defendant, who is in the wrong, is apt to simply pay up if he is to the left of line D_c'. In that area, the legal system justifies its existence by bringing about a correct result. On the other hand, to the right of line P_c', where the present discounted value of collection minus the litigation costs is less than zero, the plaintiff will not bring suit; therefore, in this case the legal system not only does *not* justify its existence, it will be positively perverse.[1] In the area between P_c' and D_c', which is the area in which most litigation occurs,

1. Perversity is particularly likely if the plaintiff who is in the wrong is able to get the court to compel the defendant to commit an illegal act.

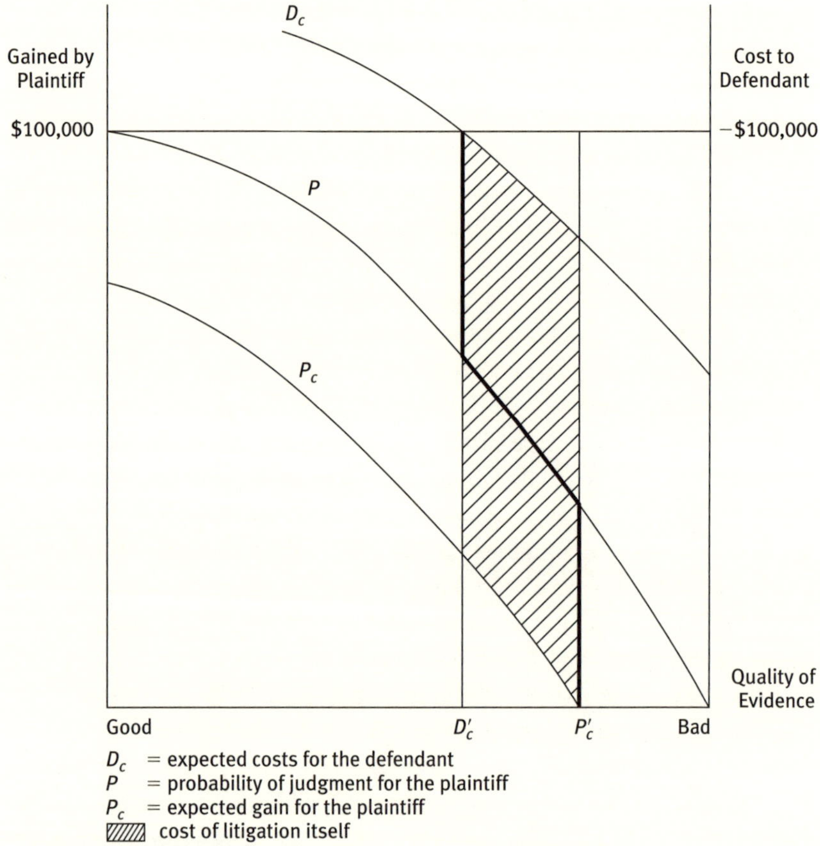

FIGURE 1
Social cost of litigation

we only have a probabilistic idea of whether the court will promote or hinder justice.

Fortunately, the probability line permits us to get an idea of the total number of cases which are carried out correctly. Specifically, the area below P and between D'_c and P'_c is the ex ante value of the correct decisions reached by the court, and the area above that line is the ex ante value of the cases in which the system goes wrong. Thus, below and to the left of the thickened line, we reach the right result; above and to the right of that line, the court is wrong. To repeat what I have said before, these lines are drawn for drafting convenience; I would not like to be on my oath that the comparative sizes of the areas to the left and below the thickened line and those to the right and above *in fact* represent the error propensity of our courts. As an offhand guess, I would think that the errors would be less prominent than shown in the diagram, but, in the absence of empirical evidence, this is merely a guess.

The benefit we receive from the court proceedings, then, is the area below and to the left of the thickened line. There are two costs. First are those costs in which the system goes wrong—those above and to the right of the thickened line. Note that there may not be any net social cost as a direct result of the court's decision. The defendant's success means that the defendant is wealthier and the plaintiff less wealthy, which, no doubt, is regarded as a cost by the plaintiff, but, from the social standpoint, the two cancel out. Inaccuracy of the court, in this case, simply means that opportunities in the form of possible bargains, which could have been made if the court were more effective, or laws could have been socially adjusted, are missed. On the other hand, there are cases in which the decision itself imposes positive costs on society: for example, suppose that the defendant had the duty to undertake some action which had a social benefit, and the court erroneously fails to compel him to do so.

The second cost is the cost of litigation itself, shown in figure 1 by the shaded area. Thus, the total opportunity cost is the sum of the area above and to the right of the thickened line *plus* the shaded area. This means that in the point where these two overlap, as they do above the thickened line and left of P'_c, there is a double cost; i.e., there are the errors of the court *and* the costs of the lawyers who talk them into making the errors.

I suppose it is obvious that an improvement in accuracy will lower the total costs. Figure 2 is identical to figure 1, except that we assume that the court is more accurate—that it is less likely to be misled by deceptive evidence, etc., and therefore it achieves a higher P line. The area above and to the right of the thickened line is smaller, and the area below and to the left of it is larger. Thus, one element of cost is reduced.

The element of cost involved in the actual court proceedings themselves can be larger or smaller, depending essentially on the slant of line P in the range between D'_c and P'_c. In the diagrams 1 and 2, it is roughly the same size, but, as an offhand guess, it would tend to be smaller with the more accurate court. There would be less litigation, even if the cost of each case were the same as before. Thus, improving the accuracy of the court leads to an unambiguous gain. Further, a large part of this gain accrues to people who do not participate in the litigation. All those cases which lay to the right of line D'_c in figure 1 and to the left of D'_c in figure 2 have been shifted from litigated cases to nonlitigated cases by the improvement in accuracy of the court. The shrinkage of the number of cases in which there is no litigation because it is

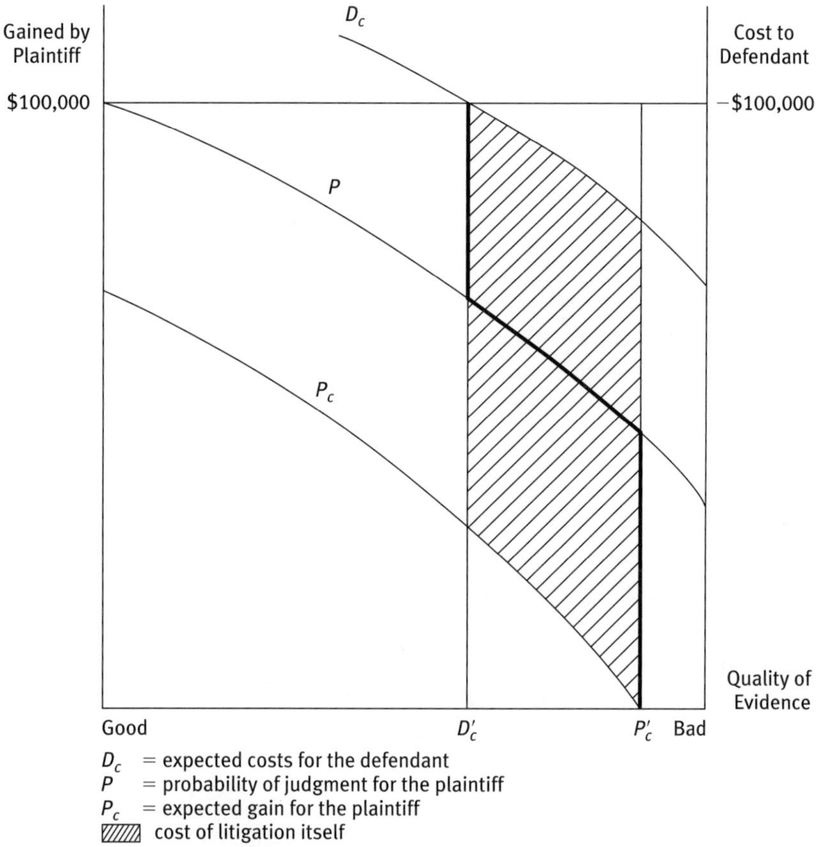

FIGURE 2
Social cost of litigation with more efficient court

predicted by both parties that the court will go wrong is also an important variable here.

It could be argued that my cost structure here is too simple. Many cases are settled out of court. Further, those cases which are never actually carried to the point of litigation—ones lying left of D'_c or right of P'_c—may in fact involve high legal costs as the parties inform themselves of the actual legal situation and perhaps engage in preliminary legal sparring. Thus, the real cost would not be my lozenge but a canoe-shaped structure along the *P* line. I do not think there is any great damage in using my approximation, but any reader who disagrees with me is free to draw in the canoes and use them instead of my lozenges.

While improvements in accuracy clearly lead to social gain, it is obvious that reduction in cost of litigation with *no* change in accuracy can also reduce social cost. Unfortunately, although this is true, the reduction in cost has to be handled carefully in order to avoid imposing indirect costs on society. The point is shown in figure 3, where I have used the same accuracy curve as in figure 1, but assume that there has been a very sharp reduction in costs, so the costs to the defendant in refusing to pay the just claims of the plaintiff are only D'_c, and the plaintiff's costs in suing are only P'_c. As a result, the number of cases where it is sensible for the defendant to refuse to pay is greatly increased, and the number of cases in which the plaintiff also should refuse to drop his claim, because the evidence is perverse, is reduced;

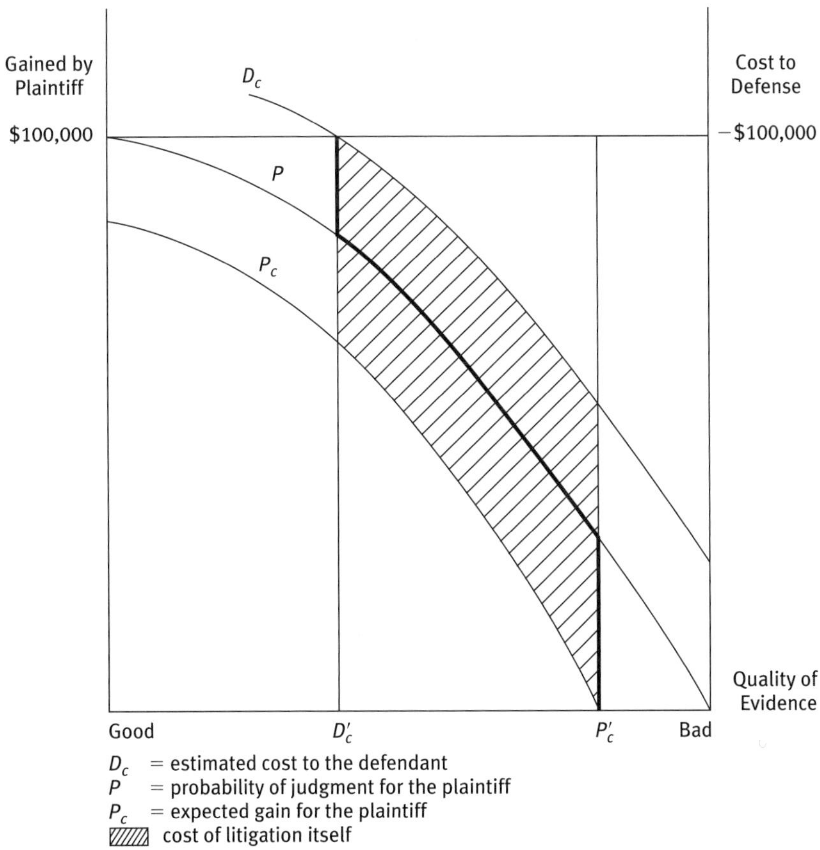

FIGURE 3
Social cost of litigation with cheap but inaccurate court

consequently, there is very much more litigation. In this particular diagram, there are actually more total legal expenses when the cost of litigation per suit has been lowered than there were in the higher-cost conditions of figure 1. This is an artifact of the drawing, but it does not seem to be a particularly improbable event.

The increase (if there is one) in total legal expenses, however, is not the major problem here. It is clear that the area above and to the right of the thickened line has been greatly increased by this reduction in cost. The number of correct decisions by the system has been lowered and the number of incorrect decisions raised.

Obviously, this is not an inevitable result of lowering court costs. It comes not from the reduction of the court costs but from the way in which the saving from the cost reduction was allocated. Suppose, for example, that the real resource cost of court proceedings was reduced as much as the reduction shown between figures 1 and 3, but there was a tax placed on the two parties so that their cost remained the same. Under these circumstances, we would have an unambiguous social gain, because there would be no change in outcome or costs for the parties, and the government would obtain a revenue. I do not, of course, argue that such a tax would be socially optimal.

This obviously brings me to an important characteristic of lawsuits. The cost of the lawsuits is not only a direct cost, but it is also a factor in deciding which suits will be brought. Granted the court does make errors, the decision as to which cases will be brought also affects the efficiency of the system. Suppose, and I realize this is an unrealistic assumption, that a tax was imposed on legal proceedings, carefully calculated so that in all cases in which the probability of success to the plaintiff is more than 50 percent he could anticipate a positive return, ex ante, on his investment, but he would lose if he brought a case where the probability of success was less than 50 percent. Assume the converse set of institutions for the defendant. Under these circumstances, the only cases brought would be those in which the probability of success to both parties was exactly 50 percent (which would be a very small number of cases), the thickened line of figures 1, 2, and 3 would become vertical, and we would minimize social costs for a given level of court accuracy.

Obviously, no one feels that lawyers' judgments on probable outcomes are accurate enough so that this kind of institution would be sensible. Still, when we discuss changing court costs, we must always keep in mind that this will change the number of cases that are brought, as well as change the costs of those cases which actually do get to court. Both effects are socially significant.

Further, cases may be settled out of court at their ex ante value. For these cases, this 50 percent rule would lead to a rather bad disposition, with the plaintiff receiving only half of what is actually due him minus his costs. Further, for those cases to the right of the 50 percent line, a guaranteed perverse result would occur. Altogether, this institution could reduce the efficiency of the basic law or contract, and that, too, would have costs.

The problem is particularly severe if we have a program for reducing the costs of the actual parties by subsidizing their legal expenses. If we subsidize both sides' legal expenses, then the results can be extremely perverse. For example, suppose that the real legal expenses are as shown on figure 1 but that subsidies reduce the legal expenses to the parties to those shown on figure 3. Under these circumstances, not only do we get the reduction in the social payoff to the law-enforcement scheme shown by the shift of the thickened line, but we also pay a resource cost in the form of lawyer's time, etc., which is about three times as high as it was in figure 1.

Another "reform" that is frequently recommended is subsidization of the legal expenses for only *one* side. The arguments for doing this may be arguments for bias, and discussion of this will be delayed for a few pages. For example, if we want the courts to be biased in favor of the accused, then paying the accused's legal expenses may be one way to acquire that particular bias. In making such a decision, we should realize that it will mean that the accused is much more likely to go to trial, even if the evidence is against him, than if we do not subsidize his defense. Once again, this will be discussed later.

The other situation, in which we subsidize both sides (the poverty-program lawyers, for example, representing both parties in a divorce case), is perverse *unless* there is some kind of preselection of the cases. If there is preselection, then the actual total legal procedure must include the preparation for, and activity in, the preselection process. In essence, as I have said before, we have two proceedings—the first of which is entered into for the purpose of obtaining government payment of one's legal fees, and then, once one has convinced the government that he is eligible for subsidization, a regular trial.

In sum, then, the benefit derived from court proceedings is the enforcement of the law or the contract, and a very large part of that benefit is derived from cases where the law or the contract is simply carried out without ever going to court. Of course, in many cases, it would be carried out even *without* the threat of legal proceedings, and if we had data, we could eliminate those cases. The costs are (a) the actual cost of the procedure itself, and (b) those cases in which the court goes wrong, in the specific sense that the parties are ordered to do something which they normally would *not* do and which imposes social costs. Thus, for example, an innocent man is imprisoned, or specific performance of a contract is erroneously ordered.

There is another element of opportunity costs. If the law were better enforced, then many contracts that are now considered undesirable could be undertaken. Further, the substantive law could be adjusted in such a way as to obtain greater benefits. These are opportunities for gain which we could hope to obtain if we improved the efficiency of the law, but it is hard to argue that they are positive costs for court errors. After all, if the court did not exist at all, these lost opportunities would be greater than they are now. Still, we should keep in mind that the efficiency of the court affects both the efficiency with which the contract-negotiation process is carried on (because the parties will have in mind the probable efficiency of the court enforcement of the contract) and the efficiency with which the substantive law can be drafted, for the same reason.

Actual measurement of the cost and benefit of a court system would be difficult, even at the conceptual level. Still, generally speaking, we can recognize improvement when we see it. Improvement in accuracy is an unambiguous gain, and reduction in costs is also an unambiguous gain, unless the savings are allocated among the parties in such a way as to perversely change the pattern of litigation. Such a perverse change must, of course, be large enough to offset the reduction in costs.

So far, I have not said anything at all about the problem of bias. Almost all discussions of judicial matters strongly urge that the procedures should be biased in some way. Normally, the bias in criminal actions is supposed to be in favor of the accused. For example, in Anglo-Saxon countries, the accused is not to be convicted unless he is "guilty beyond reasonable doubt." In Continental countries, the slogan is, "If there is doubt, acquit." Lenin thought that in cases where people were accused of opposing his government, the bias should be in the other direction.

Our procedure in some cases imposes fairly strong biases against the "accused." To pick an empirically important example, the so-called Dohaney Amendment provides that drugs, additives, and a variety of other things must be removed from the marketplace if there is any significant evidence pointing in the direction of their being a carcinogen.[2]

2. Specifically, if any animal test has shown development of cancer.

Application of this amendment led to the abolition of the cyclamate industry (in the United States only; cyclamate is still readily available in Europe) on the basis of what now appears to be erroneous—and what, even at the time, must have seemed very inadequate—evidence. Obviously this is not a criminal penalty, but the costs imposed can be extremely high. In a cyclamate case, the cost imposed on various chemical companies appears to have been in excess of $100 million. This is a clear-cut legal case of very strong bias against the company or individual producing the product alleged to be a carcinogen.

Somewhat the same procedure is apparently used by the Food and Drug Administration (FDA) in the certification of new drugs. There are two parties at interest—the manufacturers and the potential customers. So far as I know, no studies have been made of the effect of the Dohaney Amendment on consumers, but the studies on the FDA seem to indicate that the withholding of drugs from the market by the FDA kills far more people than it protects. The delays in the introduction of new drugs, although such delays certainly make it less likely that defective drugs will come on the market, also lead to people dying because the new and successful drug is not available; it would appear that the excess deaths from the delay are more numerous than the lives saved by keeping defective drugs off the market.

It is not very obvious, however, that magic phrases like "beyond reasonable doubt" have any great effect on the behavior of judges and juries. The only empirical evidence on the subject of which I am aware is contained in two articles, one by Rita James Simon and one by her and Linda Mahan.[3]

In the Simon and Mahan article, various groups of people, including jurors and judges, were asked to translate "beyond reasonable doubt" into a percentage probability statement. The translations were extremely various, running from 50 percent to 100 percent, but, roughly speaking, the mean was 85 percent. Interestingly, in the same study, the standard rule for civil proceedings—"a fair preponderance of the evidence"—was also translated by the respondents, and the mean result here was about 75 percent. Thus, it would appear that in actual practice, judges and juries probably use a rule in deter-

3. Rita James Simon, "'Beyond a Reasonable Doubt'—An Experimental Attempt at Quantification," *Journal of Applied Behavioral Science* (1970): 6(2):201–9; Rita James Simon and Linda Mahan, "Quantifying Burdens of Proof: A View from the Bench, the Jury, and the Classroom," *Law and Society Review* (February 1971): 319–30.

mining transfer of funds from the defendant to the plaintiff in a civil suit that is very similar to, but not quite as stringent as, the rule they use in determining whether to imprison someone for a crime. In both cases, it would appear that the plaintiff bears a substantial burden of proof if we believe that this, the sole empirical investigation of the subject of which I am aware, is in fact correct.

Once again, the fact that this is the only investigation of which I am aware, and the fact that it contains many defects,[4] is, I believe, a very serious criticism of the present state of both the social sciences and the legal system. We should have a great deal more empirical evidence upon which to make decisions than we now do. The immense number of people engaged in "legal research" have produced almost nothing that is of any real value in determining whether our procedure is good or bad. In general, they have simply elaborated on court decisions or argued, usually on the basis of rather cloudy ethical ideas, that previous court decisions should be changed. There are almost no properly controlled studies of the actual impact of different types of procedure.

But let us consider this problem of bias a little more formally. For this purpose, I should like to turn to a diagram which I introduced in the *Logic of the Law*.[5] In figure 4, on the vertical axis is shown the likelihood that people in a given category of evidence are, in fact, guilty. On the horizontal axis, then, the cases are arranged in accord with the weight of evidence. Line *E* shows the percentage of persons in each evidence category who are, in fact, guilty. The shape of the line carries with it an assumption that the evidence is normally distributed, which seems a good null hypothesis, although once again, I would like empirical evidence.

Note that there are some guilty people at the far left, even though in this case there is practically no evidence against them. Similarly, there are some innocent people at the far right, even though the evidence is very strong against them. Both are cases where the evidence is perverse. On the other hand, the individuals who are at the far right, and are in fact guilty, are examples of the evidence being strong and correct, and those at the left who are innocent benefit from strong evidence.

4. The principal defect is the failure to realize that many of their experimental subjects may not be very familiar with the percentage method of presenting probability. I should say, however, that my statement that this article contains defects is not intended as a criticism of its two authors. The first study in almost any field inevitably contains defects, simply because it is the first study.

5. Gordon Tullock, *The Logic of the Law* (New York: Basic Books, 1971).

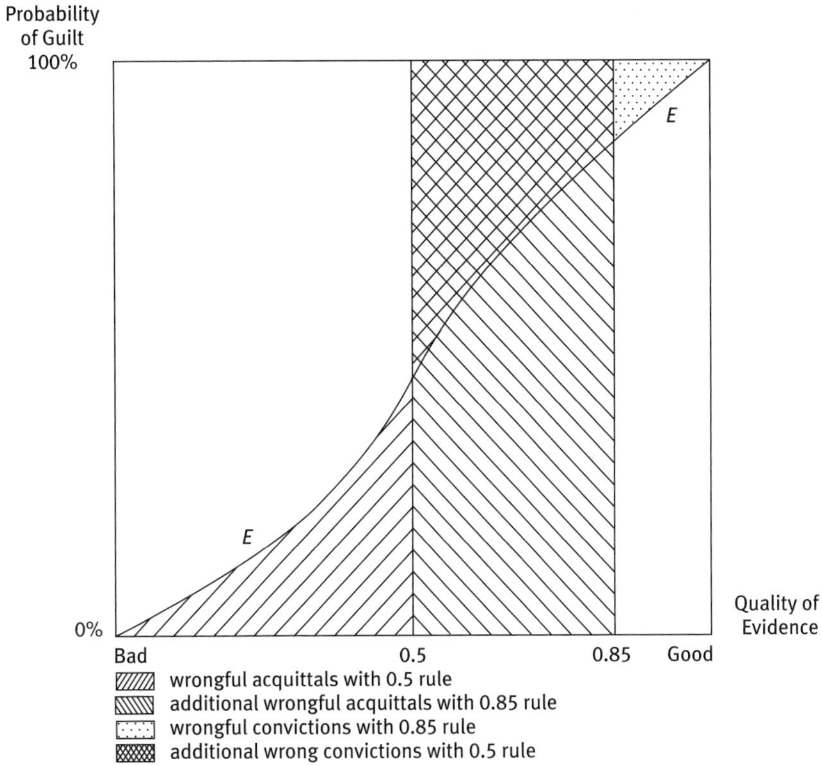

FIGURE 4
Bias in favor of the accused

There seem to be two obvious ways to decide on the weight of the evidence needed to convict. The first would be simply to try to choose that required weight of evidence which minimizes total errors. As a general rule, this means that weight which gives about as many erroneous convictions as erroneous acquittals, which in our particular shape of the curve is 0.5.[6] Using this 0.5 weight of evidence, we would acquit in all cases to the left of line 0.5. Cases at the left of 0.5 and above line *E–E* are correctly decided, and those which are to the left and below (those that are ruled slanting downward to the left) are in error. Similarly, those to the right of 0.5 are convicted, and all those which lie below line *E–E* are cases where this is correct. Those cases in the cross-hatched area and the dotted area are errors.

6. It is possible to put line *E–E* in such a location that equalizing the numbers of type 1 and type 2 errors does not minimize the total errors, but, in most cases, the 0.5 rule will work.

Suppose we bias the proceedings by moving the weight of evidence line to 0.85, which is about the mean of the one and only empirical study of the matter. This lowers the number of improper convictions to the dotted area, but it increases a number of improper acquittals by the area ruled slanting downward to the right. Clearly there are more total errors. Is this increase in total errors compensated (or overcompensated) for by the reduction in the particular errors in which the defendant is unjustly held guilty?

Most people who have been indoctrinated in the conventional wisdom will regard the answer to the question as so obvious that it is foolish even to raise it. In fact, it is not at all obvious, although the conventional wisdom may well be correct. If we wish to use the threat of punishment to deter crime, then the present discounted value of the crime, including the chance of punishment, must be negative. If we bias proceedings in favor of the defendant, then, of necessity, we reduce the number of guilty persons who are convicted. It will be noted that the area on figure 4 which is shaded down and to the right (i.e., the area where guilty people are acquitted because of the change in the weight of evidence) is much larger than the area which is cross-hatched (which represents the *innocent* people who are acquitted). The minimum punishment which will deter is therefore necessarily increased.

Look at the matter entirely from the standpoint of innocent persons. The decision to bias the proceedings in favor of the defendant reduces the likelihood that he will be convicted, but it increases the penalty that he will suffer if he is convicted. It is not immediately obvious that innocent parties are benefited by this change.

Suppose there is a movement from 0.5 to 0.75 in the weight of evidence required to convict. Let us assume that this reduces the likelihood of conviction of a randomly selected innocent person by one-half. Suppose, also, that the reduction in frequency of conviction of guilty persons which was caused by this increase in the burden of proof on the prosecution required that sentences be doubled in order to retain the same deterrent effect. The increase of the sentence for the guilty people is sensible, and the fact that it cancels all of the gain to the innocent is unfortunate.

The real issue here would be whether increasing the burden of proof does or does not reduce the likelihood that innocent persons will be convicted *more* than it reduces the likelihood that guilty persons will be convicted. Assume that movement from 0.5 to 0.75 halved the probability that guilty persons would be convicted but cut the probability that innocent persons would be convicted by 0.75. Doubling the penalty would leave the deterrent effect of the court and punishment system unchanged.[7] On the other hand, the innocent person who previously would have faced, let us say, a 0.5 chance of one year in jail now faces a 0.125 chance of two years. Clearly, he has benefited.

The real issue, of course, is the relative reduction in the likelihood of punishment of guilt and innocence as we raise the burden of proof. Once again, that is an empirical issue upon which, so far as I know, nothing has been done. It does not seem particularly improbable, however, that innocent persons do gain from increasing the burden on the prosecution. Note, however, that the gain would be lower than it first appears, since the increase in the sentence certainly eliminates a good part of the expected gain and may (once again, our empirical knowledge is scanty here) more than cancel it.

I began this discussion by saying it was by no means obvious that we should bias proceedings in favor of the accused, and that seems to me a correct statement. The very common and very strong statements that this is a desirable policy, I think, have to be put down to the fact that before I wrote *The Logic of the Law* no one had noticed the implication of biasing proceedings for the length of sentence. For reasons which will be discussed below, judges and juries are in fact apt to act in this way—giving the benefit of the doubt to the accused or the defendant—but the rationalizations which have been used for this activity are erroneous. However, further investigation may well lead to the conclusion that it was a correct policy, even if it had been reached by corrupt reasoning methods.

Before turning to why we observe this type of behavior on the part of the judges and juries, let us discuss briefly the situation in civil cases. As I have said, the only empirical study we have seems to indicate that the behavior of judges and juries in civil cases is not very much different from that in criminal cases. "A fair preponderance of the evidence" is translated as being 0.75 probability, whereas "beyond reasonable doubt" is translated as 0.85. Clearly, these are not very different.

In my opinion, juries, in general, are not willing to bring in large damage cases against ordinary citizens unless the weight of the evidence is considerably better than 0.5000001. This is, of course, an example of bias for the defendant. On the other hand, there are cases in which the jury may be biased

7. Actually, it would increase it slightly because the choice between committing the crime and not committing the crime also involves a measure of the likelihood of being unjustly convicted as a cost on the "don't commit crime" side. In most cases, it is trivial.

in the favor of the plaintiff. If the defendant is a large corporation [8] or the government, then the jury may exhibit prejudice against the defendant. Note that it is also apparently true that corporate or government plaintiffs have trouble under similar circumstances. Needless to say, this is only a *large* corporation or government. A small corporation—let us say, a local grocery store—does not seem to suffer from this particular kind of difficulty.

The result of this bias against plaintiffs is clearly perverse. Assume, for example, that we are talking about a contract which is allegedly breached and for which large damages are claimed by the plaintiff. If the judge and jury use the rule under which there must be a 0.75 probability of being correct before a damage claim can be brought in, this means that many more just claims will be rejected than with a 0.5 rule. However, in this case there is no increase in the penalty to offset this reduction. Thus, the application of this rule means that the present discounted value of a claim is almost always less than the actual damage caused. Out-of-court settlements, then, tend to go against the plaintiff much more strongly than one would anticipate.[9]

The result is that many otherwise profitable contracts will not be negotiated, which surely imposes considerable social cost, and that many laws either will be enforced in a rather ineffective way or must be drafted with the idea that this type of bias exists. They are therefore less efficient than they could be if the courts maximized their performance by using the 0.5 rule.

The only attempt in our law to offset this kind of thing is the occasional use of triple damages in civil suits. This is an unusual expedient, and, as far as I can see, the particular cases in which it is used are frequently badly chosen. For example, it is frequently possible to sue for triple damages in monopoly and Sherman Act cases. In these cases, the jury and judge are almost certainly biased against the defendant to begin with. Thus the triple-damage claim, instead of offsetting the bias in the proceedings, actually magnifies its effect.

Why do we observe a general bias against the prosecution in criminal cases? In spite of Lenin, it does seem to be very widespread in almost all legal systems. The standard arguments for it ignore the effect of the rule on the necessary punishment. Thus, the first assumption would be that this type of bias involves intellectual error.

8. And, of course, in many cases, although the plaintiff nominally is a private citizen, it is in reality an insurance company.

9. Needless to say, I am using the contract case and plaintiff-defendant only as an example. Where the plaintiff is a large corporation, suing an individual in tort, the bias would likely be in the other direction.

I think, however, it is not quite that simple, although intellectual error is surely there. The real problem here is analogous to public goods in economics. Suppose I am making a decision as to whether or not a particular accused shall go to prison for twenty years. The decision to send him to prison is a clear-cut, straightforward imposition of specific, very great harm on a person I see before me. The contrary decision raises the total crime rate in the community by some small amount. The effect is highly dispersed, since it amounts to a slight reduction in the average well-being of the rest of the population as a whole, and it is hard to see. Under the circumstances, it is fairly easy for any individual to pay careful attention to the concentrated effect and very little attention to the highly dispersed effect.

This same line of reasoning would apply both to civil cases and to criminal cases. My decision that the defendant in this case shall pay $100,000 in damages, which will mean that he will lose both his business and his house (to say nothing of his car), inflicts a very definite harm on him. The social benefit obtained by a contrary decision is much less clear and direct; therefore, it is easy to overlook.

In civil suits between two individuals this effect is not as clear. It is still true, however, that the defendant is likely to be badly harmed by a decision against him, while the plaintiff simply suffers an opportunity cost—i.e., he does not gain as much as he otherwise would—in a decision against him. If the plaintiff has already been very badly injured in an automobile accident, perhaps bias might go the other way; but, in practice, such cases normally involve an insurance company as the defendant.[10]

The bias against large corporations and the government can be explained in a similar manner. The cost of a large judgment against a corporation, or the failure by a corporation to collect, is actually widely dispersed in very small units to the stockholders of that corporation. Further, many citizens would think that really the cost does not get passed on to the stockholders anyway, because they do not understand how corporations work. Much the same can be said about the government, which is also subject to bias of this type.

Thus, if what I have said above is correct, the basic explanation for the "beyond reasonable doubt" rule in the criminal law and the effective, although

10. In those cases where the insurance company is not a defendant, it is doubtful that the jury knows it. In general, it is not possible to say in the court proceedings that the defendant is actually an insurance company. It is likely that juries assume that all such cases involve insurance companies.

not properly rationalized, bias in civil law is not a carefully thought-out line of reasoning but a fairly natural and normal way of thinking on the part of judges and juries. They are wrong in the sense that the social optimum is not achieved in the civil case, but it is possible that the rule is correct in the criminal case.

Finally, I should like to deal with one set of cases in which the bias is in the other direction—the bias is very heavily in favor of the prosecution and against the defendant. This is a collection of minor cases, mainly traffic violations, in which the cost to the defendant of conviction is usually quite small. The proceedings in this area are very heavily biased against the defendant. It is nearly impossible for the defendant to win the case, unless the officer who gave him the ticket admits that he has done something which is clearly improper. Note that in this case, although the cost to the defendant is usually very small, it can be very high—he may lose his driver's license. The loss of a driver's license to a cabdriver in Washington, D.C., is really a serious penalty.

Once again, I think this can be explained in terms of the dispersed and concentrated effect. In most cases, the cost of a traffic violation is very modest for the person convicted. The possibility of serious damage from auto accidents is clear to everyone, and hence this particular bias is not terribly hard to understand. It is notable that in most cases, the actual deprivation of the individual's driver's license is not done by the court. Courts are very reluctant to convict people of traffic offenses if it will lead to the revocation of their driver's licenses. The actual severe penalty that is then imposed on people, usually as a result of repeated convictions, is done by a completely anonymous agency, before which the individual has no right to a hearing. The outcome, I think, would be held unconstitutional by the Supreme Court were it not for the fact that Supreme Court justices can be killed by a careless driver, too. They are, therefore, less tender than with defendants accused of murder or robbery, crimes to which high-level jurists are very rarely subject.

TECHNOLOGY

THE ANGLO-SAXONS VERSUS THE REST OF THE WORLD

Turning to the technology of courts, we see that among Western countries there are two basic procedural systems.[1] One, which descends from the Roman law, is used by most Continental countries; and the other, which mostly descends from medieval precedents, is used in the Anglo-Saxon countries. There are a number of differences between these two methods, but only one will be discussed in this chapter. The Anglo-Saxon procedure is called the adversary system, because the proceeding is dominated by the two parties to the litigation with, in most criminal cases, one of the parties being a prosecuting attorney. It descends in part from trial by battle, in which the government official present at the trial simply refereed the contest. Under modern circumstances, the evidence and arguments are presented by the two sides, and a judge, board of judges, or a group of conscripted private citizens (called jurors) decides which one has won.

The other system, used on the Continent, is usually called the inquisitorial system. In this system, the judges or judge are, in essence, carrying on an independent investigation of the case, and the parties play a much more minor role. I should warn the reader that I argue that the Roman jurists were right and that the medieval feudal lords were wrong. The line of reasoning used will not rigorously prove this proposition.[2] Further empirical research will be necessary to prove that the inquisitorial system is superior to the adversary system. I shall merely establish a theoretical structure for the analysis of the two systems and present a strong argument that the inquisitorial system is better.

In practice, of course, the inquisitorial system of necessity has some adversary elements, since the parties are given some role in court; and the adversary system has some inquisitorial elements, because the judge (and, in some rare cases, the jury) also engage in some direct investigation of the case. The judge, for example, may occasionally ask questions of the witness.

Reprinted, with permission, from *Trials on Trial: The Pure Theory of Legal Procedure* (New York: Columbia University Press, 1980), 87–104. Copyright 1980 Columbia University Press.

1. The next few pages are drawn largely from Gordon Tullock, "The Efficient Organization of Trials," *Kyklos* (1975) (Fasc. 4), 28:745–62.

2. See Gordon Tullock, *The Logic of the Law* (New York: Basic Books, 1971), for a "commonsense" argument for the European system as opposed to the Anglo-Saxon system.

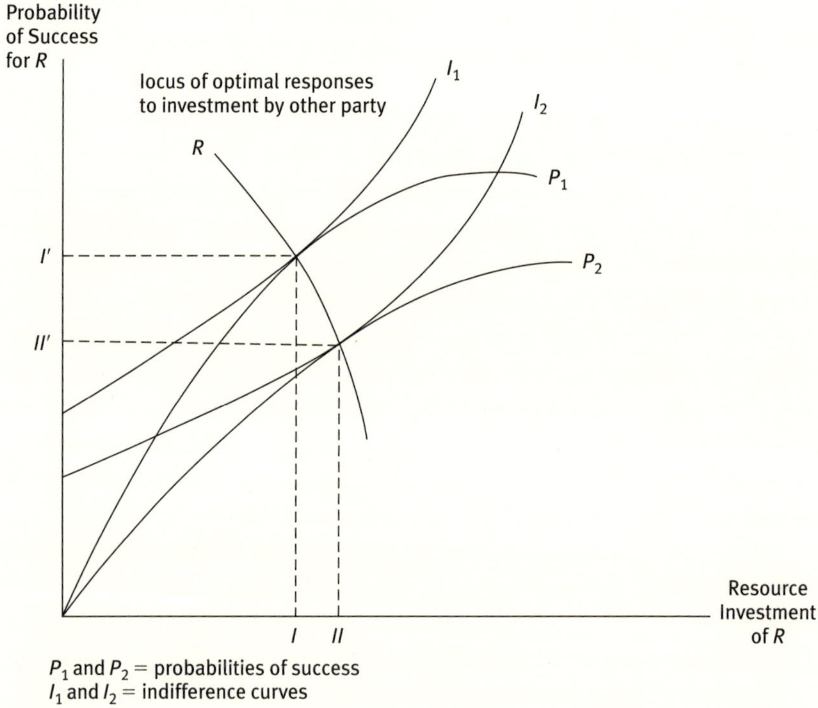

FIGURE 1
Resource adjustment of one party

Consider the situation of a party in the adversary-type proceedings. He can invest various amounts of resources in hiring lawyers, investigating the facts, testifying himself—either truthfully or falsely, etc. Since he knows a good deal about the facts of the case and can make an estimate of the resources the other party will invest in his case, he should have an idea of the likely probability of success for various investments of resources. On the basis of this estimate, figure 1, line P_1, shows for one party, Mr. Right, the probability of success for various resource commitments in a particular litigation.

We assume that there are two parties, Mr. Right and Mr. Wrong, and that, as their names suggest, Mr. Right is the one who (if we had divine justice) would win. Line P_1 then shows the probability of success that he can purchase by each investment of resources. The investment exhibits the usual declining marginal productivity. *R*'s tastes are depicted by a set of indifference curves, I_1 and I_2, and his bliss point is in the upper left-hand corner, with certain success at a zero resource investment. He chooses the resource commitment where his highest possible indifference curve is tangent to the production function line, with the result that he invests I resources and obtains a probability of success at I', as shown on the diagram.

If we consider the evidence available for the case, there are two meanings to the term. First, there is whatever still remains in the world which might have bearing on the case. This is more or less unchanging. Second, however, there is the evidence that is actually dredged up and presented in court. This is a function of the resources put into the case, and there should be better evidence actually presented to the court if more resources are invested. Suppose that Mr. Right thought Mr. Wrong would put in more resources and, hence, that there was a lower probability of success with each investment by Mr. Right. This would produce curve P_2. Mr. Right is forced to be satisfied with the lower indifference curve I_2. Under these circumstances, he would invest II resources and obtain II' possibility of success.

In this case an increase in resources invested by Wrong leads Right to both increase his resources and reduce his likelihood of success, but this is not general. In cases in which the resource commitment or evidence is very one-sided, an increase in resources by the party in the stronger position may lead the other side to reduce his resource commitments and take the corresponding increased probability of losing the suit (see figure 3). It depends on the payoff to the marginal dollar of resources invested, and where it is less than \$1, there is a motive for reducing instead of increasing expenditures.

If we consider all possible resource commitments by Mr. Wrong, each would be accompanied by a risk-production function, like P_1 or P_2, for Mr. Right, and Mr. Right would have an indifference curve tangent to it at some point. A line can be drawn connecting all such points. A segment of such a line is shown as R in figure 1. It is the reaction curve of Mr. Right to various possible investments of resources by Mr. Wrong. In figure 2, reaction curves for both of the parties are shown. On the vertical axis are the resources invested by R, and on the horizontal are those invested by W. The probability of success in this diagram is a fan of rays from the origin. The straight line running through point 0, for example, shows those pairs of resource investments which all give the same probability of success for Mr. Right. Granting declining marginal returns and that the evidence is reasonably close to equal, the two curves will have the shape shown and will intersect as shown in the figure. The point of intersection is the equilibrium of the model, which would occur with Mr. Right investing R resources and Mr. Wrong investing W.

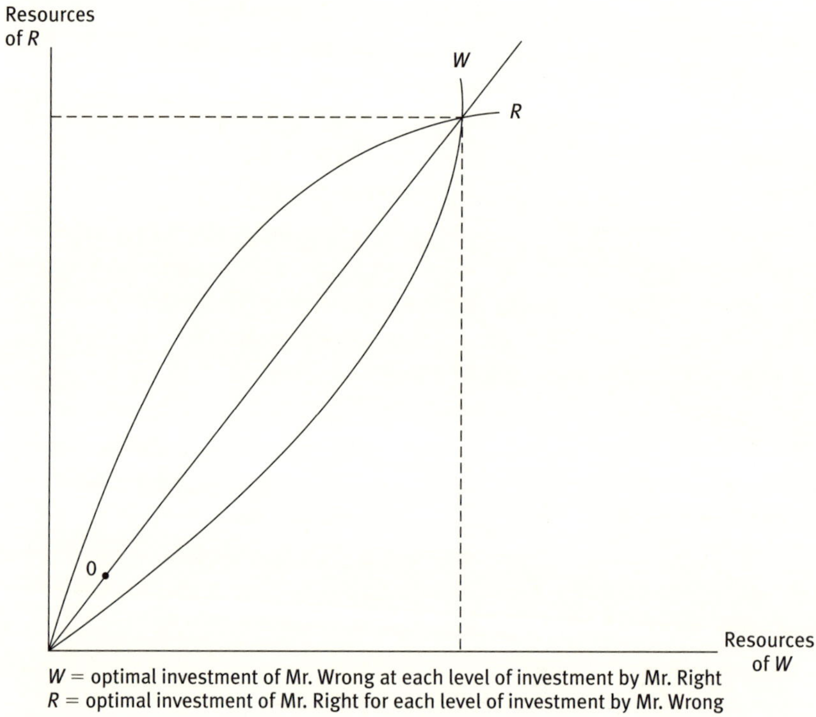

FIGURE 2
Resource investments by two parties

In figure 3, I have shown by line *P* the situation in which the evidence happens to be very strong for Mr. Right and, hence, that he can purchase a high probability of success with a relatively modest investment of resources. Line P_1 goes up very steeply and is, of course, tangent to a very high indifference curve with a relatively low resource investment and a high probability of success. It might be, however, that the evidence is positively misleading and, hence, that Mr. Right would have a low marginal return on resources invested in raising his probability. Line P_2 shows these circumstances, and the indifference curve tangent to it, I_2, which is a low one, shows the best that Mr. Right could do under these circumstances. It will be observed that Mr. Right would choose to put fewer resources into his suit in the unfavorable case than in the very favorable cases; but this is simply an artifact of the particular lines I have drawn. The reaction curves for the later case are shown on figure 4, and the equilibrium point is, of course, very near to the horizontal axis.

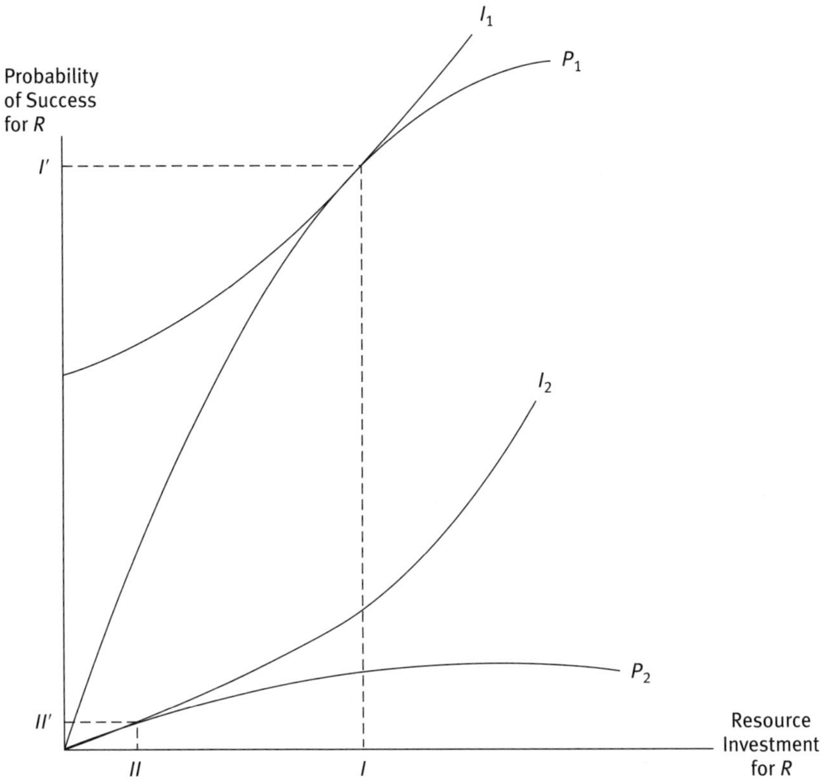

P_1 and P_2 = probability of success for Mr. Right
I_1 and I_2 = indifference curves

FIGURE 3
Response of Mr. Right at different levels of evidence

Looked at from the economic point of view, it is immediately obvious from figure 2 that the outcome is not ideal. I have drawn an equiprobability line from the equilibrium point to the origin and put a point 0 on it. Point 0 has the same probability of success for the two parties, but with a much lower investment of resources. Clearly, it dominates the equilibrium solution. This is also true of point 0 on figure 4. The only question is whether an institutional structure can be designed which will reach 0.

I should now like to introduce a game which is helpful in analyzing court proceedings. Suppose that a sum of money is put up as a prize for a particular form of lottery. The lottery has only two contestants and each of them

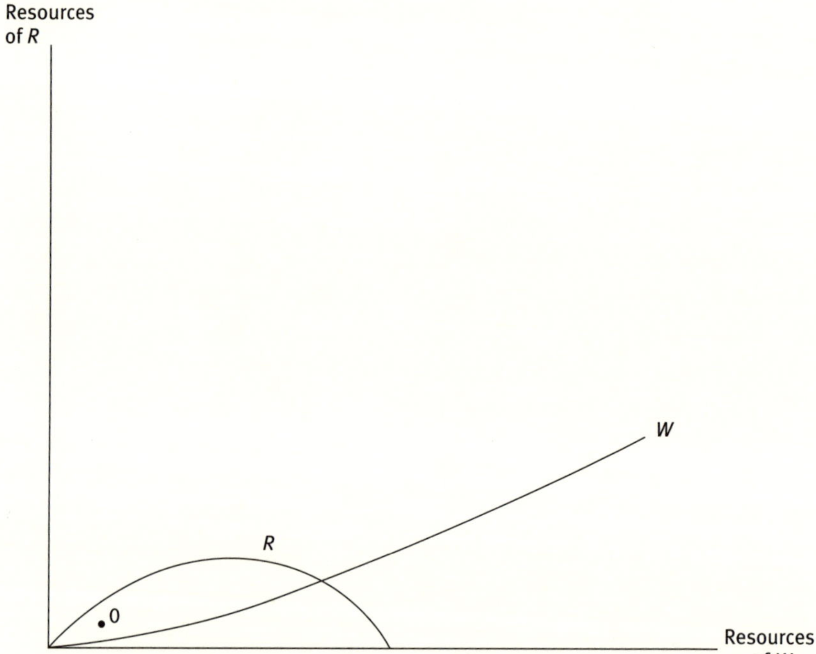

FIGURE 4
Response of Mr. Right at different levels of evidence

may buy as many tickets for the lottery as he wishes for $1 each. One ticket is drawn at random, and the owner of the ticket receives the prize. Note that the payments for the tickets are not added on to the prize. The payoff to this game for our two parties is shown on the set of equations (1).

$$V_R = D \cdot \frac{R}{R + W} - R$$
$$V_W = D \cdot \frac{W}{R + W} - W \qquad (1)$$

The ex ante value for Right, for example, is the prize (D) multiplied by the probability that the ticket purchased by Right will be drawn [$R/(R + W)$] minus the amount of money put in by Right (R). Wrong's value is symmetric.

It is obvious that we could solve this equation set, although in the real world we might want to add in risk aversion.[3]

This set of equations, of course, would generate a set of lines of the same nature as those drawn in figure 1 and a set of reaction functions similar to those shown in figure 2. The probability of success is a function of both resources invested by the player and those invested by the other party, and exhibits declining marginal returns.

This game can be changed so that it maps many different types of trial institutions. Temporarily we are interested in only one particular type here. The equations as given are egalitarian; i.e., they indicate that two parties, in the nature of things, have the same inherent likelihood of winning. In the real world, the physical evidence available in a case is rarely evenly balanced. This can be easily dealt with by adjusting the equation.

For example, we might alter the rules of the game so that Mr. Right can purchase two lottery tickets for $1, whereas Mr. Wrong must still pay $1 for each one. This would increase the value for Mr. Right. Indeed, there are many complications of this sort that can easily be put into the game; but since we do not know a great deal about the real-world parameters, there is no great reason for us to be extremely complex in our discussion of the matter. No doubt the payoff to various conditions which may make the trial less than completely equal—such as evidence in favor of one side—is quite complex; but, for the moment, let us use a very simple function. A variant of the game, in which the number of tickets Mr. Right can buy for $1 is R multiplied by some function (f) of the evidence (E), is shown in equation set (2).

$$V_R = D \cdot \frac{f(E)R}{f(E)R + W} - R$$
$$V_W = D \cdot \frac{W}{f(E)R + W} - W \qquad (2)$$

To make it easier to deal with some matters to which we will turn shortly, I should like to further simplify these equations and change them from

3. For calculation method and a set of results, see Gordon Tullock, "Efficient Rent Seeking," in James Buchanan, Robert Tollison, and Gordon Tullock, ed., *Toward a Theory of the Rent-Seeking Society* (College Station: Texas A&M University Press, forthcoming).

statements as to the payoff of the game to the probability of success. This permits me to drop part of the equation as in equation set (3).

$$P_R = \frac{f(E)R}{f(E)R + W} \qquad P_W = \frac{W}{f(E)R + W} \tag{3}$$

Note that the reason I have attached the evidence function to R instead of to both R and W is simply that they would be different functions, and, without any knowledge of their exact shape, it seems a waste of time to make the matter more complicated than is necessary.

In this form, the equation shows in a particularly pure form the externality associated with adversary proceedings. If I increase the likelihood that I will win by 1 percent, I automatically reduce the likelihood that you will win by 1 percent. Under the circumstances, the likelihood that I will choose the resource investment which is socially optimal is, to put the matter mildly, slight.

So far, we have discussed almost exclusively the adversary proceeding rather than the inquisitorial, and hence I have not fulfilled my promise that the two will be compared. To make a comparison, I would like to introduce another set of equations, set (4).

$$P_R = \frac{f(E)R}{f(E)R + W} + g(F) \qquad g(F) > 0$$

$$P_W = \frac{W}{f(E)R + W} - g(F) \qquad g(F) < 0 \tag{4}$$

This is, of course, the same as set (3), except that another term has been added on at the right. This term shows the investment of resources in the actual judging process, something which, up to now, we have not considered. This function is assumed to improve Mr. Right's chances as the resources invested in judging (F) are increased simply because he is right.

With this modification, we can now deal somewhat more generally with the problem. It is clear that increasing the skill or diligence of decision makers will increase the likelihood of accuracy, and this is not subject to the kind of externality we were discussing earlier. The difference can perhaps best be seen from considering a rather unusual way of investing resources in a trial. Suppose that instead of permitting the parties to decide how much they were going to spend on legal fees for their own attorneys, we let them decide how much they would like to put in to hire a judge. Each one could contribute whatever he wished, and then the authorities would purchase for this trial the best judge that could be obtained for the sum of the two contributions. Of course, the judge would not be told which of the two parties put up the most money.

Unless we assume that in making selection of judges we are random or, perhaps, systematically perverse, surely a better judge would be hired if there were more resources available.[4] If, then, with larger amounts of money we get a decision maker who is better qualified and more likely to reach the right conclusion, it will be contrary to the interests of Mr. Wrong to have a very good judge, and he would tend to put no money at all into the pot.[5] Mr. Right, on the other hand, would want a good judge and would be willing to make a suitable payment. Presumably, the amount he would be willing to pay would be less if the case looked to him to be an easy one and, hence, suitable for a rather poorly qualified judge.

The interesting feature of this little *Gedankenexperiment*, however, is not Mr. Right's investment but Mr. Wrong's. Mr. Wrong would have no motive to try to improve the quality of the judiciary, because the better the judiciary, the worse off he is going to be. Whereas he might have very strong motives to hire excellent attorneys and put a lot of money into his legal defense under the adversary system, under this system he would have no motive for investment at all. A good judge, in essence, changes the production function of the initial parties, as shown on figure 1, in the sense that he raises the production function for Mr. Right and lowers the production function for Mr. Wrong. Thus, each improvement in the quality of the judge tends to move cases in the proper direction.

The point of this chapter has been to compare the European-type procedure (inquisitorial) with that used in Anglo-Saxon countries (adversary). It can be seen that the basic difference between these two is the amount of resources put on the two parts of our set of equations. The adversary proceeding puts almost all of its resources on R and W in (4); and the inquisitorial proceeding puts almost all of them on F. I have, so far, been simplifying the situation when I talk about the adversary proceedings by assuming that $g(F)$ is zero, and I could take the complementary simplification and assume that, in Europe, R and W are zero.

4. Needless to say, it might be wiser to hire a board of judges rather than an individual, a technical specialist rather than a legal specialist, etc.

5. Contributions would have to be restricted to positive contribution. Presumably, Mr. Wrong would be delighted with the opportunity to make a negative contribution.

An American attorney who read this section accused me of setting up a straw man. He claimed that the system is not anywhere near as pure as the model would indicate. Judicial-supervision control of the process is already significant and growing more important. There are, in fact, now rules that penalize a party for the cost caused to an adversary who is forced to prove a fact that should have been admitted.

The lawyer's comments are both correct and incorrect. It is certainly true that judicial control is somewhat greater than zero. It is also true that just at the moment it is growing. The history of law in the United States shows phases in which judicial control grows and phases in which it is reduced. We are in one of the growth phases right now. A point the lawyer did not mention is that in England judicial control on the proceeding is very much stronger than in the United States.

Nevertheless, the difference between the system in the United States, or even in England, and Continental procedure is still very large. We can say that there are elements of inquisitorial proceeding in American procedure and much stronger elements in England, but, nevertheless, they are still basically adversary. It is, of course, also true that there are elements of the adversary approach in Continental courts, but these are relatively minor compared with the strength of the adversary procedure in Anglo-Saxon law.

The basic difference between the two, as will be seen, is the W which appears in all of the equations. In the adversary proceedings, a great deal of the resources are put in by someone who is attempting to mislead. Assume, for example, that in the average American court case, 45 percent of the total resources are invested by each side and 10 percent by the government in providing the actual decision-making apparatus. This would mean that 55 percent of the resources used in the court are aimed at achieving the correct result, and 45 percent at reaching an incorrect result. Under the inquisitorial system, assume that 90 percent of the resources are put up by the government which hires a competent board of judges (who then carry on an essentially independent investigation) and only 5 percent by each of the parties. Under these circumstances, 95 percent of the resources are contributed by people who are attempting to reach the correct conclusion, and only 5 percent by the saboteur. Normally, we would anticipate a higher degree of accuracy with the second type than with the first.

This line of reasoning is so simple that I always find it difficult to understand why the Anglo-Saxon court system has persisted. Its origins, from trial by battle, are obvious enough, and, at a time when the law quite literally was the will of the stronger, it was indeed quite rational. Its persistence can perhaps be explained in terms of the inertia of established custom, but customs do change.

There is, of course, an immensely powerful interest group favoring the preservation of the present situation in Anglo-Saxon courts. The number of lawyers per capita in Anglo-Saxon countries (and, in particular, the United States) is a high multiple of the number in systems using the inquisitorial system. We also probably have more judges per capita than such countries as Switzerland and Sweden, in spite of the greater emphasis put on judicial decision-making in those countries. The higher inherent accuracy of their court system means that there are fewer cases brought before the courts; and, once the case is brought, the judge makes the decision as to how much time will be spent on it, rather than the parties, with the result that cases are frequently disposed of quite quickly with good accuracy.

A change from our system to the Continental system would eliminate a sizable part of the demand for lawyers. This statement is not, of course, made under the assumption that our lawyers spend all of their time in court; indeed, they spend relatively little of their time in court. The advice they give, however, is very heavily affected by the type of judicial proceeding they anticipate if a court case does arise. Further, they spend much time negotiating cases and preparing cases. All of this is less expensive in Europe.

A sharp fall in the demand for lawyers would, of course, impoverish the present profession. Many lawyers would become vacuum-cleaner salesmen, law schools would be compelled to close, immense bodies of accumulated personal capital would cease to be of any relevance, and, altogether, the legal profession would suffer a major disaster.[6] Under the circumstances, the opposition of the lawyers to the type of legal system used on the Continent is understandable.

Lawyers defending our current system do offer some arguments for it. The first I usually encounter in talking to the average American lawyer is an expression of incredulity that any other system exists. They will then tell me a few myths about European procedure, such as that the defendant is compelled to prove his innocence rather than the prosecution being compelled to prove his guilt; but, once one has penetrated through this smoke screen, there is an intellectually possible defense of our system.

6. It is my personal opinion that the social benefits would be large enough so that a Pareto optimal move is available; i.e., we could fully compensate them for this loss and still make a gain.

The point of this defense is that the judge may be undermotivated and, hence, will not work hard enough. The two sides, whatever else may be said about them, are strongly motivated; hence, they can be expected to put a great deal of resources into influencing the decision. The judge has nothing personal riding on it and may not put much effort into his decision, according to this argument.[7] This matter will be discussed in considerable detail in chapter 8.

One of the problems in research of this type is, of course, that the courts have the power to prevent themselves from being investigated. In general, we take the view that people who try to avoid investigation do so because the investigation would turn up things that are not to their credit; but it must be admitted that courts may have a valid reason for not wanting to be investigated. It is possible to argue that the judicial system works better if it is surrounded by myths and magic than if everyone concerned knows that the court regularly makes mistakes.

Regardless of this, I now turn to a second issue, which is how hard judges and juries work. It seems fairly certain that judges and juries are not particularly highly motivated in law cases, and hence there is something to be said for the view that leaving everything to them would be undesirable. It should be pointed out that there are various methods used in Europe to provide stronger motives for judges than are provided under the Anglo-Saxon system. The judicial career is organized with promotion, regular transfers, etc. This would normally motivate judges under this system more strongly than the judge under the Anglo-Saxon system. Certainly the jurors, who are conscripted amateurs, have practically no motives to work hard.

In fact, there is no reason to believe that judges and juries under either system are optimally motivated. Research should be undertaken for the purpose of developing institutions which will give them a better motivation. But the undermotivation is more extreme with respect to the jury and the Anglo-Saxon judge than with respect to the European judge. In Anglo-Saxon adversary proceedings, the parties have every motive to put great resources into presenting their case; but this case is to be presented before a group of people who, in the case of the jury, are amateurs, of average intelligence, and are not strongly motivated to hard intellectual labor to understand the case. As a result, the parties' arguments are unlikely to be designed in such a way as to put

7. For a discussion of the general problem of the undermotivation of government officials, see Gordon Tullock, "Public Decisions as Public Goods," *Journal of Political Economy* (July/August, 1971), 79:913–18.

great strain on the minds of the listeners, even if the situation is such that truth can only be obtained with such great strain.

Still, the weak motivation for the public officials concerned is a defect in both court systems. It is not obvious that it is less of a defect for the Anglo-Saxon than for the European system, but it is clear that public officials play a larger role in the European system. Thus, it is at least conceivable that the undermotivation of the judges more than counterbalances the overinvestment of resources by the parties, with which this chapter has been mainly concerned.

It will not have escaped the reader that, personally, I favor the European system. It seems to me the theoretical arguments in its favor are much stronger than those against it. But I cannot be sure. The whole field of legal research has been dominated by essentially unscientific techniques. This has been particularly true of the comparison of these methods of reaching decisions in lawsuits. This chapter has been an effort to set the matter on a sound theoretical basis. Without further research, particularly empirical research, it is not possible to be certain that the Continental system is better than the Anglo-Saxon, but the presumption is surely in that direction.

Appendix. A Digression on Arbitral Geography

When a portion of this chapter appeared in *Kyklos*, my argument that the European system was basically better than ours apparently upset a great number of people, and, in particular, there were two comments on it, one by McChesney and one by Ordover and Weitzman.[8]

Frankly, I did not think that either comment made much of a dent in my basic reasoning. This may, of course, simply represent the usual author's vanity, but, in any event, my reply to them was rather brief.[9]

In general, the arguments offered by these three critics seem to have had very little impact. One particular argument by McChesney, however, has since been repeated by other scholars. In my opinion, once again, this is a

8. Fred S. McChesney, "On the Procedural Superiority of a Civil Law System: A Comment," *Kyklos* (1977), 30 (Fasc. 3):507–10. J. A. Ordover and Phillip Weitzman, "On the Efficient Organization of Trials: A Comment," *Kyklos* (1977), 30 (Fasc. 3):511–16.

9. Gordon Tullock, "Reply to McChesney, and Ordover and Weitzman," *Kyklos* (1977), 30 (Fasc. 3):517–19.

rather weak argument, but granted the support it seems to have, I do not feel I can simply pass over it in silence. On the other hand, I do not see why all of my readers should devote their attention to what I think is basically a fallacious argument. Hence, this appendix, which can be either read or skipped.

Let me begin by quoting McChesney's argument.

> Arbitration permits parties to agree beforehand that any disagreement between them in the course of future dealings will be settled, not in court, but in prearranged private proceedings whose result is binding on the parties. Most importantly, the parties are able to stipulate the procedures, including those relating to evidence, that will be followed. To quote from one legal source:
>
> > "The essence of arbitration is its freedom from the formality of ordinary judicial procedure, and unless it is stipulated that the arbitrators should follow legal rules of procedure, the courts have no jurisdiction to set aside and award for failure of the arbitrators to follow court rules. . . . Where *unrestricted by the agreement* or by statute, the arbitrators are allowed much latitude in their procedure, and there is no requirement that they observe technical rules and formalities, so long as the proceedings are honestly and fairly conducted."
> >
> > "All questions as to the admission or rejection of evidence as well as the credit due to evidence, and the inferences of fact to be drawn from it, are matters for the arbitrators to decide in the exercise of their honest judgement. Formal rules as to the admissibility and the weight and sufficiency of evidence do not bind them . . . unless a statute or the *agreement so directs*."
>
> There are other differences as to rules of evidence that are important: arbitrators may minimize total costs by stipulating the time within which evidence must be produced and refuse to hear that brought in too late. They may limit the number of witnesses to be heard, and need not rely solely on the evidence brought forth in arbitration proceedings but may draw on their own experience or knowledge, and even testify themselves. But the important point is that these provisions are all matters of negotiations between the parties, such that the externalities claimed by Tullock can be internalized.[10]

10. McChesney, "Civil Law System: A Comment," 507–10.

McChesney then goes on to point out that parties to international contract can frequently contract in such a way as to have the case tried in a selected jurisdiction. He then continues:

> In fact, this is no idle theoretical game. It is precisely the sort of contracting that occurs when parties form an international sales agreement. Legal commentators note:
>
> "The parties to a contract for sale of goods abroad are well advised to provide expressly which legal system they desire to be applied to their contract. . . . The parties may submit their contract to any legal system which they like to elect and, in particular, they are not limited to a legal system with which the circumstances surrounding their contract have an actual connection.
>
> ". . . The parties to the contract are permitted, if they so wish, to nominate the law of a particular country as the proper law of the contract. If they do this, their choice is conclusive. . . ."
>
> Given this situation of free contracting, it is of great interest for the controversy at hand that the majority of such international contracts, regardless of the nationality of the parties, specify that litigation is to take place in England. If Anglo-American common law is inferior, its inferiority is not borne out by the behavior of the parties able to select the most efficient jurisdiction for themselves.[11]

Let me begin with a problem of fact. McChesney gives no source for his statement about the courts chosen.[12] On being asked, he said he had been told this by one of his law professors (he was a law student at the time). It seems likely that that law professor's sample of cases from which he made his subjective judgment was drawn in the United States and England. The superiority of the courts of England over those in the United States is, of course, strictly speaking, not relevant. Nevertheless, for reasons I will discuss below, I would not be surprised to discover that international litigation was very commonly carried on in an English-speaking court.

11. Ibid.

12. According to the *Economist* (August 12, 1979, p. 94), the British government drastically changed its arbitration act in 1979 because a great many cases were being heard in Switzerland, Paris, and the United States, and they wanted to improve the competitive status of the English arbitration system.

Before turning to these matters, however, I should like to go on to a second rather similar comment contained in an article by Landes and Posner.[13] They say:

> Notwithstanding all the above reservations, the use of arbitration as a benchmark for evaluation of the judicial system may help resolve a recent controversy between Gordon Tullock and others regarding the relative efficiency of the Anglo-American adversarial and Continental inquisitorial procedural system. It appears that most arbitrators are conducted according to English or American arbitration procedure—and, as mentioned, a nation's arbitration procedures tend to follow its judicial procedures. Here then is some, albeit limited, marked evidence of the superiority of the adversary system.[14]

Note that Landes and Posner are not endorsing McChesney's point of view. Indeed, instead of saying most cases take place in England, they say that most arbitration cases follow either English or American arbitration procedures. Once again, however, there is a question of fact. They footnote three sources,[15] none of which contains any statistical evidence. The basic problem with their remark, however, is the phrase about arbitration procedures tending to follow judicial procedures, for which they state no source at all. Indeed, in the next paragraph, they point out a number of rather radical differences between arbitration and standard procedures of Anglo-Saxon law.

The theory underlying the McChesney, and Landes and Posner, argument is that if people are free to choose the type of judicial procedure they will face in enforcing a contract, they will tend to choose the most efficient one. I agree, and indeed took the same point of view in *Logic of the Law*.[16] We might expect technological progress, in the sense that new techniques are discovered which are better than existing ones, and some inertia, in the sense that the parties will

13. William M. Landes and Richard A. Posner, "Adjudication as a Private Good," *Journal of Legal Studies* (March 1979), 8(2):235–84.

14. Ibid., pp. 251–52.

15. Michael Marks Cohen, "A Venue Problem with the Arbitration Clauses Found in Printed Form Charters," *Journal of Maritime Law and Commerce* (1976), 7:541; Lynden Macassey, "International Commercial Arbitration: Its Origin, Development, and Importance," *Transactions of the Grotius Society* (1939), 24:179, 199; Donald E. Zubrod, "Arbitration from the Arbitrator's Point of View," *Tulane Law Review* (1975), 49:1054, 1055.

16. Tullock, *Logic of the Law*.

not instantly switch to the most efficient method, but on the whole we would expect parties to choose the most efficient course of action if they have a choice available to them. I would argue that the rapid growth of arbitral proceedings in the United States[17] is evidence that we have had here a technological change[18] to which the commercial community is adapting. All this is evidence of the superiority of the arbitral technique over the regular courts. It is, of course, the evidence of the superiority of arbitration over the Anglo-American courts, not over Continental courts. Nevertheless there is, in fact, a good deal of arbitration on the Continent too. This is clear evidence that the Continental procedure is not optimal, even if it is better than the Anglo-Saxon.

To demonstrate from statistics on arbitration that Anglo-Saxon procedure is better (or worse) than Continental, we need fairly good statistics. The total number of arbitrations is of little or no use, because the overwhelming majority of these arbitrations are fairly minor matters, which are handled very quickly and easily by arbitration, and in which the parties have not made any real choice as to what arbitral tribunal they will take. They will simply take the one that is readily and immediately available, because the issue is not of such importance that they make a worldwide search for the best tribunal and then run all across the world to take the case to London or, for that matter, Tokyo.

Most large-scale commercial contracts are in English simply because that is the language of international trade. This would point toward an English-speaking tribunal to interpret them. Further, an arbitral tribunal is not capable of enforcing its decisions and must turn to the regular courts for this purpose. We need, then, an arbitral tribunal located in a country where the courts will enforce its decisions, and where the loser is apt to have enough assets on hand so that the enforcement can proceed even if he objects. This tends to lead toward England, or better yet, the United States, as the place of arbitration. In this connection, it should be said that Anglo-Saxon law puts very few restrictions on what one can contract to do and, hence, gives greater freedom to the parties. Presumably, a French court in enforcing an arbitral tribunal would only enforce it if the contract itself were legal in France.

Probably as a result of these factors, together with the fact that London used to be the commercial center of the world, and English courts were much

17. See Table 1, Landes and Posner, " Adjudication," p. 251.

18. When I was in law school, we were told that courts would not enforce arbitration contracts, and I remember personally feeling horrified at being informed that the English courts would. That was a long time ago.

kinder to arbitration in the early years than American, the development of a set of external economies for arbitration procedures in London has occurred. It is simply somewhat easier to run arbitration there than almost anywhere else. We should not be particularly surprised then to find many cases in London.

Finally, however, the question arises as to whether the fact that an arbitration procedure is carried on in London is any evidence at all with respect to common law as opposed to Continental procedure. Clearly the procedure is different from the common law, or the parties would have no motive to seek arbitration. Indeed, Landes and Posner point out no less than six major differences between the common-law procedure and arbitration.[19] In essence, they are saying that the common-law version of arbitration is superior to the Continental version of arbitration. Whether there is very much difference between the two is not in any way examined empirically. My own impression from scattered reading is that arbitration resembles the Continental procedure for civil suits, although it does not resemble the procedure for criminal actions. This, however, is a mere impression.

It does seem to me that looking into what parties choose when they are given freedom to choose—i.e., the type of arbitral procedure that they select—is a valuable research technique. Further, I would rather anticipate that improvements in legal procedure would be more likely to come out of arbitration procedure than out of the regular government courts. Nevertheless, in order to engage in this kind of research, we actually have to do the research and not simply speculate. I must admit that I have been as casual here as McChesney, Posner, and Landes, but at least I have not claimed any particular conclusions from my lack of research. I simply suggest that we look into this area to find out whether the law can be improved.

19. Landes and Posner, "Adjudication," p. 252.

VARIOUS WAYS OF DEALING WITH THE COST OF LITIGATION

In the last chapter, on the basis of the cost-accuracy trade-off, I argued that the Continental system of procedure is better than that used in Anglo-Saxon countries. I find that this normally shocks lawyers.[1] This chapter will be devoted to the adversary system and an investigation of different methods of paying lawyers' fees. For this purpose, I will use the gambling game which I introduced in chapter 6 as a simple model of court procedure. The reader will recall that I promised a demonstration that the model could be used to investigate other methods of paying for litigation; we will proceed to that task now.

In the models that follow, I will make certain simplifying assumptions. First, the costs of judges, juries, courtrooms, etc., will be ignored. Normally the parties do not pay these expenses; and adding figures into our equations for the minor "court costs" which they *do* pay would be an unnecessary complication. Since these publicly provided resources are not taken into account by the parties, the actual social investment of resources is greater than that shown by our equilibrium points. In arbitration proceedings, of course, the parties *do* pay for the cost of the "judges," and presumably there is a more rational allocation of resources under those circumstances. Arbitration will be dealt with later.

No doubt the most common way of reallocating legal resources in the United States is the "contingency fee." A lawyer takes the plaintiff's case in return for a promise that he will receive some percentage of the proceeds (usually one-third) if he wins and nothing if he loses. It is not very clear in the discussion of this situation in the legal literature whether or not the court is supposed to take this fee into account in fixing the damages. In some cases—for example, some antitrust cases—Congress has provided that the defendant may pay the plaintiff's fees; and in civil rights cases, some courts have recently required a defendant to pay the plaintiff's fee even when the

Reprinted, with permission, from *Trials on Trial: Pure Theory of Legal Procedure* (New York: Columbia University Press, 1980), 105–19. Copyright 1980 Columbia University Press.

1. But not all lawyers. See, for example, Mirjan Damaska, "Evidentiary Barriers to Conviction, Two Models of Criminal Procedure: A Comparative Study," *University of Pennsylvania Law Review*, 121:506.

defendant wins. In these cases, the fee is added onto the decision (at least in theory). In most automobile damage suits, it is subtracted from the decision. This may or may not make a difference in the size of the fee and/or the amount actually received by the plaintiff. But leaving this unsolved question unsolved, it is clear that under these circumstances there are three parties at interest—the defendant, the plaintiff, and the plaintiff's attorney. Their interests are shown by equation set (1).

$$
\begin{aligned}
D_v &= \frac{D}{D+P+L} \cdot M - D \\
P_v &= \frac{P+L}{D+P+L} \cdot \frac{2}{3} M - P \\
L_c &= \frac{P+L}{D+P+L} \cdot \frac{1}{3} M - L
\end{aligned}
\tag{1}
$$

In this case, D is the defendant, P is the plaintiff, and L is the lawyer.

In practice, L, the resources invested by the lawyer for the plaintiff, are larger by quite a wide margin than P, the resources invested by the plaintiff himself; so the real issue in bringing the system of equations into equilibrium is primarily that D and L each maximize their return (minimize loss in the case of D). The plaintiff (in most cases) does not have enough money so that he could pay the fee of a really first-class attorney under any system other than the contingency-fee system. In a way, the attorney is acting as a banker for the plaintiff. Presumably the reason that the credit market covering plaintiff fees in this case has developed in this way is simply that bankers would have much less knowledge as to the relative likelihood of success in a case than will a skilled attorney. The fact that younger attorneys usually have a lot of spare time—hence, the opportunity cost of taking a case is low—may also be significant.

As a first approximation, I would tend to say that this system leads to underinvestment of resources for the plaintiff. The lawyer will receive only one-third of the damage suits he wins and hence will only invest resources up to the point where it pays, granted that one-third payoff. Under the circumstances, there are fewer resources supplied than would be the case if both of the parties were able to hire an attorney out of their own funds, but there's no reason to believe that the system is unfair to the plaintiffs.

There is, however, something that I have glossed over here. The plaintiff invests relatively little in actual cash and may get a great deal out of it. Under the circumstances, one would anticipate that plaintiffs would make every effort to obtain a leading lawyer. Thus, there is a preliminary decision by the attorney as to whether or not he will take the plaintiff's case. This decision can be decisive. If the plaintiff cannot get an attorney to take his case, he has lost.

I have been unable to find any serious discussion about how attorneys make their decisions in these matters. Certainly there is no formal hearing with both parties represented. The potential defendant would be particularly anxious to be represented if it were permitted. I imagine that the attorneys in fact investigate these cases very carefully, since they do not want to waste their own time on a poor case. One might even hope that they would only take those cases in which they were personally convinced that their client was in the right. Their investigative methods, I am sure, are not adversary but inquisitorial.

Under these circumstances, the potential plaintiff provides any information that the lawyer requests; and the lawyer either investigates—or sends out junior members of his office to investigate—the actual circumstances. The plaintiff does not really have control, although he may devote a good deal of energy in attempting to attract the attention of a lawyer, and indeed may even hire a lawyer for the purpose of making approaches to another more highly qualified lawyer. The resource investment, therefore, is probably much smaller than we see in court. But there is no reason to believe that the decision is any less accurate.

Indeed, the attorney probably makes a much better decision than the judge and the jury, albeit on a different subject. He is going to invest his own resources in this case, and he will lose them if he makes a mistake. This is a totally different situation from that of the judge and jury, who will be out not one single cent if they reach the wrong decision.[2] Thus, the decision by a plaintiff's attorney as to whether the situation in a given case is such that the present discounted value of his fee is greater than his own investment is a matter which he considers much more carefully than the judge and jury will later consider the actual case.

Since a large part of the cost of such a case is in the time of a very skilled man—i.e., the plaintiff's attorney—and his assistants, one would anticipate that the cases would tend to be distributed in such a way that the most skilled of the attorneys took those cases which had the highest probability of large judgments and the less skilled took those which involved smaller judgments

2. The judge might suffer in reputation from a bad enough decision. How frequently this happens and how important it is, I have no knowledge.

and/or smaller probability of success.[3] Of course, this is rational, and it improves the efficiency of the court system if we assume that these lawyers are adept in determining what is a sound case. I see no reason to doubt this, and the fact that they use inquisitorial methods rather than adversary proceedings in order to make that estimate seems to me a point in their favor, rather than a point against them.

In any event, the procedure is fairly straightforward. The plaintiff seeks out a plaintiff's attorney. The plaintiff's attorney then investigates the issue and decides whether he wishes to take the case. This part of the proceeding, which may be very important indeed for the plaintiff (and, for that matter, for the defendant), is not covered by our equations, because they deal with adversary proceeding. If the attorney turns down the plaintiff, the plaintiff is free to seek out another attorney. In part, the shift from attorney to attorney would be merely random, with attorneys making different judgments. In the long run, however, the plaintiff is apt to work his way down to less-and-less-skilled attorneys. The less-skilled attorneys tend to be less busy, and, hence, the opportunity cost to them of taking even a bad case is less. On the other hand, of course, they are less likely to win, and presumably know that.

If the attorney accepts the case, then the matter goes to trial (or negotiation), with the plaintiff's attorney putting up most of the resources and making substantially all of the important decisions. Under the circumstances, the P equation more or less drops out, because P, although he is the principal beneficiary if he wins, puts in few further resources. He has already invested his resources (wisely, we hope) in securing the services of the attorney. That this was relatively inexpensive simply reflects the fact that inquisitorial proceedings are usually more efficient than adversary proceedings. As a reasonable approximation, equation set (1) could be solved by omitting the P equation and solving the D and L equations.

Whether this system is an improvement over the system in which the two parties put up the resources is not clear. The usual argument is that it permits impecunious clients to sue. Note, however, that it only assists impecunious *plaintiffs*. Perhaps it is assumed that impecunious persons are not likely to be

3. In recent years, some of the attorneys have begun to charge a higher fee than the traditional one-third. It is only the best attorneys who are able to do this. Thus, the tendency discussed above is now less strong than it used to be. A very skilled attorney, for example, might be willing to take a rather poor case in return for a much higher than normal percentage of collections. This would reduce the efficiency of the system as described above.

defendants, because they have few assets. It also clearly leads to a situation in which lawyers who happen to have a little free time can bring suits of little merit if they think that the court system is inherently inaccurate. For example, assume that the court system with respect to some particular type of case is apt to go wrong one time in four. A young attorney just starting out in the business would be well advised to try to find a client for whom he could act as a contingency-fee attorney, even if the client's case was poor. Still, as I said before, it is by no means obvious that this is either a poorer or a better system than one in which each party pays his own expenses.

The "crime" of barratry is relevant here. Surely if the court system were both accurate and cheap, the person who instigated lawsuits would be performing a public service for which he should reasonably be paid. Lawyers would be the obvious persons to perform this particular type of service for society. It is only if the legal system is both expensive and inaccurate that this type of activity is socially undesirable.

There is another example of the same problem—suits against judges for bringing in erroneous decisions. If court proceedings were inexpensive and reasonably accurate, such suits would be rare, for judges would rarely bring in erroneous decisions, but this would surely be a sensible institution to have as a way of motivating judges to concentrate on the cases. Indeed, a special court for the specific purpose of imposing this kind of discipline on judges would probably be desirable. If, on the other hand, court proceedings are expensive and uncertain, then it would be almost impossible for judges to perform their duties if this sort of lawsuit were permitted. Suppose, for example, that incorrect suits could hope for success one time in eight. The expected cost to a judge bringing in a decision which inflicted injury on anyone, even a mass murderer, would be high. Thus, the errors of the court system are one of the reasons why the court is protected against suit, although I have never seen any of the judges discuss the matter using this particular argument.

We now turn to a system for paying the costs of adversary proceedings that is in vogue in England. In England, after a decision is made in a civil suit, the legal costs of the winner are usually paid by the loser. A simplified version of this cost structure is shown in equation set (2).

$$\begin{aligned} P_v &= \frac{P}{P+D}\cdot M - \frac{D}{P+D}\cdot(P+D) \\ D_v &= \frac{D}{P+D}\cdot M - \frac{P}{P+D}\cdot(P+D) \end{aligned} \tag{2}$$

Each party has some chance of winning the prize and an inverse probability of paying both parties' legal fees. In general, one would anticipate that this system would lead to parties being reluctant to bring litigation, because of the greater risk involved, but fighting very hard once litigation has been undertaken.

In practice, however, things are not quite this simple. The winning party does not simply present all of its bills to the defeated party for payment. A "taxing master" is appointed, and this official is usually a lawyer (barrister) and may be generous to other lawyers. In any event, he decides how much should be paid. Exactly how he decides is not clear, but it is clear that he does not necessarily award all expenses. It seems quite probable that he awards expenses in the amount that seems to him reasonable in those areas which are traditional. But this is merely an external estimate; I honestly do not know how taxing masters decide what to allocate. Granted this complication, however, the actual situation faced by the parties is shown by equation set (3).

$$P_v = \frac{P}{P+D}\cdot M - \frac{D}{P+D}\cdot(P_R + D_R) - P_E$$

$$D_v = \frac{D}{P+D}\cdot M - \frac{P}{P+D}\cdot(P_R + D_R) - D_E \qquad (3)$$

In these equations. I have put in P_R and D_R to indicate the reasonable expenditures for P and D, and P_E and D_E to designate any expenditures they chose to make beyond the "reasonable" amount. All of this is, of course, ex ante. The parties must make estimates of how much the taxing master is apt to permit when deciding whether or not to sue and what resources to put into the suit.

Clearly, under these circumstances, the litigants would attempt to game the system. Until we have a better idea of how the taxing masters actually decide the reasonable "expenses" of the parties, I do not see any way to say much more about this problem. There is another complication here. The barrister is required to collect his fee in advance. This may have been intended as another way of reducing the amount of litigation. It certainly meant that impecunious people could not bring actions.

In recent years, the British government has remedied this situation in some cases by providing legal aid for the barrister's fees. This, of course, raises the question of how government decides who will get legal aid. The problem of outsiders paying for all, or part, of the legal expenses is an important one. Let us begin our discussion not with impecunious people but with people whose cases are of such political importance that some outsider or group of outsiders is willing to pay the legal fees.

Both Angela Davis and the Watergate defendants (up to the time of their first trial) had their legal expenses paid by political allies.[4] This system can be analyzed by equation set (3a) which is a modification of (1), assuming that P_v is the prosecution and D and L represent, respectively, the defendants in the case and the people who are actually putting up the money; L_v represents the satisfaction obtained by the financiers.

$$
\begin{aligned}
P_v &= \frac{P}{P + D + L} \cdot M - P \\
D_v &= \frac{D + L}{P + D + L} \cdot M - D \\
L_v &= \frac{D + L}{P + D + L} \cdot M - L
\end{aligned}
\tag{3a}
$$

Once again, the defendants play a relatively minor role because the bulk of the resources are contributed by other people who thus gain basic control over the case.[5]

4. There is a small and, in my opinion, unimportant organizational difference. In the Angela Davis case, her attorneys played a part in raising the money. In the Watergate case, this was not true. Outside political sources raised money; the attorneys confined themselves to spending it. It does not seem to me that this is of much importance.

There is another difference which might conceivably be of more importance, and which had to do with the publicity given to the two operations. Although it certainly was no secret that the Republicans were paying the legal expenses and living costs of the Watergate defendants, there was no deliberate publicity given to the operation. In the Angela Davis case, there was a public fund-raising drive. The outcome, in effect, involves an interesting inversion. We now know all of the people who made the contributions to the Watergate defense case, but we do not know all of the people who made the contributions to the Angela Davis case, because secrecy, for at least some donors, was better preserved there.

5. In the original Watergate case, this turned out not to be true. Hunt and four Cubans, motivated by heaven only knows what, chose to plead guilty on the first day of the trial. Judge Sirica then prohibited the attorneys for the two remaining defendants from presenting the defense that they had prepared, with the result that, for all intents and purposes, there was no defense at all. In this particular case, it cannot be said that the people who paid for the attorneys actually had any control. Clearly, this was a most unusual case; indeed, I can recall no case in which there has been such obvious judicial bias. Since I am in favor of systems which quickly and easily reach the correct conclusion, and since I do think that the defendants were guilty in this case (also in the case of Angela Davis), I am not objecting to this bias. See Walter Rugaber, "Liddy and McCord Are Guilty of Spying on the Democrats," *New York Times*, January 31, 1973, p.1.

All of my equation systems so far are readily solvable for any given case. I have left out the variables dealing with the strength of the evidence and of the commitment of judicial decision-making resources, because they are not the subjects under discussion, but adding them would cause no difficulty. All of the sets so far would lead to the same type of equilibrium as the simple set of two equations introduced in the previous chapter for ordinary adversary proceedings. These proceedings differ from those simple adversary proceedings only in that the amount at issue is greater (in the case of the English system) or that some third party chooses to pay part of the costs of one of the two original parties. No doubt from the standpoint of one of the original parties, the latter is a great advantage—and to the other, a great disadvantage—but looked at from the standpoint of the whole system, it makes little difference. In essence, in these cases there is simply another party interested on one side.

In these cases, however, we have private persons making their contributions to the side they prefer. The use of government money raises somewhat different issues. In general, we do not want the taxpayers to take a partisan role.[6] We would like to have the judicial system, as a whole, reach relatively impartial conclusions. Thus, if we decide to subsidize someone's legal fees, we would prefer that this only be done where it is more likely to lead to a just conclusion than not. It is not at all obvious that any of the existing set of institutions under which the government pays one side's legal fees have this characteristic; but let me take them up one at a time.

Suppose someone comes to one of the new government-financed neighborhood law clinics in a poor district and asks for legal help in getting a divorce. If the divorce is contested, the other party might also want legal help, but let us (for the time being) confine ourselves to cases in which only one side is to be given legal assistance. This is simply so that I can continue to use equation set (1). First, the aid is going to the plaintiff rather than to the defendant. Hence, it should be $P + L$ instead of P in the first equation, with a similar alteration below. Second, M represents a divorce in this case rather than a pure monetary payment. The divorce, of course, does not accrue to the aiding agency, and, hence, the bottom equation should be dropped off and the two-thirds in the second from the bottom equation should be eliminated.

Success in this particular litigation will, once again, be partially determined by the resources put up by the plaintiff and by the government

6. In some cases, politicians or bureaucrats may indeed want the government to take one side for strictly partisan reasons. In general, however, this is undesirable.

attorney, on the one hand, and by the defendant on the other. Since I am assuming that the government helps only one side, this means that the defense must pay his entire cost himself.[7]

Once again, the plaintiff is going to use very few of his own resources in court; the bulk of the costs will be borne by the government. The government, however, presumably does not wish to allocate infinite resources to helping people win cases. In practice, these neighborhood law clinics have resources which are distinctly limited, considering the demand, and they must decide which cases they will take, and how much energy they will put into them, in terms of the inability to take other cases or the necessity of skimping on cases.

Obviously the government attorney must undertake some kind of an investigation to determine whether or not to undertake this particular case. The possibility of simply taking cases as they come in and then putting maximum resources behind the first few is too foolish to give any serious consideration. Another possibility is that of appropriating enough money so that all cases anyone wishes to be brought *can* be brought, and maximum resources can be applied to each one. But this is politically implausible.

Thus, there is a restriction on the resources, and some decision must be made as to how these resources are to be used. One hopes that the attorneys look into the matter and select the "best" cases. Since they are using the taxpayers' money, one would indeed hope that they only accept cases in which they feel their client is "in the right." In those cases where they feel doubtful about the rightness of their client's case, their investment of resources may lower accuracy. Thus, in general, they should aid only those cases which they think are right.

This is particularly important, since on my present set of assumptions, the government is not going to pay the other side's attorney's fee, and, hence, the other side must either face a trial without legal advice (which is costly) or acquire an attorney on his own. Thus, the attorney, in deciding to take a contested divorce case, is not only deciding how some government resources should be allocated,[8] he is also—even before any court proceedings have begun—inflicting heavy costs on a third party. One hopes that he only does this in those cases in which he is confident that he is correct. Indeed, many

7. Note, I am assuming that the government is helping the plaintiff. It might well be helping the defendant. This makes no difference in the basic principles we are going to discuss.

8. Normally the contest concerns alimony, custody of children, etc., and not whether or not the divorce will be granted.

people accuse the storefront lawyers of selecting cases not in terms of the convenience of the client but in an effort to establish precedents for future cases. This policy is particularly hard on the potential defendants, who are compelled to invest resources not so much to defend themselves as to defend a category of other people—people in their same situation—from the establishment of an unfavorable precedent.

There is another and much more important case in which the state subsidizes one side of the litigation. In this particular case, indeed, the custom is so old that most of my readers may not realize that this is what is happening. The state pays the prosecution in most criminal cases. This developed from an earlier system in which the parties paid the prosecution cost, and the earlier system still does have some legal remnants. Until very recently, private parties were perfectly free to bring actions against people they believed to be criminals in the British courts, and if they were successful, the convicted person would be imprisoned. In the United States, this is not the case; but it is still true that, as a general rule, the police are legal agents of the victim of a crime in making arrests.

But this is merely a brief and inadequate discursion into the history of the law. The resulting situation is that the government does pay the full cost of prosecuting criminals. In most cases, no private party directly benefits from the prosecution; but there are cases in which private individuals will benefit substantially if conviction is obtained. An obvious example of this is in the antitrust cases.

Since, once again, the resources available to the district attorney—and, for that matter, the court—are not infinite, he must make decisions as to which prosecutions he will bring. Looked at overall, these decisions are far more important than the decisions undertaken by the court itself. Of all people charged with crimes by the police, the district attorney characteristically decides not to proceed against about six in seven, who are thus "acquitted." Among those he does decide to prosecute, approximately 95 percent are convicted. Thus, his initial decision as to whether or not to proceed with the matter is, for the average defendant, very nearly decisive of the outcome. It is genuinely decisive if the district attorney decides to drop; and if he decides to proceed, the defendant faces a 95 percent chance of conviction.[9]

9. This 95 percent chance of conviction requires a little explanation. Somewhere between 80 and 90 percent of all people who are prosecuted choose to negotiate a plea of guilty. This

This important decision is made entirely in an inquisitorial manner. The district attorney investigates the matter and usually talks to the defendant. Sometimes he has a small detective force attached to his own office which will investigate the issue and try to unearth evidence which will be of help to him in making this decision (and later in prosecuting the case, if he decides to prosecute it). The defendant has no right to be represented in these decision-making processes (although the prosecuting attorney normally is willing to talk to the defense attorney). In particular, none of the so-called safeguards for the accused in the judicial procedure apply here. They apply in a somewhat indirect way in the sense that the prosecutor will realize that they will affect the trial, but they are not directly controlling. The prosecutor, for example, in deciding whether or not to prosecute should (and normally will) consider any evidence the police have, regardless of whether this evidence can later be presented in court. In trying to make his estimate as to whether there will be an eventual conviction—which is important to him in making his basic decision—he should also consider whether such evidence can be presented in court.[10]

Let us now consider the situation that would occur if the government is asked to subsidize *both* sides. For simplicity, let me return to the case in which someone approaches the legal aid office for a divorce and assume that the other partner to the marriage also approaches the legal aid office seeking assistance in defending the case. If legal assistance is given, then the outcome will be determined by equation set (4).

---

normally leads to a lower sentence but, of course, a much greater certainty of receiving the sentence. Of those who actually go to trial, about three-quarters are convicted. I compound these two numbers to get my 95 percent conviction ratio.

10. It is now fairly well known that the police frequently have evidence that cannot be presented in court because of the laws of evidence. This presumably has some effect on jury behavior. Juries realize that there is a possibility that there is further evidence of the guilt of the accused, which the prosecution possesses but cannot present. Since the laws of evidence do not seem to prevent the defense from presenting anything it has, no matter how it was obtained, this particular element is one-sided. One would assume, therefore, that juries (to at least some extent) take this into account when making a decision. Thus, it is by no means obvious that barring this evidence benefits the accused. It surely benefits those particular accused for which there is such illegally obtained evidence, but the accused for whom there is no such evidence may be damaged by the rule.

$$P_v = \frac{P + G_1}{P + G_1 + G_2 + D} \cdot M - P$$
$$G_{1v} = \frac{P + G_1}{P + G_1 + G_2 + D} \cdot M - G_1$$
$$G_{2v} = \frac{D + G_2}{P + G_1 + G_2 + D} \cdot M - G_2$$
$$D_v = \frac{D + G_2}{P + G_1 + G_2 + D} \cdot M - D \tag{4}$$

The attorneys on the two sides, both employees of the legal aid office, would each obtain satisfaction from having his side win, but in other respects their situations are identical. The bulk of the resources would come from the legal aid office and not from the two parties; hence, G_1 and G_2 would be fairly large and P and D would be small.

Of course, this assumes that the case is actually litigated. If I were in charge of the legal aid office, or if the people who were in charge of it considered my well-being as a taxpayer, the result of this visit to the office by both parties would be an investigation of the issue, a decision as to the merits of the case, and a suggestion to the two parties that they accept that decision. If either of them refused, then legal assistance should be provided only to the other party. I am not at all convinced, however, that this particular prescription will be that of the reader. In any event, I have never seen it proposed before—so let us look at the alternatives.

To make matters simple, let us assume that the divorce itself is not contested but that the custody of a child is at issue. The husband first approaches the legal aid office and requests assistance in obtaining the divorce and custody of the child. Without legal assistance, he would have only a 10 percent chance of getting custody; if the legal aid office decides to assist him, he has a 40 percent chance of getting custody of the child. Now his wife approaches the legal aid office and asks them to represent her. Let us assume here that as a result of their dual representation, the odds for the wife getting custody of the child are 85 percent and for the husband 15 percent.[11]

Under these circumstances, should the legal aid office undertake the representation of the wife also? The first thing to be said the moment one

11. In order to keep things symmetrical, assuming that they chose to represent the wife only and not the husband, the odds would be 95 percent for the wife getting custody and only 5 percent for the husband. I omit the prospect of the legal aid office providing a third attorney to look after the interests of the child.

begins dealing with these problems is that representation is not of zero value. In our previous work dealing with adversary proceedings, the two parties invested resources in litigation out to the point where they reach the equilibrium point of the two reaction lines. In this case, since the parties are investing no resources to speak of, and indeed are unable to invest any resources to speak of, the government must invest the resources for both sides, and clearly each party would like to have an infinite amount of resources on his side. This cannot be provided, and hence the government must make a decision as to how much it should invest on each side. I can see no way to do this without a considerable degree of arbitrariness; but, in any event, let us assume that some kind of decision is made.

If the government decides to provide legal assistance to the wife as well as to the husband, they should increase their legal assistance to the husband. The amount of legal assistance which is appropriate in dealing with someone who will have to handle his own case is considerably less than the amount appropriate in dealing with someone who will be represented by an attorney. Thus, the decision to represent the wife not only involves a direct expenditure, but it also involves an increase in the amount of money spent representing the husband.

So far as I know, there is no way to determine the optimal amount of resources to be introduced into the litigation process under these circumstances. An inquiry into what private parties would do under the same circumstances is not helpful, because the income of private parties is one of the variables in their determination of how much resources they will invest in a divorce action; hence, one would have to decide what income one is going to allot to these impecunious customers of the legal aid office in making one's calculation.

Let us suppose that it is decided to invest $500 in representing the wife and $750 in representing the husband; this will, as we said before, provide an 85 percent chance that the wife will obtain custody of the child and a 15 percent chance for the husband. It is immediately obvious that we could obtain this 15 percent chance for the husband and the 85 percent chance for the wife in a much more economical way. Assume that if we were supporting the husband only, not the wife, it would only cost $100 to improve his chances from 10 percent to 40 percent. Instead of giving that $100, we could give him, let us say, $25 in legal assistance, thus moving his probability not from 10 to 40 percent but only from 10 to 15 percent. The wife would receive no assistance under this plan. Thus, we would have a net expenditure of $25 to purchase the same present discounted value of the outcome for the two parties as can be obtained with $1,250. Clearly, this is the dominating solution.

Although this is clearly the dominating solution, so far as I know it has never been discussed in the literature before. Indeed, it took me a very long period of thought before it came to me. It is always possible that an idea which has never been discussed has just not been thought of before. It is also possible, however, that there are very good reasons why the idea should not be applied, and the lack of discussion stems from the fact that everyone realizes that there are such good reasons. The only suggestions that I have been able to unearth as to why we might prefer to have the government paying attorneys on both sides to having them get the same probability of outcome by helping only one side are, in my opinion, unconvincing.

First, there is the possibility that we just have some primitive ethical idea involved here. For example, perhaps it is thought that adversary procedure is right in some metaphysical way, regardless of the outcome attained.[12] If this is the explanation, then people who do not happen to have that particular moral set would not agree. People who do have that moral set should at least be willing to consider the costs.

There are two other possible explanations. In a way, they are closely related but not identical. The first is that we might feel that the adversary process, with good representation on both sides,[13] is an efficient way to reach the truth. It might be argued that the more resources we invest on *both* sides, the more likely we are to achieve an accurate outcome. Not everyone seems to argue this way. When discussing matters in which the accuracy was important, I have sometimes been corrected by lawyers who tell me that improving the quality of the legal representation does not increase accuracy. I am somewhat

12. This is apparently the view of Arthur Okun: "In some important noneconomic areas, we do regard whatever results emerge as untouchable, because they are generated by an explicitly accepted ideal process. I do not believe that the winner of an election is always the best candidate, but I believe that it would be wrong to overturn the results. Similarly, I do not care whether a jury finds a particular defendant guilty or not; I care only that justice be done. And I am prepared to respect the jury's verdict, unless I learn that the intended process was violated by tampering or the like." Arthur Okun, "Further Thoughts on Equality and Efficiency," in Colin Campbell, ed., *Income Redistribution* (Washington, D.C.: American Enterprise Institute for Public Policy Research, 1977), p. 25.

13. This assumes, of course, that the free representation provided to impecunious parties by the various government agencies is, in fact, good representation. I am not convinced that this is so.

puzzled by this, partly because it seems to me that it should, and partly because it seems to me that it would be in the interest of the lawyers, or at least the best lawyers, to argue that it does.

It seems likely that we are indeed improving the accuracy of the court procedure when we increase the resources put into the adversary proceeding. Unfortunately, the increase is a very slow one. Doubling the resources of both the man who represents the truth and the man who represents falsehood may make it more likely that the court will recognize the truth from the falsehood, but it surely does not double the probability. Indeed, I would anticipate only small improvements in accuracy from quite large increases in resource investment.

The second reason is, in a way, a derivative of the first. We could always, by reducing the resources being invested on one side of the case, obtain the same probability we can obtain by increasing the resources on the other; hence, it is always possible to obtain the same probability of a correct outcome by a cheap method as by an expensive one. It might be difficult, however, for us to predict accurately the result of changing the resources on both sides. In our simple divorce case, if there are no legal representatives, the odds are 9 to 1 in favor of the wife obtaining custody. If both sides are represented, the odds are 85 to 15. Without running the case a hundred or so times, it might be difficult to determine what those odds are; hence, it might be difficult to duplicate them by reducing resources for one side only.

I am not at all sure that this is true; what little experimental work has been done seems to indicate that lawyers are quite good at estimating the odds. But if the odds are indeterminate, it is not at all obvious why we would regard one resource investment as better than another unless we had an implicit belief that the adversary proceeding does increase accuracy as the resources invested in it are increased. To repeat what I said before, I am inclined to go along with this assumption, but I think that the accuracy is purchased very expensively.

THE MOTIVATION OF JUDGES

In this chapter, I will reverse field and talk about the decision-making apparatus itself and not the efforts of the parties to influence it. Although I have entitled the chapter "The Motivation of Judges," I intend to use the word "judge" in a very broad way. It will include jurors, lay assessors, arbitrators, and, for that matter, boards of judges as well as individual judges.

If we look around the world, there is quite a variety of ultimate decision procedures. Perhaps the United States has the widest variance of any country. We use a board of conscripted citizens or a single judge in our basic decision-making procedure. Most countries in the world tend to use some compromise between these two—either a board of judges or a board composed of judges and lay assessors. The American custom of either the single judge or the jury of conscripted citizens presumably comes from the historical development of law in England, although at the present time in England the jury seems to be in the process of being phased out in favor of a single judge.

The arbitrator is characteristically a judge or a member of a board of judges who is called an "arbitrator" because of historic accident. In most cases, he is selected by the parties rather than appointed by the government, and this probably makes considerable difference in his motivation; some arbitrators are former judges—indeed, a prominent one in the United States is a former Supreme Court justice. Thus, there seems no strong reason to distinguish between arbitrators and judges in our current discussion.

In general, the people who are used to decide court trials fall into two categories, amateurs (who are usually conscripted) and professionals. The American jurymen and the lay assessors in the European courts are amateurs. American judges, judges in European courts, and many arbitrators are professionals. There are advantages to both professionalism and amateurism, but, on the whole, one would think professionalism would work better. After all, the professional does have a good deal of experience, and hence he is less likely to make errors than the amateur. On the other hand, it must be admitted that he is more likely to make systematic errors than is the amateur; for example, if he gets something in his head, he may repeat it again

Reprinted, with permission, from *Trials on Trial: Pure Theory of Legal Procedure* (New York: Columbia University Press, 1980), 119–34. Copyright 1980 Columbia University Press.

and again. The amateur will not have any opportunity to repeat the same error.

As I turn to the motivation of these decision-making officials, there is another classification scheme which crosses my previous classifications. The member of the board of judges in European courts is motivated, to some extent, by the desire for promotion, which will be obtained by behaving in a manner his superiors think is efficient. (In Germany, officials rather systematically take into account the number of reversals by appellate courts in deciding on promotion.) No doubt he is also interested in finding the truth, serving the public interest, etc., but an altruistic approach is not relied on as the sole drive for obtaining good performance. If we consider, however, American judges (who are rarely, if ever, promoted), lay assessors in Europe, or jurymen in the United States, their income and prospects are little, if at all, affected by their performance in court.[1]

The argument for not rewarding good performance is that any reward system for the judges is apt to lead them to try to do what the people manipulating the reward system want rather than to "seek justice." Of course, if the people who are operating the system are in favor of "justice," then this argument does not apply. It must, therefore, be based on the untested theory that for some obscure reason, one particular set of government officials—the judges—are less "corrupt" than others—the higher officials—who could be higher-ranking judges, as they characteristically are in Europe.

Another explanation for the sole dependence on "virtue" of judges would be a distrust of democracy, and I believe that this motive, at least in part, impelled the founding fathers of the United States. They did not want the judges subject to "political" criteria. Of course, they were not naive and realized that the President and Senate would consider political matters in making the initial appointments; but they felt that by guaranteeing judges lifetime tenure and fixed salaries, they would lead them to gradually move away from their friends and into a position in which political influence would be much less important than the objective nature of the cases. They may very well have been right.

1. With elected judges in the United States, this is not entirely true, since it is at least possible to remove them by the election process. However, most judges are fairly well shielded from any real risk of this kind by a set of local customs or laws. Thus, on one hand, their own future is well insulated from the consequences of any mistakes they may make on the bench, and, on the other hand, particularly brilliant and effective service will not benefit them.

The most political of all decision-making processes, if we are thinking of democratic politics, is the jury. Many people think of the jury as being a random sample of the population. It is not, partly because it is small enough so that the variance of the sample would be great in any event, and partly because the people who compose the jury are by no means a random sample. It is also likely that the jury contains relatively few highly intelligent or very stupid members of the community.

The selection process tends to weed out people who would suffer a significant financial loss from their service on a jury, those who are particularly knowledgeable about anything with which the jury might deal, those who seem to be either a little dumb or peculiar, and, last but not least, anyone who does not want to serve on that jury and is bright enough to realize that exhibiting bias will get him out of it.

The people who act as juries in those cases which are expected to be very long, and in particular those cases where the juries are to be sequestered, must be really quite an unusual group of people. In actual practice, no one who does not wish to serve on such a jury has to do so, although some people may not realize that indicating bias will get them off.[2] An interesting empirical study could no doubt be made of these people who have chosen what must be an unpleasant and boring experience. Probably they go into it under the impression that it will be exciting and only later discover how dull legal proceedings are.

In any event, however, the jurymen are motivated entirely by their curiosity as to what actually happens in a case and by their feeling for justice. In this respect they are thus like the professional judge, who can be neither promoted nor fired. On the other hand, they see only a very few cases. This means they lack experience, which has both advantages and disadvantages. The disadvantages, I suppose, are obvious; the advantage is that they are apt to be more interested in the cases simply because they have never seen them before.

There does not seem, however, to be any reason at all to believe that the jurymen devote any great effort to understanding the case. Indeed, trial practice is very largely based on the implicit theory that jurymen are mainly impressed by image and only to a rather modest extent by facts. Convincing the jury that your opponent is a rat is far more useful than convincing them that he actually defaulted on his contract. Once they are convinced he is a rat,

2. It should be noted that this does not involve dishonesty, since almost everyone is biased about almost everything to some extent.

they are apt to believe he defaulted; and if they are convinced he is an honest man, they are apt to believe he did not, almost regardless of the objective evidence.

The above point, although generally true, should not be exaggerated. Jurymen, of course, do not totally disregard objective evidence, and, indeed, the objective evidence is one of the things which gives them the impression that the defendant is or is not a rat. Still, so far as I know, there is no other walk of life in which we make important decisions by dragging twelve persons off the street and permitting two highly paid people to make arguments in front of them. Normally, we have better ways to reach the truth.

The final type of judge is the professional arbitrator. He receives a fee for each case.[3] It seems likely, however, that his major motivation is not his fee for this particular case, but the fees he hopes to receive for future cases. Thus, he should attempt to carry out his duties in this particular case in such a way as to motivate people to hire him as an arbitrator in the future. In my opinion, this particular motivational system, although a long way from perfect, probably works better than any of the ones I have so far discussed.

But this chapter is about the motivation of judges. Although telling them that they should do right, be virtuous and industrious, surely can do no harm (and might do some good), normally we try to motivate people by giving them rewards for good behavior and penalties for bad behavior. How can we apply this system to judges? The obvious problem is that in any individual case, we have no automatic mechanism for determining who is right and who is wrong. Further, we not only want the judges to make the right decision, we want the right amount of resources invested in the decision. We do not want minor traffic offenses to involve lengthy hearings with the jury sequestered and the Supreme Court eventually involved, even if all of that would mean a higher probability of accuracy. The cost of the proceedings should be offset against the importance of the accuracy which results. Of course, in the Anglo-Saxon system, the judges or jury do not have very much

3. Note that a very large number, indeed the vast majority of all arbitration cases, are not decided by a professional arbitrator but by some businessman who is an expert in the particular trade concerned. A colleague of mine, for example, recently decided that the contractor had done an inadequate job in building his house. Arbitration was proposed, and it would have consisted of asking another contractor in the vicinity to look over the house and decide whether it had, in fact, been badly built. The arbitrator would not have received a fee in this particular case. Even if he had received a fee, he would hardly have been a professional arbitrator for whom future arbitration assignments would be an important part of income.

control over the total resource investment; but in other systems (particularly the Continental system), they have a good deal, and we would like our motivational scheme to work there as well.

It will not surprise the reader to discover that, although I think we can do better than we now do, this is not a problem to which I can give (or, indeed, think anyone can give) a highly sophisticated and guaranteed efficient answer. Nevertheless, there are some things we can do. First, it would be sensible to avoid giving perverse incentives. Most judicial systems are rather good on this score, although there are occasional exceptions. A justice of the peace, for example, used to be (and, indeed, still is in some cases) paid only from the fines he collects; hence, he had an incentive to find the defendant guilty. In some cases, judges may find a situation confronting them where a particular decision will greatly reduce their workload; they are likely to move toward the lower workload because their pay is not affected by the number of hours they put in on the job.

But note that even these cases are not necessarily perverse. Presumably, the justice-of-the-peace payment institution described above increases the number of convictions, but it is not at all obvious that it increases the number of errors, in the sense of decisions which are different from those which God would have made had we been able to consult Him. Similarly, in the second case, it certainly should reduce the total amount of time that judges devote to legal activities; but, once again, it is not clear that it increases the number of errors. In both of these cases, it presumably leads to errors being distributed differently.

The two examples above are simply special cases of the general problem of conflict of interest. The judge has a personal interest in deciding in one direction—in one case, because it increases his income; and in the other, because it reduces his workload. There are many other cases in which he may have such a motive, and the efforts to reduce "conflict of interest" are efforts to reduce their frequency. The judge may be related to one of the parties, have a direct or indirect financial interest in one side or the other, or merely be personally friendly with one of the parties. In all of these cases, the judge is removable, although in the particular case of federal judges in the United States, he normally decides himself whether he is biased.

This is a particularly bizarre rule, since, presumably, if he is really biased, he either will not notice that fact (since he believes he simply knows the truth) or if he does notice it, he will be strongly motivated to conceal it. Most state judges in the United States are subject to a rule under which the parties suspecting bias can have them removed from the case without the necessity of convincing the judge himself that he is biased.

It should be pointed out that it is by no means obvious that this type of conflict of interest actually leads to any high degree of inaccuracy. Suppose, for example, that Judge Sirica is convinced before the trial begins that the defendants in the Watergate case are guilty and refuses to concede his own bias—he knows that he is right, and hence it is not bias but simple devotion to the truth. He also arranges a jury, the bulk of whom have been watching the Watergate hearings on television, and who were very heavily favorable to McGovern in the election to which Watergate was relevant; then, during the course of the trial, he makes a number of rulings which are clearly beneficial to the prosecution. This does not lead to error if the defendants were guilty (and most people do think they were).

Suppose that a judge believes, as Judge Sirica apparently did, that almost everyone brought before his court is guilty. Suppose, further, that this leads to a conviction rate of 90 percent in his court as opposed to the more normal 80 percent rate in a federal court. It does not follow from this that his court makes more errors than the more normal court. It simply means that the distribution of errors is different. It might be, for example, that 95 percent of all defendants brought before both courts were guilty; that the normal court found, of every 100 defendants, 77 guilty persons guilty, 3 innocent persons innocent. They would have gone wrong in 20 of the 100 cases. This is somewhat above what I would regard as a normal error rate; I merely use these numbers for illustrative purposes.

Judge Sirica, on the other hand, might find 86 people who are in fact guilty guilty, 9 people who are guilty innocent, 4 people who are innocent guilty, and 1 person who is innocent innocent. Errors are less frequent in Sirica's court than in the more normal court. The distribution of errors between the innocent and the guilty is different, and if the reader is one of those who believe that the court should be biased in favor of the accused, he would regard the normal court performance as better than Judge Sirica's. Surely, however, it is not more accurate.

The above numerical example illustrates the point that the conflict of interest problem is more complicated than it appears at first glance. This is one of the many areas where what is normally referred to as "fairness" is not necessarily identical to minimization of error. "Fairness" essentially means sticking to a set of rules which are thought to put the two parties on an even footing. In the trials by combat, from which our trials in a way descend, it would have been unfair to give one knight a lance longer than the others. If, however, we assume that the ability to win in combat is unrelated to guilt or innocence, then it is fairly obvious that this would not have led to a more erroneous set of outcomes. Regardless of the length of the lances, the relationship between the outcome of the combat and the "correct" outcome would be random.

The objection to bias or conflict of interest, then, is not as straightforward as it normally appears. In order to object to it, we have to feel that judicial or jury decision-making proceedings are normally accurate enough so that the introduction of what is essentially a random factor (because bias can be on either side) lowers total accuracy. Most of us would feel that this is true, but the effect is probably fairly weak. Nevertheless, we attempt to eliminate conflict of interest because it is a very cheap and easy thing to do. Note that this is, in fact, the way our law operates. In those cases where it would be very difficult to find a court without bias, we simply accept biased courts under a doctrine going back almost five hundred years.

So far, we have been examining possible incentives which might have a perverse effect and have judged them not all that important. But if there are few positive incentives to actually go wrong, there is very little in the way of incentive to go right, except the desire to be virtuous, diligent, and just. As we shall see below, the arbitrator is a partial exception to this, but even in his case, the incentives are hardly simple and straightforward.

If we knew what the truth was in every case, we could provide for differential rewards, depending on whether the judge and jury reached the correct conclusion. We could also save money by omitting them. At a somewhat more mundane level, it is possible to make certain that the judge and jury have paid careful attention to the case by a fairly simple, although radical, change in our present institutions. If, at the end of the trial, the judge and jury were given a short examination on the strictly factual side of the evidence and then rewarded for their knowledge, it is likely that they would concentrate much more on the details of the case than they now do. Note that there would be no particular problem of bias or, for that matter, complexity in the examinations. In any lawsuit, there are a great many uncontroverted facts, such as how old the defendant is, the address where the murder allegedly took place, whether the body had two or three bullet holes in it, etc.

But this is clearly a rather minor reform, the only purpose of which is to make judges and jurymen pay careful attention. Further, in the case of the European-type procedure, where the judges play a major role in investigating the facts, we would want to ask at least some questions aimed at determining whether they had engaged in a sensible investigation rather than simply whether they remembered what they had uncovered.

Still, the fact that they know some of the simple facts of the case does not prove they are reaching the correct conclusion. Another technique which might be used to deal with this problem would be to draw a random sample of cases and rerun them with a much higher investment of resources in the second run. Presumably, this would mean that the second time cases were run through, more accurate determinations were made. A statistical comparison between the behavior of the original judges in these cases and the more accurate decisions would indicate which judges were better, and which judges were worse, in determining what had happened. Their pay could then be varied accordingly. The judicial promotion system in Germany roughly approximates this system.

Unfortunately, only the judges in the first series would be subject to this type of pressure. The judges who were applying greater resources in the second round would not be subject to it.[4] Hence, they might not be motivated to pay careful attention, do a good job, etc. As a result, in practice, the first round could have about as many real resources invested as the second, even though budgetary costs of the checking-up round were much greater.

There is another problem. It might be that the judges in the first round of cases would have some idea of the foibles and special prejudices of the judges who will be checking on them, and therefore they would incorporate these foibles and prejudices into their own decisions. Thus, although this procedure would mean that the judges in the first round were under pressure to behave in the way that the judges in the second round thought they should, it might not reduce the total number of errors. Suppose, for example, that the judges in the first round know that the judges in the second round, who are very senior and therefore elderly judges, do not understand statistics. Under the circumstances, they might disregard statistical evidence because they know that it will be disregarded when their accuracy is evaluated.

The basic problem with this procedure, however, is the one I have mentioned earlier in a note. It might provide a technique for policing the behavior of the judges in the first round, but eventually we would come to a stop—a group of judges who are not being checked by other judges. This would be true even if we did not have a set of levels of judges but simply reassigned an

4. We could put on a third round, but that would simply move the problem one stage back.

occasional case from any given judge to another judge, at random, to rerun. This would mean that there would not be a first and second level of judge, but it would still be true that the judge taking the second round would know that he would not be supervised, and the judge taking the first round would know that he was. Nevertheless, although this system is far from perfect, I would think that it would tend to move the current legal system to a higher standard of accuracy, simply by providing an automatic and completely unpredictable check.

Note that I have talked mainly about judges here and not juries. Presumably the juries would not care very much whether they were found to have been inaccurate after the event, because it would not affect their future income. If they were given an additional payment in the event that their cases were selected for examination, and they were found to have been right, this would provide them with an incentive. Granted the stochastic nature of the process, however, they might treat this mainly as a simple gamble rather than as a motive to be more careful.

When we turn to the arbitrator, the incentive system is quite different. The professional arbitrator is unlike a judge in that his decision in a given case increases or decreases the likelihood of his being employed in the future. Since he wants to be employed in the future—he is making money from his arbitration practice—he will attempt to choose that decision which is most likely to lead to his being selected for arbitration in the future. Where the two parties to any future contract have roughly equal levels of information, I shall argue below that this leads him to choose an economical and accurate procedure if that is possible for him. If, however, one of the parties to future contracts is apt to hold superior information, it may lead to a very strong element of bias on the part of the arbitrator.

This point is, I suppose, fairly obvious; but a little discussion may not be out of place. If the arbitrator, for example, deals exclusively in small-scale consumer complaints, he may feel that most consumers will not know anything at all about the arbitrator and therefore will be willing to accept the arbitrator suggested by the retailer. Under the circumstances, a bias toward the retailer might be the arbitrator's profit-maximizing course of action. It might not, however, because the retailer might be interested in his general reputation and want an arbitrator who was either impartial or, for that matter, actually procustomer.

I have noticed that when I have a complaint in my dealings with retail establishments, their usual reaction is not one of making a fair judicial decision between themselves and me but one of giving me every benefit of the doubt. Presumably one reason for this is that careful consideration of the issue would be an expensive process, and the complaints desk would have to be greatly enlarged if they attempted it. Even more important is their feeling that damaging their relations with the customer is a good deal more expensive for them than the cost of replacing some piece of merchandise which the customer claims is defective. They do not accept the customer's position in every single case, but they very decidedly tend to favor him. They might select arbitrators with the same set of biases. On the other hand, the fact that their complaints desk is lenient, and therefore that only cases the complaints desk thought were fake were transferred to the arbitrator, might mean that they would want an arbitrator who normally decided for them. In any event, the arbitrator would not aim at true accuracy but at whatever outcomes were favored by the retailer. The customer might or might not benefit from that.

Most cases where arbitrators are now used, however, are cases where both sides are reasonably well informed. The typical case is a commercial contract between two businessmen or two corporations, either under circumstances in which the two parties regularly make use of arbitrators or where the contract is large enough so that it is worth their trouble to become well informed for that particular contract. In many cases, of course, both of these conditions apply.

Under these circumstances, the parties will know fairly accurately the capacities of the arbitrators, and we can therefore reasonably pause to inquire what type of arbitrator they will choose. Note that at the time the contract is undertaken, the two parties have no significant conflict of interest with respect to the desirable qualities of an arbitrator, although later, when and if a violation is alleged, their differences may be very great. At the time the contract is negotiated, the two parties want the joint profit of the contract to be maximized, albeit they have differences of opinion as to how this profit should be divided. Therefore, selecting an arbitrator who, in terms of both cost and accuracy, maximizes the value of the contract is in their mutual interest.

It is not at all obvious that either of the parties would, in fact, want an arbitrator who is biased in his direction if the other party knew that the bias existed. The other party could insist on the other terms of the contract being changed in such a way as to compensate him for the bias of the arbitrator. Thus, only if hiring an arbitrator with a particular kind of bias was efficiency-promoting would the person who is to benefit from the bias be willing to pay the other party the cost of that bias.

There are special cases where this condition is met. If, for example, one of the two parties is more risk averse than the other, he might be willing to pay for an arbitrator who is biased in his direction by giving the other party to the contract advantages in other areas of the contract. In a way, this is like the policy mentioned above by which most retail merchants give the customer the benefit of the doubt in complaints. The merchant can combine a whole number of such complaints into an actuarially predictable cost, and hence he runs no significant risk. He provides for his customers, then, a reduction in their risk, because they do not have this possibility of actuarial combination.

In most cases, however, it seems likely that the two parties would prefer an unbiased arbitrator who would invest the "optimal" resources in determining the outcome and who would use the most efficient methods. The use of the most efficient methods would probably mean that the personal characteristics of the arbitrator—especially intelligence—would be taken into account.

Once an issue arises between the two parties, it is no longer necessarily desirable for both of the parties that the arbitrator be intelligent and impartial. Since we are currently talking only about issues of fact and not issues of the law or interpretation of the contract, it is highly likely that the party in the wrong knows that he is in the wrong but sees a good chance to profit from pushing this particular case.[5]

At this point, both of the parties would like to win, and both will be disappointed if they do not. Under the circumstances, the arbitrator, of necessity, is going to annoy one of them. It is not at all obvious that this will reduce his future business. Remember that, ex ante, both parties to a contract want much the same thing from the arbitrator.[6] Thus, even the party who is very disappointed by the decision of an arbitrator in a given case may regard the decision of the arbitrator in that case as good grounds for hiring him in the future.

The arbitrator, then, under the circumstances we have described, has a good reason to do an efficient job, in the sense that the cost-accuracy ratio of

5. With large corporations, this will be true with respect to "the corporation," but not necessarily with respect to its senior officials. It may be that the junior official responsible is falsely reporting to his superiors in order to protect his job, and his superiors believe him, with the result that the people who actually initiate the litigation on both sides each honestly think that they are in the right.

6. Unless one of the parties has special knowledge which indicates that the arbitrator is biased in his direction, and this knowledge is not available to the other party. The publicly announced decision in a case of this sort would not be an example.

his decision is optimized for the two parties. In the real world, it is not always true that arbitrators are well known by all parties to the arbitral contract. In many cases, there is some differential knowledge. The same is also true, however, of professional judges; and indeed judge-shopping is one of the activities of a good lawyer. Further, most contracts can be drawn in such a way that the actual court to decide is determined in the contract. When this is so, the same problem of differential knowledge of prejudice of judges would apply. Although this is a real problem, it does not seem to be a major one either with regular courts or with arbitrators.

The major problem with respect to the use of arbitrators as a general technique, however, is simply that by no means all litigation concerns contracts. In a very large number of cases, the litigation occurs between two parties who have not made any preliminary agreement, and whose first contact is the act which causes the legal dispute. There is an automobile accident, and A wishes to sue B. At this point, there is no motive for either A or B to favor an impartial arbitrator. Each would want one prejudiced in his favor, if that was possible.[7] A second example is the average crime. The district attorney and the man he is prosecuting might have difficulty agreeing on a suitable arbitrator. There are many other cases. Parties to a dispute over property very commonly have no previous contract. Parties to a dispute over a will may not have, although in this case presumably the testator could specify an arbitrator.

In all of these cases, there is no point at which both parties would have motives leading them to select an efficient and impartial arbitrator. We have thus turned to a social contrivance in which the parties, in essence, agree to a system under which arbitrators—hopefully efficient and unbiased—are automatically provided. We call this system the courts and the agreement was made very long ago.

Note, however, that although we do have this system to provide some means to adjudicate disputes between parties who have not made a specific contract, there is no strong reason to believe that it is optimal or that it must take the form it does take. Under present circumstances, the dispute is settled either by a permanent government official or by a group of conscripted private citizens. There is no reason why other techniques might not be tried.

7. Of course, it might be a case which is clear enough so that one of the two parties would feel confident that an impartial arbitrator would decide in his favor. In this case, he would favor the impartial arbitrator, although he might wish to buy a little insurance by choosing his brother.

To take an extreme example, in Roman law if the case turned out to involve a difficult point of law (not of fact), it would be referred to a private citizen, called a *jurisconsultus*. He was prohibited by law from receiving any direct payment by either party but could anticipate that the party for whom he decided would eventually make a suitable provision in his will. Since this technique of turning over part of the law cases to a private citizen was the foundation of the great Roman law, it is hard to argue that it is impossible. It was, after all, these *jurisconsulti* whose decisions and general writings shaped the Roman law, not any formally appointed official.

Thus, there is no intrinsic reason why we could not use some method under which the government, instead of maintaining a set of judges and juries, simply maintained a procedure for appointing an arbitrator for each case. But if there is no reason why this could not be done, it is not at all obvious that it would be a desirable system either. The arbitrator would presumably be primarily interested in his fee, not for the instant case but for future cases, and therefore he would tend to behave in a way which would make it likely that whoever appointed him (in this case, a government official) would reappoint him. Presumably, the appointing official would have no reason for wanting the arbitrator not to be efficient in the strict sense, but he might prefer some sort of bias. Since the same type of officials appoint our present judges, there is no reason to regard this as necessarily a fatal objection.

Assume, then, that we have a system under which, when a case arises, the parties may agree on an arbitrator, or a board of arbitrators or, for that matter, a board of twelve citizens with no special training. In cases in which they reach agreement, we simply respect that agreement unless there is reason to believe one or the other party has been defrauded. In cases in which they would not reach agreement—the district attorney, for example, and the murderer having great differences of opinion as to who would be a suitable person to decide whether or not the murderer shall be hung—we must turn to another procedure.

The second procedure involves two steps, the first of which is determining the compensation for the arbitrator(s), and the second is actually selecting the individual(s). The first one is fairly simple. We could permit the two parties to decide individually how much they will contribute. Presumably the one who is in the right would be interested in contributing more, because he is interested in hiring a more accurate judge, and therefore he wants more resources invested in the trial. There is no reason why the two parties must put up the same amount. Indeed, in the case of the district attorney and the murderer, presumably the murderer will be unwilling to put up anything, unless he was given a guarantee that the judge would be biased in his favor. The arbitrator would know how much his fee was, but would not know which of the two parties had contributed the larger amount to it.

The total fee of the arbitrator now being determined by simply summing the amount that the two parties are willing to invest, each party recommends one person or group as arbitrator. The arbitrators are then interrogated as to whether they are willing to work for the fee suggested, and assuming that all agree,[8] the choice between the two arbitrators is referred to some government official, perhaps whoever selects our current judges.

Let us look at the incentives which this system provides for the parties. First, the judge who makes the ultimate decision between the two nominated arbitrators has no more incentive to do a good job or work hard or be unbiased than our present judges, but he also has no less. Those who have confidence in our present judges should have confidence in his judgement; and those of us who do not, should not. For the second group, however, it should be pointed out that the choice is both a relatively easy one and, as we shall see, not all that important. It is fairly easy to keep abreast of the general reputation of a limited group of men engaged in this kind of activity.

Where it is not easy to do it directly, there presumably would be reference books, as there are today for labor arbitrators in the United States. These catalogues as they now exist for labor arbitrators, and as they would exist for general arbitrators under the proposed procedure, simply attempt to transmit information, because that is what the person who might buy such a catalogue wants. Under the circumstances, they are likely to present a fairly good picture of the capacity of the arbitrator, although not a perfect one. However, they generally provide better information than is available when a man is appointed as a judge under our present system, simply because they are based not on a guess about his character as to how well he will do but from observation of his performance in a number of actual cases. Someone trying to break into the arbitration profession, instead of trying to get a politician to back him as he does today if he wants to be a judge, would simply have to start with small cases, which he offered to handle at low prices. As his reputation improved, he would rise to better and more important cases.

I said above that the job of choosing between the arbitrators would be neither very difficult nor very important. The reason it would not be very

8. If one or both disagree, the party would be permitted to substitute another.

important has to do with the motives of the parties themselves. Each will present a potential arbitrator, and the final decision procedure is simply to choose between these two. Each party is motivated to choose as his nominee someone who is at least reasonably likely to be acceptable to the judge. If my cousin is my candidate, it is likely that the person chosen by my opponent will be selected. This technique was originally suggested for labor cases, in which it was proposed that both parties to the labor dispute simply present their demands and that a government board then make a selection between the two—the board being prohibited either from trying to compromise or from working out its own decision. It was pointed out that this would put pressure on both parties to be moderate in their demands, because it is likely that the more moderate of the proposals will be adopted.

Similarly, the technique I have just suggested would lead each party to suggest someone who was just a trifle on his side—perhaps simply because he had selected him as his nominee—in hopes that he would be the one selected, rather than the one nominated by the other party. We would anticipate, then, that the two people suggested to the judge would be reasonably competent people with no very obvious defects. The decision between them would not be a very important one, since either would do.

This brings us to the question of the motivation of the arbitrators themselves. They are going to make the ultimate decision and are, therefore, the important people in the system. They would think, when making their decision, of its effect on employment in two stages: their nomination by one of the parties to a dispute; and the selection between the two by the government official who makes the ultimate selections. It is clear that diligence and accuracy would pay off in both of these decision processes; bias, on the other hand, would not.

We thus have a system in which the people making the decisions are, to at least some extent, offered positive rewards for accurate decisions, albeit not in an ideally efficient way. Whether it is better or worse than the existing systems is a question I will leave for future consideration.

As a general rule, then, most legal systems have depended not on positively motivating judges and juries to reach the right conclusion, but on attempting to avoid perverse motivation. The substitution of positive incentives clearly would be highly desirable; the only problem is whether we can design an institutional structure which does offer such positive incentives at a reasonable cost.

DEFENDING THE NAPOLEONIC CODE OVER THE COMMON LAW

I. WHY I PREFER NAPOLEON

Although I do prefer the Napoleonic code to Anglo-Saxon procedures, I do not think that it is in any sense ideal. The point of my criticism of Anglo-Saxon attitudes in the procedural area (of which this paper is simply a continuation) is not that I am convinced that Napoléon was right and Blackstone wrong but that I think we should open the whole discussion to scientific investigation. I feel reasonably confident that scientific investigation would list Napoléon as a greater expert on procedure than Chief Justice Warren, but I would anticipate that the ultimate outcome would be procedures that are better than any existing system.

Having thus jettisoned my title, let me turn to the main subject of this paper, which is essentially my reasons for believing that the Anglo-Saxon legal procedure is inferior. I have made most of these arguments at much greater length in my *Trials on Trial*.[1] Since this is a brief article of necessity, I cannot develop the full argument, but the book is available to anybody who wants a more elaborate presentation.

Let us begin by considering how we would evaluate a procedural system if we were offered, perhaps through divine favor, all the data that we wished. May I temporarily assume that the purpose of the legal procedure is to carry out the law, although, in a moment, I will point out that it may not be to carry out the law but to implement an ethical code. Assuming then that we are trying to evaluate a procedural rule, we would have really two basic objectives; one would be to have as high a level of conformance to the law as possible, and the second would be to have as low a cost as possible. Obviously these two objectives would be laid off against each other according to some function, but we need not concern ourselves now as to the way in which these two desired data would be reconciled.

Reprinted, with permission, from *Research in Law and Policy Studies*, ed. S. S. Nagel (Greenwich, Conn.: JAI Press, 1988), 2:3–27.

1. Gordon Tullock, *Trials on Trial: The Pure Theory of Legal Procedure* (New York: Columbia University Press, 1980). Note that although I do make this argument at considerable length in the book, that is not the only subject. It deals with other aspects of legal procedure as well.

The actual carrying out of the law is something that is done by private citizens in their daily life. The legal system exists simply for the purpose of giving them a motive to carry out their legal duty when it, for one reason or another, conflicts with their private interests. But note that if they are to carry out the law, they must know what it is. This indeed is one of the arguments for having them carry out an ethical code rather than the law. Presumably most of them know what the ethics of their society are, because they have been taught in the family, the church, and the school. Of course, under modern circumstances in which the school has ostensibly, although I think not in reality, abandoned ethical indoctrination as one of its objectives and where the church is losing influence, the ethical codes held by different people may be quite radically different from one another. Under these circumstances, the ethical code method becomes difficult to enforce in those areas where different members of the society have different ethics.

We do not, in the United States, have anything very much in the way of formal apparatus to teach people the law. Since I started out long ago as a China specialist, I should say that traditional China did better than we in this area. One of the duties of the local magistrate was to educate the people in the law, and there would be parades, public meetings, the Chinese equivalent of billboards, and so on instructing the citizenry in their legal duties.[2] We do not do this, and I think that on the whole in this respect, the Chinese were better than we are. Fortunately, our court system, to a considerable extent, ignores the law and simply enforces the ethical code, and, at the moment, most Americans know pretty well what are the basic ethical principles in important areas. With the present educational standards, it is not clear that will continue to be the case, and indeed some younger people may not only have ethics different from those of the jurors but may not be aware of the details of the ethical code held by the average juror.

Assuming that people know what the law is, the purpose of the enforcement procedure is simply to provide them with a motive for carrying out the law by providing punishment when they do not. This, of course, is particularly applicable to the criminal law; the civil law, at least nominally, does not punish. Still, the prospect of getting involved in a lawsuit is always to some extent a factor to be taken into account when one is thinking of breaching a contract or driving dangerously. Unfortunately, here the "punishment" goes

2. In China it would have been called their ethical duty, but the rules enforced were imperial decrees.

both ways. If I breach a contract, the victim has to make a conscious decision to go to court, which in the United States is an expensive and inconvenient procedure. The fact that I know he must do so may give me more incentive to breach the contract than I would have if we had a cheaper and more efficient method of dealing with the matter.

We can list, more or less, the various costs of enforcement once we assume that people know what the law is. There is, first, the apparatus used to detect breach. In the case of the criminal law, this is largely but not entirely a police force or neighborhood guard force responsibility.[3] There is then the actual court procedure itself. It should be noted that in the Napoleonic system, the detection apparatus and the court system are to a large extent melded into one, with a judicial official conducting the investigation of important crimes. The "trial" that then occurs is in a way an appeal from this initial judicial proceeding.

In addition to the trial process itself, there are the private expenditures involved in the procedure. In the case of a criminal action, that is mainly on the defense.[4] In civil actions, both sides spend a great deal of money on this subject.[5] There is then the cost of actually implementing the decision. If this is, for example, imprisoning someone, the cost can be quite considerable, although there does not seem to be any intrinsic reason why prisoners should not be compelled to work and provide the bulk of the cost of confining them. If it involves a fine or a court order for someone to pay, then this is a transfer, and the only real social cost lies in the rather modest police cost of getting the order carried out, together with the possibility that the person required to pay will either be driven into bankruptcy or will, one way or

3. It is intriguing that we seem to have gone back about two hundred years in our protection apparatus. The large condominium apartment house in which I live has a fairly elaborate private police force.

4. Which may be paid for by the state if the defendant is impecunious.

5. Until recently I have used an estimate obtained from a number of trial lawyers, which is that the cost of each party is about one-third of the actual amount issued. I am happy to say that there is now better research, although it is still far from complete. This new research implies that my one-third is an underestimate, perhaps a sharp underestimate. See James S. Kakalika, *Costs of Asbestos Litigation* (Santa Monica, Calif.: Rand Corporation, 1983); and David M. Trubek, Austin Sarat, William L. F. Felstiner, Herbert M. Kritzer, and Joel B. Grossman, "Costs of Ordinary Litigation," *UCLA Law Review* 31(1) (October 1983): 72–126. Let us hope that further research indicates that the total costs are not quite so disastrous as implied by Trubek et al.

another, fail to pay, which usually, but not always, involves a considerable resource loss.

These costs are, of course, small compared with the costs of not having the law enforced at all, or at least that should be so.[6] If the law itself is a desirable one, then there are social costs from its violation, and unless these costs in the event of nonenforcement would be greater than the cost of enforcement, we should not have the law. Thus in a way, the total costs of the legal system should include not only the enforcement costs I have listed but also the cost of the law's not being enforced where our procedure has functioned badly.

There is another item here. Courts will inevitably bring in wrong decisions, at least occasionally. I have been able to compute a sort of minimum error term with respect to one particular set of cases—criminal cases in Anglo-Saxon countries—where the minimum error term is one in eight.[7] As far as I know there are no data from which similar calculations can be made in other countries, nor are there any data from which such calculations can be made in civil cases. There is, however, no reason to believe that our court is more accurate in civil cases than in criminal cases. Legal scholars in general do not seem to be much interested in the accuracy problem. For example, Hastie, Penrod, and Pennington[8] have a table on page 60 from which it is possible to deduce that their trial juries were wrong 40% of the time. They make no such calculation themselves. Indeed, on page 62, they appear to be arguing that two juries can reach radically different decisions on a case and both be right. They appear, however, to have very low expectations of accuracy of the jury. They found that the individual jurors scored about 60% accuracy in their recall of information directly stated in testimony and remembered only about 30% of the judge's instructions.[9] Nevertheless, they say, "In their task of fact finding, juries perform efficiently and accurately."[10] They seem to feel that the "accuracy" of their juries derived from the fact that "the present study was tried by two exceptionally skillful attorneys whose competence can be partly credited with the juries' strong performance of the fact finding task."[11] One wonders what the result would be with ordinary attorneys.

6. These costs are total costs. We should hope that marginal costs balance.

7. For methods calculations, see my *Trials on Trial*, 31–33.

8. Reid Hastie, Steven D. Penrod, and Nancy Pennington, *Inside the Jury* (Cambridge: Harvard University Press, 1983).

9. Ibid., 80.

10. Ibid., 230

11. Ibid.

It should be said that the data I used in making my calculations[12] referred only to the decision of innocence or guilt and not to the decision as to the length of the sentence to be given. Of course, in our criminal procedure, the judge's decision as to the length of the sentence is merely the first stage. In most cases, the parole board has more influence on how much time the person actually spends in prison than does the judge. Nevertheless, either the judge or the parole board could be wrong, and my estimate would not apply to them. Since civil cases also turn, first, on a determination of responsibility and, second, on a measure of that responsibility in damages,[13] my statistics should apply only to the first of these two decisions.

In general, it is preferable that courts should not make mistakes in either civil or criminal cases. At least in the formal law, however, we distinguish between treatment of error in criminal and in civil cases. In criminal cases, courts feel that bias should be introduced in such a way that the errors in favor of the accused are more common than errors against. I have critically discussed this issue elsewhere.[14] In the rest of this paper I assume agreement that the procedure should be biased in favor of the accused. This implies that the cost of unjustly imprisoning someone who is innocent is higher at the relevant margin through some kind of social externality than its apparent cost.[15]

But all of this assumes access to perfect data. In practice, such data do not exist. Indeed, when we turn to the actual functioning of court procedures, we find very little data relevant to the central issues. There is an immense apparatus of government legal machinery, law schools, and so forth, yet the system fails to generate relevant data.

The comparison, then, is between two systems: a rather idealized version of the Napoleonic system and a rather idealized version of the Anglo-Saxon procedure. I must begin, however, by pointing out that I have said nothing so far about a just procedure. I have only referred to errors and to cost.

12. See note 6.

13. See James K. Hammitt, Stephen J. Carroll, and Daniel A. Relles, "Tort Standards and Jury Decisions," *Journal of Legal Studies* 14 (1985): 751–62. They prove fairly conclusively that a jury's allocation of damages suffers from a number of different biases.

14. A brief explanation of my criticism here may be found in *The Logic of the Law* (New York: Basic Books, 1971), 225–27. For a more elaborate discussion, see my *Trials on Trial*, 78–86.

15. It is interesting that in some cases we use the civil law—such as lawsuits to enforce the law by such methods as providing for triple damages. Whether such cases should be biased in favor of the accused seems to be a very debatable question in the conventional wisdom.

The reason for this omission is that most people's views of a "just procedure" are simply whatever they happen to be accustomed to. Khomeini, for example, has severely criticized all Western jurisprudence for using what he regards as highly unjust procedures.[16] He is, of course, correct from the standpoint of the Sharia legal tradition. Most Americans are disturbed when they become acquainted with continental law. Continentals are also frequently upset by U.S. law. The bail institution in particular impresses them as tremendously unjust.

It is not my concern to criticize any of these quaint customs. If it is indeed true that you feel happier with a particular procedure, then changing that procedure would in fact inflict cost upon you. But if we are talking about changing the law, of necessity, this particular type of externality has to be discounted. Any change involves costs, and a people who think that the current structure is just because they have become accustomed to it are going to suffer. Those who think the present procedure is just, because they regard it as accurate and with the right degree of bias in favor of the accused in criminal proceedings, will avoid such cost if they are persuaded that the accuracy level can be improved by other procedures. Further, although they probably do not feel that lowering costs is a matter of justice, if cost can be lowered without lowering accuracy, they would no doubt accept that as an improvement. It is only those who feel that the present procedures are just per se who will continue to suffer this external cost.

II. THE JURY

There are three basic differences between the Anglo-Saxon and the continental procedures. The first of these is the presence of the jury; the second is the accusatory rather than the inquisitorial method of proceeding; and the third is our particular laws of evidence. Let us begin with the jury.

Napoléon himself believed in the jury, and the Code Napoléon as originally set up made wide use of it. Over time, however, most continental countries gradually abandoned the jury. There are, here and there, remnants; but basically the jury has been abolished. Recently, continental countries have been adopting another way of obtaining nonlegal inputs to the court in the

16. Ayatollah Ruholla Khomeini, *Islamic Government*, trans. The Joint Publications Research Service (New York: Manor Books, 1979).

form of assessors. For example, in West Germany two laypersons sit on the bench with the judge, and when the case is completed, the three retire to their chamber and reach a conclusion by simple majority vote. This is not a jury, but it does have some slight resemblance to it. In a more extreme way, the Soviet comradely courts consist of a set of laypeople all of whom sit on the bench and act as a corporate body of judges.

In all of these cases, there is no formal distinction between fact decided by laypeople and law decided by a judge. In practice, I presume that the assessors are likely to defer to their legally trained colleagues on legal matters even if not required to do so.[17] This probably makes relatively little difference since juries predominantly do what they think is right rather than follow the law. The instructions by the judge are normally unintelligible anyway. The law to most juries probably is relevant only in those cases where ethics do not seem to lead to any definitive conclusion and where the jury understands what the judge is saying.[18]

Let us consider the jury itself. Its historical origin is, like so many other things that go back to the Middle Ages, a little hard to define. It does have one clear advantage over the courts: it is harder to bribe a jury than it is to fix a judge. My own personal opinion is that although this, perhaps, in the early history of the jury, may have been of some significance, today it is more or less irrelevant. It is fairly easy to constitute the court system in such a way that judges will not accept bribes; and hence it is not necessary to turn to the jury for protection against this particular abuse.[19] This is in fact an advantage for the jury, however trivial under modern circumstances.

17. In Sweden, in cases involving serious matters, a district court consists usually of three legally trained judges. Sometimes, however, there is no judge but instead three special elected assessors. These elected officials normally take part in judging cases for about ten days each year and tend to remain in office for very long periods of time, so they normally have considerable experience even if they're not legally trained. ("Law and Justice in Sweden," Fact Sheets on Sweden, Swedish Institute, Stockholm, 1984).

18. Hastie, Penrod, and Pennington found that their trial juries remembered only 30% of the legal instructions: "Comprehension, memory, and application of the law are major problems for juries." *Inside the Jury*, 231.

19. Professor Rose-Ackerman seems to be dubious about this point—probably because she lives in New York—and asked me to explain. The reason that it is easy to prevent judges from accepting bribes is simple. If a judge is to make any significant revenue out of bribes, litigants must know that the judge can be reached. If litigants know it, it is not very difficult for an enforcement body to find out.

The second argument for the jury that is genuine but rarely pushed very far is that we do not want a government of law; we prefer a government of ethics. We do not really like our law code and would prefer to have twelve randomly chosen citizens in a position where they can overturn it if they wish. Since, as a matter of practical fact, they do not know much about the law, they may frequently overturn the law unconsciously. According to this argument, we are better off having a body of men and women who are not outstanding for intelligence, devotion to duty, or anything else; in fact, they are average, making essentially ethical decisions rather than following the law with great precision. People who hold this point of view, by the way, frequently also believe that the United States and England have a government of law rather than people, and they do not see the contradiction.

In my view, it is preferable to have the law so drawn up that it can be enforced by courts rather than having a code of law and a code of ethics that are separate. If ethics are thought to dominate the matter, then the law should be changed so it fits our ethical principles. This is clearly superior to having a law that conflicts with ethics and then a procedure that in fact brings out results in accord with such ethics.

For the purposes of this paper, the issue is essentially irrelevant. There is no reason why the United States should not utilize the usual European panel of three judges or the English, American, and Mohammedan single judge presiding over a case, simply told to follow his, her, or their own conscience, if it conflicted very sharply with the law. In my view, judges in fact do this. The difference between judges and juries in this area is simply that the judges are more likely to carry out the law rather than follow their own ethical code than is the jury. If this is thought to be an objectionable feature of the judicial temperament, then appropriate changes in the judges' instructions should make them as careless of the law as the juries.

Sometimes it is alleged that the jury is biased in favor of the accused and, hence, that this is a precaution against unjust convictions. The general problem of bias in favor of the accused is one I discuss later. It is not really relevant in deciding between a jury and any other procedure. Procedure can be biased at will in favor of the accused to any degree desired.

It should further be said that it is not obvious that juries are biased in favor of the accused. In connection with some recent expert testimony, I had a conversation on the matter with an experienced trial lawyer in Virginia. He informed me that, under present circumstances in Virginia, the prosecuting attorneys always insist on a jury in drunken driving cases because the jury, as he put it, "throws the book" at people accused of that particular crime. I suspect, although I cannot prove, that there are many other cases in which the jury, with its tendency to be more emotionally involved than a judge, and its further tendency to be more shocked on hearing their first rape case than a judge who has heard two hundred and regards this one as routine, may be less likely to give a defendant the benefit of the doubt in certain types of cases. What little evidence there is[20] seems to indicate that, on the whole, the jury is more likely to find a person innocent than is a judge. This may be changing. It is really a question of the climate of opinion among judges, or the average people, who make up the jury.

Recently I have encountered what I frankly regard as an astonishing argument for the jury. Putting this argument in an accurate, if rather uncharitable form, it assumes that the judges are upper class and that the juries and people who appear before courts are lower class. The upper-class judges have difficulty in evaluating the testimony of the lower-class witnesses. I find this an astonishing argument, but let me take it seriously, and in particular let me accept the statement of "fact"—that is, upper-class judges find themselves trying lower-class litigants. It seems to me that the only thing demonstrated in this argument is that judges should have special training. Surely, someone of well above average intelligence, which I take it most judges are, and adequate training would be better at evaluating the testimony of lower-class witnesses[21] than would be an average person of average intelligence with no special training, or even a board of twelve such average people.

Having given what I believe are the strongest arguments for a jury as opposed to a judge, it will not have escaped the reader that I do not think they are very strong. Juries are a rare method of investigating problems, whether of the fact or of the law in the present-day world. This is true not only outside the United States but also within the United States. Let us look at areas where we can use a jury but where we are not constitutionally required so to do.[22] If we set up some organization to make factual inquiries about

20. See Harry Kalven, Jr., and Hans Zeisel, *The American Jury* (Boston: Little, Brown, 1966); John Baldwin and Michael McConville, *Jury Trials* (Oxford: Clarendon Press, 1979); S. McCabe and R. Purves, *The Shadow Jury at Work*, Oxford University, Criminal Research Unit (London: Blackwells, 1974).

21. This follows some training in lower-class mores, but that is easy.

22. The Supreme Court has in general refused to enforce the constitutional requirement of juries in all cases at common law involving more than twenty dollars. This is very sensible of them.

substantially anything, we turn to nonjury methods. Our administrative tribunals, for example, either hold direct hearings with the administrative board acting as a board of judges or use trial examiners who function without juries. Perhaps the closest duplicate of our normal court system is arbitration. In this case, the parties have considerable freedom in choosing their procedural method, and so far as I know, none of them has ever chosen a jury. When Congress wants to obtain information, it either holds hearings in which the congressmen themselves directly question witnesses[23] or establishes an investigating body that seeks out the truth, once again without the use of the jury.

Nor is it true that we avoid the jury only in nonjudicial roles. At the time the Constitution was drawn up, one whole branch of law, equity, normally functioned without juries, and its descendants still do today. The courts in those days also had, as they still do today, some hangovers from the royal power directly to punish people, and to this day most contempt proceedings are without a jury.

This last, from my standpoint, is a mildly amusing phenomenon, because when I was in law school, the more liberal law professors and the more liberal part of the Supreme Court seemed bound and determined to make most contempts triable by jury.[24] Then came *Brown vs. Board of Education* and the realization by the court that their integration policy would not be carried out if juries were necessary in order to put a southern school superintendent into prison for contempt of court. The whole move going on when I was in law school to put contempt in control of the jury simply vanished.

This last item—the contempt of court power—is a particularly clear-cut case because almost all contempts are in the nature of crimes. The apparent reason that the person charged with contempt is not given a jury trial is simply unwillingness on the part of judges to let a board of laypeople overrule their judgment. I understand that perfectly. There is almost no issue on which I would regard a board of twelve jurors selected at random from the population as having better judgment than I do.[25]

England, the home of jury trial, has gradually restricted it over time. At the present, for all intents and purposes, you cannot obtain a jury in civil

23. Many of the witnesses are volunteers.

24. My professor of constitutional law, a standard liberal jurist, was particularly determined on this point.

25. Possibly a board of twelve of the readers of this paper might have such better judgment.

cases, and there has been a long-term though slow tendency to restrict its availability in criminal cases. In both England and the United States, although a criminal defendant can still insist on a jury if the charge is serious, the bench trial is on the whole more common than a jury trial.

I presume most trained lawyers regard all of this as beside the point. They are so accustomed to juries in one area and no jury in others that it seems to them like a law of nature rather than a policy decision. A little thought, however, will convince them that there is nothing impossible about convening a group of twelve randomly selected citizens to consider whether the Kansas City school board has violated the law and the Constitution by segregating its schools. So far as I know, there is no significant reasoning indicating that the jury is better than a board of judges in this (or any other) case.

If we confine ourselves to problems of accuracy, it really is quite hard to think of a mechanism that we would anticipate would be less accurate than a random selection of individuals who know nothing about the matter. The only thing we do that even remotely resembles it are occasional government commissions appointed to look into some general problem and report. These commissions, although they are called fact-finding commissions, actually have as their goal looking into the matter and proposing something that might be politically feasible; and for that reason they are heavily weighted with people thought to represent political opinion in the community. Even here, there always are at least some people on the commission who are experts on the subject matter and who would, if they were a jury, be removed on the grounds that they were not suitably ignorant of the material to be examined.

Further, in these commissions, normally there is a professional staff of people selected for expertise who carry on a more or less normal investigation (sometimes a very detailed one with a lot of research contracted out) and write the report. It is signed normally after a few minor revisions by the public members of the commission. Among our institutions for fact finding, I think this one resembles a jury more than any other, but it certainly does not resemble it very much.

Think of the matter a priori. The average person is of only average intelligence and average information. The jury process begins by removing from its sample anybody who is well informed with respect to whatever it is the jury is supposed to look into, thus ensuring ignorance. The jury has no strong economic motive to work hard and understand the material presented to it. Presumably, in criminal cases, the jury is interested (almost everybody reads the crime news in the newspapers) but probably not interested enough to devote a lot of careful attention to the case. In civil cases, they may not even be interested.[26] If the matter is complicated, it is unlikely that the jury will understand it at all.[27]

When we have the combination of an average level of intelligence, probably somewhat below-average information, and weak motives for hard work to understand the situation, clearly the general social decision not to use this mechanism to determine factual or other information is sensible. What has to be explained is why we in fact use it in some criminal and civil cases. The only apparent explanation is tradition. The process started long ago when the pope ruled out trial by ordeal; and the trial by jury has remained in Anglo-Saxon countries, more or less, ever since.[28]

When I was in law school, I was advised that the jury was useful in court because its practical experience offered advantages in determining factual matters. Occasionally, this is stated by judges. I have great difficulty in believing that anybody seriously believes this particular rationalization. There is, of course, no reason why the average jury member is any more practical than anyone else. The average judge probably has as much experience driving a car as the average jury member, perhaps more. When it comes to judging crimes, he or she no doubt has massively more experience than the juror. Altogether, I think this has to be put down simply as an ex post rationalization invented by people who could not think of any better reason for favoring the jury.

As a final set of remarks on the jury, I should like to recur to the problem of bias in favor of the accused. Of course, this is quite irrelevant in civil cases.[29] Nevertheless, if one does feel that the court should be biased in favor of the accused, it must be admitted that jury members seem to be more biased in that direction than are judges.[30] Since no one has measured the degree of bias of the jury, if we *assume* that the jury has the right degree of

26. My only recent experience in court involved an appearance as an expert witness. One of the six jurors kept falling asleep.

27. "As a result, many fraud cases never reached the courts. In those that do verdicts are often inconsistent. Juries convict or acquit at whim, because jurymen are out of their depth." *Economist*, April 21, 1984, p. 16.

28. See Charles Rembar, *The Law of the Land* (New York: Simon and Schuster, 1980), esp. 116–71.

29. Hammitt et al., "Tort Standards and Jury Decisions."

30. See Kalven and Zeisel, *The American Jury*; Baldwin and McConville, *Jury Trials*; McCabe and Purves, *The Shadow Jury at Work*.

bias, then the use of the jury seems justified. That *assumption* is not very reasonable, and in any event, there is no reason that we could not set up experiments to measure the degree of bias that juries evidence. The problem here is that there does not seem to be any specific statement anywhere as to the degree of bias that is desirable. Once one has determined the degree of bias that is desirable, it can be built in almost anywhere in the procedural rules and does not have to depend on the jury. Most people argue that our procedure, in particular the law of evidence (which will be discussed below), helps protect innocent persons. I am by no means convinced this is true, but there is no doubt that that kind of bias could be easily built into the procedural rules without a jury. Further, there is no doubt that a jury's bias in favor of the accused varies a great deal from jury to jury and from time to time.[31]

Since we can, if we once decide how much bias we want, build it into the procedure with no difficulty, there is no reason to use this as an argument for the jury. The only counterargument is that the amount of bias we want is simply defined by the use of the jury.

But this, of course, assumes that the amount of bias that the jurors impose (and to repeat, it varies a good deal from time to time and place to place) is somehow known to be the right amount. This is sufficiently bizarre that I shall not pursue it further. Altogether there do not seem to be any arguments for the use of the jury except that is has been used for some time. In Argentina, the same argument has supported torture.

III. ADVERSARY PROCESS

Let us turn now to the second problem: adversary proceedings, or, as it is usually referred to, accusatory as opposed to inquisitorial proceedings. The first thing to be said about this is that the word *inquisition* has a negative connotation in English because of the long period of wars between England and Spain and the role of the Holy Office in Spain. I hope that this matter can be put aside for the current discussion.

31. The Reverend Moon will be recalled as presenting really quite good evidence that any jury from the district in which he was being tried would be prejudiced against him as an argument against being tried by jury. The judge, who apparently did not like the reverend, went along with the prosecutor's insistence on a trial by jury. It would seem reasonable that in this case everyone concerned thought that the jury would be biased against the defendant.

Another essentially false issue is the myth that the use of the jury requires an accusatory rather than an inquisitorial form of trial. Napoléon introduced juries into his procedure. But they gradually died out in Europe over the nineteenth century. There are, in fact, still a few special nooks and crannies where the jury is used. These juries, however, were used in an inquisitorial type of court. In both the inquisitorial and the accusatorial systems, a jury, if there is one, simply listens to evidence gathered and presented by other people. In the accusatory system, it is the opposing attorneys, with the judge occasionally intervening. In the inquisitorial system, it is the presiding judge, with the attorneys occasionally intervening. When lay participation in court is obtained by use of assessors rather than a jury, assessors, of course, are seated on the bench and play an active role in questioning the witnesses. A legally trained presiding judge, however, normally dominates the proceedings.

The adversary proceeding, in its strong form, is more or less unique to Anglo-Saxon countries. We find it almost nowhere else. This is, of course, some evidence that it may not be the best procedure. If we look at domestic activities in the United States, then adversary proceedings are in use more widely than the jury. Proceedings before administrative bodies or before their trial examiners not infrequently take on adversary form, although that is by no means universal. Congressional investigations are not formally adversarial; but it sometimes happens that the Republicans and the Democrats will take the two sides and conduct the investigation in a way that looks adversarial. The formal investigating committees constituted to investigate special problems almost never actually follow adversary proceedings, but they sometimes permit outsiders to call witnesses; and if there happen to be only two such outside groups and they are strictly opposed, the outcome can look rather adversarial. Here, however, the questioning of the witnesses will normally be done by members of the commission and not by attorneys for either side. The procedure thus resembles closely a procedure under an inquisitorial court in a civil lawsuit. It differs in that, in a civil lawsuit, attorneys for the adversaries have some rather restricted rights to cross-examine witnesses after the judges have finished. There has been some effort to establish a similar right before commissions in the United States.

Thus the general practice within the United States would seem to indicate that the adversarial procedure is a little more sensible than the inquisitorial, because we certainly do make more use of it. I believe, however, that here all we observe is a spread of custom. The courts have enforced "due process" on quite a lot of our procedures, and even where there is no such enforcement, a sort of habit has developed of following it. Congress is largely composed of lawyers, and they, in the Administrative Procedure Act, imposed some aspects of Anglo-Saxon procedure upon administrative tribunals. In general this does not mean a jury, because the courts and legislature do not seem to think that the jury is worth enforcing outside of the areas where it has traditionally been used. It does, however, frequently mean adversarial proceedings.

The existence of the custom of commercial arbitration provides at least a potential test. The parties there have considerable, although not complete, freedom to choose their legal procedure. We would assume that over time, they would tend to move towards the most efficient procedure. Unfortunately, there seem to be substantially no empirical data from which we can draw conclusions here.[32]

Normally, however, if we are interested in finding out what happened with respect to some particular matter, we investigate it; we do not appoint attorneys on each side to present arguments and collect and present evidence. Consider, for example, the situation which not uncommonly turns up in universities in which it is desired to determine the facts with respect to a contentious issue. An individual or a committee is appointed to look into it and proceeds to use inquisitorial methods to do so. This is indeed the normal procedure. Indeed, scientific investigation is an example of inquisitorial methods. Certainly, parents invariably use it in disciplining their children, and we allot grades to our students by a purely inquisitorial procedure.[33]

The argument for this procedure is simple. If information is sought, properly qualified individuals are commissioned to find it. This procedure has appealed to almost everyone throughout history. Our particular procedure seems to have descended in a rather obscure and complicated way from trial by battle.[34] But its historical origins are less significant than its disadvantages.

The standard argument for the adversarial system is that if there is to be an investigation, the investigator must of necessity be motivated by initial ideas. These are likely to hold as he continues; and so, in essence, the half-formed

32. See Gordon Tullock, "A Digression on Arbitral Geography," in *Trials on Trial*, 100–104.

33. The last remark may be a puzzle to some of my readers. The basic characteristic of inquisition is that somebody inquires, collecting such evidence and asking such questions as he or she wishes. An examination is an almost perfect expression of this, although I presume most of you have never thought of it in those terms.

34. See Rembar, *Law of the Land*.

ideas with which he started exert undue influence on the final outcome.[35] Since I frequently change my mind about problems during the course of research, I tend to feel that this is a psychologically weak argument. I must admit, however, that at the moment, we do not have any positive evidence one way or the other. Since it is the only significant argument for the accusatory as opposed to the inquisitorial method, the people who favor the accusatory method should feel it incumbent to produce genuine evidence. If there is no genuine evidence, obviously the argument is weak.

The arguments against the accustatory and in favor of the inquisitorial method so far given are the traditional ones. I am the inventor of another one.[36] Briefly, a legal proceeding in which the two parties are in control of the proceedings (that is, each one of them introduces evidence, calls witnesses, cross-examines the other's witnesses, and so on) is a case in which each of them can generate a Pareto-relevant externality on the other. The net social cost of my calling someone as a witness has several components. First, there is his or her time and trouble. Second, there is the cost of maintaining the court for the time the witnesses testify. Third, there is injury that he or she will do to my opponent's case. The advantage is solely the benefit to my case. But note that the benefit to my case and the injury to the other case are identical. In other words, there is an externality falling on my opponent of exactly the same size as the benefit I receive.

It can, however, be argued that there is another benefit: that calling more witnesses, questioning them, and so on, whether done by the parties or by the courts, increases the accuracy with which the ultimate decision is made. This means that the law itself will be better carried out; people in the future will be more likely to obey the law; thus there is a gain.

Nevertheless, when a litigant calls witnesses, cross-examines, and so on, he or she is ignoring a very large part of the cost. He or she will invest resources

35. It is also true that juries may be impressed by the first thing that comes to their mind. Robert G. Begam, a trial lawyer of immense experience and president of the ATLA, said, "The University of Chicago conducted studies some years ago that revealed that 80 percent of all jurors make up their minds on the subject of liability and never change their minds after the opening statement." *Trial* (July 1980): 36. I have been unable to find the University of Chicago study, but the fact that it's believed true by a prominent trial lawyer is probably more important than the study itself. In any event, I do trust Begam's word that such a study exists. See also James A. Yonker, "The Effect of Decision Time and Argument Complexity on Legal Judgment," *International Review of Law and Economics* 3 (1983): 161–78.

36. *Trials on Trial*, 49–86.

in the case up to the point where the private return to him or her equals the private cost. The litigant ignores both the possible social gain from accurate enforcement of the law,[37] and the direct effect on this particular case, which surely in most cases is a much larger matter. After all, one more contract, the breach of which is healed or not healed by a court action, does very little to affect the likelihood that people will keep their contracts. Nevertheless, if the litigant is likely to overinvest socially, the opponent will do the same, and the outcome will depend to a considerable extent on how expensive the lawyers are.[38]

The judge in the inquisitorial system takes care of this problem: The judge is as interested in the social effects of the law as the judge in an accusatory system. The judge takes into account the total cost of the proceedings because he or she bears a good part of them.[39] The judge is the one who decides which witnesses will be called and how much they will be questioned, and indeed he or she does the basic questioning.[40]

Thus, the externalities are dealt with in the inquisitorial system, and they cause considerable difficulty in the accusatory system. I suspect that this is one of the major reasons why accusatory proceedings are so expensive—although in England, where the judge generally completely dominates the trial even if he or she does not play a large overt role, they are cheaper. A British barrister would do almost anything to avoid seriously annoying a judge who not only is presiding over this trial but who will preside over many more in which the barrister participates.

Continental legal proceedings are massively less expensive than American proceedings, as can easily be seen from the fact that the total size of the legal profession is so much smaller there. However, the basic difference here may not be the choice between adversary and inquisitorial proceedings but other

37. Fifty percent of the resource investment is on the side of the party that loses.

38. As an amusing aside here: In my original work I always said that the more the two sides put into hiring expensive lawyers, the more likely it was that the outcome in fact would be correct. I always pointed out that the improvement would be small but, I thought, real. Among the serious criticisms that my theory has received, the statement that this is not true—that very expensive lawyers on both sides do not lead to more accurate proceedings—is, oddly enough, one of the commonest. Interestingly, it is the lawyers who normally make this criticism.

39. It could be said that it is not he but his employer, the state, that bears the cost. In either event, the externalities are internalized.

40. There are some powers in all inquisitorial systems for the two parties to provide witnesses and do supplementary questioning. Basically, however, it is the judge or board of judges that determines the proceedings in the trial.

matters. In England, which uses adversary proceedings but does not use the jury in civil cases, there are about half as many judges as in the United States. Most of the continental systems have far fewer lawyers per capita than that of the United States but somewhat more judges.[41] The last fact is presumably a consequence of the use of panels with three judges rather than the single judge. Basic reliance on a single judge is characteristic only of Anglo-Saxon and Mohammedan countries. In any event, the immense size of the American legal establishment is prima facie evidence that something is wrong.

The arguments here for the inquisitorial system are not overwhelming.[42] I rarely run into any real arguments on the other side. There is a feeling that the inquisition is wicked. A misunderstanding of Napoléon is also apparently important. The view that in Europe "court proceedings are an opportunity for the defendant to prove his innocence" is quoted repeatedly. As a matter of fact, European courts in general use the slogan "If there is doubt, acquit," whereas in our case it is "reasonable doubt." Further, even if it were the truth that our system protected the defendant better in criminal cases, that is no argument for using it in the civil law.

IV. EVIDENCE

The third topic is the laws of evidence, which, in fact, are a large collection of different rules, not all of which are motivated by the same considerations. Further, although the laws of evidence are rather minor and insignificant in most European procedures, they are not totally nonexistent. Indeed, in countries where the pre-Napoleonic legal system still maintains its sway (mainly in those parts of the Spanish Empire that broke away without adopting the Napoleonic code), there are rules of evidence that, on the whole, are worse than ours. Arbitral tribunals, where the parties have a good deal of freedom in choosing their procedure, normally get by with little or nothing in the way of rules of evidence.

But let me return to our rules of evidence. I would like to classify them into two categories: those that have some reasonable chance of benefiting the accused, whether he or she is guilty or innocent, and the "others." The United States Fifth Amendment right not to testify against oneself and the

41. Earl Johnson, Jr., and Ann Barthelmes Drew, "This Nation Has Money for Everything Except Its Courts," *Judges Journal* 17(3) (Summer 1978): 9. See charts on p. 10.

42. For further arguments, see *Trials on Trial*.

"fruit of the poison tree" doctrine are both biased in favor of the accused. The "others" all change procedure, but it is not obvious that the accused gains or loses.

Note that I have said "the accused"; that was the original meaning of the privilege against self-incrimination. It was simply that the person accused of a crime could not be called upon to testify. Indeed, in the early days of the Republic, not only could the person not be called upon to testify, it was illegal to testify on his or her own volition.[43] The somewhat dubious privilege of not being permitted or compelled to testify was restricted to the people who were accused of crime. Other witnesses did not have this privilege.

As a result of various historic developments in the middle of the nineteenth century, the situation has been largely reversed. Legislative acts of Congress gave the accused the "right" to testify, and since the jury knows that he or she can, they are likely to feel that a defendant's failure to testify indicates that he or she thinks the testimony would be likely to be damaging. They may, of course, be told by the judge that they are not to consider this in their deliberations. It is conceivable that his advice has some effect. Nevertheless, there clearly is considerable pressure on the accused to testify because of the general feeling of most defense lawyers that the jury is likely to be suspicious of defendants who do not testify.

On the other hand, the privilege is now of considerable use to witnesses who are called in other kinds of cases. If called upon to testify before Congress or to appear as a witness in a lawsuit, they can freely use the privilege without prejudicing any jury, because there is no jury considering the case. The situation is roughly the reverse of what it was at the time the constitutional amendment was adopted.

Nevertheless, I think that we have to concede that the situation offers the defense some advantages. The defendant and his or her lawyer can consider whether the testimony is more likely to benefit his or her case or injure it, granted that the jury will be made suspicious by his or her nonappearance. DeLorean did not testify, and I think that we can feel confident that he and his lawyer made an intelligent decision. Thus, there is some bias in favor of the defendant.

The "fruit of the poison tree" doctrine also is biased in favor of the accused, at least pro forma. As a rule, this prevents the prosecution from offering various kinds of evidence that they otherwise might offer and has no

43. See Dean Griswold, *New Leader*, October 29, 1956.

effect on the defendant, since, in practice, the defendant can offer anything in evidence no matter how he or she got it. The bias in favor of the defendant is clear, but it may well be that the wide publicity this rule has received means that the whole proceeding is biased against the defendant. The problem is that most jury members must be under the impression, if they have read newspapers and watched television, that the prosecution commonly has evidence that it is not permitted to present because of this rule. If they allow for this (and they may or may not), this might lead to a net bias against the defendant. This matter will be discussed in more detail below.

European procedure is quite different. The defendant is put on the stand (although not sworn) and questioned by the judge. He or she is free to refuse to answer any question the judge asks, but the judge will take any refusal into account.[44] I take it that there can be no doubt as to which of these two proceedings is more likely to reach the truth, but if you want a system biased in favor of the accused, in particular, of the guilty accused,[45] one should be in favor of this particular stricture. Once again, this depends on the degree to which one wants the proceedings biased. There does not seem to be any serious discussion of this point, and therefore it is impossible to say whether any particular procedure offers the "right" degree of bias in favor of the accused.

Still, if a degree of bias in favor of the accused is wanted and yet accuracy also is desired in the sense that this bias shall be the same over all cases, then the present U.S. scheme is clumsy. The degree to which a given defendant benefits from the existence of this privilege is not necessarily—in fact is unlikely—to be the same degree to which some other defendant benefits. In other words, there is a level of bias that varies from case to case. It seems far better to determine the degree of desired bias and then to specify such bias as instructions to the court rather than to provide various more or less random provisions that give bias in favor of the accused but in different amounts to different accused.

An opposite bias may exist. Every jury member who watches television knows that a good deal of potential prosecution evidence is refused admission under the laws of evidence, while the defendant is much less handicapped. Dealing with illegally obtained evidence is a particularly clear example. As a

44. It is sometimes said that the privilege is protection against torture of the accused. As a matter of fact, the United States retained sporadic torture of suspects in the form of the third degree long after the continental democracies using inquisitorial method had given it up. I take it there is no one today who really fears torture if arrested by the Swedish, Dutch, or Swiss police.

45. It's rare, although not totally unknown, to have a situation in which the innocent defendant's testimony will actually injure the case.

rough rule of thumb, the defense can in fact obtain admission while the prosecution cannot.

The juror may think, quite rationally, that there is more evidence against the accused than has been presented in court. If he or she does so think and acts on that suspicion, the procedures may in fact be biased against the accused. Further, once again, this bias would be a sort of helter-skelter matter. Assume that the average juror thinks the prosecution's case is normally 15% better than is presented in court, with the missing 15% being accounted for by the evidence prohibited by the laws of evidence. In some cases, the prosecution's case in terms of the evidence they actually have would presumably be much more than 30% stronger, and in other cases there would literally be no evidence that the prosecution had not been able to bring into court. The 15% correction by the juror, then, would underestimate the actual bias introduced by the laws of evidence in one case and overestimate in the other. Thus, if the laws of evidence do lead to bias against the accused, the bias varies considerably from case to case.

Turning to my second division, all the other rules of evidence, I perhaps should begin by pointing out that they are, in general, quite impartial in ruling out evidence for both the prosecution and the defense. Hence, they do not bias the case in favor of the accused.

In this field, the popular statement recurs: "How would you like to be convicted on hearsay evidence?" Obviously I prefer not to be convicted, but I should as soon be convicted on hearsay evidence as convicted because hearsay evidence that otherwise would have been on my side was barred by the court.

Hearsay will do as a sample of the kind of laws of evidence that are so different in our court from those on the continent. It is clear that if there is a choice between hearing D testify about something he saw or hearing W testify as to what D said about what he saw, we would prefer D:

> Suppose D . . . was the only eye witness and he is now dead; and there is no other evidence either way on the issue. It would seem that the jury is more likely to reach a correct result (if W's testimony) is admitted than if it is excluded. This becomes highlighted if we further suppose that his statement is the only thing that can clear Mr. Q of a charge of murder. Remember that all that is needed to acquit is a reasonable doubt. But considerations such as these seem to have no part in the official doctrine, except to the formalistic extent that need and reliability are recognized in the exceptions to the hearsay rule. If it's hearsay, and it does

> not come within one of the recognized exceptions (which this probably would not), it is inadmissible. And yet, citizens, in making important decisions in their daily lives, commonly rely on their ability correctly to evaluate hearsay.[46]

European courts hear the hearsay and discount its importance. The explanation for the Anglo-Saxon deviation normally offered is that jurors are simple people who might be easily misled. This explanation is not used as much these days as it used to be, because language has become more democratic. In any event, the laws of evidence, having once been adopted on this particular reasoning, are also used if the trial is being conducted by a judge without a jury, apparently on the grounds that judges also are simple people and can be easily misled.[47]

It can be argued, first, that jurors are not all that simple. In fact, this procedural restriction was adopted long ago in England at a time when the jury was composed exclusively of members of the upper class because of rather high property restrictions.[48] They, in fact, came from the same social class as the judges.

More important, if the jury's ability to make judgments with respect to the evidence is not trusted, there is no reason to be selective and to look at only certain types of evidence. We let the jury judge all sorts of complicated technical problems. Suppose that the prosecution and defense expert witnesses disagree on whether chemical tests show the existence of poison in a corpse. It may be that the average person is much better in discounting hearsay than in judging which of two professors of chemistry is right.

Further, the laws of evidence introduce what amounts to a random element of bias in any case. Consider in a lawsuit between A and B that some of the evidence that the parties would like to use is banned by the laws of evidence. There is no law of nature, or even of probability, that this evidence will be evenly divided. These are small sample problems, and the odds are not unconvincing that the evidence banned by the law of evidence should be heavier on one side than the other.

46. Paul F. Rothstein, *Evidence in a Nutshell* (St. Paul, Minn.: West Publishing, 1970), 119–20.

47. There is another explanation for the extension of the rule to judges, which is simple muddle.

48. "Property, Authority, and the Criminal Law," in *Albion's Fatal Tree: Crime and Society in Eighteenth-Century England*, ed. Douglas Hay, Peter Linebaugh, John G. Rule, E. B. Thompson, and Cal Winslow (New York: Pantheon Books, 1975), 38–39.

All of these rules are aimed at protecting rather obscure "civil liberties," which do not seem to have much to do with the accuracy or inaccuracy of the trial. A wife, for example, cannot be forced to testify against her husband.[49] Whether this helps the accused is not clear. Suppose that Mr. Jones is on trial for murder. The murder was actually committed by Mr. Smith, and Mrs. Smith witnessed it. Should Mrs. Smith be compelled to testify in Jones' defense?

The remainder of evidence rules are rather similar to hearsay. They are a number of specific rules that, if they have any justification at all, have the justification of making it less likely that dull people will be misled by poor evidence. Consider, for example, our current method of detecting dishonest witnesses. It is sometimes possible to prove that a witness is dishonest by producing physical evidence, and we may have witnesses testifying in opposite directions about some matter, with the result that at least one of them must be in error, whether he or she is consciously lying or mistaken. The basic method for determining who is lying, however, is simply to look intently at the person's face and draw deductions from that. This is not a convincing method.

There is, however, another method of detecting lying, which also is not strong but is almost certainly better than looking at the person's face. This is the lie detector. Empirical evidence indicates that the lie detector is right roughly three-quarters of the time.[50] There does not seem to be any empirical test of accuracy of judgment by looking at people's faces, but it would be doubtful that it could be more than 75% accurate. The basically honest person who lies on the stand is probably unusual. The people who lie on the stand tend to be those who have lied a great deal in the past and gotten away with it. Indeed, it is likely that a professional con man will stand up better under cross-examination than the ordinary honest but naive citizen.

Why, then, do we refuse to use the lie detector? It should be said that at the moment the European courts also make very little use of them. The

49. When I was in law school she could not testify, whether she wanted to or not.

50. There is considerable dispute as to the accuracy of lie detectors, and 75% is a conservative estimate. In "Validity and Reliability of Detection of Deception," David C. Raskin, Gordon Barland, and John A. Podlesny (Washington, D.C.: National Institute of Law Enforcement and Criminal Justice, June 1978, United States document J262V23) find a 90% accuracy rate. Benjamin Kleinmuntz and Julian J. Szucko, "On the Fallibility of Lie Detection," *Law and Society Review* 17(1) (1982): 85–103, are vigorous opponents of the use of lie detectors and devote the bulk of their article to severe criticism. Nevertheless, their data show that when lie detectors are used appropriately, results have a correlation with the truth equivalent to something like 72% or 73% accuracy. See pp. 94–96.

answer seems to be simply its novelty; additionally, it is hard to integrate it into the U.S. procedure. It would be much easier to integrate it into the European procedure. The sensible way of using the lie detector is not to have someone who is called an expert on lie detectors determine whether given witnesses are lying but to inspect the witnesses' blood pressure while testifying. If this was done to all witnesses and the procedure was 75% accurate, it could sharply improve the quality of the proceedings. This, however, requires that whoever is inspecting the blood pressure or other physical measure used by the lie detector be someone who understands it, and this is unlikely to be the jury. There is no reason that judges could not be trained in this not terribly obscure art. Thus the law of evidence that rules out lie detectors in general in the United States in this case guarantees that a poorer rather than a better form of evidence be accepted.

Most people are ambivalent about lie detectors. They tend to think that a person they suspect of ill doing and whom they dislike should be compelled to face the lie detector while people they think are nice should not. The *Washington Post*, for example, has been indignant about proposals of the Reagan administration to require high-ranking civil servants in the Department of Defense to undergo lie detector tests to determine who is leaking information. They feel equally indignant about the reluctance of the Reagan administration to have all of its high officials take lie detector tests with respect to the Carter campaign briefing papers that appear to have been leaked to the Republican campaign headquarters. The Reagan administration is, needless to say, no more consistent. It differs only in having opposite values on these two uses of the lie detector.

This is a general characteristic. When Mayor Rizzo of Philadelphia voluntarily underwent lie detector tests some years ago and failed, the ACLU and its supporters did not immediately dash forward and say that whether he had failed was irrelevant because they were not accurate.[51] It had something to do with the political position of that particular mayor of Philadelphia and the political position of most members of the ACLU.

But since I am here defending the European procedure and not the lie detector, all of this has been a digression. The European procedure, which is to let almost anything in, provided only that it is relevant, and then to let the judges decide whether it is good evidence or bad evidence and how much weight to give it, is surely superior to our system under which some kinds of

51. "Rizzo Is 'Baffled' at Lie Test Result," *New York Times*, August 5, 1973, p. 15.

evidence are simply barred. This is particularly so since in the small number of cases of an individual trial, it surely regularly prejudices one side or the other.

V. IN CONCLUSION

I have taken as my brief today the defense of Napoléon against Justice Warren. In practice, of course, I have not taken the original Code Napoléon but the more modern version of it. Some form of inquisitorial procedure is the norm throughout the world, not only in the Napoleonic code. It was the norm in Rome. It is normal in a lot of places whose judicial schemes we dislike, such as Poland and Khomeini's Iran, but also in most of the democratic countries of Western Europe. It is almost inevitably what people who are attempting to find out the truth turn to if they are not stuck with a bunch of ancient traditions.

On our side, we have a legal system that, in essence, developed without much thought in the late Middle Ages and has been slowly changed without any serious research on whether its basic structure might be erroneous. Its hold is partially tradition and partially the fact that it guarantees large incomes to almost everybody now connected with it. Those people are the "experts" whom we turn to in discussing changes.

It is always hard to convince people that something they were brought up with, and for which respect is continuously reinforced by the fact that most of the people they associate with were also brought up in it, is, in fact, wrong. Biologists currently find creationism a problem of this sort. In their case, however, they have the advantage of a good deal of scientific evidence. In the comparison of different methods of procedure, there is substantially no scientific evidence on either side. This is not because such scientific evidence could not be developed but because it has not been. One of the characteristics of modern governments is that they do not do much research in their own functioning. I have therefore been forced to fall back on what I would call general reasoning, obviously inferior to careful scientific studies. My opponents, however, also depend on general reasoning; a priori it seems to me that general reasoning leads in my direction. Only tradition works the other way.

NEGLIGENCE AGAIN

Since Learned Hand's famous Carroll Towing decision,[1] an idea that the standard negligence–contributory negligence rules of Anglo-Saxon tort law are efficient[2] has been important in the literature. The idea was formalized by Brown in a truly path-breaking article which led to an immense body of further research.[3] This literature also shows that what is rather misleadingly called "strict liability" is at least equally efficient. "Strict liability" does not mean that anybody is really strictly liable, but that the person causing the injury is liable not only if he has been negligent, but also when neither has been negligent. The injured person remains responsible for his own injuries where he has been negligent, even if the injurer has also been negligent.[4]

To put the problem in modern terms, we have a non-cooperative game between two parties in which the individual strategies are investment of resources in preventing accidents. Looked at from the standpoint of the society, there is a clear-cut Pareto optimum which occurs when the sum of the cost of the resources invested by the two parties for prevention of accidents and the cost of the accidents that actually do occur is minimized. Instead of attempting to directly regulate the investment of these resources, society turns to allocation of damages after the accidents occurred and attempts to do this allocation in such a way that both parties will have motives to invest the right amount. In other words, it attempts to change the rules of the game so that the equilibrium investment for each of the two parties and the social optimum are the same. A rather surprising outcome of research in the area is that this trick can be done, granted assumptions of perfect calculations on the part of everybody concerned, and in particular the courts.

While I have never questioned the strict line of reasoning used by Hand

Reprinted from *International Review of Law and Economics* 1 (June 1982): 51–62, copyright 1982, with permission from Elsevier.

1. *United States* v. *Carroll Towing Co.*, 159 F. 2d 169 [2d Cir. 1947].

2. "Two Kinds of Legal Efficiency," Hofstra Law Review, forthcoming.

3. J. P. Brown, "Toward an Economic Theory of Liability" (1973) 2 Journal of Legal Studies 323. For European readers, I should point out that the American rule making contributory negligence a complete defence is assumed.

4. At least this is what I think is meant in the theoretical literature. Fortunately, for the purposes of this article the issue of exact meaning of "strict liability" is not important.

and his successors, I tend to doubt whether our institutional structure is such that we can actually attain these advantages. In particular, it seems to me the probability of error, both in the calculations of risks by the parties and in the *ex post* determination of the situation by the courts, is so high that basically different, more rough and ready rules should be adopted.[5] For the bulk of this article, however, I am going to accept the "Hand" tradition in these areas and assume that courts and parties can make these very fine distinctions. The point of this article is not, then, to disagree with the efficiency arguments of Hand, Brown, etc., granted their assumptions, but to point out that under those assumptions there are several other institutional structures which are equally efficient. The choice among this set of institutions has to be made on rather different grounds than those used by Hand and Brown.[6] But more of this below after the structure has been laid out.

Although Hand's argument was simple and straightforward, most of his successors have used highly sophisticated mathematical tools. Here, I propose to use a fairly simple argument which is, I think, as rigorous, albeit not as mathematical.

But first a few preliminaries. Assume that an accident has occurred in which two people were involved and one of them was injured and the other not. This is not a particularly uncommon form of accident, although accidents in which both parties suffer at least some injury are more common. Nevertheless, our simple accident with only one injured makes the reasoning easier to follow, and the reader who is curious will be easily able to extend it to situations in which there is some injury on both sides.

Under the Anglo-Saxon law, if the uninjured person has been negligent, thus causing the accident, and the injured person has not also been negligent (contributory negligence), then the uninjured person must pay the cost of injury to the injured person. Unless this particular combination of events has occurred, the injured person must bear his own injuries without payment.

5. G. Tullock, *Logic of the Law*, Basic Books (1971), pp. 105–35, and *Trials on Trial: Pure Theory of Legal Procedure*, Columbia University Press (1980).

6. J. L. Croyle, "The Impact of Judge-Made Policies: An Analysis of Research Strategies and Application to Products Liability Doctrine" (1979) 13 Law and Society Review 949. R. A. Posner, "Utilitarianism Economics and Legal Theory" (1979) 8 Journal of Legal Studies 103. A Stern, "Divergent Liability Rules and Economic Integration" (1979) 89 Economic Journal 385.

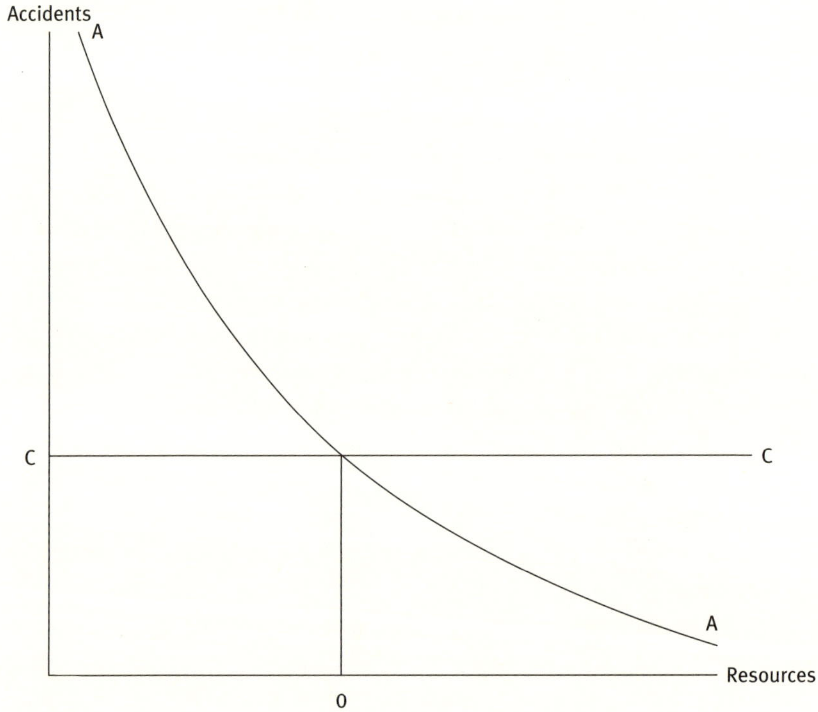

FIGURE 1

Why this system is efficient is readily explicable on the basis of Figures 1 and 2. In Figure 1, we show the *ex ante* situation from the standpoint of one party, who assumes that the other party has invested a certain amount of resources in preventing accidents. For this party—who can be the injured or the uninjured; it makes no difference—the line AA shows the expectancy of accidents with various levels of resource investment on his part to prevent accidents. The line CC shows the cost to him of investing such resources, and the socially optimal amount of resources for him to invest is, of course, 0.

However, this assumes that there is a fixed amount of resources invested by the other party, and what we want is a system under which both parties *ex ante* will invest the optimum amount. In other words, we want the sum of the cost of the resources invested by each party, together with the expectancy of the accidents, to be minimized. The intent is that the decisions on the allocation of the cost of the accident, after the accident, will be such that they give the parties the right *ex ante* incentives to invest the appropriate amount.

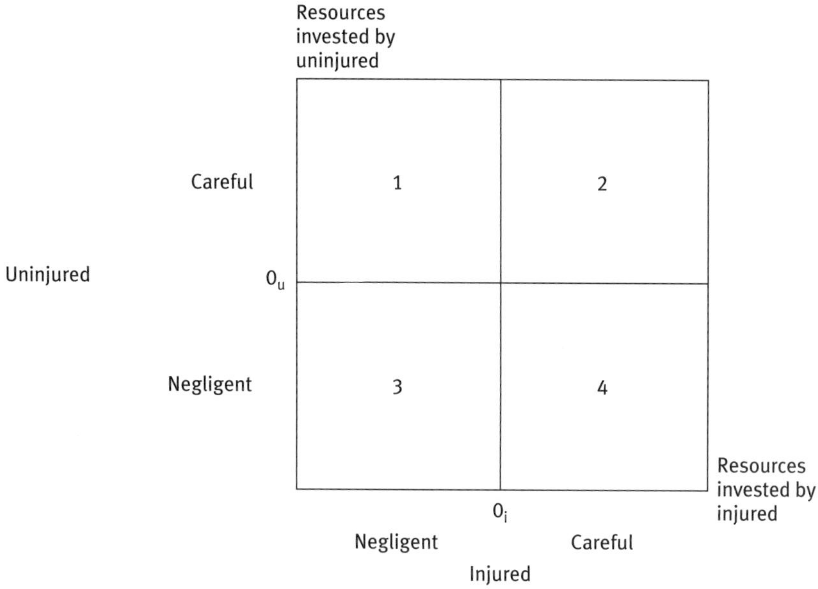

FIGURE 2

In Figure 2, we show the resources which had been invested to prevent accidents by the injured on the horizontal axis and those by the uninjured on the vertical axis. Expectancy of injury and the cost of prevention, in essence, are presented on a vertical axis sticking out of the paper, but we need not draw them in. It is clear that there would be one point on this figure which minimizes the net social cost. This is the point where the lines 0_i and 0_u cross and is in the center of the diagram for drafting convenience. Thus, good social policy should aim at getting each party to invest that appropriate amount of resources. Note that this puts an extreme burden of calculation on the individuals who have to guess what the other is doing, and on the courts, who, *ex post*, have to make all these calculations.[7] This is indeed the basis of my general dislike of this system, but for this article we will assume the calculations can and will be made.

I have numbered the four quarters of this diagram in order to simplify discussion. Square 3 is where both have been careless—i.e., have underinvested

7. The difficulty is increased when concern is given to the possibility that it is often cheaper for the parties to act jointly to avoid the harm than for either to act on his own. See Gary T. Schwartz, "Contributory Negligence: A Reappraisal" (1978) 87 Yale Law Journal 697.

in resources—and, hence, there is a socially inadequate amount of resource investment and too many accidents. Square 2 is the counterpart, the case in which both parties have been careful; but note that all points in Square 2, except the point at the intersection in the middle of the diagram, actually involve an excessive investment in accident prevention.

Square 4 is the square where the uninjured has invested an inadequate number of resources to prevent accidents, but the injured has invested an adequate amount. It is the one case where under traditional tort law[8] the uninjured is compelled to pay the injured for his damages. The remaining square, Square 1, is one that has largely been ignored in the discussion of this problem but, as we shall see below, is of very considerable importance. Here the injured person has been negligent and the uninjured person exerted care—for example, a pedestrian stepping in the way of an oncoming car. The law is perfectly clear that in this case the injury is entirely borne by the injured and the uninjured person has no liability.

Why then is this system efficient; i.e., why does it lead each party to invest exactly the optimum amount of resources? The answer is simply that the intersection of the two lines of optimum is an equilibrium for each party as well as the social optimum. Consider, for example, the injured person. Before the accident occurred, if he was contemplating how much resources he should put into accident prevention, he would realize that there is some probability of his being in an accident and, using the reasoning of Figure 1, if the uninjured had invested 0_u resources, he would find that the AA curve was so positioned that optimum for him was the 0_i of Figure 2. If he invested more resources than 0_i, he will purchase less in accident prevention than its cost. If he invests less resources, he will fail to avert some accidents whose costs were greater than the cost of avoiding them. Since he pays the full cost of the accident, he should make the right marginal decision.[9]

The situation is similar with respect to the uninjured. If the injured person, in the period before the accident, has invested the socially optimal amount, or 0_i, then if the uninjured invests less than 0_u resources, this will lead to additional accidents which will cost more than the cost of preventing them. Further, under the negligence rule, the uninjured will have to pay for these accidents and therefore is motivated to the optimal investment. If he invests

8. *United States* v. *Carroll Towing Co., supra*, n. 1.

9. These efficiency arguments implicitly assume that the parties do not have insurance. The point is further discussed below.

more than 0_u resources, he is preventing accidents, which will have a lower expectancy than the cost of prevention. Further, in this case, the cost of these accidents will fall entirely on the injured rather than on him, so, in a way, the actual cost to him of accidents drops to 0 at 0_u.

Note that if either party thinks that the other party is adopting a resource investment different from the social optimum, then his own optimum is characteristically not the social optimum. But, following the kind of reasoning usually used in this kind of game situation, the optimum of the second party is such that the first party should change his investment, et cetera, et cetera, and the eventual outcome (assuming perfect knowledge, et cetera) will inevitably be the intersection between 0_u and 0_i.

Since the sum of the expectancy of the accident and the investment resources by the two parties in accident prevention is always higher as you move away from the social optimum, it will always be to the interest of at least one of the parties to change his resource investment to be closer to his social optimum if, by chance, the two parties have chosen resource investments other than that at the optimum. Only at the optimum is each party playing the best strategy, granted the strategy of the other party. We do not, of course, assume that such a game is taking place, but that the parties each anticipate that the other will anticipate his decision. This leads to the same outcome. In a way, this simply is another version of the perfect information assumption.

Note that so far I have not mentioned Square 3, where both parties are negligent. The situation here is, as we shall see at greater length below, rather complicated, but for our current strict equilibrium argument the area can largely be ignored. If the uninjured has invested 0_u, then the best reply is 0_i. It would be so even if the rule for Square 3 was that the uninjured had to pay damages, because as long as the injured invests 0_u there is no way of getting into Square 3.

Nevertheless, Square 3 does have some effect if either party, instead of following a strict equilibrium strategy, acts on the suspicion that the other may have made a mistake. For example, the injured might feel that it is likely the uninjured will have underinvested and, hence, will be found negligent. Then the arguments for the injured investing 0_i are even stronger, since there will be additional accidents, and he can only be compensated for them if he invests at 0_i.

For the uninjured, the reasoning is interesting enough in the other direction. If he suspects that the potentially injured person is underinvesting resources, then the optimum for him is to underinvest also because in at least some of the accidents caused by his underinvestment he will not have to pay the damages, and, hence, the cost of accidents for him, although not the actual number of accidents, is reduced. However, these would not be equilibria.

So much for the standard system. Let us turn now to "strict liability." Under this system, the uninjured pays the full cost of the accident unless the injured person has been negligent.[10] On Figure 2 he will pay damages, not only if the situation is in Square 4 but also if it is in Square 2, i.e., in the situation where both parties have been careful. This system is equally efficient on the same assumptions. We can, however, go through the reasoning ourselves. Once again, assume that the person who is going to be injured when the accident occurs thinks the person who will be uninjured has invested 0_u resources. Under these circumstances, if the injured person has invested 0_i, then he will be reimbursed for all accidents; whereas if he has invested less than 0_i, he will not. Clearly, his incentives to invest 0_i are high, and if he invests more than 0_i, the only effect is to reduce the number of accidents, which lowers the liability of the uninjured.

Similarly, for the uninjured. If he assumes that the person to be injured in the accident has invested 0_i, then he is going to pay the full cost of all accidents. Under the circumstances, he should invest 0_u, which is the amount which gives him the lowest combined accident prevention and expectancy of accident cost.

Once again, in the contributory negligence square, i.e., 3, we have the same rather peculiar circumstance. If the person to be injured believes that the uninjured person has been negligent and underinvested, this gives him a stronger incentive to invest 0_i, but if the person who is not to be injured believes that the person who will be injured has underinvested, this would lead to a decision to invest less than 0_u on his part.

So far we have simply duplicated the existing literature, but now we suggest the existence of several additional efficient schemes. For simplicity, I have outlined four schemes on Figure 3. In each of the four panels of Figure 3, one of the various possible rules is shown by shading those squares in which the uninjured is compelled to pay the injured. Thus, in Figure 3a, the square in which the uninjured has been negligent and the injured has been careful is the only one shaded. This is the traditional system. In Figure 3b, both that

10. Note that "strict liability" in the theoretical literature is not identical to the concept in those law codes which actually make use of it.

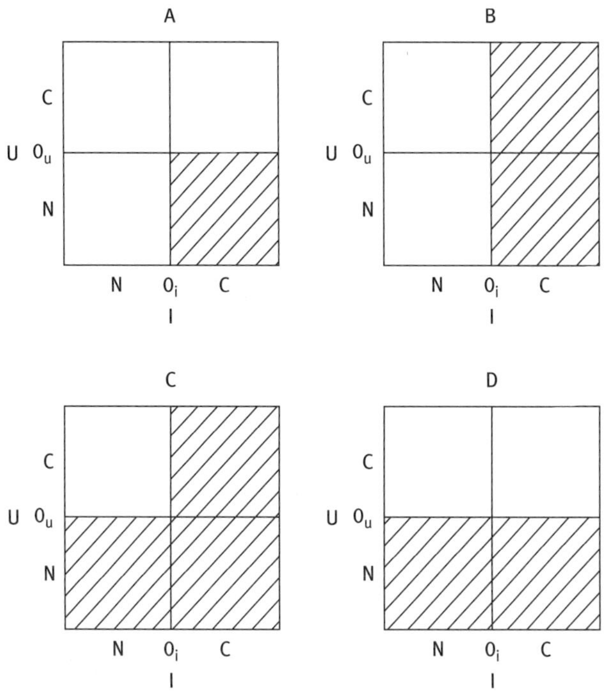

FIGURE 3

square and the square in which both have been careful are shaded, because under strict liability the uninjured is compelled to pay damages in this case too.

Let us now proceed to Figure 3d, which is in many ways the converse of Figure 3b. In Figure 3b, the injured person bore the full cost of the damages if he was careless and was reimbursed by the uninjured if he was not careless, regardless of the behavior of the uninjured. In Figure 3d, the uninjured person bears the full cost if he is negligent and no cost if he is careful, regardless of the behavior of the injured person. Once again, let us go through our familiar line of reasoning. If the person who will not be injured has invested 0_u resources, then the injured will bear the full cost of any injury and, hence, is motivated to invest exactly 0_i because that is the quantity which minimizes the sum of the cost of accident prevention and expectancy of injury to him. Similarly, if the person who will not himself be injured thinks that the person who is potentially to be injured has invested 0_i, then if he invests less than 0_u he will bear the full cost of all accidents caused by his negligence, and the expectancy of this cost is greater than the cost of taking 0_u precautions.

There is, however, here one minor reversal. We considered, above, the possibility with respect to accident prevention activities. In this case, it will be the uninjured whose estimate that the other has underinvested leads him to even more strongly favor investing 0_u. On the other hand, the person who is potentially the injured should respond to his estimate of an underinvestment for resource prevention by his counterpart by reducing his own investment below 0_i.

We now proceed on to Figure 3c, which is the converse of the standard negligence–contributory negligence system of tort law. In this case, the uninjured must pay damages unless he has been careful and the injured person has been negligent. In all other cases he pays damages. This is the converse of standard tort law, where the person who is physically injured bears the full cost unless he has been careful and the other party has been negligent. I shall not try the patience of the reader by going through a demonstration that this is efficient. It follows the same rules as before. Note that in this case, as in Figure 3d, the incentives in the square where both are negligent are the opposite of those in Figures 3a and 3b.

Here we have four basically efficient systems using the standard lines of reasoning, and, as I shall show in a few moments, there is a fifth. Let us pause here and consider this set. Using the payoffs of Figure 2, it is obvious that it makes no difference for efficiency at this level what is done with accidents falling in Square 2.[11] It is a simple wealth transfer from one party to the other. Distributive justice is involved here, but in this article I propose to avoid such ethical considerations. On the other hand, squares 1 and 4, where one party has been careful and the other has been negligent, are of vital importance, and it will be noted in all four of our systems, squares 1 and 4 are treated the same way. The person who has been negligent bears the full cost, and the person who has not been negligent bears no cost. The final square, the one where both have been negligent, apparently makes relatively little difference. We have demonstrated efficiency, with the entire burden of accidents in this square falling on the uninjured and with them falling on the injured. There are other systems in which the damages are divided 50–50, as in traditional maritime law or according to relative negligence. These also are efficient. It will always be true that since the sum of the accident prevention cost and

11. Polinsky's argument for efficiency on different grounds will be discussed further below. A. Mitchell Polinsky, "Strict Liability Versus Negligence in a Market Setting" (1980) 70 American Economic Review 363.

expected cost of accidents for the two parties is greater in this square than at the optimum point, one of them has an incentive to move from this square to the optimum. If he so moves, then the other also has such an incentive. The details of the incentives, however, may lead to oddments in this square, such as the one we discussed above, where one party, if he assumes that the other party has made a mistake by underinvesting resources, may be led to underinvest himself. There doesn't seem much point in discussing these details, however, because the institutions in this area are so varying and they are all efficient.

Let us now turn to our fifth efficient system.[12] Under this system, the uninjured party is assessed the full cost of the accident to the injured party regardless of why the accident occurred. This cost, however, is not paid to the injured party but instead is paid to all other people who might have had accidents but didn't. This rather bizarre-sounding rule, which frankly I do not believe any court would ever enforce, has very good efficiency characteristics because both parties would pay the full cost of the accident, and, hence, both parties would invest resources out to the point where their marginal return on prevention of accidents is equal to the expectancy. Hence, we will end up at the optimum.

I have always had difficulty taking this particular rule seriously, because of the enforcement difficulties. The police would have to detect accidents, and an individual badly injured, largely through the carelessness of someone else, might find himself presented with a large bill which would be the quantity of the injuries suffered by the careless person in the accident. It would not go to the careless person but would be distributed to all other drivers. Juries would surely refuse to enforce the law.

The actual payment of these funds to other people who are in the same industry, or driving cars, or whatever caused the particular accident and were not involved in the accident, is necessary in order to make certain that this payment which involves imposing double cost on the people participating in the accident does not have the effect of reducing the total volume of activity in this industry or activity below its social optimum. It is bizarre but theoretically efficient.

We thus now have five different systems, all of which can be argued to be efficient in the same sense that the current literature indicates the

12. This system was apparently first invented by Earl Thompson, but like so many things invented by Thompson, it has been circulated as part of the oral tradition at the University of California–Los Angeles rather than being put in print.

negligence–contributory negligence system is efficient. We obviously must choose among them by some method other than efficiency, since they are all equally efficient under these schemes. Before we turn to discussing how such choice should be made, however, let us briefly mention several systems which would be inefficient. The first of these is, in essence, the opposite of our last one—one in which the full cost of the accident is paid from a tax on all other participants in whatever activity it was in which the accident occurred. This is more or less the spirit, albeit certainly not the practice, of the no-fault insurance scheme. Obviously, it is inefficient, since individuals would lose when they invested resources in accident prevention.[13]

A second scheme is one in which there is automatic liability for the uninjured party regardless of fault of the two parties. This is more or less what our current industrial accident laws normally provide and, once again, is inefficient by the rules we have been describing so far, although, like the no-fault insurance, it may indeed be efficient on other considerations. Lastly, it would, of course, be possible to leave the injured person with no remedy against the other party to the transaction. This also is clearly inefficient, although we do use it in a number of areas.

We thus have eight possible ways of dealing with accident costs. This list of eight is, of course, by no means comprehensive. Further, I have confined myself to those accidents in which only one party is injured. Nevertheless, even among this set of eight, we have five that are, by the assumptions which have become conventional since Learned Hand's decision, efficient and three that are inefficient. If we look at the real world, however, we find that two of the efficient schemes—contributory negligence and "strict liability"—are in actual use, together with all three of the inefficient systems. Three of the efficient systems, my figures 3c and 3d and the double liability system, are, so far as I know, used nowhere.[14]

How do we choose among these various systems? The first thing to be said is that if we assume that everybody is able to make the perfect

13. One of the referees suggested that if the tax were assessed in terms of investment of resources in accident prevention, then the system would be efficient. This is, of course, true but administratively probably impossible.

14. Something like the double liability system is used for many crimes. The person responsible is fined or otherwise hurt, but the person injured is not reimbursed. It is arguable that Figure 3c does feature in those systems which use the device of *res ipsa loquitur* in their negligent action. Under this, Figure 3d is presumed to be negligent unless he can show that he was sufficiently careful.

calculations, which the reasoning normally used to indicate that the negligence–contributory negligence system is efficient does rather assume, then, the wealth transfer which we would observe as we worked from my Figure 3a to my Figure 3c would be cancelled. If I sell someone a potentially dangerous product which may injure him, then under the legal structure as shown in Figure 3a, I would have to charge him less than I would if the actual structure was as in Figure 3c. *Ex ante* we would be indifferent between the two situations.

Polinsky argues that the perfect calculation of this sort is not likely and, in fact, that purchasers are apt to underestimate their likelihood of damages.[15] Thus, if we are using the system of Figure 3a, sellers will actually be bearing less of the risk than they should, and the industry will be expanded to a larger size than is desirable even though each individual accident will have the right investment of resources in prevention.

I don't agree with Polinsky about the purchaser's inability to make these calculations, but it seems to me that at the present stage neither of us can offer much beyond a personal opinion here. Empirical research would be desirable. Nevertheless, I feel that the kind of consideration that Polinsky raises should be taken into account in making decisions even if I disagree with him in this particular case.

Epstein argues for a very broad liability, essentially on the grounds that it is easier for the courts to enforce. They need only inquire whether the injured person was injured and not whether anyone was negligent.[16] This is clearly an easier task than the standard tort damage system. Here again, although I am not sure that empirical tests would show all that much was gained in simplifying court procedure, I think that he is on the right track. In both of these cases we need further investigation, and in making this investigation we should not confine ourselves to just two of the efficient schemes but consider all five and, for that matter, consider schemes that are inefficient in the rather narrow parameters of the problem as conventionally discussed. After all, the

15. A. Mitchell Polinsky, "Strict Liability Versus Negligence in a Market Setting," *supra*, n. 11.

16. In a way, Epstein reintroduces contributory negligence through the back door. It is my understanding that a pedestrian who carelessly stepped in front of a car and was injured by the car would not be able to collect, because Epstein would say that he had not been hit by the car but had hit the car. It seems a bizarre use of the English language, and I would prefer to say the pedestrian was careless whereas the driver had not been. Richard A. Epstein, *A Theory of Strict Liability*, Cato Institute (1980).

social decision to use industrial accident codes, no-fault insurance, and total absence of liability in some cases is at least some indication that these two may be valid choices.

Looking at the matter more generally: Accidents can be divided into two categories, one in which the injured and uninjured parties are involved in some kind of transaction in which, from the beginning, it is obvious which of them is going to be injured if anyone is. For example, if I buy some of Mrs. Stouffer's frozen food, she is not going to be poisoned but I might be. The employment contract is another example of the same thing. In these cases, at least in theory, parties can enter into an efficient arrangement among themselves. I do not normally recommend this, but for that minority of contracts which are the result of careful and lengthy consideration between skilled parties on both sides, this does indeed seem the best arrangement.

The existence of law codes which set up liability for injury in these cases will, if everyone makes perfect calculations, have an effect on the price at which the transaction is carried out but on nothing else. The parties will fully discount the liability so that the price, after liability has been taken care of, will remain constant as we move over the first four of my efficient cases. For the fifth efficient case, we have to prevent negotiation between the two parties; if they reach agreement they are certain to invest too much money in accident prevention, because the accident will cost them twice as much as its true social cost. The inefficient systems would also lead to different prices, but, of course, they would also have certain other elements of inefficiency.

The second type of accident is one in which the parties have no previous contact. The automobile accident, the commonest single cause of tort litigation, is the obvious case. In this case, I can see no significant argument for any one of my five efficient systems except that some of them are somewhat easier for the courts to enforce.

Normally, the above argument assumes that everybody is perfectly informed and, hence, that the market price always exactly discounts the situation. This assumption is probably not perfectly accurate but, I suppose, is the natural one to follow if one is using the kind of perfect information which the traditional line of reasoning we have been using so far implies for the people making decisions as to how many resources they will put into preventing accidents. As a matter of fact, it seems to me that it is far more likely that the price system will properly discount the institutions, whatever they are, than that the individuals will in fact make the perfect decisions as to the resources to be invested in accident prevention under these rules.

Simplifying the task of the courts and making them more accurate is, of course, a second argument to be used in choosing among systems to deal with arguments. Since I have talked a great deal about this in my two books,[17] I shall not discuss it more here, but only say that under various circumstances it does provide fairly strong arguments for each of the three inefficient systems that I have listed above. They may reduce the probable litigation cost in areas where errors by the courts are highly probable.

So far we have ignored a final argument which was much pushed when I was in law school. Insurance against accidents is readily available, and we used to talk about various liability rules, primarily in terms of who was the most convenient person to buy the insurance. Note that this consideration is different from another reference to insurance which is found in the literature. It is frequently suggested that although nobody ever pays an automobile accident claim himself, it is always paid by his insurance company, nevertheless the system is still efficient because it puts appropriate pressure on the insurance company to put the appropriate pressure on its policyholders. I am rather dubious about this argument because it seems to me that the control that insurance companies have over their policyholders is far from detailed, and, hence, although they can do something by varying rates across various risk clauses, the amount they can do is not very great. Nevertheless, this particular "use" of insurance is a part of the negligence–contributory negligence efficiency argument which has been discussed above.

What I wish to talk about here, however, is a somewhat older argument which assumes, more or less, that people don't want accidents, regardless of the distribution of liability, and, hence, that the decision as to who is the most convenient purchaser of the insurance is to be made simply on administrative terms. For example, a restaurant owner does not want people poisoned in his restaurant for obvious business reasons, regardless of whose insurance company will actually pay the cost. Moreover, in a competitive market, presumably he can recover his insurance premiums without difficulty. It was therefore argued in tort classes in law school that it would be fairly easy for the restaurant owner to purchase an insurance policy governing all customers in his restaurant for a year, whereas expecting each individual to purchase a little insurance policy when he entered the restaurant was obviously an administrative impossibility. Retrospectively, I find this argument

17. G. Tullock, *The Logic of the Law*, Basic Books (1971). G. Tullock, *Trials on Trial*, Columbia University Press (1980).

embarrassingly inadequate, but I must say that, at the time, it seemed to me convincing.

The fallacy in the argument, of course, is the assumption that the person who is worried about being poisoned in restaurants must buy a set of separate individual policies every time he enters a restaurant. There is no reason why he cannot simply, on an annual basis, buy coverage against accidental injury, including accidental poisoning. Such policies are apt to be very much more efficient administratively than having the restaurant do it, because of the much greater simplicity involved in dealing with your own insurance company as opposed to dealing with an adversary insurance company.

Although insurance companies do not always make payments to their own policyholders, they have every incentive to see to it that litigation costs are minimized and that their reputation for paying promptly is maintained. Further, there will be no problem determining negligence or contributory negligence, because the insurance policy would simply cover injury regardless of cause. Lastly, there would be no problem of determining the actual value of whatever injury occurs, because the insurance policy at the time of purchase can have incorporated in it a list of payments for various kinds of injuries. This is, in fact, characteristic of personal injury policies.

Perhaps I should digress a little bit here and remark that this kind of policy does not seem to be very widely held. This may be because of the almost universal ownership of medical insurance, but, still, people should be interested in coverage against pain and suffering of accidents. They don't seem to be. I myself, for example, carry liability insurance for my automobile but no collision insurance to cover my own car. I also have a comprehensive policy on my home which, in addition to giving me fire protection, protects me against being sued by anyone who is injured on my property. I think my coverage is rather typical.

Why people do not have personal injury policies in much larger numbers than they do is something of a mystery. I suspect it has to do with problems of the way courts, in fact, would treat damage suits subrogated to the insurance company by people holding this kind of insurance. This is a mere suspicion, and, once again, empirical investigation would be sensible.

Returning to our main theme: The point of this article has been very largely to indicate that a very large part of the current economic discussion of tort law is misplaced. Attaining efficiency in the perfect information context of these discussions is fairly easy; indeed there are five ways of doing it. The choice among those five must be made on some grounds other than this kind of efficiency. Further, once we turn to other criteria, then additional methods of dealing with accidents which are not "efficient" in the same way that negligence–contributory negligence is are brought into the discussion. There has been too much concentration on a narrow definition of efficiency in this area. I have been unable here to offer proof that one system is better than another. I regret this, but although I cannot solve the problem, I have tried here to put the discussion on a more comprehensive basis.

WELFARE AND THE LAW

I propose in this paper to explain what I think are the proper criteria for judging law. The early part of the paper, however, is to be devoted to the more negative task of a critique of what are perhaps the most widely used welfare criteria. These criteria are used by Posner[1] in almost all of his work and, in view of his influence in the field, have been copied by many other people.

Let us begin, however, with matters upon which Posner and I agree. We both accept the Pigou point that the government should internalize externalities, and the Coase point that many externalities can be internalized by private agreement. The role of government, then, is internalizing externalities in those cases where transaction costs make private arrangements difficult or impossible.

Posner and I are in agreement so far. There is some difference between us, however, in our attitude towards the other major function of the law, which is transferring wealth back and forth in the population. In part, this wealth transfer is generally approved. Most of us favor some help for the poor, although there are great differences as to how much and who should pay for it. The very large transfers that exist in most modern societies, however, are not aimed at helping the poor, whatever the rationalization that is used. In fact, they are transfers to people who have succeeded in manipulating the political machine in order to receive them and from people who have been less successful. Posner has done little research in this area. In one important article, however,[2] Posner indicates that, like me,[3] he understands and disapproves of these transfers. His major work, however, turns almost entirely on those cases where transfer is a sort of by-product of a lawsuit on some other topic.

Reprinted from *International Review of Law and Economics* 1 (June 1982): 151–63, copyright 1982, with permission from Elsevier.

1. His book summarizes his general position and has been read by more people than most of the things he has written. See R. A. Posner, *Economic Analysis of the Law*, 2d ed. (Boston and Toronto, Canada: Little, Brown, 1977).

2. "The Social Cost of Monopoly and Regulation," *Journal of Political Economy* 83 (1975): 807–27. Reprinted in *Toward a Theory of the Rent-Seeking Society*, ed. J. M. Buchanan and R. D. Tollison (College Station: Texas A&M University Press, 1980).

3. I have a considerable number of articles and a forthcoming book, *The Economics of Redistribution* (Boston: Kluwer-Nijhoff, 1982), which summarize my position.

In any event, I regard these transfers as part of the positive law, although normatively I disapprove.

We now come to a criterion which is more controversial. Posner feels that the law should attempt to provide whatever relation between the parties they would have chosen had transactions cost not prevented it. He appears to believe that this, in general, would be the wealth-maximizing choice. Leaving aside transfers, I also think the law, and indeed government as a whole, exists for the purpose of providing an institutional alternative to private contract in those areas where private contract is too expensive through transactions cost.[4] But he further believes that the law should attempt to provide that bargain which would have been reached without transactions cost. On this point, I disagree.

Before explaining why I disagree, however, I should like to discuss further the other criteria which Posner has used. He has argued very strongly that wealth maximization should be the objective of the law and, in essence, argues that this is an appropriate moral goal. I have no particular objection to the view that, in general, law should be designed so as to maximize total wealth in society;[5] but I doubt that it is correctly defined as a moral goal.

There are two problems. The first, essentially a false one, is that I would, of course, prefer increasing utility to increasing wealth. In this I am like most economists and, I believe, like Posner himself. He, like most economists, frequently aims at maximizing wealth simply because it is very difficult in the multi-person society to determine just which variables will increase utility. There are a few cases where a definitive judgment decision is possible; for example, most people are risk averse, but frequently we are forced to use wealth or income as a proxy for increasing utility.[6] The second problem is a real one and involves the nature of moral judgment.

I think one could argue that the true moralist would not object to wealth maximization provided it did not contravene whatever moral code the

4. See G. Tullock, *Private Wants, Public Means: An Economic Analysis of the Desirable Scope of Government* (New York: Basic Books, 1970).

5. The use of total terms here is somewhat inconvenient, since, obviously, what we are really interested in are individual utilities which are not very easily comparable, but the total term does not lead to any great difference from the more complex building of the rule from individual utilities. See G. Tullock, *The Logic of the Law* (New York: Basic Books, 1971).

6. Occasionally Posner seems to actually prefer wealth maximization to increasing utility. See, for example, "A Reply to Some Recent Criticisms of the Efficiency Theory of the Common Law," *Hofstra Law Review* 9 (1981), 775–94, especially the second paragraph on p. 791.

moralist happened to have. Further, most moral codes aim, in part, at making people better off, and wealth maximization, of course, does have that characteristic. Nevertheless, insofar as I know, no moralist would agree with Posner that wealth maximization is in and of itself the ultimate moral rule. There are innumerable different moral codes in the world, but I think that all of them have at least some goal which is held higher than wealth maximization, so that wealth maximization should on occasion be abandoned to meet that higher goal. What this higher goal is, of course, varies immensely from culture to culture and from individual moral philosopher to individual moral philosopher, but they agree in denying wealth maximization as the ultimate moral goal. It seems to me, in this particular area, Posner can fairly easily rescue himself by adopting the more modest claim that wealth maximization is desirable.

Let us turn to the proposition that government should exist solely to take care of those situations where voluntary contract is impossible because of high transactions costs. I have no quarrel with this position. It does not, however, completely describe government activity. It would appear that governments originally were constructed for the specific purpose of transferring funds, specifically from the governed to the governors. They have retained transfer functions throughout their history, and some of these transfer functions, modest assistance to the poor, are favored by a substantial majority.[7] If we remove from consideration, at least temporarily, the assistance to the poor or general transfer to politically influential people, then we are left with a government performing acts where the transactions costs are so high as to prevent private contract.

In some cases, however, "transactions costs" have to be rather severely distorted in order to put government activity under that rubric. In the case of crime, for example, we can regard the law against burglary as a way of reducing transactions cost, but it involves a rather bizarre way of looking at reality.[8] The same is true of military activity, funding of research, and such direct government services as road construction and weather prediction. Nevertheless, all of these can, "with a sort of mental squint,"[9] be regarded as government action where transactions costs are too high. But it seems to me that this is less informative than saying that these are areas where wealth can be increased by government action.

7. Many people would, of course, favor vastly more in the way of transfers by government.

8. G. Tullock, "The Welfare Cost of Monopolies, Tariffs, and Theft," *Western Economic Journal* 5 (1967), 224–32.

9. Lewis Carroll, "Poeta Fit, Non Nascitur," *The Lewis Carroll Book* (Tudor, N.Y., 1939).

Posner's approach in this area in essence originated with Ronald Coase's article, "The Problem of Social Cost." This article dealt with an example in law of torts, and in many ways the problem is most readily examined in that field. Let us then turn to a particular example which I used before.[10] Posner says:

> Another common law rule was that a railroad owned no duty of care to people using the tracks as paths (except at crossings). The cost to these "trespassers" of using alternative paths would generally be small in comparison to the cost to the railroad of making the tracks safe for them. The railroad's right, however, was a qualified one: the railroad was required to keep a careful lookout for trespassing cattle. It would be very costly for farmers to erect fences that absolutely prevented cattle from straying, so we would expect that, if transactions between farmers and railroads were feasible, farmers would frequently pay railroads to keep a careful lookout for animals on the track.[11]

Note that in this case Posner argues that the law should achieve the goal which would have been achieved had the farmers been able to make an agreement with the railroads. In the above-cited comment, I argued that it is by no means obvious that that would have been accepted as the wealth-maximizing rule or what the farmers would agree with the railroads on. Let us, however, leave that problem aside and assume that Posner is correct here, because I am interested in his welfare procedure, not in the details of this application. So, we shall assume that if the parties had reached a voluntary and transaction costless agreement they would have agreed that it was cheaper for the railroad to keep a sharp lookout for cattle than for the farmers to build fences. Further, they agreed that it was cheaper for humans either to not trespass or to keep a sharp lookout if they did than it was for railroads to keep a sharp lookout for human beings.[12] Does this prove that that is the right law? I would

10. G. Tullock, "Two Kinds of Legal Efficiency," *Hofstra Law Review* 8 (1980), 659–68.

11. R. A. Posner, *Economic Analysis of the Law*.

12. I believe that Posner misunderstands the idea in the minds of the judges. I suspect very strongly that the judges who created this particular rule thought that only an extremely negligent person would be on the railroad tracks at a time when a train, making large amounts of noise and, for that matter, making the tracks and roadbed vibrate ahead of it, hit him. I realize that this is not what the judges said, but when I was in law school I was taught to pay less attention to what judges said than to the facts of the case and their actual decisions. Thus, in my opinion, this is a simple illustration of the usual contributory negligence rule which Posner, as well as most other writers in this field, thinks is efficient.

say the answer is clearly no, because a great many costs have been left out. In other words, it is not truthfully wealth maximizing.

Let us consider the existence of this law from the standpoint of the two parties and look at all the costs that they face. The first cost would obviously be that both parties must invest at least some resources in finding out what the rule is. In this case, the resources would probably be very small; but we should not totally ignore them. Secondly, the parties will then invest resources to some extent in carrying out the rule. That is, the people or potential trespassers will avoid getting on the railroad track under conditions in which they could not get off quickly if they heard a train coming. The railroad company will, insofar as it is physically possible to do this, take precautions against running over animals but not against running over adult human beings. The latter distinction might be a rather fine one for them to make.

Let us suppose that an accident does occur, and the law must be applied. The two parties will consult attorneys. There may be a settlement out of court or there may be a settlement in court. In any event, total legal cost is apt to be quite sizeable. The best estimates that I have been able to uncover, admittedly not very good,[13] indicate that the total legal costs at this stage are apt to be in the general range of one-half to the full amount of damage done by the accident.

There is eventually, in this case, a decision. There may be some costs involved in complying with the decision; but there is another and more important cost. The decision may be wrong. If the court does reach a wrong decision, and surely courts do occasionally, that decision in a direct sense imposes costs. In an indirect sense it imposes even further costs by reducing the estimate of the probabilities that the law will be carried out correctly in the minds of the two parties. This should affect their behavior.

The rule used by Posner attempts to minimize only a small part of this total chain of costs. The part which he minimizes, admittedly an important part, is by no means all. We would anticipate that a truly efficient rule would attempt to minimize this whole chain of costs and, hence, maximize wealth. But even if we consider only the portion of the transaction which Posner minimizes, the sum of the cost of preventing action by the two parties and the damages, it is not obvious that the decision he gives is the correct one.

13. They are simply the estimates offered by a number of experienced lawyers with whom I have discussed the matter.

I do not quarrel with its efficiency within this particular narrow scope. Unfortunately, however, there are five other rules that are efficient.[14] These five separate rules, all of which are efficient under the specific circumstances, differ in their distributional impact. If we consider a voluntary transaction between the railroad and people who might conceivably trespass, one can assume that the trespassers would prefer that rule which transferred the most resources to them,[15] while the railroad would favor that which had the most favorable distributional consequence for it. There does not seem to be any efficiency motive for choosing between the two. Thus, strict liability, which is one of these rules, or negligence–contributory negligence cannot be distinguished by this very simple efficiency criterion.[16]

Voluntary transactions would clearly involve the use of resources by each party to attempt to distribute the gains from an efficient solution to himself. Such bargaining costs are probably not very important in the law of negligence, but they are of real importance when we turn to contracts below. Meanwhile, we should simply note that there is no obvious outcome to a voluntary transaction in this particular case. Let us, however, skip the point; assume that one of the five systems has been selected, perhaps arbitrarily, and continue with our line of reasoning.

We can perhaps summarize the various types of costs which are involved here under five categories.

1. There is the cost of calculation, of determining what is the appropriate course of action by each party.
2. There is the cost of the actual precautions taken by the two parties.
3. There is the cost of the accidents.

The second and third of these costs are those which are used in the conventional economic discussion of negligence. As we have noted above, they do not necessarily lead to any specific outcome, since there are a number of

14. See G. Tullock, "Negligence Again," *International Review of Law and Economics* 1 (1981), 51–62.

15. Unless they were also customers.

16. In this particular case it is conceivable that one could choose among the five rules because they would have different effects on the frequency with which the trespassers and the railroads undertook their activities. I doubt that it is important here, but certainly, in the overwhelmingly commonest case of tort liability, automobile accidents, this particular factor has no effect.

different solutions, all of which minimize them. We have, however, at this point, by no means finished our discussion of the costs.

4. There is, then, a legal cost which grows out of the accident if an accident occurs.
5. There are the costs of errors. Here we are considering, in terms of errors, only errors made by the court. The individual parties may make errors in their initial calculation as to what is an appropriate course of action, and these errors also impose costs, but we include them back in our first calculation category.

The errors made by the court will be discussed here as simply imposing costs by compelling the innocent party to pay damages or, alternatively, relieving the guilty party from paying damages. The prospective error, i.e., the fact that the parties know that the courts do make some errors, will be put into an earlier stage in the reasoning. Specifically, we shall assume that the parties, when they make up their minds as to what their legal duties are, include an error term on the theory that the courts will not be perfect, in addition to the error term which represents the possibility that the other party will have made a miscalculation.

Once the parties begin calculating the possibility that the courts will be in error, their own behavior will not be the same as it would be had they assumed the courts would perfectly carry out whatever the legal rule is.[17] Thus, the cost-minimizing rule which would be required, assuming that this kind of error should be taken into account, would be different from that which involves the assumption that everybody behaves perfectly.

Clearly this collection of costs is quite different from that in general use in the conventional economic discussion of negligence. Further, it is not at all obvious whether these additional costs may not be much larger than the costs taken into account in conventional discussion. In any event, any optimal legal system should certainly attempt to minimize all of these costs and not just that portion which was mentioned by Learned Hand in his famous decision.[18]

Let us go through them one at a time, beginning with the individual parties attempting to calculate their best course of action. The first thing to be

17. G. Tullock, *Trials on Trial: The Pure Theory of Legal Procedure* (New York: Columbia University Press, 1980), 34–48.

18. *United States v. Carroll Towing Co.*, 159 F. 2d 169 (2d Cir. 1947).

said here, with respect to most cases of negligence (perhaps not the specific problem of the trespasser on the railroad tracks), is that if people in their daily lives regularly calculated the course of action on their part which would lead to lack of liability or, alternatively, which would permit them to collect in the event that the other party is found careless, an immense amount of energy would go into this activity. Further, most of us would not even be able to make the appropriate calculations while, for example, driving a car. This is no doubt a good rationalization for the reasonable-man rule so widely used.

We do not compel the individual to make a series of individual calculations for every second of his driving time; we merely assume that he will act as a reasonable man would[19] in a given case, i.e., follow the habits of driving which most people have. Even where he is confronted with an unusual situation in which he does not have any established habit nor do the members of the jury, we do not assume that he should put a great deal of time into thinking over the efficient system. We do think that he should consider his situation in those circumstances, but only as much as a reasonable man should.

I do not argue here that the reasonable-man rule, as currently applied, is a perfectly designed instrument for minimizing the calculating costs. I merely point out that it aims in that direction and, hence, that substituting the reasonable-man rule for the complex calculations of minimizing total costs may well be socially desirable in many cases. In essence, it says that individuals should only engage in as much calculation as a reasonable man should, and we can charitably interpret this as minimizing joint costs of the accident, prevention of accident, and calculation. As far as I know, this particular formalization has never been used in any instruction to a jury.

We should pause here to point out the very general existence of liability insurance. A reasonable man who has an insurance company which will bear damage liability[20] may take this into account and underestimate the damage he will do to other people. In the particular case of automobile accidents, I doubt that this is of great importance, since the prospect of very severe injury to any individual, in such accidents, makes most people try to avoid them. Perhaps drivers tend to underestimate the actual social costs of

19. In general, the reasonable man can safely follow law or custom, whatever it is and whether it is efficient or not in the particular circumstances.

20. And which may, and then again may not, increase his premiums after that event. But in any event, the increase in premiums will be much less than the payment of damages.

injuries to pedestrians for this reason. Nevertheless, the existence of insurance should be taken into account by the individual in deciding both his course of action and how much time he should spend in trying to calculate an appropriate course of action. If he does take this into account, then, at best, the cost of the accident to him is his own injuries plus some possible change in his insurance premium. If he lives in one of the states that have adopted a no-fault insurance system, then the impact on him of an accident is radically different from the social costs, and, if he is sensible and makes correct calculations, he would take this into account. This would lead to more accidents, but the reduction in legal costs might more than compensate socially for the increase in accidents.

But, here, when individuals are calculating their appropriate activity and considering the likely legal outcome, they certainly should take into account the prospect that the court will make errors. If we assume that the court will go wrong about one time in eight—a rough rule of thumb which is based on quite poor research—then clearly this would make a difference to the parties. As a rough generalization, the party who is likely to be sued could lower the amount of precautions he takes, and the party likely to sue should increase them with this estimate of judicial error.[21]

There is another possibility of error here, which is error by the other party. We are now talking about a negligence case, and, if the other party has miscalculated, then this changes the appropriate resource investment for the first party. The obvious case is that of a potential tortfeasor who feels that there is at least some probability that his potential victim will miscalculate and, hence, be contributorily negligent. This lowers the optimal amount of resource investment by the potential tortfeasor in accident avoidance, because he will be excused from paying damages in at least some cases in which he is negligent. All of these costs can be affected, at least to some extent, by changing the liability rule. Thus we can easily imagine circumstances in which the liability rule should be aimed at minimizing, among other things, the costs of calculation and the probability of error at the beginning. Once again the reasonable-man rule is, in part, such a procedure.

We now proceed to the other costs—the actual costs of preventing accidents and the costs of the accidents themselves. I have no quarrel with the proposition that if these are the only costs to be considered we should try to minimize their sum. Minimizing the sum of all costs, including the costs

21. See G. Tullock, *Trials on Trial*.

of calculation before the accident and the legal costs after is, however, a better rule. It could very easily lead to a law which did not minimize the sum of accident costs plus the costs of preventing accidents by themselves.

Let us now proceed to the legal proceedings after an accident. In part, these proceedings, of course, are settlement negotiations, and, if the accident is a minor one, these are usually quite quick and straightforward. Insurance companies tend to be prompt and generous in dealing with minor injuries and slow and miserly in dealing with large. This is a perverse pattern of behavior from the standpoint of society as a whole, but it is the appropriate rule for a profit-maximizing firm facing the current legal system.

Ignoring that matter, however, let us consider briefly the legal costs themselves. As I said above, in those cases in which the matter actually goes to trial, the total costs of the legal proceedings are somewhere between a half and three-quarters of the amount at issue. This is a large cost, and a procedure which attempts to minimize other costs of accidents and does not touch this is clearly deficient.

Nevertheless, it should be pointed out that the bulk of all accidents do not go to trial, but are settled out of court. The settlement process, however, is also expensive, even if not as expensive as the trial. Indeed, a plaintiff's attorney, as part of his negotiations for a settlement, will go through a good deal of preparation of his actual case, and the insurance company's attorney, as part of their negotiation technique, will also put a good deal of resources into preparing a case for trial. Thus there is a considerable cost even in those cases that do not go to trial.

Rules aimed at minimizing this cost can very well be sensible, even if they do not minimize the sum of accident prevention together with accident costs. Take two examples, both of which have been enacted into law: the industrial accidents codes and the no-fault insurance programs for autos. These programs provide that the factual situation surrounding the accident can, to a very large extent, be ignored, and compensation (usually much less compensation than would be obtained in a standard tort action) is paid to the person injured. Note that the person injured is compensated under both of these circumstances even if he was negligent and, indeed, even if his negligence is the sole cause of the accident. To take a suggestion (not enacted into law) on the other side, in *The Logic of the Law* I propose that tort liability in automobile accidents simply be abolished and that individuals be permitted, if they wished, to take out personal injury insurance policies to cover the possibility of being injured in such an accident.

All three of these proposals are efforts to avoid the costs of legal action, and of legal error, by simplifying the legal situation. The factual problem is much more simple; in fact, really all that has to be proved is that somebody has been injured. It is also true, however, that they are, in essence, removed from ordinary court proceedings and put in the hands of other quasi-judicial bodies. The insurance companies handle most no fault and would, of course, handle the personal liability under the Tullock proposal. Industrial accidents are handled normally by a state board which does not use judicial procedure. Thus, those factual and legal problems that do come up are characteristically handled by non-court procedures and, hence, are handled much more cheaply.[22]

What we should aim for then is a legal rule that minimizes this whole set of costs.

1. The costs of calculation.
2. The fact that a given legal rule, granted the prospects of miscalculation by the other party and judicial error, may lead individuals to courses of action which are not optimal even though the rule would lead to optimal outcomes if no one made any mistakes.
3. The actual costs of the accidents and whatever precautions are taken against accidents.
4. The legal costs which come from the accident itself.

What we want is a procedure, or rule, which minimizes the sum of this whole series, and there is no reason to believe that the negligence–contributory negligence rule is an example. I have to admit, however, that I do not know what the appropriate rule is. This is a case where we must have further empirical research and probably further theoretical progress.

Let us now turn to contract law. As a rough rule of thumb, we permit people in Anglo-Saxon countries to make almost any contractual arrangement among themselves that they wish, provided only that we feel that the parties are sane and reasonably well informed about what they are doing. It is true that we put some restrictions on this freedom, but I would prefer to leave these restrictions for another time. Let us talk about the problem of what we do when a contract which provides for something which is perfectly legal turns out not to cover a contingency which, in fact, arises. Assume we

22. There is no reason to believe they are handled less accurately.

have an absolutely clear-cut case in which the contract says nothing whatsoever about the issue. In the more normal case, the contract has some vague hints as to what the parties had in mind, but let us take a case in which they simply have totally and completely ignored it. There are several things one can do here.

1. Simply flip a coin and make the decision that way. I shall argue below that under some circumstances this is the optimal procedure.
2. One could turn to the law of contracts and see what it has to say about the matter. Let us assume that in this case there is a clear-cut legal provision which takes care of the matter.

The normal approach here would be to say that the legal outcome is clearly superior to flipping the coin. Let us consider it a little more, however. If the two parties knew that this particular outcome was provided by the law, then we could assume that the reason there was no clause in the contract dealing with it was that they had simply decided to save time in drawing up the contract by depending on this legal provision. Suppose, however, the two parties had not known of the existence of this legal procedure. In this case, from their standpoint, the outcome would be exactly the same as flipping a coin.

3. The third possibility would be that one of the parties knew about this provision of the law and the other did not. If there is this kind of assymetrical information, then in the bargaining process in which a contract was drawn up, the better informed party would have a distinct advantage. If the legal provision in question was to the advantage of his opposite number, he could suggest that a specific provision be put in the contract, with the result that the legal provision was not brought into play. He might or might not win on this particular bit of bargaining, but surely he would have an advantage over his opponent, who would not realize what the debate was actually about. If, on the other hand, it was in his favor he could remain silent.

Look at the matter socially. The first situation, one where both parties are in ignorance, is simply the same as flipping a coin in terms of the efficiency with which the original contract will be drawn up. The parties will not take the legal provision into account, and, hence, the contract will be drawn up as if it did not exist. If one particular provision was, in fact, for some reason superior to another, the parties would not be able to take advantage of that in their initial negotiations.[23]

The second situation in which both parties know the provision in the law is the one where the law for "interpreting" contracts is most likely to have a social payoff. It permits the parties to have a basically shorter contract without giving either side any special advantage.

The third case, however, is one in which a long, detailed law of interpretation is apt to inflict social costs. We earlier pointed out that one of the costs of a legal system is the calculating costs: the determination of what the law actually is by the parties concerned. If the party whose lawyer is best informed about the law of contracts has a distinct advantage over the other, then there will be a competition in becoming well informed about the law of contracts. This competition may be entirely wasteful from the social standpoint. The individual parties will carry their research into contract law beyond the point where there is mutual gain from that research, i.e., the point where they simply shorten the contract, in search of individual gains. Each bit of research by party A's lawyer benefits him, but it inflicts an injury on party B if they are simply engaging in competitive efforts to outwit each other. There is an externality, and there will be an over-investment of resources in searching the law.

Now note that legal research to find out what the law actually means and, hence, to shorten the contract by not putting unnecessary clauses in does have a payoff, albeit not a gigantic payoff, in efficiency. Almost all legal research has at least some aspects of this efficiency gain. In general, however, the cost of competitive research in which the two parties are attempting to out-maneuver each other by becoming better informed will immensely outweigh the benefit if the law is long and detailed. What we would like is to have the parties obtain only that information for which the joint benefit is greater than the joint cost of search. We do not want them engaging in a competitive search for information which, jointly, is worth less than the cost but which from the standpoint of one of the parties is worth more than its cost.

There is a simple procedure to deal with this problem, which is to turn to our first legal rule in which a coin is flipped. The parties cannot predict how the coin will come out, and, hence, they do not engage in research beyond a certain point. In other words, we would have the law of contracts detailed enough so that parties interested simply in saving space in drawing up their

23. All of this is dealt with in greater detail in *Trials on Trial*.

contracts could leave out a number of standard clauses but not detailed enough so that there will be much prospect of competitive legal research in order to obtain unilateral advantage. Putting it differently, a long and detailed law of contracts increases the calculating costs of the parties and carries with it only the very slightest social benefits from permitting the parties to leave clauses out of their contracts.

Of course, I am not seriously proposing that coins actually be flipped, particularly since in most cases the problem is not the kind of complete ambiguity in which the contract has no reference to whatever happened at all, but is what might be called partial ambiguity, in which the fitting of the contract to the actual occurrence is ambiguous and unclear, but there is at least some enlightenment in the contract as to what the parties had in mind. The appropriate procedure in these cases, however, is to have a short law, not a long law, and to introduce a legal system which prevents the parties from wasting resources on dealing with these ambiguous cases. I have discussed such procedures at some length in both *Logic of the Law* and *Trials on Trial*, and so I shall not present them here. Basically, they consist of conceding that the law or the contract is not clear—and, hence, that any outcome will have a stochastic element—and then preventing competitive investment of resources by each of the two parties to increase their individual likelihoods of success.

This scheme at the time when the matter finally comes to trial will mean that each informed party is compelled to invest fewer resources than he would like to at that time. He is, however, compensated by the fact that the other party is also investing fewer resources. The outcome, at least theoretically, can be optimized, and we can obtain the appropriate amount of resources on both sides. In practice, fairly arbitrary restraints would no doubt be necessary, but they could certainly do much better than the present very extensive legal costs.

This leads us on, of course, through the actual contract itself, which we can, I think, assume the parties have at least very strong motives to arrange in a manner which is most efficient, and to the proceedings after the contract in the event there is a breach or in the event that something happens which the contract does not cover. Here again, the arguments for enforcing the contract, where it is clear, are extremely strong, but the arguments for spending much time and effort on determining what the contract should have provided, if it does not provide anything, are very weak. Further, there is every reason to believe that the parties would prefer a quicker and easier procedure to the ones that are now used in our courts. The rapid expansion of the use of arbitration, even though it is still not possible to simply select your own procedure freely,[24] indicates this.

Thus, the law of contracts should not only attempt to design contracts which are of maximal efficiency, a goal which, in general, can be reached by permitting the parties to a contract for anything they wish,[25] but it should also take into account the costs imposed on the parties by the need to find out what the law with respect to their contract is and the legal costs once the contract has been, or is alleged to have been, broken. The legal rule which minimizes this chain of costs is apt to be different from a legal rule with respect to an existing contract, and ignoring both the calculation costs which come when the contract is made up and the costs of legal proceedings is most inefficient.

These two examples from tort and the law of contracts have been selected as examples, not as exhaustive discussions of the law. They do, however, I think, indicate that deciding on the welfare test for the law is a little more complicated than simply choosing that law which minimizes costs, assuming that it is applied costlessly and that everybody knows about it costlessly. Both the costs of becoming informed about the law and the costs of the proceedings themselves, including the probability of error, are important. Further, in many cases, a rule which by itself is efficient is inefficient when we add on these additional factors.

Turning to more general considerations—i.e., what is the appropriate welfare test—I am naturally biased in favor of the test which I proposed in the first two chapters of *The Logic of the Law.*[26] It is, however, not too far different from Posner's wealth maximization. I, needless to say, never implied in my book that it was good morals, merely that it was practically the right rule. But in practical application it would not be too far from wealth maximization.

Consider a situation that all of us are in if we are thinking about new laws. Firstly, it may be possible to install a new law that benefits us rather directly, either by name or by some class of which we are a member. Democratic, and indeed dictatorial, politics are very heavily aimed at this particular objective. I happened, rather by accident, to be reading a book on faculty tenure at the time I was preparing this paper, and it is clearly, in part, a history of the way academics have acquired special legal privileges. If I were non-academic

24. The courts frequently say it is, but there are always modifying clauses which the draughtsman of the arbitration agreements and the arbitral judges themselves take into account.

25. Once again, there are areas where this is not true.

26. G. Tullock, *Logic of the Law.*

I might be highly annoyed about it.[27] Clearly, these provisions are not wealth maximizing for society as a whole, but they are apparently wealth maximizing for the existing members of the teaching profession.

Mostly, however, we shall not be in a position where we can bend the law for our own special interests. Needless to say, I do not say we should not, merely that mainly we cannot. Under these circumstances, we should favor a law which will, on the whole, give the best present discounted value to ourselves, assuming that we are more or less a random member of society. Thus, we do not know whether we are more likely to be the tortfeasor or the tort victim in future accidents. We do not know whether we are more likely to be the person who is injured by a breach of contract or the person who would gain from being able to breach contract. Since we do not know, choosing the best present discounted value on the assumption that we are a random individual is our best bet.

But it should be pointed out here that we should be trying to maximize, strictly speaking, not wealth but utility. In particular, if we are, as most human beings are, risk adverse, we would favor rules which had at least some tendency to equalize risk in the future. This would, of course, have to be set off against the fact that normally equalizing risk costs money and, hence, that the present discounted value in monetary terms would be lower.

So much for my partial agreement with Posner. Turning to the second portion of his welfare system, what the parties would agree on in the absence of transaction costs, I doubt that this really has much meaning.[28] Almost always, when two parties are reaching agreement for something or other which has at least the potential of increasing the well-being of both of them, there are two problems in the negotiations.

1. Choosing that particular distribution of duties, responsibilities, and benefits which maximizes the total well-being of the two regarded as a group.
2. The distribution of the potential profit between the two parties.

27. Commission on Academic Tenure in Higher Education, *Faculty Tenure: A Report and Recommendations* (San Francisco: Jossey-Bass, 1973). See sections 3 and 4, "Academic Tenure in America: A Historical Essay," by Walter P. Metzger, p. 60, and "Legal Dimensions of Tenure," by Victor G. Rosenblum, p. 160, respectively.

28. Although I must admit that I have used it myself on occasion, I believe that in all cases where I have used it, replacing it with the welfare procedure suggested above would lead to no substantial changes in the argument. It is easy for an economist—both Posner and I are

Large-scale resources are normally invested in attempting to affect the second. These resources are completely wasteful socially, but we know no mechanism for avoiding their investment.

It seems that the statement that there are no transactions costs is ambiguous. Characteristically, what we actually mean is that the special transactions cost associated with public goods, or perhaps some peculiar problem of information spread, is left out but that the two parties engage in normal bargaining. Normal bargaining, however, is a costly business. We observe that parties frequently can reach agreement, but we should not assume that the agreement is reached at zero cost. There is no known zero cost way of dividing the profits of a bargain between the parties. Even flipping a coin requires a previous agreement, and obtaining that agreement is costly.

There is, however, a more serious problem here. In general, the manipulation and maneuvering which goes into bargaining will take, in part, the form of the parties misinforming each other. Under the circumstances there is no very obvious reason for believing the ultimate outcome will maximize their joint wealth. If I can change the outcome of a given contract in such a way that my return goes up by a dollar, I am not particularly concerned about the fact that the wealth of the man with whom I am dealing may go down by two. Since he is not perfectly informed (because I am systematically misinforming him), this is never impossible.

Actually, I think that Posner really knows this about real-life bargains. When he talks about the bargain that the parties would make, he is implicitly assuming that they always choose the most efficient set of relationships between themselves and that they then divide the profit by some method, probably the result of bargaining, but that the choice of bargaining techniques never affects the optimality of the bargain itself from the joint standpoint. I believe this is empirically wrong. If we accept this interpretation of Posner, however, then his agreement between the parties is, in essence, exactly the same as his wealth maximization. However, I would prefer that we stick to wealth maximization because the agreement between the parties, in general, would not lead to the conclusion that he proposes. I must, of course, concede that in the real world there is no reason why you should not attempt to get institutions adopted which will benefit you, even though the injury they impose on others is greater.

---

economists even if we both had legal training—to slip into the contract terminology because of the frequent use of simplifying assumptions in economics.

The Case against the Common Law

CHAPTER 1

INTRODUCTION

This monograph provides an unusually comprehensive critical evaluation of the common law—a term, like many other legal terms, that is ambiguous. As Posner has noted, the common law is used to encompass the body of principles applied by the royal courts of England in the eighteenth century; the fields of law that have been created largely by judges as the by-product of deciding cases, rather than by legislatures; or any other field of law shaped largely by judicial precedents.[1] In this monograph, I shall concern myself primarily with the common law in the second sense outlined above, focusing primarily on the criminal law, the law of property, the law of contracts, and the law of torts, branches of the law that many of my colleagues in the law and economics movement view as being economically efficient. As the reader will readily determine, I beg to differ with respect to this Panglossian rush to judgment.

The institutional principles both of common law and of civil law adjudication are grounded in the social functions of courts. Like other complex institutions, courts serve many functions. However, two of these are paramount.[2] The first function concerns the resolution of disputes that derive from a claim of right based on the application, meaning, and implications of a society's existing standards. In the U.S. system, the resolution of such disputes is a central function of the courts. To this end, courts are structured to be passive, acting only when set in motion by a party with a claim. Similarly, courts are limited to actions that are responsive to the actionable claims. I shall contend in this monograph that the U.S. court system under the common law has largely failed to honor its responsibilities with respect to the cost-effective resolution of disputes.

The second major function of the courts is the enrichment of the supply of legal rules that private individuals can live, plan, and settle by. In many areas, the slowly evolving judicial rule has apparent advantages over legislative rules

Reprinted, with permission, from no. 1, *The Blackstone Commentaries*, ed. Amanda J. Owens (Fairfax, Va.: Locke Institute, 1997), 1–70.

1. R. A. Posner, *Economic Analysis of the Law*, 4th ed. (Boston: Little, Brown, 1992), 31.

2. M. A. Eisenberg, *The Nature of the Common Law* (Cambridge: Harvard University Press, 1988).

that tend to be less flexible in form, but more susceptible to sudden change. It is a widely held judgment[3] that the common law upholds the rule of law more effectively than the civil code, and that the courts should consciously take on the function of developing certain bodies of law, albeit on a case-by-case basis.[4] I do not deny that the U.S. courts have pursued this second function. Indeed, I shall assert that they have done so with a vengeance, and that in so doing they have largely emasculated the rule of law in this country.

Four foundational principles allegedly govern the manner in which law is established and changed by the courts in a common law system—namely, objectivity, support, replicability, and responsiveness. Let me review them each in turn.

In a complex, impersonal, and unofficially religious society, like that of the United States, courts derive legitimacy, in substantial part, from their objectivity. Objectivity derives in part from evident impartiality, which requires the courts to be free of ties to the parties, and from universality, which requires the courts to resolve disputes by establishing and applying rules that are applicable not only to the immediate dispute, but to all similarly situated disputes. I shall contend that late twentieth century U.S. courts have failed to maintain such objectivity on a consistent basis.

Even when courts sustain high standards of objectivity, as defined above, the rules that emerge should also be supported by the general standards of the society or by the special standards of the legal system.[5] For, if the courts resolved disputes by reasoning from other types of standards, there would be no institution to which a member of society could go to vindicate a claim of right on the basis of existing standards. The rooting of common law rules in existing standards provides important support and legitimacy for an institution that is not conceived as representative, and that is deliberately structured in a way that limits its accountability and responsiveness to the citizenry as a whole. In the absence of such support and legitimacy, disputes over past transactions will be resolved by applying rules that have been articulated after the transaction has occurred. I shall contend that the erosion of the role of precedent and of the application of *stare decisis* by the U.S. courts during

3. F. A. Hayek, *Law, Legislation, and Liberty*, vol. 1 (London: Routledge and Kegan Paul, 1983).

4. Eisenberg, *Nature of the Common Law*, 6.

5. Eisenberg, *Nature of the Common Law*.

the second half of the twentieth century has severely eroded, if not entirely destroyed, the support and legitimacy of the common law.

In a complex society, private citizens who desire to resolve disputes or to make plans on the basis of the law normally must consult a lawyer. In the vast majority of instances, the institution that determines the law is not the courts, but the legal profession. In such circumstances, it is important that lawyers should be able to replicate the process of judicial reasoning. The principle of replicability serves as a coordinating device through which the reasoning of the profession can flow.[6] An important aspect of the principle of replicability is that the courts employ a consistent methodology across cases. I shall contend that the U.S. common law system has failed to preserve such replicability across major and growing areas of the law.

Given that the courts are not structured to be directly responsive to the citizenry as a whole, they should be responsive to, though of course they are not obligated to follow, what the legal profession has to say. The discourse to which courts are obligated to be responsive basically occurs in two areas. The first is in the context of a particular case in which discourse is effected through briefs and oral argument and through lawyers' decisions whether to raise claims or defenses. The second is in the wider context of the profession as a whole, entered after final decision in the particular case is rendered. Discourse in this wider arena takes the form of law reviews, books, and monographs, together with other exchanges among members of the bar. I shall contend that responsiveness to the wider arena has significantly deteriorated in the U.S. common law system, not least because of the increasing politicization of the bench and the widening role of the non-specialist jury during the second half of the twentieth century.

Central to the social functions and the foundational principles of the common law system is the concept of doctrinal stability as encapsulated in the institutional principle of *stare decisis*. Under that principle, the *ratio decidendi*, holding, or rule of a precedent is binding upon subsequent cases, within broad limits, if the precedent satisfies certain formal conditions, such as having been rendered by a court of a relevant level in a relevant jurisdiction.

Stare decisis clearly gives effect to the principle of objectivity, requiring the courts to behave impartially and universally in dispensing the law, and discouraging a court from deciding cases on the basis of propositions that it would be unwilling to apply to all similarly situated disputants. It also rein-

6. Ibid.

forces the principle that the rules that emerge will reflect the special standards of the legal system, on which legitimacy is derived, and that such rules will be responsive to legitimate legal discourse. Self-evidently, *stare decisis* supports the principle that the law should be replicable throughout the legal profession. For these reasons, *stare decisis* plays a major role in supporting the social function of the courts in the resolution of disputes.

Stare decisis also plays a major role in supporting the social function of the courts in enriching the supply of legal rules. The most salient aspect of this role is the protection of justifiable reliance, without which there can be no rule of law. A tension between *stare decisis* and the evolution of new legal rules in response to changing circumstances inevitably exists. Nevertheless, the standard of doctrinal stability cannot survive any general retreat from the principle of *stare decisis*. It will be my contention in this monograph that the retreat from *stare decisis* in the U.S. common law system is a predictable consequence of the institutional characteristics of the U.S. legal system and that this retreat is now sufficiently extensive as to challenge the validity of the common law system. For what is left now—the surviving kernel of a once robust system of law—is a high-cost, subjective, unresponsive, non-replicable, and essentially illegitimate legal system predicated more on the rule of men than on the rule of law.

CHAPTER 2

THE IDEAL OF THE COMMON LAW

Among the nations of Western Europe, the English alone successfully conveyed the essential elements of their medieval customary legal system into a modern common law system. They did so by overcoming powerful criticism and almost insurmountable obstacles.[1] The English common law system survived several periods of political crisis which seriously disturbed the balance of three elements fundamental to the English constitution—the prerogative of the Crown, the privileges of Parliament, and the individual rights to personal security, personal liberty, and private property.

The general rules of the common law might well have disappeared in the fifteenth century as a consequence of dynastic disputes known as the Wars of the Roses. The central powers of governmental law enforcement were so eroded by these disputes that the weak could no longer secure justice in the royal courts. Disintegration back into feudalism was avoided only after 1485, when King Henry VII acceded to the throne and established the House of Tudor. The common law again might have succumbed in the sixteenth century, when certain English monarchs nurtured Roman law at the expense of medieval customary systems. King Henry VIII favored Roman law but was satisfied instead to manipulate the medieval constitution, especially after the break with Rome and the onset of the English Reformation.

The common law again was threatened throughout much of the seventeenth century by theories of divine right monarchy that greatly influenced the House of Stuart. Government by unrestrained divine right surely would have produced subservient judges sitting in prerogative courts responsive to the monarch's will. The common law escaped such emasculation as a consequence of the Glorious Revolution of 1688 and the flight of King James II.

Perhaps its most serious challenge (yet unresolved), however, was the emergence in the eighteenth century of the legislative sovereignty of Parliament, which created the possibility of the emasculation of the common law by means of statute. In 1783, William Blackstone, justice of the Court of Common Pleas and Vinerian professor of English law in Oxford University, claimed that the competence of Parliament was so great that he knew "of no

1. A. Hogue, *Origins of the Common Law* (Indianapolis: Liberty Fund, 1985), 241.

power in the ordinary forms of the constitution that is vested with authority to control it."[2]

In the view of many common law scholars, however,[3] the legislative sovereignty of the English Parliament has not destroyed the common law doctrine of *stare decisis* nor has it emasculated the common law doctrine of established legal principles. Its early maturity and technical complexity have provided the common law with formidable protection in the form of a powerful special interest, namely, the judge and lawyer lobby. Economic interests, in the form of property owners, also resolutely defended the common law from legislative overthrow, at least until the early twentieth century, when economic interests became more diffuse and the common law defense of property rights became less unambiguous.

The expansion of Western European civilization from the late sixteenth century onwards and, most significantly, the widening reach of the British Empire scattered elements of the English common law across much of the globe. Notably, from the perspective of this monograph, English colonists on the Atlantic seaboard introduced common law to the American continent, while French and Spanish colonists introduced laws originally derived from Roman law. As the British Empire asserted its dominance, the common law traditions predominated, with the exception of Louisiana and also of certain territories acquired from Spain.

The English colonists brought to America the law of England as it stood in the seventeenth and eighteenth centuries. When the colonies broke away from England in the course of the American Revolution, they framed arguments about their rights taken straight from Blackstone's *Commentaries*, the classical statement of the common law: "The enormous popularity of Blackstone in the most formative period of American national institutions may go far to explain why American law kept close to English law."[4]

What then was the *ideal* eighteenth-century vision of the common law that eventually evolved out of medieval England and how effectively was this ideal transported to the United States following the War of Revolution? It is important to address these issues before proceeding to critique the *reality* of the common law as it now manifests itself in late-twentieth-century America.

2. W. Blackstone, *Commentaries on the Laws of England* (London: Macmillan, 1973).

3. Hogue, *Origins of the Common Law*, 244.

4. Ibid., 250.

Foremost among the ideas that constituted the eighteenth-century vision is the idea of the *supremacy of law*, a concept also captured by such phrases as *the rule of law* and *due process*. This idea implies that there are limits to the power of ruling, that all government agencies and the law courts themselves must operate according to known rules and procedures. The rule of law is always difficult to apply in the face of ideas of sovereignty, be they from medieval kings or from the modern U.S. Congress, which admits no limitation on the power of ruling. Yet, this idea was at the heart of the ideal version of the common law.

In his influential magnum opus, *Introduction to the Law of the Constitution*, Albert Venn Dicey cited the supremacy of the law as the chief characteristic of the old law of the English courts: "The law is the highest estate to which the king succeeds, for both he and all his subjects are ruled by it, and without it there would be neither king nor realm." According to Dicey, the supremacy of the law, in turn, was a principle that corresponded to three other concepts, namely: (1) the absence of arbitrary power on the part of the government to punish citizens or to commit acts against life or property; (2) the subjection of every individual, whatever his rank or condition, to the ordinary law of the realm and to the jurisdiction of the ordinary tribunals; and (3) a predominance of the legal spirit in English institutions.[5]

Despite the fact that Americans appeared to derive their individual rights from the general principles laid down in their Constitution and in the first ten amendments, Dicey considered the United States to be a typical instance of a country living under the rule of law, because she had inherited the English traditions. Leoni strongly endorses Dicey's judgment, noting that a written bill of rights was not considered to be necessary even by the Founding Fathers and that judicial decisions have always been accorded high importance in the political system of the United States insofar as the rights of individuals are concerned.[6]

Hayek centered attention on four features of the rule of law that coalesce largely with Dicey's description. According to Hayek, the generality, equality, and certainty or replicability of the law, as well as the requirement that administrative discretion always be subject to review by independent courts are "really the crux of the matter, the decisive point on which it depends whether

5. A. V. Dicey, *Introduction to the Law of the Constitution* (London: Macmillan, 1987).

6. B. Leoni, *Freedom and the Law* (Los Angeles: Nash Publishing, 1961).

the Rule of Law prevails or not."[7] This idea implies that there are limits to the power of ruling; that all government agencies, including the law courts themselves, must operate according to known rules and procedures; that adherence to the rule of law may be the only means of preserving the enjoyment of private rights and personal freedoms.[8]

A second idea passed down from the Middle Ages relates to the work of the courts in the legal system and the doctrine of judicial precedent. The dignity of medieval royal courts was impressive. The royal judges, the repositories of the legal tradition, exercised the right to control all matters of procedure, from judging the initial grounds of a legal action to the enforcement of any judgment on that action. When judges failed to maintain the high standards of learning and disinterested action expected of them, the English feudal barons, churchmen, and merchants insisted on reform.[9]

In the Middle Ages, common law court decisions were recorded, and occasionally the record would be consulted. For the most part, however, the common law lived more in the memories of judges and practitioners than on plea rolls and reports. The law was largely judge-made, and even when the law was changed by action of the king's council or by Parliament, judges participated in the change. It is an essential feature of the common law system that its principles are derived from decisions in actual cases, in which judges play the predominant role.

A third important element underpinning the common law is the writ system. This is so even though the writ system was abolished by legislation in England during the nineteenth century. English lawyers were content to dispense with those old forms of action because they had become embedded in the common law. The full catalogue of writs, known as the *Register of Writs*, was the framework of the common law.

Let me briefly review the central elements of the common law as they had evolved by the late nineteenth century towards the end of what may be loosely referred to as the *classical period*. These elements best reflect the ideal of the common law that has been advanced in this chapter.

There is no concept more central to the common law than that of property. The legal conception of property is that there are a bundle of rights over

7. F. A. Hayek, *Law, Legislation, and Liberty*, vol. 1 (London: Routledge and Kegan Paul, 1983), 54.

8. Hogue, *Origins of the Common Law*, 252.

9. Ibid., 253.

resources which the owner is free to exercise and whose exercise is protected from interference by others. Property thus creates "a zone of privacy in which owners can exercise their will over things without being answerable to others."[10] As individuals depart from the state of nature, where natural law allows them to defend property from interference, into civil society, where they surrender this right to government, they enter into an agreement which commits government to uphold their natural rights to life, liberty, and property.[11] This agreement is the social contract which includes the fundamental laws of property.

The two normative principles of property law that governed the ideal of the common law were: (1) minimize the harm caused by private disagreements over resource allocation and (2) minimize the obstacles to private agreements over resource allocation. In pursuit of these principles, the courts developed two alternative responses to situations where illegal interference came from another *private* citizen, namely *legal* or *equitable* remedies.

The principal legal remedy was the payment of compensatory damages by the plaintiff to the defendant. The general rule in common law courts was that legal remedies would be applied unless there was clear evidence that the award of money damages would under-compensate the plaintiff.

Equitable relief, often in the form of an injunction, consisted of an order by the court directing the defendant to perform an act or to refrain from acting in a particular manner.

Economic analysis now informs us that legal remedies tend to be efficient when transactions costs are high and that injunctions tend to be efficient when transactions costs are low (the *Coase theorem*).[12] Put differently, owners should be protected against externalities of the private-bads type by the injunctive remedy and against externalities of the public-bads type by compensatory damages.[13]

All property owners in a civil society are concerned by the prospect that they may be required to sell their property to the government, without any guarantee that they will be paid their reservation price. The *takings power* thus

10. R. Cooter and T. Ulen, *Law and Economics* (Glenview, Ill.: Scott, Foresman, 1988), 91.

11. J. Locke, *Two Treatises of Government* (1690; New York: Cambridge University Press, 1991).

12. R. H. Coase, "The Problem of Social Cost," *Journal of Law and Economics* 3 (1960): 1–44.

13. Cooter and Ulen, *Law and Economics*, 17.

described is also called the right of *eminent domain* or the right of *condemnation*. The common law in England, where there is no written constitution, deals with the sovereign's right to condemn private property and compel its sale to the Crown by requiring that the taking must be for a public purpose and that the owner must be justly compensated. In the United States, this common law presumption was codified into the Constitution through the Fifth Amendment. State constitutions generally impose similar constraints.

By the late nineteenth century, the U.S. common law had enunciated the central principles of a *bargain theory of contracts* as the basis for contract law. The approach adopted was that of isolating and abstracting the minimal elements of a typical bargain and of asserting that those elements were necessary for a binding contract in every case. This approach was so widely adopted that it is often referred to as the *classical theory of contract*.

The classical theory of contract asserted that a promise was legally enforceable if it was given as part of a voluntary bargain and was unenforceable otherwise. In determining whether or not a bargain had been struck, the common law developed three necessary and sufficient conditions, namely the presence of offer, acceptance, and consideration. "Offer" and "acceptance" had the same meaning in this context as in ordinary speech. The doctrine of consideration was a technical concept describing what the promisor received in the exchange from the promisee. This element perfected a bargain and made it legally enforceable.

Under classical theory a court would not inquire as to whether the consideration was adequate. Hard bargains, even bargains that a reasonable man would regard as unfair, were enforceable under this doctrine. The court's sole concern would be the presence or absence of consideration, not its adequacy. It was enough for the court that the contracting partners had found the consideration to be adequate at the time the bargain was struck.

The classical theory also had an answer to the question: what should be the remedy for breaking enforceable promises? The answer was that the victim was entitled to *expectation damages*, defined as a payment by the breaching party of a sum of money just sufficient to make the victim as well off as he would have been had the promise been kept. Only rarely would the courts grant the alternative equitable relief of *specific performance*, whereby the parties would be ordered to perform their sides of the bargain. According to classical doctrine, the existence of a bargain established enforceability; and the expected value of a bargain measured damages.

The term *tort* is French, derived from the Latin word *torquere*, to twist, and means a private wrong or injury.[14] Under the ideal of the common law, torts were of limited reach and achieved legal status only where contracts failed to regulate relationships. There was a classical theory that specified the essential elements of a tort, much as did the classical theory in contracts. This theory enjoyed substantial acceptance in America at the end of the nineteenth century.

The purpose of classical theory was to protect the interests of individuals in their property and to protect persons from damage by others. Three elements were distinguished, namely (1) breach of a duty owed to the plaintiff by the defendant; (2) harm suffered by the plaintiff; and (3) the breach being the immediate or proximate cause of the harm. Although the distinction between intentional and unintentional harm was important, going to the magnitude of the remedy, the focus of tort law itself was not on the mental state of the wrongdoer (or tortfeasor) but rather on the fact that a duty of care had been violated.

The duty of care to which potential tortfeasors were held was the negligence standard of reasonable care which depended on the norms, practices, and values of ordinary people. The breach of duty had to give rise to measurable damages, which were prescribed narrowly. Thus, doing something dangerous that caused no harm did not constitute an actionable tort. The courts were willing to compensate for medical costs, but reluctant to compensate for emotional harm, distress, or loss of companionship. Until the nineteenth century, a person's action died with him, affording no remedy for a victim's estate.

The third element of a tort concerned the connection between the wrong and the harm; the former must cause the latter. This was strictly required. For the plaintiff to recover, the defendant's breach of duty to the plaintiff must be, not just the cause-in-fact of the plaintiff's injury, but also the *proximate cause*. There had to be a natural and continuous sequence of events which linked the act to the injury, unbroken by any new independent action which produced its own event and injury. Historically, common law would not countenance tort suits directed at deep-pocket defendants where proximate cause could not be established.

Although criminal law is largely governed by statutes, many of these statutes are codifications of earlier common law. The minimal elements of a

14. Ibid., 326.

crime were defined by the common law courts. Fault is the failure to fulfill an obligation. In every crime there is fault. However, fault was not sufficient to justify criminal prosecution. The intent to harm (or *mens rea*) was necessary to justify criminal prosecution in cases involving personal injury. The first element of a crime, therefore, was intent.

The second element of a crime concerned the physical act(s) which created the harm. In torts, the harm is private, whereas with crimes the harm is public. This explains why tort suits are brought by victims (the plaintiffs), whereas criminal prosecutions are brought by the state.

The elements so far described—criminal intent and public harm—characterize the criminal act. Two further elements characterize the legal consequences. The first is punishment, which can take several forms, ranging from fines in excess of compensation to probation, imprisonment, or execution. The second is the standard of proof required by law. In a civil action, the plaintiff must prove his case by the preponderance of the evidence, or in certain tortious actions clear and convincing evidence. In a criminal action, the state must prove its case beyond a reasonable doubt. Taken together, these four elements constituted the ideal of the common law with respect to crime and punishment.

The ideal of the common law, then, is the development of law by means of judicial precedents, the use of the jury to determine the material facts of a case, and the definition of numerous causes of action. These ideals constitute the principal, valuable legacy of the medieval law to the modern law notwithstanding a number of oddities (e.g., the inability of heirs to sue for compensation in cases where the victim was killed in an accident) that were rectified, if at all, by legislation. Unfortunately, these ideals have been eroded and disfigured by the U.S. judicial system during the second half of the twentieth century, not least because the erosion of the U.S. constitutional republic by the forces of democratic majoritarianism has exposed law and justice to the pressures of the political marketplace.

CHAPTER 3

THE COMMON LAW IN PUBLIC CHOICE PERSPECTIVE

The U.S. common law system is appropriately analyzed, as part of the more general political marketplace, from the perspective of the interest group approach to politics.[1] In this approach, politicians are modeled as providing a brokering function in the political market for wealth transfers. Voters, confronted with individual incentives to abstain from voting or at least to remain rationally ignorant of political activity, tend not to be decisive in the wealth transfer market.[2] Relatively small, homogeneous special interest groups, capable of effective political organization, "demand" wealth transfers. Other more general, heterogeneous groups, incapable of effective political organization, "supply" such transfers. Politicians effect political market equilibrium, balancing benefits against costs at the margin, in return for some balance of expected wealth and expected votes. The public bureaucracy, which includes the court system, enforces the deals that are struck in the political marketplace.

The concepts of "demand" and "supply" in this stylized model require a somewhat special interpretation.[3] "Demand" consists of the willingness to pay, in the form either of money transfers or of votes, by well-organized special interests, in return for wealth transfers carrying a positive net present value. Such positive expected returns, which represent rent and not profit, induce rent-seeking behavior.[4] "Supply" consists of the unwillingness or inability of those from whom wealth transfers are sought, at the margin, to protect themselves by making countervailing offers of money transfers or votes to the balancing mechanism. Evidently, there are connotations of coercion associated with this concept of "supply."

1. R. McCormick and R. D. Tollison, *Politicians, Legislation, and the Economy* (Boston: Martinus Nijhoff, 1981).

2. G. Tullock, *Rent-Seeking*, Shaftesbury Paper 3 (Aldershot: Edward Elgar, 1993).

3. C. K. Rowley, W. F. Shughart, and R. D. Tollison, "Interest Groups and Deficits," in *Deficits*, ed. J. M. Buchanan, C. K. Rowley, and G. Tullock (Oxford: Basil Blackwell, 1987).

4. Tullock, *Rent-Seeking*; G. Tullock, "The Welfare Cost of Tariffs, Monopolies, and Theft," *Western Economic Journal* 5 (1967): 224–32.

Many of the public institutions of the U.S. legal system were developed to facilitate the monarchy's efforts to centralize and consolidate their power.[5] These institutions now operate in representative democracy. Yet, because the legal system is intimately bound up in the legitimate use of coercive force in society, it must be viewed as an integral part of the political process. Special interest groups have strong incentives to try to influence the behavior of the legal system. All areas of law are subject to interest group manipulation through the legislative process. Moreover, once laws are passed, the administration of justice is also influenced by interest groups. Attempts are made to influence the courts, the police, the juries, the prosecutors, the witnesses, and the rest of the legal system to assure that laws favorable to special interest groups are enforced.

5. B. L. Benson, *The Enterprise of Law* (San Francisco: Pacific Research Institute for Public Policy, 1990), 87.

CHAPTER 4

ALL THE WORLD'S A STAGE

The U.S. legal system is based on adversary proceedings which are unique to the Anglo-Saxon tradition. It provides a stage on which many players perform, each responding to specific incentives and constraints in a rational expected utility-maximizing way. In this chapter, I subject the behavior of each of the principal players to public choice analysis, setting the scene for a review of the common law play itself in Chapter 5.

A. *The Courts*

Courts in the United States are publicly owned facilities provided to the general public at zero or near zero prices. Courts that are composed of long-term appointee judges (all the federal courts and approximately half the state courts) are full-fledged bureaucracies. Courts that are composed of shorter-term, elected judges confront incentives and constraints that render them directly vulnerable to electoral pressures. In the latter courts, the lower the level of the judge and the shorter his term of office, the more intense his political involvement predictably will be.

Courts are like any form of public property. When ownership rights are not clearly assigned, and when prices are not charged to ration its use, the resource is over-used and inefficiently allocated. Ostensibly available on a first-come, first-served basis, the tragedy of the commons results, ameliorated only by an implicit pricing system that favors wealthy individuals and well-heeled organizations that gain privileged access to the justice system. Those who administer the court system typically do not comprehend the nature of the problem. Chief Justice Burger, for example, complained that the courts were overcrowded and that there was an excess demand for courts' services.[1] In fact, the existence of a queue simply indicates that the service is under-priced.

The over-crowding of the courts implies that rationing must occur, a process which favors those who can most afford to stand in line. Since places in line cannot be auctioned off or traded, at least overtly, all litigants pay

1. B. L. Benson, *The Enterprise of Law* (San Francisco: Pacific Research Institute for Public Policy, 1990), 99.

essentially the same price for use, a price that bears no necessary relationship to the importance of the case. The rationing process can be manipulated, especially in civil court cases where customers come in competing pairs. Delay is often an attractive product to a better-heeled customer, allowing him an opportunity to wear down a less-well-heeled opponent. Given that courts do not efficiently price their services, an incentive is provided for customers to outspend their opponents, driving the latter into disadvantageous settlements by the threat of ever-escalating legal costs. In criminal cases, the court system encourages foot-dragging by criminals and unwarranted prosecution by prosecutors and the police.

Excess demands on the civil court system often spill over and downgrade the criminal system and vice versa because civil and criminal lawsuits compete for essentially the same resources. Thus the waste and inefficiency associated with common access also distort justice across the common law system. In this sense, the public production of the common law imposes negative externalities upon society at large.

The tragedy of the commons manifest in the U.S. court system could be avoided by the introduction of market-clearing prices. Such a price mechanism would discourage frivolous, low-valued use of the justice system, just as it would deny access to those who could not pay. Predictably, a number of special interests would resist such a solution. The legal profession, through its mouthpieces, the American Bar Association and the Association of Trial Lawyers of America, would lobby powerfully against any measure that reduced the volume of litigation. City and state governments would also lobby to avoid the bankruptcy that might ensue if civil cases against abuses were to be concluded successfully against them in a timely fashion. Insurance companies clearly have a major stake in slow-moving litigation, as do tenant associations defying the eviction of members for non-payment of rent.[2] Many special interests actively seek (and seek successfully) mediocre, or even downright incompetent, court performance.

B. The Judges

It is widely believed that U.S. judges (federal judges most especially) enjoy considerable independence from the interest group pressures that dominate the marketplace of politics. The independence is derived both from the

2. Ibid., 118.

rules that govern judicial tenure and from the rules of judicial procedure. It is supposedly fortified by the oaths of loyalty to the Constitution that all judges—state as well as federal—are required to swear before assuming office.

Article III of the U.S. Constitution provides for the appointment, rather than for the election, of federal judges, guarantees that such judges have life tenure in office, and provides that Congress may not reduce their salaries while they remain in office. In a number of states, similar provisions exist, although protection is not as extensive as that offered to the federal judges. These constitutional guarantees certainly protect federal (and some state) judges from flagrant political pressure, though a guaranteed nominal salary offers only limited financial security in an inflationary economy. They do not provide an absolute barrier against political pressure.

First, each federal judge is appointed to office only following nomination by the President and confirmation by the Senate—a uniquely political route to judicial office. In the case where the presidency and the Senate are under single-party control, the path is open for appointments that reflect a common ideology and that are susceptible to a particular group of special interests. Where power is divided, only extremely compliant, flexible, and nonassertive individuals will make their way to office. Such personalities will respond equally flexibly to the prevailing winds that blow across Capitol Hill throughout their terms in office.

Special interest groups have obvious incentives to influence the recruitment of judges. Eisenberg found that bureaucrats, lawyers, bar associations, and various other organized interest groups actively seek to influence judicial appointments at all levels of government.[3] The special interest circus occasionally reaches farcical levels in Supreme Court appointments, notably, in recent years, in the successful attempt to derail the nomination of Robert Bork and in the ultimately unsuccessful, but vicious attempt to derail the nomination of Clarence Thomas. Many judgeships in the United States are political rewards for individuals who have demonstrated past support for powerful interest groups. Such individuals often have little understanding of the law itself and little or no respect for precedent and *stare decisis*. Usually, the latter qualities are not attractive to the special interests.

Second, even though individual judges cannot be removed from office once appointed, the integrity of the judicial system itself may be threatened if

3. M. A. Eisenberg, *The Nature of the Common Law* (Cambridge: Harvard University Press, 1988).

judges attempt to uphold the Constitution against the combined authority of Congress and the President. This indeed was the case in 1937 when Justice Roberts of the U.S. Supreme Court dishonored his oath of office and switched position in *West Coast Hotel Co. v. Parrish* to uphold a state minimum-wage statute.[4] This "switch in time that saved nine" avoided an all-out attempt to pack the Supreme Court with New Deal protagonists by increasing the number of justices from nine to fifteen. Such a threat need be leveled only rarely to bring the judicial system to heel for several decades and to impose an attitude of judicial deference that is inimical to the concept of separation of powers.

Third, even though the salaries of federal judges cannot be lowered by Congress, their offices are entirely dependent on the flow of annual appropriations from Congress. If the judiciary were to stand resolutely against unconstitutional behavior by Congress (as it attempted to do throughout the early 1930's), budgets might be sharply reduced to the discomfiture of individual judges. If the judiciary resisted the unlawful behavior of the executive branch, it is not inconceivable that the executive branch would refuse to enforce its judgments. Threats of this kind, however implicit, may sharply influence the judicial behavior of judges and justices who were not appointed in the first place because of their jurisprudential brilliance or the firmness of their independent resolve.

Fourth, although the salaries of the judges cannot be lowered, they need not be increased to keep pace with inflation and rising living standards. In consequence, the annual salaries of all federal judges are substantially lower in real terms than they were in 1900 and about one-third lower than they were in 1940, despite massive increases in per capita U.S. income over these time periods.[5] Current salaries are unattractive to high-flying lawyers in private practice, further downgrading intellectual quality and personal vigor at all levels of the federal judiciary, notwithstanding the prestige attached to appellate court judgeships and (especially) to positions on the Supreme Court.

All judges are required to take an oath "to support the Constitution," and all federal judges another oath to decide cases "agreeably to the Constitution." So the lawful judge is constrained by the Constitution. Where the Constitution is unambiguous, the lawful judge, in principle, has no option but to up-

4. *West Coast Hotels Co. v. Parrish*, 300 U.S. 379 (1937), 19; C. K. Rowley, "The Supreme Court and Takings Judgments," in *Taking Property and Just Compensation*, ed. N. Mercur, 79–124 (Boston: Kluwer Academic Publishers, 1992).

5. R. A. Posner, *The Federal Courts: Challenge and Reform* (Cambridge: Harvard University Press, 1985), 32.

hold its meaning, even though he may disagree with that meaning, and even though majority opinion may be hostile to that meaning. If a judge or justice cannot accept the burdens of this constraint, he has two options, namely either to refuse or relinquish office or to become unlawful and betray the oath of office. Few have taken the former route. Many have taken the unlawful route and have abandoned the text of the Constitution, whether in pursuit of private political agendas or in deference to special interest pressures.[6]

As Posner makes clear: "in a system in which judges are appointed by politicians, it would be unrealistic to expect all or most judges to be apolitical technicians."[7] It is not surprising, therefore, to find that the most influential U.S. judges—John Marshall (who received only six weeks' training in law), Oliver Wendell Holmes, Louis Brandeis, Benjamin Cardozo, William Howard Taft, Felix Frankfurter, Robert Jackson, Hugo Black, Earl Warren, William Brennan, William Rehnquist, and Learned Hand—were all politically motivated rather than jurisprudentially learned. Few of them would have made their way to high judicial ranking under peer review of the kind practiced in England and Wales.

Posner challenges the normative validity of the "faithful agent" notion of the good judge,[8] evidencing doubts as to whether there is any moral duty to obey the law.[9] He makes it clear that judges, even Supreme Court justices, will not be bound by rules, at least not completely, and that they will impose their own preferences in the shaping of the law. Judicial independence, which in England guarantees the insulation of judges from politics, in America fosters the exercise of political power by individual judges. "Judicial independence has not taken our judges out of politics; in our political culture, it has put the judges securely in politics."[10]

If the so-called *judicial titans*, who are revered or hated for creating U.S. law, are essentially creatures of politics, what is the predictable motivation of the ordinary appellate judge with secure tenure (be it a federal court of appeals judge or a Supreme Court justice)? This question has been answered empirically and theoretically, with fairly consistent results.

Higgins and Rubin developed and tested a theory based on the assumption that judges maximized some combination of personal wealth and

6. Rowley, "The Supreme Court," 97.

7. Posner, *The Federal Courts*, 17.

8. R. A. Posner, *The Problems of Jurisprudence* (Cambridge: Harvard University Press, 1990), and R. A. Posner, *Overcoming Law* (Cambridge: Harvard University Press, 1995).

9. Posner, *The Problems of Jurisprudence*, 137.

10. Posner, *The Federal Courts*, 19.

ideology subject to constraints imposed by judgment reversals, politics, and seniority. In this theory, judges are assumed to benefit from imposing their values upon society through precedent-setting opinions. They also benefit from increased wealth, which is enhanced by an absence of judgment reversals by superior courts and by promotion within the judicial system.[11] Empirical tests decisively rejected this theory. Judicial discretion appears to be unconstrained, with age and seniority insignificant, precedent unimportant, and no evidence of effective policing through appellate review.

Kimenyi, Shughart, and Tollison focused more narrowly on personal economic reward as the factor that motivates judges. They determined empirically that judicial output is influenced by economic factors. They concluded that the presence or absence of incentives to economic efficiency are as relevant to the judiciary as they are to other areas of human behavior.[12]

In a far-reaching theoretical study, Posner outlined a positive economic theory of judicial voting. Essentially, he argued that rational judges pursue instrumental and consumption goals of the same general kind and in the same general way as private individuals.[13] The vast majority of judges are not Prometheans, intent on changing the world, or saints, devoid of human weaknesses, biases, and foibles. They are not, for the most part, either power seekers, like some politicians, or truth seekers, like many scientists.

The judiciary operates on a non-profit basis, and so judges, on average, do not work as hard as lawyers of comparable age and experience. The enormous caseload increases in recent decades have been accommodated mainly by expansions in staff, who are eligible for quality increases and bonuses. Federal judges of the same rank are all paid the same, regardless of stature and productivity. Leisure predictably has a lower opportunity cost than is the case in private practice. Those who do work hard are motivated by the desire for popularity (with the bar rather than with litigants) and by the desire for prestige among their peers.

Judges do not like to be reversed, but this aversion, according to Posner, does not figure largely in the judicial utility function. It is non-existent in the case of Supreme Court justices, and fairly unimportant in the case of court of

11. R. S. Higgins and P. H. Rubin, "Judicial Discretion," *Journal of Legal Studies* 9 (1980): 129–39.

12. M. S. Kimenyi, W. F. Shughart, and R. D. Tollison, "What Do Judges Maximize?" *Journal of Public Finance and Public Choice* 3 (1985): 181–88.

13. R. A. Posner, "What Do Judges and Justices Maximize? (The Same Thing Everybody Else Does)" *Supreme Court Economic Review* 3 (1993): 1–41.

appeals judges. Reversal rates do not appear to affect district judges' chances of promotion. Judges do like to vote, however, not least because this is the symbol of their power, and to be published, which is their best prospect of immortality. By voting with the majority—what Posner calls "going along voting"—a judge can maximize the pursuit of leisure without noticeably sacrificing the deference that his voting power attracts from the bar.

Posner's theory helps to explain why judges adhere to *stare decisis*, but not rigidly. Rigid adherence would eliminate discretion and would reduce the perceived power of office. "Going-along voting" and "live-and-let-live opinion-joining" are leisure-seeking activities, even though they are not far distant from judicial logrolling, which would attract public hostility.

However, Posner's theory ultimately does not allay suspicion that judges who cannot be removed from office and whose salaries cannot be cut retain considerable discretion to pursue personal agendas in their judicial decision-making. There is no obvious reason why judges should be enamored of economic efficiency for its own sake. Law and economics scholars, therefore, have been forced to fall back on dubious arguments concerning the nature of the litigation process itself (Chapter 5) to justify their assertion that the common law is economically efficient.

C. The Lawyers

Lawyers did not always play a significant role in the evolution of the common law. Until the thirteenth century, indeed, legal advisors, professional councilors, and pleaders were not allowed by custom. Individuals not skilled in the art of pleading were seen to be less likely to be able to conceal their guilt. Moreover, one litigant might be unable to hire a skilled spokesman, while another could, providing the one with an unfair advantage over the other. Ancient principles thus retarded the emergence of the legal profession.[14]

The earliest records of a pleader identify John de Planez as pleading on behalf of King Henry II. King Richard I employed a permanent contingent of pleaders. As with other common law developments in England, the legal profession was established to provide an additional advantage to the king. The king not only gained an advantage in his own suits but was able to sell the same privilege to others. King Edward I had a large number of servants

14. Benson, *The Enterprise of Law*, 57.

or sergeants at law under retainer and a large number of appointees who were their pupils. By 1292, these legal practitioners had acquired some exclusive right to audience. In that year, Edward ordered his justices to provide for a sufficient number of attorneys and apprentices in each county so that the king and the powerful might be well served.[15]

London had already begun to license two groups of legal professionals—attorneys and pleaders—in 1280. However, the king's justices assumed control of the licensing function in 1292 and severely restricted entry in order to secure monopoly power for those appointed. The legal profession began to take shape. Attorneys and counters became licensed court appointees and formed into a professional group. Those who wished to learn the profession joined the guilds or fraternities that eventually would develop into the Inns of Court, the English law schools. Legal procedures became much more complex, and litigation more prolonged. Lawyers, rather than ecclesiastical clerics, became the primary candidates for royal judgeships. Lawyers slowly but inexorably began to tighten their stranglehold over the common law.[16]

Lawyers have practiced in America since early colonial times, with early settlers enjoying a period of free entry into the legal profession. Dispute resolution services were made available by a wide range of *scriveners* drawn from such diverse occupations as the clergy and the taverns.[17] This informal bar provided little by way of special training in the law, emphasizing instead skills in penmanship and in dispute resolution. As the colonies became more established and populated with new immigrants trained in English law, pressure mounted for regulation, on the basis of claims that the law had been overrun by *untrained pettifoggers* who posed a nuisance to society. In essence, the main goal of the colonial bar was to restrict access into the profession through a licensed barrier to entry.[18]

In its bid to establish exclusivity for the legal profession, the colonial bar established three tiers of regulation. The first, the establishment of training standards and educational requirements for all individuals seeking to practice law, is still an important entry barrier, with accreditation procedures

15. Ibid., 58.

16. Ibid.

17. W. Brough and M. S. Kimenyi, *Rites of Passage: The Bar Examination as Central Enforcement Mechanism* (Washington, D.C.: Legal Services Corporation, 1987).

18. C. K. Rowley, *The Right to Justice* (Aldershot: Edward Elgar, 1992), 272.

allowing the bar associations not only to restrict entry but also to police the curricula of accredited law schools.

The second tier of regulation, the bar examination, is designed to restrict the number of attorneys permitted to appear before the courts. Maurizi estimated that, between 1940 and 1950, a 10 per cent increase in excess supply of lawyers generated a decrease in bar examination pass rates ranging from 1 to 10 per cent.[19] Royack determined, in the case of ten out of twelve licensing systems under review, that bar examination failure rates increased systematically over a fifty-eight-year period in response to increases in the general unemployment rate. Brough and Kimenyi found a positive, statistically significant relationship between pass rates in the bar examinations and prior increases in attorney incomes. They also detected an inverse statistical relationship between excess demand for entry and pass rates in the bar examination.[20] Such results are consistent with the hypothesis that the bar examination is used as an entry barrier and not exclusively as a protector of legal standards.

The third tier of regulation, licensure, established the bar as the exclusive enforcer of standards and as the exclusive authority over the number of lawyers who can practice. This is characteristic of the present U.S. legal system. All state bars police the profession through the use of unauthorized practice of law statutes, which make it illegal for unlicensed individuals to practice law. All states have legislated to impose mandatory bar examinations, one section of which is uniform nationwide and the other section of which is written by the state bar association. These examinations are graded by licensed members of the legal profession who are exempt from antitrust regulations following the favorable ruling of the U.S. Supreme Court in *Hoover v. Ronwin*.[21]

Despite the enforcement of entry barriers, the United States has far more lawyers per capita than any other country, 700,000, or 70 per cent of the world's entire supply. Recent studies suggest that, after correcting for other factors, a nation's economic growth is positively correlated with the number of engineers and negatively correlated with the number of lawyers.[22] Where there are too many lawyers in a country, incentives exist for them to press for inefficient laws in order to manufacture fee income. The fault lies not only

19. A. Maurizi, "Occupational Licensing and the Public Interest," *Journal of Political Economy* 82 (1974): 399–413.

20. Brough and Kimenyi, *Rites of Passage*.

21. *Hoover v. Ronwin*, 466 U.S. 442 (1984), 25.

22. Posner, *Economic Analysis of the Law*, 589.

with the legal profession itself, however, but with the growing taste in America for wealth redistributionist litigation. Many Americans have become the world's leading socialists, paying lip service to capitalism while pursuing the socialization of all risk through the legal process.

There are two different types of lawyer in the United States. The trial lawyer has evolved into an expert at debating the law and swaying the jury (and/or the judge). Court proceedings tend to be dominated by debates over points of law between opposing attorneys (often with the jury excluded).[23] Some attorneys specialize in manipulating the ordinary people who comprise the jury.[24] In some cases, attorneys seek to persuade the jury to bring in verdicts that are contrary to the law, to fall back on what are called the *fireside equities*, for example, to nullify a clear criminal conviction. Judges sometimes make efforts to discipline such breaches of legal ethics. Unfortunately, many judges are tarred with the same feathers as the lawyers and favor the fireside equities over the established law.

The Anglo-Saxon system allows the parties (or more correctly the attorneys) basic control over the proceedings, with the judge acting as arbiter or referee. Courtroom strategy is extremely important in the adversarial system, which is governed by a complex system of procedural rules. For example, skillful attorneys use procedural objections primarily to interrupt the judge's and jury's train of thought in order to diminish the effectiveness of witness testimony.[25] In such circumstances, the relative ability of the lawyers hired by the two parties becomes extremely important in determining the outcome of a case. The adversary system places little or no value on searching for the truth. It is a combat system in which winning is the sole objective. Indeed, the smaller the role played by trial lawyers, the more likely it is that the outcome will be in accordance with the facts.[26]

There is a significant element of rent-seeking in the adversarial legal system. Trial lawyers can be viewed from the same perspective as special interest lobbyists. In both cases, government is involved as a vehicle of wealth redistribution. The basic difference between the two is that legal proceedings

23. G. Tullock, *Trials on Trial: The Pure Theory of Legal Procedure* (New York: Columbia University Press, 1980), 11.

24. G. Tullock, *Trials on Trial Reconsidered*, working paper, University of Arizona, Tucson, 1990, 16.

25. Tullock, *Trials on Trial*, 52.

26. G. Tullock, *The Logic of the Law* (New York: Basic Books, 1971), 92.

are subject to more stringent procedural rules. Such rules may serve to increase rather than to ameliorate the social waste from rent-seeking and rent-protection. As with much lobbying of Congress, litigation offers some prospect of a genuine social product. However, the social product itself tends to be lost in a sea of social waste.[27]

The second kind of lawyer does not engage in litigation, but rather specializes in interpreting the current law and in advising clients, for example, on drafting contracts or skirting the edges of the criminal law. This is a large-scale enterprise which accounts for the major part of legal work in the United States. Unlike the trial lawyer, who benefits from ambiguities in the law in order to manipulate juries, the writing specialists usually prefer long and detailed codifications that they must master in order to service their clients at high billing rates. Even in this aspect of the law, however, competing attorneys vie in interpreting contracts to exploit unanticipated loopholes.[28]

Do we want our resources to be put to competitive rent-seeking? There is a real possibility that the rent-seeking costs of a transaction may exceed the social product.[29] The cost of employing attorneys to enforce a contract may increase the accuracy of the outcome by an amount valued at less than the attorneys' costs (in aggregate). In such circumstances, eliminating attorneys entirely would boost the nation's wealth, since the work of one attorney to some extent simply cancels out the value of the other.[30]

D. *The Jury*

The purpose of a jury system—whatever its form, at whatever time—has been either to buttress or to buffer official power. The buttressing jury simply confirmed the view of the holder of power. The buffering jury evolved when accusations needed to be proved to a collection of people and the jury came to represent the wisdom of that community. When that wisdom opposed the ruling power, the jury became a political institution. When it

27. G. Tullock, "Rent-Seeking and the Law," in *Current Issues in Public Choice*, ed. J. Casas Pardo and F. Schneider (Aldershot: Edward Elgar, 1995), 17.

28. G. Tullock, "On the Desirable Degree of Detail in the Law," *European Journal of Law and Economics* 1 (1995): 17.

29. G. Tullock, "Court Errors," *European Journal of Law and Economics* 1 (1994): 17.

30. Tullock, "Rent-Seeking and the Law," 16.

acquired the freedom to disagree with the ruling power without retribution, the jury became a political force.[31]

Most historians place the origin of the Western jury system in classical Athens. The Greek jury, called a *dicastery*, little resembled a modern jury. The jurors, or *dicasts*, had to be male, over thirty years of age, full and free citizens, and free of debt. Normally 501 dicasts would serve in a public, or criminal, case and 201 in a private, or civil, case. Verdict was by majority vote, and the ballots—black and white stones—were placed in urns for secrecy. Jurors' names were drawn by lot by the magistrates. Fee-paying, introduced by Pericles in the fifth century, encouraged the poor and elderly to make up the majority of the dicasts, serving essentially as professional jurors. Jurors might be chosen, or volunteer, for a specific case precisely because they had knowledge of it. The dicasts were free to ask questions of parties to a case and were provided with all available evidence. The dicasts decided both fact and law and often passed sentence too.[32]

The modern jury system, however, is of Anglo-Saxon origin, based on the English jury system introduced when the Normans invaded England in 1066 A.D. There were several precursors to English trial by jury. In the ninth century King Alfred divided the country into tithings, each composed of ten neighboring households. When a dispute occurred, every member of the tithing would debate it. Trial by oath required that a defendant should retell his case repeatedly. Any wavering from the original version would forfeit the case. Compurgation was another mode of trial in which the defendant had to find eleven persons who would swear to his side of the dispute, adding his own vote to make twelve.

At the time of the Norman conquest, trial by ordeal was the most common form of judgment. A defendant would be subjected to such rituals as walking barefoot on hot iron plowshares or reaching into a pot of boiling water. If his skin remained unblemished or uninjured, he would be declared innocent. During most of these rituals, priests and other clergy were present. In the early thirteenth century, Pope Innocent III forbade churchmen to participate. Thereafter, trial by ordeal increasingly gave way to trial by jury.

Throughout the twelfth century, the jury system was restricted mostly to civil matters, primarily property disputes. King Henry II, who reigned from

31. P. DiPerma, *Juries on Trial: Faces of American Justice* (New York: Dembner Books, 1984), 21.

32. Ibid., 25.

1154 to 1189, established the Grand Assize, a court of four knights and twelve neighbors, who ruled on challenged claims to land. Juries that found against the king could be charged with attaint, and, if their judgment was reversed by a second jury, attainted jurors could lose their property and/or be imprisoned.

In 1215, the English nobility challenged the supremacy of the king and forced King John to sign the *Magna Carta*. The contemporary idea of the right to jury trial derives from this document. Article 36 of the Magna Carta guarantees the right of inquisition or trial. Article 39 sets out that "no free man shall be taken or imprisoned . . . nor shall we send upon him unless by the lawful judgment of his peers, or by the law of the land." These newly guaranteed rights brought jury trials into prominence in England. The right to a trial by jury was supposed to make tyranny impossible, imposing a buffer between the king's will and application of the law.[33]

Colonization of British America brought the English jury system to the New World. Trial by jury was guaranteed in some form by the incorporating charters of each colony. Though unanimity among jurors in criminal case verdicts had become English rule, some colonies had provisions for majority rule decisions. The First Continental Congress in 1774 asserted that the colonists had the right to be tried by their peers. The Declaration of Independence declared among its grievances against King George III that he had been depriving colonists "in many cases" of the right of jury trial.

Following victory in the War of Revolution, the Sixth Amendment to the United States Constitution specifically guaranteed the right to jury trial in all federal criminal cases punishable by more than six months' imprisonment. The Seventh Amendment provided for this right in civil trials. In 1968, a Supreme Court decision, *Duncan v. Louisiana*, held that the Sixth Amendment had been incorporated into the Fourteenth Amendment and, therefore, applied to the individual states.[34] At the time the Constitution was written, one separate branch of law, equity, functioned without juries. Its descendants still do so today.

The Fifth Amendment to the Constitution provides that no person shall be held to answer for a capital, or otherwise infamous, crime, unless on a presentment or indictment of a grand jury. Grand juries are used to investigate crimes committed within a court's jurisdiction. Persons are indicted if there is sufficient evidence to warrant holding them for trial. The grand jury has the

33. Tullock, *The Logic of the Law*, 85.

34. *Duncan v. Louisiana*, 391 U.S. 145 (1968), 29.

right to subpoena witnesses, to question them privately without the presence of their lawyer, and to conduct any investigation that it chooses. As a normal rule, the grand jury performs its duties quickly and tends to follow the direction of the prosecuting attorney.[35]

Until 1835 the American jury retained its colonial right to decide the law as well as the facts of a case, always assuming the law decided was constitutional. From 1835, the jury lost that right, although defense attorneys frequently attempt to persuade juries to behave unlawfully through nullification of the law. They are successful in such subversive attempts more frequently than most legal scholars choose to acknowledge. In large part, the problem arises because of the low average intelligence and dysfunctional nature of many juries, especially those drawn from inner city populations.

The right to trial by jury in criminal cases is guaranteed constitutionally both at the federal and at the state levels, with exceptions for trials in juvenile court and for petty offenses. The Supreme Court has ruled that defendants may waive their right to a jury trial and that plea bargains are not an unconstitutional violation of the defendant's right to trial by jury. The Federal Criminal Code states that a defendant may waive a jury trial only with the approval of the court and the consent of the government. In many state courts, the consent of the prosecutor is not required for a waiver of jury trial rights by the defendant.

Jury verdicts are all but sacrosanct.[36] In criminal cases, only convictions can be appealed to a higher court and only then on points of law—often alleged errors in the judge's charge to the jury. The jury's verdict itself is never the basis for an appeal. Civil cases, however, are somewhat different. The right to trial by jury in civil cases is guaranteed by the Sixth Amendment. Both parties in a civil suit must agree if the jury right is to be waived. However, the judge may set aside a civil verdict on appeal on the basis either of points of law or of a review of the evidence. The judge may also change the amount of monetary damages awarded by the jury.

Twelve-member juries are still common in the United States, especially in criminal cases. In 1970, the Supreme Court ruled in *Williams v. Florida* that the number twelve had been an "historical accident, unrelated to the great purposes which gave rise to the jury in the first place."[37] Currently, seven

35. Tullock, *Trials on Trial*, 14.

36. DiPerma, *Juries on Trial*, 19.

37. *Williams v. Florida*, 339 U.S. 78 (1970), 30.

states permit juries of fewer than twelve for misdemeanors. In civil cases, twenty-two states permit juries of fewer than twelve. Six-member juries are the minimum number allowed.

There is inconsistency in the law concerning whether verdicts must be unanimous. The U.S. Supreme Court has ruled that the Constitution does not require unanimous verdicts in criminal proceedings. In practice, all federal verdicts, criminal and civil, must be unanimous. A number of states have moved to less than unanimity verdicts at least for some crimes. In civil cases, thirty-one states permit non-unanimous verdicts, and some require only a simple majority. There is a growing interest, nationwide (trial lawyers excepted), in favor of moving away from unanimity in criminal trials as a means of lowering the incidence of hung juries.

The jury selection process is a controversial aspect of the jury system. There is a large and growing gap between theory and practice in jury selection. In theory, jury selection is supposed to be a random procedure drawing names from some relevant population. That is what is now implied by "a jury of one's peers." Practice is far different. The first stage in jury selection, both for criminal and civil trials, is the *venire*. The *venire* lists eligible jurors drawn from the population of the United States, age eighteen or older, who can communicate in English ("communicate" is broadly interpreted). Most common is the use of voter registration lists.

Since only 60 per cent of eligible voters register, a large part of the population, often minorities, are excluded from this list. A number of jurisdictions attempt to improve the reach of a jury list, not necessarily in any scientific manner. In *Glasser v. United States*, the Supreme Court ruled that jury selection procedures, even though intended to secure competent jurors, had to comport with the concept of the jury as a cross-section of the community.[38] From this judgment the law evolved so that under-representation of "cognizable classes" is now ground for reversal of a verdict if it can be proved that those who prepared the list had the opportunity to discriminate as well as the intent. Racial and ethnic groups and women are held to be unquestionably "cognizable." Others, such as the young, poor, religious, and under-educated, are argued to be such. Inevitably, run-down inner-city communities, pressured to build juries that reflect the diversity of their populations, end up with juries that are too inept and dysfunctional to dispense justice.

38. *Glasser v. United States*, 315 U.S. 60 (1942), 31.

Once the list has been called and the summons sent out, intelligent potential jurors with a significant opportunity cost of time find excuses, including perceived bias, to be excused from duty. Some 60 per cent of summonsed jurors are successful in avoiding service in this way. Others are rejected by counsel either for cause or by peremptory strikes. Counsel are increasingly advised by experts on the psychological profiles of potential jurors and strike to win, not to ensure justice. The *voir dire* process through which potential jurors are investigated with varying intensity is costly in time and devastating for any notion of "a jury of one's peers." Jury lists are routinely manipulated by counsel. Any unevenness in the quality of opposing counsel thus tilts the jury selection in favor of one party or the other.

Juries typically consist, therefore, of individuals of below average intelligence, of below average income, and of below average productivity. They are made up disproportionately of the old, the lame, and the unemployed. They are selected to reflect racial and ethnic diversity and implicitly encouraged, therefore, to think of their role in such terms. Lost completely in this potpourri is the notion of a jury trial as a "trial per pais" or, in the famous words of Lysander Spooner, as a "trial by the country—that is by the people."[39] The people who serve on juries, most especially those who serve on high-profile, sequestered juries, tend to be extremely non-random, unusual representatives of the population at large.

If the average jury is made up of individuals of below average intelligence, below average income, and below average productivity, the jury system has additionally evolved to ensure that it operates with low levels of information. Potential jurors with above average information concerning the matter in hand tend to be stricken from the panel. Potential jurors who are well versed in the law find it easy to have themselves removed from consideration. Jurors are so deprived of real information in the courtroom, because of arcane rules of evidence (see Chapter 5), that many of them literally (maybe even productively) sleep their way through the trial. Juries convict or acquit at whim because jurymen are out of their depth, especially in complex financial trials.[40]

This goes to an important issue in the debate over jury trials. Those who strongly favor jury trials frequently argue that the United States is a

39. L. Spooner, *An Essay on Trial by Jury*, 1852.

40. G. Tullock, "Defending the Napoleonic Code over the Common Law," in *Research in Law and Policy Studies*, vol. 2 (New York: JAI Press, 1988).

government of law and not of men. They are grievously mistaken in this perception. Jurors who do not understand the law often overturn it unconsciously. Those who do understand the law and choose to nullify it do so with malice. Those who understand the law but are not presented with the undiluted facts grope blindly for a judgment based on the rhetoric of opposing counsel. To argue for the continued use of the jury suggests a dislike of the current legal code and a desire to have it overturned at will and/or by chance. This is the rule of men and not of law. It may even disintegrate into rule by a very costly and time-consuming lottery.

E. The Witnesses

In medieval times, witnesses to a crime often acted as jurors to the case, enhancing the relevant information that could be accessed to bring in a true verdict. In late-twentieth-century America, genuine witnesses are excluded from jury service and are so hobbled by rules of evidence (see Chapter 5) that they become pawns moved by rhetoric of counsel. In their place, so-called expert witnesses, mostly professional liars who repeat under oath whatever counsel has trained them to say, seek to mislead the judge and jury on matters of financial or technical complexity.

The entire problem of dishonest testimony and its prevention bristles with difficulties.[41] The basic problem is that it is extremely difficult to detect whether people are lying. Even if there was developed some perfect method of detecting lies, there would still be many reasons why decisions might be incorrect. The human memory is fallible; most people are poor observers; and judges make their own errors. Nevertheless, eliminating lying testimony would be a major advance.

The principal method of detecting lies used in American courtrooms involves a combination of examination and cross-examination by counsel and looking intently at the witness's face in the hope that his expression will indicate that he is lying. This method is not very good. Contrary objective evidence or conflicting testimony is another method, although that also may be suspect. Even if a witness is discredited on one point, that may not mean that the remainder of his evidence is also tainted. The average individual is not a good

41. Tullock, *The Logic of the Law*, 97.

observer, a fact that has been proven by innumerable experiments, and may well be mistaken on part of his evidence simply because he observed badly.

Better ways of telling whether witnesses are lying are currently available, though they are much under-utilized.[42] Falling under the general heading of "lie-detectors," they are the subject of heated debate, despite evident technical advantages. Lie detectors measure a witness's blood pressure, evaluate the electrical conductivity of his skin as well as several other phenomena that are not visible to the naked eye. They are not foolproof or error proof. But to a much less degree is the naked eye. A sensible procedure would be to take all the evidence, including the lie detector test, into account simultaneously, allowing the judge, the jury, and opposing counsel to see the dials as well as the witness's face.

In a court system where the loser does not pay the winner's costs, there is a constant temptation to call too many witnesses, to strengthen one's case and to confuse the jury. This is another weakness of the adversary common law system that I shall address in Chapter 5.

42. Ibid., 100.

CHAPTER 5

THE PLAY'S THE THING

In the view of Posner, three factors lead to wealth maximizing efficiency in the common law: (1) wealth maximization is closely related to utilitarianism, and the formative period of the common law as we know it today, roughly 1800–1950, was a period when utilitarianism was the dominant political ideology in England and America; (2) judges lack effective tools for enriching an interest group or social class other than by increasing society's wealth as a whole in which the favored group presumably will share; and (3) the process of common law adjudication leads to the survival of efficient rules.[1]

I take issue categorically with Posner's viewpoint. It is true that the early-twentieth-century common law (classical law) contained many efficiency-enhancing factors. As I shall demonstrate in Chapter 6, however, the benign nineteenth-century influence of utilitarian philosophy has been swept away dramatically during the twentieth century under the influence of socialist ideology combined with pervasive legal rent-seeking.[2] The consequence is a late-twentieth-century common law that is scarcely recognizable as a descendant of its classical predecessor. Judges indeed have found it possible to change legal rules to benefit favored special interest groups, most notably the Association of Trial Lawyers of America, and they have done so with a vengeance. Where the judges have not moved, federal and state legislators, dominated by lawyers, have enacted statutes to ensure that legal rent-seeking is profitable for an ever-growing cohort of American attorneys.

Let me focus briefly on point (3) in Posner's argument, which offers a more subtle, if equally unfounded, process-oriented justification for common law efficiency.[3] It is argued that the courts will be utilized more frequently to resolve disputes when the existing rules relevant to that dispute are inefficient, and less frequently when the rules are efficient. Once efficient rules have evolved, their existence lowers the incentive for future litigation, thus raising the probability that such rules will endure.

1. R. A. Posner, "Utilitarianism, Economics and Legal Theory," *Journal of Legal Studies* 8 (1979): 103.

2. G. Tullock, "Legal Heresy," *Economic Inquiry* 34, no. 1 (1996): 1–9.

3. P. H. Rubin, "Why Is the Common Law Efficient?" *Journal of Legal Studies* (January 1977): 51–63.

In this perspective, efficiency is the outcome of evolution generated by the myopic utility-maximizing decisions of potential litigants rather than by any efficiency predilections of judges. Rubin applies this theory to accident liability law and demonstrates that where both parties to a dispute have an ongoing interest in efficient outcomes (e.g., insurance companies), efficient evolution is a predictable consequence of litigation. His result is not general. If only one party to a dispute is far-sighted, precedent will evolve in favor of that party, as occurred, for example, in nineteenth-century nuisance law, which tended to favor large corporations. If there is no far-sightedness, the status quo may persist despite the imposition of significant efficiency losses on both parties to the dispute. High litigation costs, imposed by legal rent-seeking, may also impede litigation on inefficient rules and obstruct the efficient outcome.

Cooter and Kornhauser abandon the suspect assumptions of Rubin and model legal evolution as a Markov process.[4] They determine that blind evolution will not take the legal system to an efficient equilibrium. Instead, the common law settles down to a stable state in which each legal rule prevails for a fixed amount of time. The system never settles down to a situation in which the best rule prevails forever, even when bad rules are litigated more frequently than good rules, and even when judges are more likely to replace bad rules by good rules than vice versa. In an environment where precedent and *stare decisis* have been all but jettisoned, as is the case in the United States, this interpretation has the commendable advantage (at least to the non-specialist) of corresponding with common sense.[5]

It is not possible in this short monograph to review in detail the institutional deficiencies that lead to continuing inefficiencies in the entire common law process. Let me instead focus attention on the nature of such deficiencies in one important branch, namely the criminal law. I shall attempt to draw together the implications for criminal law efficiency of what we now know (from Chapter 4) about the principal actors playing out their individual roles under the arcane rules that dominate the criminal litigation process.

Crime was once a rarity in the typical person's life. In late-twentieth-century America, it has become a pervasive social phenomenon, with nearly one in three households directly affected by a crime each year, and with more

4. R. Cooter and L. Kornhauser, "Can Litigation Improve the Law without the Help of Judges?" *Journal of Legal Studies* 9 (1980): 139–63.

5. C. K. Rowley, "The Common Law in Public Choice Perspective," *Hamline Law Review* 12, no. 2 (1989): 355–83, esp. 377.

than one million convicted criminals currently behind bars. A person commits a crime by violating a criminal statute, and, in this sense, criminal law is less judge-made than other branches of the common law. However, many criminal statutes essentially codify earlier, judge-made law. Moreover, all statutes are subject to judicial interpretation and review. Therefore, although criminal law is likely to be more diverse than most bodies of common law, making a unified account difficult, it is possible to identify key common institutional elements and to evaluate their impact on the efficiency of the law.

Let me begin by acknowledging the validity of a key assumption in economic analyses of crime, namely that the criminal mind is largely rational and that most crimes are deliberately committed for material (or at least for utilitarian) gain. This implies that changes in the expected cost of a crime, whether effected by changing the probability of apprehension and conviction or by changing the severity of the punishment, will have a perceptible impact upon the rate of criminal activity (*ceteris paribus*). An efficient criminal justice system will seek to minimize the joint cost of crime and punishment, not, of course, to eliminate crime entirely.[6] In so doing, it will not handicap itself by rules designated to make it difficult to apprehend and convict those who engage in criminal behavior. (Maas shows how rules of evidence handicapped the government in bringing its case against the master spy Richard Ames in 1994.)[7]

This ideal is in no way descriptive of late-twentieth-century American criminal procedures, which are designed to make it exceptionally difficult and costly to convict the guilty and which place an unacceptably high value on ensuring that the innocent are not incorrectly convicted. It is my belief that almost all the institutional barriers erected against efficient criminal law procedures have their foundations in a deep-rooted skepticism about the ability of jurors to do their jobs (a skepticism which may be well-founded, given the process of jury selection). In itself this constitutes a powerful argument in favor of the civil code procedure in which juries play no role.

The legal system is flawed, in the case of criminal law, from pretrial investigation to appeal. Indeed, in most criminal cases in the United States there is no trial. Police ineptitude is obvious, given the large budgets allocated to police departments and the fact that the overwhelming majority of all crimes go unsolved. If the police and prosecuting attorney become uncertain about

6. G. S. Becker, "Crime and Punishment: An Economic Approach," *Journal of Political Economy* 76 (1968): 169–217.

7. P. Maas, *Killer Spy* (New York: Time Warner, 1995).

their case, either they drop further investigation or the accused pleads guilty in return for a lower sentence. The defendant is formally charged in only a relatively few cases, and trials occur in only a tiny fraction of crimes.[8]

Plea bargaining in itself is not necessarily an inefficient procedure. It need not deny the defendant the right to the procedural safeguards of a trial, nor need it lead, on average, to reduced sentences. If the trial procedure itself is efficient (which I suggest is not the case), plea bargains must be efficiency-enhancing, since either party can elect to go to trial if it so prefers. Given a fixed prosecutorial budget, average sentences may actually increase where plea bargaining is allowed, because the prosecutor can use resources saved by plea bargains to build stronger cases where such bargaining fails.[9] Plea bargaining that occurs under the shadow of an inefficient criminal law system, however, is quite another story.

The law of evidence is at the root of this inefficiency, mired in the most procedurally complex set of rules in the Anglo-Saxon system. Many of the laws have evolved on the pretext (or reality) that jurors are simple people who are easily misled. Rightly or wrongly, the U.S. courts distrust juries. Many, if not most, of the exclusionary rules of evidence exclude evidence because judges consider that juries would be inclined to attach more weight to it than they ought.[10] That is, judges believe that juries could not be trusted to give the evidence its logical, rational weight, or to perceive that it had none, but instead, perhaps because of the emotional impact of the evidence, would allow it to be more persuasive or influential than they should.[11]

Interestingly, judges are bound by the same rules of evidence as juries. Judges not infrequently review pieces of evidence to determine whether they have been submitted in violation of procedural rules. If they so find, they announce that they will not pay attention to such evidence in the proceedings. I doubt that many judges have the kind of mental discipline necessary to fulfill that kind of promise. In any event, judges are much less likely than juries to react emotionally to evidence currently excluded from consideration.

Many of the widely accepted ground rules that have become part of the criminal process following court decisions interpreting the Fourth, Fifth,

8. G. Tullock, "Court Errors," *European Journal of Law and Economics* 2, no. 2 (1994): 14–15.

9. Posner, *Economic Analysis of the Law*, 562.

10. P. F. Rothstein, *Evidence in a Nutshell* (St. Paul: West Publishing, 1970), 4–5.

11. Tullock, "Legal Heresy," 7.

and Sixth Amendments of the Constitution allow obviously guilty and often violent criminals to go free. The Supreme Court requires judges to advise jurors that no adverse inference may be drawn from the failure of a defendant to testify. It also requires judges to exclude illegally obtained evidence from criminal trials. The result of such rulings is a menaced society, unprotected by the legal system.

The laws of evidence encourage courts to reach erroneous outcomes because they are not allowed to take account of relevant evidence. From this perspective, it is possible to distinguish rules of evidence that are intended to benefit the accused, whether or not he is innocent, from rules of evidence that have no obvious bias, ruling out evidence for both the prosecution and the defense. The Fifth Amendment right not to testify against oneself and the fruit-of-the-poisonous-tree doctrine are prime examples of bias in favor of the accused. Other rules, as we shall see, change the procedure, but it is not obvious whether the defendant gains or loses.

The original meaning of the common law privilege against self-incrimination was simply that a person accused of a crime could not be called upon to testify. Indeed, in the early days in the colonies, not only could the accused not be called upon to testify, but it was illegal for him to testify on his own volition. The somewhat dubious privilege of not being permitted or compelled to testify was restricted to people who were accused of a crime. Other witnesses did not have this privilege.

The origins of this right to silence come from the sixteenth-century maxim "*nemo tenetur prodere se ipsum*," or, "no one should be required to accuse himself." The right was applied haphazardly until the Fifth Amendment became law in 1791. For example, during the Salem witch trials of 1692, the judges believed that torture and death were appropriate persuasive techniques for recalcitrant defendants.[12]

The Fifth Amendment provides that no person shall be compelled in any criminal case to be witness against himself. The due process clause of the Fourteenth Amendment extends this privilege to state law. The privilege extends to civil proceedings if there is any threat of criminal sanctions associated with incriminating testimony. This privilege tends to be to the advantage of the accused. The defendant and his lawyer can weigh whether the former's testimony (and exposure to cross-examination) is more likely to benefit or to injure

12. E. H. Griswold, *The Fifth Amendment Today* (Cambridge: Harvard University Press, 1955); M. Berger, *Taking the 5th* (New York: Lexington Books, 1980).

his case, given that the jury will note his failure to testify. Whether or not the judge should instruct the jury to ignore the defendant's failure to take the stand is itself a controversial question.

The fruit-of-the-poisonous-tree doctrine is biased in favor of the accused, at least *pro forma*. The doctrine prevents the prosecution from presenting evidence against a defendant when that evidence is the direct result or the immediate product of illegal conduct on the part of public officials responsible for extracting it. Examples of the application of this doctrine include the inadmissibility of evidence obtained from an illegal search and of confessions resulting from an illegal arrest.

The bias in favor of the defendant appears clear. However, the widespread publicity that the doctrine has received may actually bias the whole proceeding against the defendant. Jurymen may labor under the apprehension, based on newspaper and television accounts, that the prosecution typically is in possession of evidence which is barred because of this doctrine. If so, they may over-compensate for this perceived bias in their own deliberations, despite instructions from the bench.

Assume that the average juryman believes that 15 per cent of the prosecution's case is prohibited by the laws of evidence. In some cases, the prosecution's case might be 30 per cent stronger, and in others there might be no prohibited evidence. The jury correction factor, in such circumstances, would under-estimate the actual bias introduced by the laws of evidence in the former cases, and over-estimate it in the latter.

If the objective is accuracy, in the sense of an even bias, the poisonous-tree doctrine is a clumsy way to try to achieve it. In the absence of a jury, the doctrine would be largely indefensible, since professional judges would be fully capable of giving illegally obtained evidence an appropriate weighting. If society truly does not want illegal evidence to be obtained, it could devise appropriate penalties, including lengthy prison terms, for public officials who conspire to collect it, or who attempt to deploy it in the courtroom.

Let me now briefly comment on other rules of evidence that, in general, are quite impartial, in that they rule out evidence for both the prosecution and the defense, and yet reduce the information available to reach a correct verdict. The rule prohibiting hearsay evidence is a prime example of this genre.

It is clear that if a choice is available between hearing Mr. Smith testify about something that he saw or hearing Mr. Jones testify as to what Mr. Smith told him about what he saw, we would prefer the former to the latter evidence. The problem of "whispering down the lane" suggests that information suffers from distortion as it is relayed from one person to another.[13] Yet, if Mr. Smith is not available, then Mr. Jones' testimony may be better than nothing. That is the view taken by European courts, who would hear the hearsay evidence and discount its importance. In the United States, Mr. Jones' testimony would be inadmissible.

The hearsay rule does not necessarily protect the accused. Suppose that Mr. Smith was the only eyewitness to a murder and that he is now dead. Suppose that he had testified at a previous mistrial. It would seem that the jury is more likely to reach a correct verdict if Mr. Smith's evidence is admitted than if it is excluded. The point is highlighted if we further suppose that Mr. Smith's statement is the only evidence that can clear the accused of a murder charge, by providing the reasonable doubt necessary for an acquittal. Such considerations have no part in official doctrine, except to the formalistic extent that need and reliability are recognized in the exceptions to the hearsay rule. Yet, citizens, in making important decisions in their daily lives, rely extensively on their ability to correctly evaluate hearsay.[14]

The remaining rules of evidence are similar in their effect to the hearsay rule. If they have any justification at all, it is that they reduce the likelihood that unintelligent jurymen will be misled by poor or tainted evidence. To repeat my earlier assertion, if juries really are so suspect, why not remove them in favor of bench trials. Alternatively, one might take positive steps (such as requiring minimal intelligence quota levels) to improve the quality of the average jury. Of course, trial lawyers would lobby strongly against either reform since they have invested heavily in recent years in the techniques of jury manipulation.

Evaluating the effectiveness and efficiency of jury trials is a challenging process that is yet barely in its infancy. The fact that juries are instructed from the bench not to discuss the details of cases on which they have served indicates that proponents of the jury system are concerned about the likely public reaction, once information becomes available about what went on in the jury room. In recent years, jury members have begun to sell their stories to the gutter press, and such stories do not reinforce the case for the jury system. In any event, a number of procedures have been devised to evaluate jury decision-making.

The classic study on the workings of the American jury was the 1966 report from the University of Chicago Law School. In this study, Kalven and

13. G. Tullock, *The Politics of Bureaucracy* (Washington, D.C.: Public Affairs Press, 1965).

14. Tullock, "Legal Heresy," 7–8.

Zeisel analyzed information on 3,576 criminal trials, having questioned 555 trial judges around the United States. The study used a measure of the rate and quality of judge-jury disagreements as a means of measuring jury efficiency. It determined that the judges who heard the cases would have reached different verdicts than the jury in 30 per cent of the cases studied. Disagreement was no more frequent in so-called easy cases than in "difficult" cases, a finding that Zeisel and Kalven inexplicably called "a stunning refutation of the hypothesis that the jury does not understand."[15]

According to the Chicago study, approximately 20 per cent of the judge-jury disagreement was due to juror sentiment about the law or about the defendant. Strong sentiment might even stimulate a juror to look for weaknesses in the facts or perhaps to nullify the law. As Zeisel and Kalven put it: "We know from other parts of our jury study that the jury does not often consciously and explicitly yield to sentiment in the truth of the law. Rather it yields to sentiment in the apparent process of resolving doubts as to evidence."

Disagreement between judge and jury also derives from other sources, as the Chicago study reported. One such source is the issue of witness credibility. Judges tend to be much more jaded about lying than juries. Another source of disagreement is that juries tend to have different standards than judges for *reasonable doubt*, tending to hold higher standards concerning how much proof overcomes the presumption of innocence in a criminal case. The difference is due, in part, to defense lawyers' rhetoric on the matter and in part to the greater degree of cynicism displayed by the bench. Of course, one cannot generalize about which judgment is superior. However, jury trials, from this perspective, bias cases in favor of the accused.

The Chicago study found that when the judge and jury disagreed it was usually in cases where the jury found in favor of the defendant. Factors that seem to have swayed the jury in such cases are feelings of sympathy for the defendant, perceptions of police or prosecutorial abuse, attorney performance, and lack of information about the defendant's prior criminal record. The study could not conclude objectively whether the jury system was worth retaining. It did characterize the system as a "daring effort in human arrangement to work out a solution to the tensions between law, equity and anarchy." Of course, many daring efforts have failed abysmally to achieve their objectives in the history of mankind. The jury system is one such failure.

15. H. Kalven and H. Zeisel, *The American Jury* (Boston: Little, Brown, 1966).

Theoretically, the role of the jury is to decide the facts and to leave the law to the judge. Among those who actually deal with juries, there is virtually no one who believes that this theory accurately describes reality.[16] It is customary for the judge to give legal instructions to the jury to guide them in their decision-making processes. Evidence suggests that jurors typically forget some or all of these instructions and that they ignore instructions that they do not like. In an experimental jury exercise conducted by Hastie, Penrod, and Pennington jury panelists were required to complete questionnaires, following their deliberations, which asked them about the judge's instructions on the law. Individual jurors performed only slightly better than random in their recall of the instructions.[17]

There was a period in the People's Republic of China, initiated by Chairman Mao, when specialization of labor was jettisoned and individuals were encouraged to exchange occupations at will. Janitors periodically performed operations at hospitals under this dispensation (except, of course, when the secretary of the local communist party needed an operation). It is not in any way to be critical of these janitors to admit that they achieved an abnormally high death rate. As I shall suggest in Chapter 6, the error rate in American jury trials is at least one in eight. Although I do not wish to criticize Chinese janitors or American jurors as well-meaning individuals, the error term is always much higher when you use amateurs than when you use professionals.[18]

Even the rare well-qualified jury labors under handicaps that the judge does not encounter, that extend well beyond the problems imposed by rules of evidence. For example, in some instances, rather than instructing the jury on the law, the law is deliberately withheld from the jury. This obfuscation is referred to as "blindfolding the jury." Juries usually are not informed about the consequences for criminal defendants that will follow from a verdict of not guilty by reason of insanity. Juries in comparative negligence jurisdictions usually are not informed as to when damages will be trebled or the effects of the attorneys' fees. Juries that are compelled to guess about such matters frequently guess incorrectly, compounding the weakness of the jury trial.

16. Tullock, "Legal Heresy," 5.

17. R. Hastie, S. Penrod, and N. Pennington, *Inside the Jury* (Cambridge: Harvard University Press, 1983).

18. Tullock, *Trials on Trial*, 29.

Juries are also handicapped, relative to the judge, with respect to the tools that they are permitted to use to assemble and to process the facts of the case. It is beyond rational logic to justify the prohibition imposed on U.S. juries from taking notes, reviewing evidence, asking questions, and having access to basic information resources. Perhaps such prohibitions make judges feel superior. In the kingdom of the blind, the one-eyed man is king.

CHAPTER 6

THE TRAGEDIE OF THE COMMON LAW SYSTEM IN THE UNITED STATES

As I have noted earlier, Americans are much more litigious than other peoples. There are twenty times as many lawyers per capita in America as in Japan (a civil code country), five times as many as in Germany (also a civil code country), and four times as many as in England and Wales (a common law country). American trial courts disposed of more than four million civil cases in 1981, more than 2.5 million criminal cases, and 0.6 million juvenile cases. In civil suits, contract cases dominated, producing about ten times as many trials as tort disputes, with property disputes somewhere in between. Some 95 per cent of all civil disputes are disposed of without resort to trial.[1]

The social cost of legal disputes is unknown but must be very high. In 1983, combined federal, state, and local spending on civil and criminal justice amounted to $39.7 billion, or $170 per capita. This accounted for 3 per cent of all government spending in that year. Of this total, $37 per capita was expended on judicial services.[2] This latter sum amounts to only a small fraction of the social cost of resolving disputes through the courts, since most of these costs are borne by private parties. In a back-of-the-envelope calculation of the opportunity cost of all parties to a trial (based on a $20 per hour average cost), Cooter and Ulen estimated the labor cost of a full trial to be approximately $400 per hour, to which must be added the cost of court facilities.[3] If this is even close to the mark, the costs showing up in government statistics represent only the tip of the iceberg of the total cost to society.

It is particularly instructive to compare litigation in the United States with that in England and Wales since both countries operate under the common law system. In part, the much lower rates of litigation in England and Wales occur because of cultural differences. Their citizens are much more inclined to take responsibility for their own misfortunes, much less inclined to seek socialized protection from risk through the court system than are U.S. citizens. This greater independence of spirit is reinforced by institutional factors that make litigation less attractive.

1. R. Cooter and T. Ulen, *Law and Economics* (Glenview, Ill.: Scott, Foresman, 1988), 478.
2. Ibid.
3. Cooter and Ulen, *Law and Economics*.

In England and Wales, the loser of a lawsuit must pay the litigation costs of the winner, whereas in the United States each party ordinarily pays his own litigation costs. Given risk aversion, this reduces the volume of litigation. In England and Wales, contingency fees are prohibited. This reduces the incentives for lawyers to ambulance-chase and to pressure reluctant parties into litigating for damages that truly have not been sustained, behavior that has become a pronounced feature of American trial lawyers since the 1960's. In England and Wales, all civil trials are bench trials, significantly reducing the cost of litigation and avoiding entirely the ridiculously high awards culled out of carefully selected U.S. juries by emotive trial lawyer rhetoric. In England and Wales, ethnic and race diversity does not give rise to the kind of jury tensions that lead to so many hung juries in the United States with associated high litigation costs in criminal suits. In England and Wales, the law of contract has not been destroyed by the law of tort as has occurred in certain states in America, notably California, again under sustained pressure from the Association of Trial Lawyers of America.

If litigation costs indeed are so high in the United States, does this imply that high degrees of accuracy are achieved by the U.S. courts, that truth is better served in America than elsewhere? Such evidence as is available does not support this proposition.

Errors can occur either in interpreting the law or in matters of fact.[4] Let me first address errors of fact. Under the common law system, court decisions actually make a good deal of the law, and hence the meaning of error is more ambiguous, though, as I shall demonstrate, error can be identified as unacceptable deviations from precedent and *stare decisis*. Again, let me focus primarily on the criminal law to address the issue of errors of fact.

Suppose that a prominent socialite is brutally murdered and that following a police investigation, her ex-husband is the prime suspect, albeit on the basis of circumstantial evidence. The court does not know whether or not he is guilty. It simply knows how much evidence there is against him. There are various rules that the court can use, and I shall canvass a number of them, starting with the rule now used in civil suits, not criminal: namely, take whichever is the most probable result. This minimizes total errors, type 1 and type 2. The guilty ex-husband has a three out of four chance of being convicted and a one out of four chance of being acquitted. The innocent ex-husband has a three out

4. G. Tullock, "Court Errors," *European Journal of Law and Economics* 1 (1994): 9–21.

of four chance of being discharged and a one out of four chance of being convicted in my model.[5]

To deter the crime under this rule, assuming risk-neutral criminals, a penalty levied at 1.334 times the benefit to the criminal is minimally required. The innocent ex-husband has a present discounted penalty, again assuming risk neutrality, of one-third the benefit from the crime.

The normal rule in criminal law, however, is that the defendant will be convicted only if the evidence against him is *beyond all reasonable doubt*. Assume that the weight of evidence required for conviction gives a probability of 80 per cent or higher of guilt. Under these circumstances, according to my model, 36 per cent of guilty persons and 4 per cent of innocent persons will be convicted.[6]

To deter the crime under this rule, assuming universal risk neutrality, a penalty levied at 2.777 times the benefit to the criminal must be imposed. The present discounted cost to the innocent of such a penalty is a little over 10 per cent of the assessed benefit from the crime. Although the expected cost to the innocent is lower under the criminal law standard, it is not as low as would be the case if the total magnitude of the penalty need not be increased to compensate for the lowered probability that the guilty will escape punishment. Errors with respect to the facts predictably are greater in criminal lawsuits than in civil lawsuits simply because an inefficient burden of proof is required.

One method of measuring the error rate of courts is to compare the verdicts of two independent decision-making bodies. If the two bodies disagree about a given case, one of them must be wrong. If they are in agreement, it is possible that both are wrong. A measure of court error rates based on disagreement thus provides a minimum value.[7] Two studies (one in the United States, the other in England) independently confirm that the error rate of courts is approximately one in eight.

The first such study is the 1966 report from the University of Chicago Law School by Kalven and Zeisel (discussed in more detail in Chapter 5).

5. G. Tullock, "Judicial Errors and a Proposal for Reform," *Journal of Legal Studies* 13, no. 4 (June 1984): 289–98.

6. Tullock, "Court Errors," 11.

7. G. Tullock, *Trials on Trial: The Pure Theory of Legal Procedure* (New York: Columbia University Press, 1980), 32.

In response to questionnaires, in excess of 3,500 judges were asked to mark down their own verdicts against the jury verdicts. Disagreements occurred in one-fourth of the cases. There is no way of telling from these data whether it is the judge or the jury which is in error, though the professional qualifications of the judge, in my view, generally ensure that his error rate will be the lower. In a more recent study in England by Baldwin and McConville, based on similar methodology, an error rate somewhat in excess of one in eight was reported.[8]

Of course, no system, legal or otherwise, is entirely immune from error, and there is no obvious way of determining what the optimal error rate should be. However, if a lower-cost method results in a lower average error rate, surely there should be a cost-effective presumption in favor of that method. In my view, that presumption conclusively favors a switch away from jury trials to bench trials, whether or not the common law itself is jettisoned in favor of the civil code. Recognition of court error could influence the choice among legal rules and legal remedies. This is a factor that almost universally is ignored in the law and economics literature.[9]

Perhaps the strongest argument in favor of courts rather than legislators as lawmakers is that advanced by Bruno Leoni, an Italian lawyer trained in the Italian civil code tradition. In his book *Freedom and the Law*, Leoni notes that the bulk of Roman law had been created by *jurisconsults*, who, if they were not actually judges, nevertheless had developed a common law from the consideration of real cases.[10] A judgment did not become a true precedent until it had been reached independently in separate cases by several judges. In Roman law, there was no truly binding supreme court decision, although individual cases rarely might be appealed to the senate or to the emperor. Hence, the need for a sequence of confirmatory judgments.

Until 1800, the same was essentially true of the English common law system. Prior to the Benthamite reform movement, the British government is best described as an institution that, like Topsy, "just growed" without conscious design. The English common law itself had evolved out of a competing court system and was composed of judgments that had survived repeated scrutiny. Appeals to the House of Lords, though theoretically possible, were rare events. This implied that the common law evolved only very slowly and

8. J. Baldwin and M. McConville, *Jury Trials* (Oxford: The Clarendon Press, 1979).

9. Tullock, *Trials on Trial*, 48.

10. B. Leoni, *Freedom and the Law* (Los Angeles: Nash Publishing, 1961).

that changes had to survive a sequence of independent judgments before becoming established as precedent and subject to *stare decisis*.

Unfortunately for the common law system in America, the Founding Fathers were impatient with the apparent untidiness of a slowly evolving system. They hankered for a court of last resort which could make binding rulings and hence tidy up the common law. The result was the Supreme Court, which gradually has abandoned its role as constitutional guardian in favor of a more glamorous, if dangerous, role as lawmaker. Instead of common law changes slowly evolving by surviving repeated independent scrutiny, a single simple majority ruling of the Supreme Court now changes the law instantly, in some cases to an extreme degree. Needless to say, the Supreme Court does not consider itself to be bound by its own previous judgments.

The weakness of the Supreme Court in responding to special interest group pressure has not been lost on the lower courts, both federal and state, as is evidenced by the almost complete abandonment of classical civil law principles and by the growing rush to protect the guilty through changes in criminal law procedures. Even the unambiguous wording of the Constitution has not been allowed to impede this misguided lawmaking impulse. Let me briefly illustrate by listing some of the more egregious changes in the law of property, contract, and tort.

One of the most serious invasions of the law of property was the unlawful judgment of the Supreme Court in *Penn Central Transportation Co. v. City of New York*.[11] The court, speaking through Justice Brennan, held that the state may exclude persons from the occupation of part of what they own and still not come under a prima facie obligation to pay compensation. This judgment set the pace for a decade of unconstitutional judgments which, for a time at least, effectively eliminated the Fifth Amendment protection against the seizure of private property by government for public use without the payment of just compensation.

Although there has been an uneven drift back towards constitutionality on this issue since 1988, the Supreme Court remains a less than effective defender of Fifth Amendment rights.[12] Given this example by the Supreme Court, it is not surprising that lower courts have also abandoned the defense of property rights, for example, determining disputes over property by reference to least cost avoider considerations rather than by recognition of the

11. *Penn Central Transportation Co. v. City of New York*, 438 U.S. 104 (1978), 30.

12. C. K. Rowley, *The Right to Justice* (Aldershot: Edward Elgar, 1992), 121–22.

inalienable right to property.[13] Legal rules that do not effectively protect property rights render individuals vulnerable to coercion by others and reduce wealth to society.

In the most famous passages in economics, Adam Smith set out the justification for what is now referred to as the classical law of contract:

> It is not from the benevolence of the butcher, the brewer, or the baker that we expect our dinner, but from their regard to their own interest. We address ourselves, not to their humanity, but to their self-love; and never talk to them of their own necessities, but of their advantages . . . Every individual is continually exerting himself to find out the most advantageous employment for whatever capital he can command. It is his own advantage, indeed, and not that of society, which he has in view. But the study of his own advantage, naturally, or rather necessarily, leads him to prefer that employment which is most advantageous to society . . . He is in this . . . led by an invisible hand to promote an end which was no part of his intention. Nor is it always the worse for society that it was no part of it. By pursuing his own interest, he frequently promotes that of society more effectively than when he really intends to promote it.[14]

In this view, the public interest is furthered as a mere by-product of countless self-serving individual decisions to engage in trade or exchange. The legal counterpart to this view of the market is the *will* or *autonomy* theory of contract law, where obligations by individuals to one another arise out of voluntarily assumed, self-imposed obligations reflecting convergent intentions of the contracting parties.[15] The classical law of contract, in its heyday, was viewed as simultaneously promoting autonomy (or individual freedom) and social welfare. In the United States, the courts have retreated dramatically from the classical position, *stare decisis* notwithstanding, under a combination of special interest group pressures and socialist ideology.

Under classical contract law all that was required for a binding contract was offer, acceptance, and consideration since the courts would not inquire into the latter's adequacy. Absent any one of these, a contract would not be upheld at law. Now, courts read in consideration when it is not there, in

13. D. W. Barnes and L. A. Stout, *Cases and Materials on Law and Economics* (St. Paul: West Publishing, 1992), chap. 2.

14. A. Smith, *The Wealth of Nations* (1776; Norwalk: Easton Press, 1991), 14, 421, 423.

15. M. J. Trebilock, *The Limits of Freedom of Contract* (Cambridge: Harvard University Press, 1993), 241.

order to uphold promises that individuals relied upon when they should not have done so. They strike down bargains that should be upheld, simply because some judge does not like the terms the parties agreed to.

Courts strike down bargains on the ground of incomplete information, ignoring the fact that the future is always uncertain. They strike down bargains on the ground of cognitive deficiencies on the part of one party or the other, ignoring the fact that talent is unevenly distributed across human beings. They strike down contracts on the ground that they contain terms that are "unconscionable" or "contrary to public policy," again as viewed by some judge, not by the parties to the bargain.[16] Most damaging of all, they strike down bargains on the ground that they contain third party effects, ignoring the fact that externalities are universal and that the very large majority of them are not Pareto relevant.[17] In this way, U.S. courts have allowed the law of tort to emasculate the law of contract with very serious consequences for individual autonomy and for the wealth of the nation.

Until the 1950's, the tradition with respect to the law of accidents and personal injury was to concentrate the attention of the courts on civil wrongs involving strangers, where contracts could not govern the relationships between the parties. The line between contract and tort tended to be tightly drawn, in favor of contract to the maximum extent possible. For a tort case to succeed under classical common law, there had to be a breach of a duty owed to the plaintiff by the defendant, harm suffered by the plaintiff, and proximate cause. In such circumstances, the negligence with contributory negligence standard typically was applied. Damages were narrowly construed, essentially to replace medical costs and loss of earnings.

From the early 1960's, however, the U.S. courts systematically assaulted the classical law of tort, dismantling its twin historic pillars—deterrence and compensation—in favor of notions of societal insurance and risk-spreading and undermining the concept of fault as a doctrinal mechanism for limiting tort liability to substantive tortfeasors.[18] The abandonment of proximate cause in favor of joint and several liability has fired the engines of the rent-seekers who now specifically target the deep pockets. The shift from

16. Barnes and Stout, *Cases and Materials*, chap. 4.

17. C. K. Rowley and A. T. Peacock, *Welfare Economics: A Liberal Restatement* (Oxford: Martin Robertson, 1975).

18. P. W. Huber, *Liability: The Legal Revolution and Its Consequences* (New York: Basic Books, 1988); C. K. Rowley, "The Common Law in Public Choice Perspective," *Hamline Law Review* 12, no. 2 (1989): 355–83.

negligence with contributory negligence to comparative negligence or strict liability standards has induced a sharp increase in moral hazard as plaintiffs lower their own standards of care and has stimulated a sharp increase in tertiary legal costs as the volume of lawsuits has exploded. The widening of damages to encompass pain and suffering and loss of companionship damages as well as to anticipate harms that have not even occurred has made a mockery of the law and has eliminated a wide range of otherwise viable goods and services from the American marketplace.[19]

In no sense is this retreat from classical tort law and the emasculation of contract law to be viewed as a slow evolutionary process. Rather it is the product of rent-seeking trial lawyers, activist judges, and gullible juries who together have conspired to shackle capitalism into the confines of the plantation state.[20] So diseased has the U.S. common law system become that even root-and-branch internal reform no longer is feasible. If individual autonomy and the rule of law are to be re-established, Wellington must now cede victory to Napoléon, and the common law must give way to the civil code.

19. Barnes and Stout, *Cases and Materials*, chap. 3.

20. A. de Jasay, *The State* (Oxford: Basil Blackwell, 1980).

CHAPTER 7

WHY I PREFER NAPOLEON

My principal purpose in this monograph is to outline the case against the common law, not to set out a detailed case in favor of the civil law. The latter task is better suited to a specialist in civil-code procedures, more experienced than I am in the detailed workings of the civil code in the Western European democracies. Although I personally prefer the Napoleonic code to Anglo-Saxon procedures, for reasons that I shall set out in this chapter, I do not think that it is in any sense ideal. Whether or not Napoléon was right and Blackstone wrong will be answered definitively only if the whole discussion is opened up to scientific investigation. Readers, therefore, may wish to treat my assertions in this chapter as testable hypotheses. They may even wish to take time out to test them, by engaging in the kind of comparative institutions analysis which is sorely lacking in this field.

Let me start by outlining the case advanced in favor of the common law system by its most fervent contemporary advocate, Judge Richard Posner.[1] By countering that case point by point, and by drawing upon additional arguments outlined earlier in this monograph, I shall advance my own case for adopting some variant of the Napoleonic code.

For Posner, the ultimate question for decision in many lawsuits is what allocation of resources would maximize efficiency. The market normally decides this question, but it is given to the legal system to decide in situations where the cost of a market determination would exceed those of a legal determination. Like the market, the common law uses prices equal to opportunity costs to induce people to maximize efficiency. Where compensatory damages are the remedy for a breach of legal duty, the effect of liability is not to compel compliance with law but to compel the violator to pay a price equal to the opportunity costs of the violation. Although heavier sanctions—penalties—are sometimes imposed, normally this is done in circumstances where penalties are necessary to create the correct economic activities.

Again, according to Posner, the legal process, like the market, relies for its administration primarily on private individuals motivated by economic self-interest rather than on altruists or public officials. Through the lawyer that he hires, the victim of conduct that may be unlawful in a civil case

1. R. A. Posner, *Economic Analysis of the Law*, 4th ed. (Boston: Little, Brown, 1992).

(1) investigates the circumstances surrounding the allegedly unlawful act, (2) organizes the information obtained by the investigation, (3) decides whether to activate the machinery of legal allocation, (4) feeds information in a digestible form to that machinery, (5) checks the accuracy of the information supplied by the defendant, (6) presses if necessary for changes in the rules of allocation followed by the courts, and (7) sees to the collection of the judgment.

As opposed to in criminal law, because of this private activity, the state can dispense with a police force to protect people's common law rights, public attorneys to enforce them, and other bureaucratic personnel to operate the system. Such functionaries would be less highly motivated than a private plaintiff, since their economic self-interest would be affected only indirectly by the outcomes of particular cases.

The legal process (again according to Posner) also resembles the market in its impersonality, most particularly in its subordination of distributive considerations. The invisible hand of the market has its counterpart in the disinterest of the judge. The method by which judges are compensated and the rules of judicial ethics are designed to ensure that the judge will have no financial or other interest in the outcome of a case before him, no responsibility other than to decide issues tendered by the parties, and no knowledge of the facts in the case other than what the competition of the parties conveys to him. Jurors are similarly constrained.

In his zeal to liken the common law system to a private market, Posner oversteps the mark. The common law system is not a private marketplace. It is a socialistic bureaucracy in which attorneys essentially lobby government officials—judges and juries—much in the same way that special interest groups lobby the legislature. The greater the rents at stake in an action, the more lavish will be the outlay of resources on attorney-lobbyists and on expert witness–lobbyists whose prime goal is to tilt the judgment of the judge-jury regulators in favor of their client. In some cases, attorneys will engage in judge-shopping to secure a compliant judge and in jury manipulation to secure a compliant jury. The distinction between the common law courthouse and the legislature is far less than Posner is willing to admit.

Posner is correct in asserting that the common law system economizes in the use of judges and other public officials, by substituting the private activity of the parties for the information-collecting responsibility of bureaucrats. The ratio of judges to lawyers well may be ten times higher in Sweden and in Germany than in California as Posner suggests. However, as Posner fails to note, that ratio is made up of a denominator as well as a numerator. Civil law countries resolve their legal business with between one-tenth and one-twentieth the number of practicing lawyers as in the United States, and without any significant recourse to juries. The common law is an extremely high-cost legal system by comparison with all civil code alternatives. Posner is silent on this issue, which is central to the debate, despite the fact that he relies extensively on transaction cost evidence in all other areas of his economic analysis of law.

To the extent that the common law relies on compensatory damages as the remedy for a breach of legal duty, it does make use of price as a mechanism to rectify market failure. However, as I indicated in Chapter 6, juries are extremely inefficient mechanisms for calculating compensatory damages and are prone to emotive responses to carefully targeted attorney rhetoric, responses that result in grossly excessive damage awards. If many of those awards are reduced subsequently on appeal, this is at additional legal cost and induced by a mechanism much closer to civil code procedure in that it makes no use of juries and strictly limits attorney advocacy, at least with respect to the facts of the case.

As I have argued in Chapters 4 and 5, the invisible hand of the market does not have its counterpart in the disinterest of the judge. Rather, its counterpart is the visible boot of the politically active judge and the bony knees and elbows of the semi-blindfolded, intellectually lame jury. Competition between the parties does not convey information efficiently to the courtroom, because laws of evidence are designed deliberately to obfuscate the process. In consequence, the American legal system at best is extremely capricious, and at worst is a random lottery. It would be much more cost effective, in such circumstances, to decide outcomes by flipping a coin or by rolling a die rather than by indulging in the high-cost farce of the typical jury trial.

There are three basic differences between the Anglo-Saxon common law system and the Napoleonic civil law system on which I shall focus attention in this concluding section, namely (1) the accusatorial versus the inquisitorial method of procedure, (2) the presence versus the absence of the jury, and (3) laws that limit versus laws that require full disclosure of the evidence. With respect to each of these differences, it is my contention that the Napoleonic system is superior to the common law system.[2]

2. G. Tullock, "Defending the Napoleonic Code over the Common Law," in *Research in Law and Policy Studies*, vol. 2 (New York: JAI Press, 1988).

The Anglo-Saxon adversarial process is utilized only in common law countries. The majority of countries, those that adhere to civil code procedures, utilize the inquisitorial system, whereby the judge (or magistrate) takes the lead in gathering evidence and forming the issues of a case. In such a system, lawyers have a subordinate role, much less than principal players in the litigation process.

In criminal cases, the police investigate so that a prosecutor can decide whether to proceed or to drop a case. The police have two different types of power, depending on whether the case is an ordinary investigation (*enquête préliminaire*) or a flagrant offense (*enquête flagrante*). A flagrant offense is a serious crime which can be punished by imprisonment, or a crime which is currently being committed. The police have more extensive powers to preserve evidence in such cases than in ordinary investigations. There are no search-and-seizure requirements or restrictions other than rules designed to guarantee individual rights. Once the police hand over the investigation to the prosecutor, the accused is charged or the case is dismissed.

Once the decision to prosecute has been made, the detection apparatus and the court system combine under the authority of a legally trained judicial official or magistrate. This official conducts an investigation personally if it is a serious crime or supervises the investigation if the crime is less complex. The police are available to assist the official with his inquiries. The official typically inspects the scene of the crime, conducts examinations and searches, questions all persons possibly associated with the crime, and allows witnesses to confront each other.

The suspect is involved throughout the process of gathering evidence and constructing the case. He can make representations to the official and argue his point of view. He may choose to be represented by an attorney at this stage. The suspect is interrogated (no, not with rubber hoses as many U.S. attorneys characteristically believe) to try to extract a confession. The focus of the investigation is to discharge a falsely suspected person, and there is (again contrary to U.S. attorney beliefs) a presumption of innocence. All of these proceedings are recorded in a dossier which is presented to the judges if the case goes to trial.

Magistrates formally decide the accused's guilt or innocence. If the accused is found guilty, there is a trial, normally before a bench of three, typically composed of one judge and two assessors. Committal to trial under the civil code system is more probative because the suspect has participated in all the inquiries, whereas only the police side is presented in a U.S. preliminary hearing. The trial itself, to some extent, is an appeal from the initial judicial proceeding.[3]

Once the criminal case is ready for trial, the procedure becomes somewhat more accusatorial, though the bench is much less influenced by lawyers' courtroom strategies under the inquisitorial system. When the trial is completed, the panel retires to its chamber and reaches a decision by simple majority vote. The assessors can outvote the judge on issues of fact, though they usually defer to his judgment on matters of law.[4] European courts generally apply the maxim "if there is doubt, acquit." Generally, under the civil system, a defendant who confesses and repents has his sentence reduced by 25 per cent.

The civil code tribunals admit almost any evidence, provided that it is relevant to the case, and then let the judges decide whether it is good or bad and how much weight to attach to it. Evidence is presented which would be barred under the Anglo-Saxon system. For example, hearsay is admitted but given less weight than direct testimony. The defendant can be sworn in and questioned by the judge. The defendant can refuse to answer questions, but the judge will take any such refusal into account. There is no Fifth Amendment privilege.

The judges can ask for whatever evidence they want and do not have to listen to evidence that they do not want. The president, or chief judge, decides the order in which witnesses are called and can ask questions of the witness. The bench has full access to the detailed record of evidence compiled by the magistrate. The accused may be tried *in absentia*. Judgments tend to be much better informed in civil code than in common law trials. They are also rendered by well-trained professionals and not by ignorant amateurs.

Appeals can be made from the judgment of the initial court of decision. The typical European courts acknowledge that local courts can make errors both of fact and of law and hear both categories of appeal. European supreme courts also have a wider basis of jurisdiction than the U.S. Supreme Court. For example, a legislator or other official can ask for a European supreme court's opinion on constitutional issues without awaiting a real legal dispute. In the United States, this is not possible.[5]

The code originally set up by the emperor Napoléon drew its inspiration from the laws introduced by the emperor Justinian in Ancient Rome and

3. C. J. Hanson, "The Prosecution of the Accused," *Criminal Law Review* (1955): 272.

4. G. Tullock, *Trials on Trial: The Pure Theory of Legal Procedure* (New York: Columbia University Press, 1980), 11.

5. Ibid., 37–38.

from the laws of the mercantile town of Lombardy in Italy. The code replaced the orders of the king and his courts with a concise body of rules and principles. A representative body of the people was empowered with lawmaking functions and developed the rules and principles still used today. Laws of procedure are not allowed to obstruct rules of substance. European code-based law is much briefer and much less ambiguous than Anglo-Saxon legislative laws.

Initially, the code made use of the jury for criminal cases. Over time, however, most continental Western European countries abandoned the jury system, leaving only a few remnants, and these were exclusively for criminal trials. For example, murder cases in Switzerland are tried by a fifteen-man jury. In France, the *cour d'assises* (Court of Assize) is a criminal court which utilizes a jury. There is a professional judge accompanied by two assessors and a nine-man jury. Together, they deliberate and decide questions of law and fact, the guilt or otherwise of the accused, and the appropriate sentence. A guilty verdict must be approved by a qualified majority of at least eight to four votes. If five votes are in favor of the accused, he is either acquitted or granted extenuating circumstances according to the principle of *minorité de faveur* (favorable minority). The sentencing decision must be supported by at least seven votes (eight in the case of custodial sentences, or *peine privation de liberté*).

The European procedures are far superior in clarity, precision, and implementation to the U.S. common law procedures. They lead to more accurate verdicts at a significantly lower cost. Essentially, the United States clings to an inefficient legal system which developed in the Middle Ages without much thought and which has evolved across the centuries without serious examination into whether or not its basic premises are sound. It survives, in part, because of tradition and, in part, because it guarantees large incomes to many of those connected with it.

Evidence in support of my judgment is available from recent experience in the United States, where parties increasingly contract out of the American court system, committing themselves instead to arbitration. Most commonly, arbitration takes the form of a summary inquisitorial process. Lawyers are banned, juries are not part of the process, and expert witnesses are not called. Arbitrators are selected on the basis of their professional knowledge and their independence from the parties. Usually they do not write detailed opinions supporting their verdict.

Arbitration appears to be well liked by those with the foresight to avoid the U.S. court system. In areas where it is applicable, it is set fair to supersede the common law system, introducing a private code system by default. The success of the inquisitorial arbitration system provides an ongoing challenge to those of my colleagues who continue stubbornly to defend an antiquated high-cost legal system. Like King Canute, they may order the tides to change direction. Like King Canute, their orders will be swept aside by the powerful tides of economic efficiency. By design or by default, Napoléon will defeat Wellington on this important battlefield.

INDEX

References to bibliographic information appear in italics.

The typeface used for the text of this book is Galliard, an old-style face designed by Matthew Carter in 1978, in the spirit of a sixteenth-century French typeface of Robert Granjon. The display type is Meta Book, a variant of Meta, designed by Erik Spiekermann in the 1990s.

This book is printed on paper that is acid-free and meets the requirements of the American National Standard for Permanence of Paper for Printed Library Materials, z39.48-1992. ∞

Book design by Richard Hendel, Chapel Hill, North Carolina
Typography by G&S Typesetters, Inc., Austin, Texas
Printed and bound by Edwards Brothers, Inc., Ann Arbor, Michigan